Next-Generation Ukrainian Canadian Children's Historical Fiction

This is the first book monograph devoted to Anglophone Ukrainian Canadian children's historical fiction published between 1991 and 2021. It consists of five chapters offering cross-sectional and interdisciplinary readings of 41 books – novels, novellas, picturebooks, short stories, and a graphic novel. The first three chapters focus on texts about the complex process of becoming Ukrainian Canadian, showcasing the experiences of the first two waves of Ukrainian immigration to Canada, including encounters with Indigenous Peoples and the First World War Internment. The last two chapters are devoted to the significance of the cultural memory of the Holodomor, the Great Famine of 1932–1933, and the Second World War for Ukrainian Canadians. All the chapters demonstrate the entanglements of Ukrainian and Canadian history and point to the role Anglophone children's literature can play in preventing the symbolical seeds of memory from withering. This volume argues that reading, imagining, and reimagining history can lead to the formation of beyond-textual next-generation memory. Such memory created through reading is multidimensional as it involves the interpretation of both the present and the past by an individual whose reality has been directly or indirectly shaped by the past over which they have no influence. Next-generation memory is of anticipatory character, which means that authors of historical fiction anticipate the readers – both present-day and future – not to have direct links to any witnesses of the events they discuss and to have little knowledge of the transcultural character of the Ukrainian Canadian diaspora.

Mateusz Świetlicki is Assistant Professor at the University of Wrocław's Institute of English Studies and Director of the Center for Young People's Literature and Culture. His scholarship focuses on North American and Ukrainian children's and YA literature and culture, memory, gender, and queer studies, as well as popular culture and film. He has published in English, Ukrainian, Polish, and Croatian.

Children's Literature and Culture

Jack Zipes, *Founding Series Editor*
Philip Nel, *Series Editor, 2011–2018*
Kenneth Kidd and Elizabeth Marshall, *Current Series Editors*

Founded by Jack Zipes in 1994, Children's Literature and Culture is the longest-running series devoted to the study of children's literature and culture from a national and international perspective. Dedicated to promoting original research in children's literature and children's culture, in 2011 the series expanded its focus to include childhood studies, and it seeks to explore the legal, historical, and philosophical conditions of different childhoods. An advocate for scholarship from around the globe, the series recognizes innovation and encourages interdisciplinarity. Children's Literature and Culture offers cutting-edge, upper-level scholarly studies and edited collections considering topics such as gender, race, picturebooks, childhood, nation, religion, technology, and many others. Titles are characterized by dynamic interventions into established subjects and innovative studies on emerging topics.

Representations of Children and Success in Asia
Dream Chasers
Edited by Shih-Wen Sue Chen and Sin Wen Lau

The Women Who Invented Twentieth-Century Children's Literature
Only the Best
Elizabeth West

Historical and Cultural Transformations of Russian Childhood
Myths and Realities
Edited by Marina Balina, Larissa Rudova, and Anastasia Kostetskaya

Next-Generation Memory and Ukrainian Canadian Children's Historical Fiction
The Seeds of Memory
Mateusz Świetlicki

For more information about this series, please visit: www.routledge.com/Childrens-Literature-and-Culture/book-series/SE0686

Next-Generation Memory and Ukrainian Canadian Children's Historical Fiction
The Seeds of Memory

Mateusz Świetlicki

NEW YORK AND LONDON

Designed cover image: Mateusz Świetlicki

First published 2023
by Routledge
605 Third Avenue, New York, NY 10158

and by Routledge
4 Park Square, Milton Park, Abingdon, Oxon, OX14 4RN

Routledge is an imprint of the Taylor & Francis Group, an informa business

© 2023 Mateusz Świetlicki

The right of Mateusz Świetlicki to be identified as author of this work has been asserted in accordance with sections 77 and 78 of the Copyright, Designs and Patents Act 1988.

All rights reserved. No part of this book may be reprinted or reproduced or utilised in any form or by any electronic, mechanical, or other means, now known or hereafter invented, including photocopying and recording, or in any information storage or retrieval system, without permission in writing from the publishers.

Trademark notice: Product or corporate names may be trademarks or registered trademarks, and are used only for identification and explanation without intent to infringe.

ISBN: 978-1-032-43562-6 (hbk)
ISBN: 978-1-032-43571-8 (pbk)
ISBN: 978-1-003-36791-8 (ebk)

DOI: 10.4324/9781003367918

Typeset in Sabon
by Newgen Publishing UK

This book is dedicated to three extraordinary women: my late grandmother Cecylia, who planted the seeds of memory in me, my friend Monika Czarnota, who died at 18 but is still present in my heart and inspires me to always say it right, and my mother Danuta, who is the strongest and most incredible person I know.

Contents

Preface ix
Acknowledgments xii

Introduction 1

1 Land of All Colors and Races?: Canadian Cossacks, Indigenous Peoples, and the Myth of the Founding Fathers of the Prairies 30

2 "Unspeakable. Unacceptable. Then and Now": The First World War and Canadian Internment Camps 72

3 Canadian Pysanky and the Survival of the Seeds of Memory 105

4 "You filthy little *Zaraza*!": Red Terror, Collectivization, and the Holodomor in Canadian Cultural Memory 133

5 Survivors, Oppressors, Implicated Subjects, and Entangled Bystanders: The Second World War and the Holocaust 168

Conclusion 219

Appendix 223
Index 227

Preface

My maternal and paternal grandparents survived the Second World War. When I was born, all of them were alive, but both of my grandfathers died when I was too young to remember them. I have a blurry image of my maternal grandfather, who died of cancer, lying on his bed watching me when I was looking through the window waiting for my mother to come back home. He was a tall, handsome Ukrainian man with thick, curly hair. Probably my image is distorted by the photos I used to look at with my grandmother when I was a bit older. I have only seen pictures of my paternal grandfather, who escaped from Majdanek concentration camp and survived the war hiding in the woods. At least that is the story I was told – I never found any confirmation that my grandfather was interned. My father and his mother do not often tell stories. When I was in my twenties, I finally asked my paternal grandmother about her family in Lublin and the war. She was only nine months old when Hitler and Stalin invaded Poland, and her mother was killed by the Nazis, allegedly for saving a pregnant Jewish woman. Looking at her picture with my grandmother, her only child, I can say that my paternal great-grandmother was a beautiful and elegant woman with very non-Aryan features. When my grandmother was a toddler, her father remarried. At the age of 16, he found her a husband. My educated and well-off grandfather was in his thirties, and according to my grandmother, he was short and not particularly handsome. People say he was an honest man, but my grandmother has different memories. Although she wanted to leave him, she was not granted a divorce – the only such case of which I have ever heard. The trauma of loss, abandonment, and being in an abusive relationship never left my grandmother, who continued having problems expressing her feelings. When her husband died, she remarried. Her second husband, who was of German heritage, was the only grandfather I ever knew. But he never told me his story.

I got to know more about him from my maternal grandmother. She was the storyteller. Everything I know about my family, about my heritage, about the war, about communism, I know from her. I was the only person with whom she shared her stories. My grandmother died at the age of 74, but I remember her saying much earlier that she was shocked to be alive. "I never thought I would survive to see the day I have grandchildren who are adults," she said on the last birthday we celebrated together. It was the day John Paul II died. A few months later, she had a heart attack and died in my mother's arms. I was there. My grandmother came from central Poland. Being born in 1931, she had vivid memories of war atrocities. Her father was killed by the Nazis, leaving his wife and 11 children, one of them an infant. The Nazis took away their house. Some German soldiers apologized and brought my grandmother and her brothers and sisters chocolate because they did not want to be there – at least some of them. For a while, my grandmother stayed at her wealthy aunt's place. She was abused physically and mentally until the house burned down. She survived. There were times when my grandmother had to eat grass and rotten potatoes to stay alive. More often, she would not eat anything. That is why she would never throw away any food, especially bread. After the war, she lived in Wrocław, which she helped to rebuild. It was the only place she ever called home. She disliked the small town where she later settled down. Maybe that is why I also wanted to live in Wrocław.

No one had to find my maternal grandmother a husband. She found one on her own at the age of 29, visiting one of her many sisters, who was at that time living in Głubczyce, a small town in Upper Silesia that had belonged to Germany before the war. There she met my grandfather, a 23-year-old migrant from present-day Western Ukraine. "I waited for a handsome and tall man because I did not want to have short children," my short grandmother used to tell me. Both of her children and most of her grandchildren are tall. Her mother-in-law never learned Polish, but my grandmother learned some Ukrainian. Enough to understand her saying: "Why did you marry this city lady? Why does she always wear white gloves and a hat? Why doesn't she cook *varenyky*, *borsch*, or *kutia*?" My mother remembers that for her Ukrainian grandmother, the most important thing was keeping the family line alive. That is why she never gave my mother the money her husband – my great-grandfather who fought in the First World War – would give to both of his grandchildren. She gave everything to my uncle because he was a boy. I can only imagine how surprised she would have been to see that her grandson has lived in Germany for more than 30 years. The family line continues, but it is no longer Ukrainian or Polish, as my two male cousins speak German as their first language and are married to German women who will raise their children to be German. My mother changed her last name after marrying my father, but she is the one who stayed in Poland. Moreover, my grandmother is the one who told me all of the stories. The city lady turned out to be the giver of family memories. I guess that makes me the bearer of the Polish and Ukrainian memories of my family.

My maternal grandmother loved reading. She would say that it is not important if your body stops working as long as your brain is functioning properly. Interestingly, my paternal grandmother is the educated one, but she stopped reading when she had to take care of her business. She still has an excellent little library, though. Other than us, no one else in my family shares this passion for books. I remember my mother reading me fairytales and fables when I was a toddler. I started reading at five, and I quickly fell in love because my imagination was – and hopefully still is – immense. I read everything, not always understanding. One of the first books I took from my parents' shelf was Giovanni Boccaccio's *The Decameron*. Although I did not understand a thing, fortunately, I continued reading other books. My real "awakening" happened when my mother gave me a copy of L.M. Montgomery's *Anne of Green Gables*. It was summertime, and I read it on my sofa eating fresh strawberries. The book still has some crimson strawberry stains on it. I spent that summer reading all the other *Anne* books, and since then, I have read them numerous times. *Anne of Windy Poplars* and *Rilla of Ingleside* remain my favorites. My grandmother would tell me stories about the war and post-war Wrocław, and I shared my favorite parts of *Anne* with her. When she learned that together with my mother and paternal grandmother I was going to the USA to be reunited with a long-lost relative, she was devastated. She did not believe we would return, as many of her family members immigrated to the USA or Canada before or after the Second World War and never returned. But we did return. For the final two years of my grandmother's life, I would tell her about Louisiana and Texas, and she would try to recall the names of our relatives living in New York, Chicago, and Toronto. I remember the stories, but I do not remember the names of the great-aunts and great-uncles I have there.

Mark Freeman argues that "the *history* one tells, via *memory*, assumes the form of a *narrative* of the past that charts the trajectory of how one's self came to be" (33; italics original). While I am not Ukrainian *Canadian*, considering my family story and career path, my links to Ukraine and North America are apparent. This book reflects my family's complex next-generation memory, but it is also a reflection of my interdisciplinary research and personal interests over the years: children's and young adult literature, Ukrainian and North American literature(s), memory studies, and gender studies. It is also the aftermath of my various collaborations with numerous scholars, institutions, and students.

Works cited

Freeman, Mark. *Rewriting the Self: History, Memory, Narrative*. Routledge, 1993.

Acknowledgments

First and foremost, I want to thank my family: mother Danuta, father Piotr, brother Tomasz, sister-in-law Marianna, grandmother Janina, cousin Evelyn, as well as my chosen family: my dog Toby, Piotr Ziembiński, Sylwia Kamińska-Maciąg, Łukasz Trzeciak, Monika Jaśkiewicz, Martyna Stefańska, Martyna Gliniecka, Evelina Komarnicki, and Magdalena Szymanowska – I am thanking God and Virgin Mary for having your support and love. Thank you for believing in me and reminding me of my strength even when I was crestfallen and doubted myself.

When I began working on this book, I was teaching several graduate and undergraduate courses, including ones on American, Canadian, and Ukrainian literature. To my wonderful students throughout the years – I greatly appreciate your enthusiasm and deep thoughts. However, writing and teaching at the same time is challenging. Hence I am grateful to the authorities of the University of Wrocław, who provided me with the opportunity to spend a semester on sabbatical. Parts of this book were written at the University of Florida, where I was a Kosciuszko Foundation fellow (2022), and the International Youth Library in Munich (IJB), where I held a fellowship in early 2021. I want to thank the staff at IJB – especially the incredible Nadine Zimmermann, who made sure I did not miss any primary or secondary sources. I am extremely grateful to my dear friend and colleague Anastasia Ulanowicz, who not only keeps on inspiring me in my research and made my stay at the University of Florida possible but also helped me find the voice which had been silent all these years. Ania, I am flattered to call you a friend. Kenneth B. Kidd, I appreciate your support, kindness, and hospitality. A big thank you to my friends at Fulbright Poland and the University of Illinois at Chicago – I started thinking about this project in early 2018 when I was a visiting scholar at the School of Literatures, Cultural Studies, and Linguistics.

To the editors at Routledge and the two anonymous peer reviewers of this book, I greatly appreciate your feedback and am honored that you believed in this project. *Next-Generation Memory* would not have materialized without the support and motivation I received from the authorities and colleagues from the University of Wrocław's Institute of English Studies, Center for Young People's Literature and Culture, Department of American Literature and Culture, Centre for Research on Children's and Young Adult Literature, and Department of Ukrainian Studies. A special thank you to the entire team of the Erasmus Mundus International Children's Literature, Media & Culture Master. I would like to express my gratitude to the following colleagues and friends who supported me in various ways while I was writing this book: Justyna Deszcz-Tryhubczak, Dominika Ferens, Agata Zarzycka, Dorota Kołodziejczyk, Wojciech Drąg, Katarzyna Sówka-Pietraszewska, Justyna Mętrak, Anna Pilińska, Radosław Siewierski, Dorota Michułka, Elżbieta Jamróz-Stolarska, Irena Barbara Kalla, Anna Ursulenko, Sabina Świtała, Mariusz Marszalski, Marina Balina, Larissa Rudova, Elizabeth Dillenburg, Emily Bruce, Cristina Gumirato, Katja Wiebe, Tetiana Kachak, Agnieszka Jeżyk, Junko Yokota, Aniela Radecka, Ludmila Berbenets, Tamara Hundorova, Vitaly Chernetsky, Izabella Kimak, Halyna Pavlyshyn (Rys), Catherine Ellis, Kristine Alexander, Khia Shamone, Guadalupe Arana-Roche, Katarzyna Slany, Ewa Gruda, Kamila Kowalczyk, Zofia Kolbuszewska, and Maryna Vardanian. To Marsha Forchuk Skrypuch, who provided me with advance copies of her last few novels and the original 1996 edition of *Silver Threads* – thank you for your kindness, my kindred spirit. If I have forgotten to name someone – please forgive me and do not hold it against me.

A special thank you to all of the writers and musicians whose books and songs keep on bringing back so many sad, beautiful, and tragic memories.

Short fragments of Chapter 5 were previously published as:

"'You will bear witness for us': Suppressed Memory and Counterhistory in Marsha Forchuk Skrypuch's *Hope's War* (2001)." *Anglica Wratislaviensia*, vol. 58, 2020, pp. 83–95.

Selected thoughts from the following publications issued in Polish were used in the first three chapters:

"Białe plamy pamięci. Nieopowiedziana historia Wielkiej Wojny w twórczości Marshy Forchuk Skrypuch." *Slavica Wratislaviensia*, vol. 172, 2020, pp. 111–122.

"*Daję ci te wspomnienia niczym nasiona…*" – transfer diasporycznej pamięci następnego pokolenia w powieści *Lesia's Dream* (2003) Laury Langston." *Slavica Wratislaviensia*, vol. 173, 2021, pp. 287–301.

I would like to express my appreciation to Ewa Kębłowska-Ławniczak and Ewa Komisaruk – the editors of *Anglica Wratislaviensia* and *Slavica Wratislaviensia*, respectively – for allowing me to use the previously published content.

Introduction

Oh, girls, girls, see that patch of violets! There's something for memory's picture gallery. When I'm eighty years old ... if I ever am ... I shall shut my eyes and see those violets just as I see them now. That's the first good gift our day has given us.

(L.M. Montgomery, *Anne of Avonlea*)

The title of this book was inspired by a scene in Laura Langston's award-winning novel, *Lesia's Dream* (2003), which depicts the relationship between Lesia, a first-generation Ukrainian Canadian and her great-granddaughter Laisha. When the old woman shares the story of her youth spent on the Canadian prairies in the 1910s, she says "*I give you these memories as seeds*" (xi; emphasis in original). Notably, Lesia and Laisha are representatives of the *diaspora*, a word derived from ancient Greek that originally meant scattering and planting seeds. This project studies how historical fiction for young people attempts to communicate cultural memory from one generation to the next. Specifically, it argues that children's fiction has played a particularly significant role in the maintenance and transmission of memory within and beyond the Ukrainian diaspora in Canada. Much like the elderly storyteller of *Lesia's Dream*, the authors of these books offer younger generations seeds of memory. When they are actively read – that is symbolically scattered, planted, and carefully tended – historical narratives may sustain the blossoming and survival of Ukrainian Canadian cultural memory.

In my analysis of 41 texts published in Canada between 1991 and 2021, I argue that they demonstrate what I term next-generation memory. For the youngest generations of Ukrainian Canadians, that is children born in the twenty-first century, past events central in the formation of the diaspora's cultural memory are distant. Usually the readers of historical fiction have no links to the early settlers, the survivors or witnesses of the internment, the Holodomor, or in most cases, also the Second World War. However, authors of historical fiction plant the seeds of what I call next-generation memory in both diasporic *and* mainstream readers. In formulating this notion I use concepts such as Marianne Hirsch's postmemory,

DOI: 10.4324/9781003367918-1

2 Introduction

Alison Landsberg's prosthetic memory, and Anastasia Ulanowicz's second-generation memory.

In one of her most frequently quoted texts, Hirsch maintains that the term postmemory, which she introduced in 1992, can be used to designate the connection "the generation after those who witnessed cultural or collective trauma bears to the experiences of those who came before" (105). Such experiences can only be included in the next generation's mnemonic repertoire "by means of the stories, images, and behaviors among which they grew up" (105). Hirsch highlights that this relation with the memory of the previous generation "has come to be seen as a 'syndrome' of belatedness or 'post-ness'" (105). While in her influential work, Hirsch focuses on the relationship between the survivors of the Holocaust and their children, contact with literary texts can also play a significant role in the production of cultural memory. After all, Hirsch's own inspiration came from both experience and *a book*, Art Spiegelman's graphic memoir *Maus* (Hirsch 107), which was inspired by Calvo's *La bête est morte! La guerre mondiale chez les animaux* (1944), a comic book for young readers.

Landsberg explores the mnemonic potential of various mnemonic media. Instead of emphasizing the generational belatedness, she argues that popular culture can become the source of what she calls prosthetic memory. Such memories are like artificial limbs "derived from engagement with mediated representation (seeing a film, visiting a museum, watching a television miniseries)" but are "sensuous memories produced by an *experience* of mass-mediated representations" (20; emphasis in original). Analyzing Hollywood films and other cultural texts, Landsberg highlights the active role of the recipient in the transfer of prosthetic memory.

While Hirsch writes that the bearers of memory are "*dominated* by narratives that preceded their birth" ("Family Frames" 22; emphasis mine), Ulanowicz contends that this perspective omits the historical and cultural conditions of the second generation. In Hirsch's theory, the memory of the past generation is so prevailing that it displaces the young person's recognition of their own situation in time and space. Using the term second-generation memory, which she defines as "a recent expression of memory – a production or 'generation' of memory – that exists in a contingent, 'second' relationship to earlier articulations of the past," Ulanowicz draws attention to the "*presence* and *collaboration*" (5, 12; emphasis in original) between the recipient and giver of memory in children's books. Moreover, she argues that second-generation memory is palimpsestic and involves both "recognition of the intermingling of two orientations to a past event" and "a consciousness of their difference" (124). Hence with her focus on intergenerational solidarity and collaboration, Ulanowicz's understanding of such a mnemonic practice is broader and more convincing than the ones proposed by Hirsch or Landsberg. Writing about this type of remembering, Ulanowicz also uses the notion of *ghost images*, taken from photography, which illustrates the overlapping of different mnemonic perspectives and experiences (5).[1] As she points out, "memory, particularly second-generation memory, involves narrative emplotment; thus, like all narrative, it is subject to interpretive acts informed by the specific material and political circumstances in which they occur" (124).

Although each of these notions insists on the transfer of intergenerational memory, they were coined in relation to different – and always traumatic – events and focus on diverse mnemonic objects. Unlike post-, prosthetic, or second-generation memory, next-generation memory is of *anticipatory* character. This means that authors of historical fiction *anticipate* the readers – both present-day and future – not to have direct links to any witnesses of the events they discuss and have little knowledge of the transcultural[2] character of the Ukrainian Canadian diaspora. Second, they also anticipate the readers to know a different – and sometimes contradictory – version of history which they want to challenge. Third, considering the rare meaning of the verb *anticipate* as "to forestall by taking countermeasures in advance," authors of historical books create captivating narratives that may prevent the cultural memory of Ukrainian Canadians – a nonvisible ethnic minority – from falling into oblivion. Hence, next-generation memory is cultural and beyond-textual because the transmission of memory occurs between the author, the text, and the reader. Moreover, it does not only denote the transfer of traumatic memories of singular events, but the planting of the seeds of diaspora's separate cultural memory and enabling its survival. Furthermore, I maintain that producing next-generation memory, hence *re*producing cultural memory, is one of the main tasks of Ukrainian Canadian children's historical fiction.

This book argues that reading, imagining, and *re*imagining history can lead to the formation of beyond-textual next-generation memory. Such memory created through reading is multidimensional as it involves the interpretation of both the present *and* the past by an individual whose reality has been directly or indirectly shaped by the past over which they have no influence. I argue that reading historical novels can potentially produce memories which include experiences distant from the readers, but this process is only possible when recorded memory is read and claimed by the readers. Otherwise, as Astrid Erll maintains, "books are nothing but dead material" ("Cultural Memory Studies" 5).

Children's literature published in the last three decades, especially Anglophone historical fiction, is of remarkable importance in the transcultural transfer of next-generation memory and historical discourses. With the rise of English as a global language, such books have become available to a wide range of readers representing various cultural backgrounds. Moreover, Anglophone literature is more likely to be translated into other languages. Examining books by Ukrainian

Canadian authors and tackling the complex Ukrainian–Anglo-Canadian, Ukrainian–Indigenous, Ukrainian–Jewish, Ukrainian–Polish, and Ukrainian–Mennonite relations, I explore how contemporary writers attempt to introduce untold Ukrainian voices to Canadian history and cultural memory. These voices show Ukrainians in a different way, yet one that echoes the Canadian transcultural discourse. The same historical events may have dissimilar meanings and explanations within different communities and national cultural memories. As I argue in the first three chapters of *Next-Generation Memory*, authors of children's historical fiction illuminate the diaspora's need to validate the "founding fathers" status of pioneers, which was an important element in the Ukrainian Canadian post–Second World War identity formation. Throughout the book, I investigate the entangled representations of various historical traumas: the Internment of Ukrainians in Canada, the Great Famine of 1932–1933, and the Holocaust. Insofar as I juxtapose various historical periods and perspectives, I agree with Michael Rothberg that "[c]omparison, like memory, should be thought of as productive – as producing new objects and new lines of sight – and not simply as reproducing already given entities that either are or are not 'like' other given entities" (Rothberg 19).

Next-Generation Memory explains the transcultural dimensions of the investigated historical children's books and the ways literature can shape the contours of the world of young readers; in this way narratives can help them understand the world of the past, as well as the one they live in. In all of the chapters I question how recorded memory – also traumatic memory – can shape the readers both as individuals and members of Canadian transcultural society and how the present-day reality can influence the way we read the past. As Erll remarkably observes, "all cultural memory *must* 'travel,' be kept in motion, in order to 'stay alive', to have an impact both on individual minds and social formations" ("Travelling Memory" 12; emphasis in original). If next-generation memory is to be incorporated into Canadian cultural memory, it cannot stay within the narrow frames of the social group. Rather, it has to move while crossing, overlapping, or crashing with other narratives.

Cultural Memory and Children's Literature

Historical fiction for young readers can be profoundly ideological, especially since authors often attempt to " 'forge truth' from 'facts' " (Stephens 202). Creating narratives about history, writers usually intertwine the past with the implied readers' present knowledge and experience. Then it is more likely for children to actively read[3] and identify with the protagonists' world even when it is that of the past. By forming "a sense of personal identity" through reading, children can also place themselves as individuals *and* members of particular communities in their homelands (Richter 50). This enables the transfer of next-generation memory.

Fiction about the historical experiences of characters representing ethnicities other than those of the young readers encourages children to see the world and society in a different perspective. This can allow them to understand and appreciate diversity and provoke them to question social inequalities, both past, and present, as well as the entanglements between them (cf. Richter 50). While literature helps children experience representations of transcultural societies, it can also position entire groups as the Others, as often is the case with the portrayal of North American Indigenous Peoples in books written by non-Aboriginal authors (cf. Bradford "Transformative Fictions" 195; Goldie 13; Richter 54). Even though writing accurate historical books is challenging, it becomes more difficult when the chronotopes[4] are inhabited by characters of various ethnicities and cultural backgrounds. Hence we should always evaluate whether such books are historically precise *and* pass "the criteria for good literature, as well as the criteria for *cultural consciousness*" (Yokota 158; emphasis mine). This task can be especially problematic, because, as Renée Hulan argues, differentiating "between 'knowing' and 'appropriating'" calls for recognizing the close links between "'speaking for' and 'speaking about' others" (220; qtd. in Kruk 308). Sometimes the line between these two categories becomes blurred, as is the case with most of the texts examined in the first chapter of *Next-Generation Memory*.

As Linda Hutcheon has famously written, Canadian "literature depends on the whole of culture, of history and social traditions without reducing diversity to ethnocultural enclaves" (5). However, many literary voices still remain in such enclaves and have not been transmitted to the cultural memory of the Canadian mosaic. The concept of the mosaic implies that Canada is not a monocultural melting pot of assimilated immigrants but a collage formed by various peoples' histories, cultural memories, and customs. Ukrainian Canadian author Janice Kulyk Keefer has introduced the use of a different concept: a kaleidoscope. She argues that Canada is like "the cylinder that contains" the various "shifting parts" of the kaleidoscope, that is its different peoples, "none of which is more privileged than any other" ("From Mosaic to Kaleidoscope" 16). Both of the metaphors imply an idyllic version of Canada as a place where people representing different sociocultural backgrounds "co-exist harmoniously and equally" (Howard 12). This image, however, "does not always reflect the reality of life in Canada for members of ethnic minorities" – especially visible minorities – and the place of their voices in the Canadian mainstream literary landscape (Howard 12).

Writing about Ukrainian Canadians who immigrated in the last decades of the twentieth century, Patrycja Trzeszczyńska maintains that investigating cultural memory is crucial in studies of diasporas because "its analysis reveals collective desires and needs, collective definitions, fears and traumas, and the power relations happening in the diaspora" ("Diaspora" 12).[5] As I show in my examination of Ukrainian Canadian historical books, next-generation memory is not only political and national, but also gendered, aesthetic, and discursive. Transmitting this type of memory can be done in the form of stories which form a culture's memory and play a vital role in the process of building a nation. Cynthia Sugars and Elanor Ty point to the links between Canadian literature, nation-building, and cultural memory in the introduction to *Canadian Literature and Cultural Memory* (2014). Referring to Pierre Nora's concept of *lieux de memoire* they argue that "Canadian literature as a site of memory is an extremely resonant field, for it attends to the ways that the 'idea' of Canada (and Canadian culture) is informed by interacting frameworks of memory" (5).[6] These various frameworks include the diverse, and sometimes clashing, versions of memory cultivated by ethnoreligious minorities, including Canada's Ukrainians.

The notions of "cultural memory" and "culture of memory" used by numerous scholars, including the authors of the 27 contributions in the collection edited by Sugars and Ty, are complex and multidimensional. The term cultural memory is often attributed to Jan Assmann, who notes that it consists of "reusable texts, images, and rituals, specific to a given society in a given age, whose 'cultivation' serves to stabilize and convey that society's self-image" (132). Assmann, basing on the theory of Maurice Halbwachs, who believed that memory is always socially constructed, distinguishes between three types of memory – cultural, communicative, and collective – and argues that memories of individuals and groups can become part of the cultural memory only when they are reproduced by a larger community, become relevant, and remain relevant over time. Only then can short-lived recollections have the potential to enter the general conscience of a community. It is not incidental that Assmann lists "reusable texts" first in his definition of cultural memory, because just like literature, it is narrative and involves storytelling. In order to survive, cultural memory has to be told/written and repeated/read. Hence, similar to textual narratives, the memory of social groups and nations has to be produced *and* repeatedly reproduced because when discourses are recorded but not shared, they fall into oblivion.

My understanding of cultural memory is broader than Assmann's and closer to Erll's, who calls it "the interplay of present and past in socio-cultural contexts" ("Cultural Memory Studies" 2). As she further explains, "the notions of 'cultural' or 'collective' memory proceed from an operative metaphor," meaning that "[t]he concept of 'remembering' (a cognitive process which takes place in individual brains) is metaphorically transferred to the level of culture" (4). Although cultural memory must travel, it cannot be separated from history or its representations. Hence to become next-generation memory, memory in children's historical fiction has to be anticipatory, transcultural, and multidirectional.

In my examination of historical texts, I concur with Jerry Diakiw that "shared stories lie at the heart of culture's identity" because they "provide a culture with its values and beliefs, its goals and traditions" (37). Sharing and reading stories is also directly connected to the formation of next-generation memory. I find Aleida Assmann's words that "social groups [...] do not 'have' a [collective] memory – they 'make' one for themselves with the aid of memorial signs, such as [...] texts," key in my analyses of books on the Internment of Canada's Ukrainians during the First World War or the role of the Holodomor in diaspora's mnemonic politics, examined in Chapters 2 and 4, respectively (55; emphasis in original). Written stories play an important role in the transmission of memory because creating narratives, as Renate Lachmann notes, "is both an act of memory and a new interpretation" and "every new text is attached into memory space" (301). Thus books encourage the future generations of readers to unravel and *re*imagine recorded memory and inscribe it into their own mnemonic repertoires. Through writing *and* reading, next-generation memory is continuously constructed and *re*constructed in an active interaction between history depicted in the narrative and the present-day context of the readers (cf. Erll "Literature as a Medium" 171).

The formation of next-generation memory is connected to the relationship between the author, the text, *and* the reader, which is never one-sided, as it is the author who anticipates the implied reader's needs, and the reader, who has to re-formulate textual narratives to suit their own circumstances. The textual experience can become the source of the reader's next-generation memory because the author's creative process is directed towards the implied reader and all its stages are of a dialogical nature (cf. Kaplita). Identifying with the characters is of particular importance in the context of books for young readers who are inexperienced, hence more likely than adults "to accept uncritically and appropriate the values conveyed to them in a text, so long as this text captivates them" (Richter 19). Thus it is difficult not to agree with Peter Hunt who contends that all children's books are "educational or influential in some way" (3). Literature for children, as Hunt notes, "reflect[s] ideology" and always "teach[es] something" (3). Books can also play a significant role in transmitting next-generation memory because children are most disposed to be influenced by textual narratives, especially ones allowing them to identify and build strong connections with protagonists.

The perks of storytelling allow the authors of historical fiction to intertwine exciting plots and characters with a particular mnemonic discourse they want the readers to appreciate *and* appropriate. Hans Haino Ewers maintains that young people require hearing stories for "they think in terms of stories and are able to discover the fundamental truths revealed by stories long before they are capable of thinking in abstract terms" (176). That is why stories told by authors of historical fiction have an extraordinary potential in enabling the transfer of next-generation memory and function as a means in young readers' "ethical development" (cf. Dean-Ruzicka 13). Notably, already in the 1960s Canadian educator Sheila A. Egoff argued that reading historical fiction allows children to "live" history instead of passively studying it, making its impact more permanent ("Canadian Historical" 44). This educational potential of historical novels has been studied more recently by Sara L. Schwebel, who observes that frequently students who dislike history enjoy reading books about it, which she calls "a small miracle" (3). This miracle does not come as a surprise, because historical novels for children and young adults enable "a degree of critical thinking" and encourage interest in the past by encouraging the readers to picture "themselves in, and as part of, the past" (Schwebel 3). Not every historical novel has such an education and mnemonic potential, though. All readers, even novice ones, need to be *captivated* before they can identify with the book (cf. Richter 19). Only then reading can become active. Yet making children interested in a historical narrative is a challenge many authors do not succeed in. After all, historical fiction for children and young adults can be schematic because it typically follows fixed narrative patterns. Moreover, the interdiscursive and polyvalent character of writing and the need to stand out cause some authors to *deform* history.[7]

Being historically accurate and politically correct, "sparing," yet not misinforming the child reader, is one of the greatest challenges of children's literature, which often depends on closure, happy-endings, and narratives of hope (cf. Bosmajian; Kokkola). In her influential study of Holocaust fiction for young people, Hamida Bosmajian argues that most adult writers want to "spare the child," mainly when the topics they introduce are challenging (6). However, Adrienne Kertzer asserts in her own analysis of Holocaust books that "children's fiction need not restrict itself to the predictable, and misleadingly cheerful, version of survival" (280). To captivate the reader, books about history need to be "good history and good literature" (Kokkola 47) – whatever the subjective meaning of good is.

Sparing the child is especially important in the context of "the so-called children's literature of atrocity" which has become increasingly popular in the last decades, especially, but not exclusively, in North America (Kidd 184). I concur with Lydia Kokkola who contends that scholars working on historical narratives should study how "communication takes place in order to avoid *inadvertent misrepresentations* of the events under discussion" (15; emphasis mine). While Kokkola focuses on Holocaust literature, I believe the matter of intentional and unintentional distortions is fundamental in the context of other historical texts, especially those focused on diversity and transculturalism. After all, books are frequently the child's first encounter with the complex past (and its present reflections), which cannot be explained using binary categories of good vs. evil (cf. Dean-Ruzicka 14; Gangi 163–192).

As writer Marsha Forchuk Skrypuch, whose texts I investigate in this book, argues, "young readers ingest historical fiction as history," hence the author's "responsibility to get things right is tremendous" ("Am I Ukrainian?" 65). Skrypuch's words resonate with Italian illustrator Roberto Innocenti's claims that authors of historical books for children "cannot be neutral or impartial," but rather should encourage "the reader to become a judge, to think for one's self," even as they "must be careful of creating a sermon" (30). Therefore authors always shape the next-generation memory they want to be transmitted through their books. Being "right" or "accurate" is not as obvious as it seems considering that history is also a narrative open to interpretations. Frank R. Ankersmit argues that history has to be decoded and even if its vision is shared by several historians, the dominant discourse can easily change with time and the possible social/political/cultural transformations (248–260). In *Next-Generation Memory* I explore the changes in the scope of mnemonic discourses, most notably in Chapters 2 and 4.

The same historical events, even ones well-documented, as is the case with modern history, may have dissimilar meanings and explanations within different communities and national cultural memories. As Robert Bellah et al. observe:

> Communities [...] have a history – in an important sense they are constituted by their past – and for this reason we can speak of community as a "community of memory", one that does not forget its past. [...] The stories of collective memory and exemplary individuals are an important part of the tradition that is so central to a community of memory.
>
> (153)

Usually stories are written down and become a useful tool in sharing versions of history and cultural memory because literature is an "integral part of the process by which nation-states create themselves and distinguish themselves from other nations" (Corse 7). Books in wide circulation, hence read by large numbers of individuals, are especially important in this process. That is why in *Next-Generation Memory* I investigate texts written in English and published in Canada.[8]

Ukrainian Canadians and Canadian Multiculturalism

Literature has a transcultural potential and as Miriam Verena Richter argues, "identification with literary characters whose origins lie in a different culture also prepares the readers for encounters with people of foreign cultures in everyday life" (25). Studying historical books about Ukrainian Canadians and Ukrainians, in this project I consider the ways their authors make possible the identification with such characters and their distance experiences.

While in the last few decades Ukraine has been entangled with the North American political life, most people outside of the diaspora know little of the country's complex sociopolitical position in the twentieth century (cf. Yekelchyk 1–19; Plokhy "The Frontline"). Before the First World War, present-day Ukraine was divided between two antagonistic empires,

Austria-Hungary and Russia; it was heterogenous and inhabited mostly by Ukrainians, Jews, Poles, Russians, and Germans. In the interwar period it was split between four different countries: the USSR, Poland, Czechoslovakia, and Romania. During the Second World War Ukraine was occupied by the Nazis and the Soviets, and then it was incorporated into the Soviet Union, which "had clear colonial underpinnings and produced anti-colonial resistance" (Plokhy "The Frontline" loc. 230).

Ukrainian Canadians, as I show in the first three chapters of this study, are an ethnic minority whose identity to a significant extent relies on the pioneer experience. Immigration from Ukraine symbolically started with the arrival of Ivan Pylypiw and Vasyl Eleniak in 1891, 100 years before the country gained independence (cf. Lazarenko 15; Story 806; Swyripa "Storied" 25, 91, 125). Between 1896 and 1914, under policies adopted by Clifford Sifton, immigrants from Galicia and Bukovyna, mostly peasants, settled in the prairies of Alberta, Manitoba, and Saskatchewan. At that time most of the territory of present-day Ukraine was part of the Russian Empire, and only Galicia, Bukovyna, and Trans-Carpathia were under Austro-Hungarian control. While the provinces were inhabited predominately by ethnic Ukrainians, they were the country's "most heterogeneous regions" with a large number of Poles (40%) and Jews (10%) in Galicia and Romanians (30%), Jews, and Germans in Bukovyna (Himka 11). In Canada, Ukrainians built isolated farm communities "and their distinctive sheepskin coats became a target for those who opposed foreign immigration" (Story 807). As Frances Swyripa notes in *Storied Landscapes*, the block settlement of Slavs, mostly Ukrainians, was met with hostility, as they were dismissively called "Sifton's pets" (15). Yet by 1916 Ukrainians, next to Germans, were "the largest 'foreign' ethnic group" in the prairies (Swyripa "Storied" 20). The so-called first wave of immigration stopped with the outbreak of the First World War, as immigrants from Austria-Hungary, mostly Ukrainians, were considered enemy aliens and were interned in 24 camps, a theme I further examine in Chapter 2.

Immigration continued after the end of the war and due to numerous political differences, the diaspora became "a fractured entity" (Satzewich 85). Seventy thousand people immigrated during the interwar period, including a small number of politically engaged war veterans and survivors of Polish "pacification" of Eastern Galicia and Stalinism in Soviet Ukraine (cf. Martynowych 173). Although in the 1930s some of the veterans were linked to the Organization of Ukrainian Nationalists (OUN) and were openly anti-Communist, their views were of marginal resonance (cf. Martynowych 198). They sent petitions to the government and various organizations informing them about the Holodomor and other Stalinist atrocities, which remained largely ignored by the West. I discuss the role of the Great Famine of 1932–1933 in the diaspora's mnemonic politics in Chapter 4.

The next main influx of Ukrainians, which occurred after the Second World War, consisted of displaced persons (DPs) and people escaping

Soviet occupation. Vic Satzewich argues that the DPs "further complicated an already messy situation" (85). Unlike the early immigrants, most Ukrainians arriving to Canada after the Second World War settled in cities. The third wave of Ukrainian immigrants was more diverse, as it consisted of the intelligentsia, artisans, and peasants representing various political views. The new immigrants had different experiences. Among them were victims of the Nazis, such as *Ostarbeiters* (Eastern workers or slave laborers) and child survivors of the *Lebensborn* program. Other DPs lived through the Soviet occupation, like those who before the Second World War had also survived collectivization, exiles to Siberia and the GULAG, and the Holodomor. Some risked their lives hiding Jews, like the 2,659 Ukrainians who were given the Righteous Among the Nations title; others were members of the controversial 14th Waffen Grenadier Division of the SS (1st Ukrainian), the Organization of Ukrainian Nationalists (OUN), and the Ukrainian Insurgent Army (known as UPA) accused of collaboration with the Nazis and participation in pogroms (cf. Rudling; Trzeszczyńska "Ukraińska"). The most recent wave consisted of political and economic immigrants coming from USSR, Poland, former Yugoslavia, as well as independent Ukraine (Trzeszczyńska "Diaspora" 16, 23). The last chapter of *Next-Generation Memory* discusses the entangled positions of Ukrainians and Ukrainian Canadians during and after the Second Word War.

In 2021 Canada was home to the world's third-largest population of Ukrainians – behind only Ukraine and Russia. Ukrainian Canadians have become one of Canada's most visible ethnoreligious groups and, next to the Mennonites, the only one whose story of settlement was commemorated with special stamps issued by Canada Post (Swyripa "Storied" 185). The stamps featured paintings by William Kurelek, one of Canada's most popular painters, who published a series of successful and critically acclaimed picturebooks in the 1970s. His "visual memories of a Ukrainian-Canadian childhood spent on a Manitoba dairy farm in the 1930s" won numerous awards, including *The New York Times* Best Illustrated Book (1973, 1974), sold more than half a million copies in North America, and were translated into several languages (Saltman 61; Carpenter 261).

Currently the diaspora consists of people representing different religious, economic, and political backgrounds, who came from various regions during different periods, their descendants, and new immigrants who arrived after the collapse of communism – including Russian-speaking Ukrainians. Most of them, however, were born in and grew up in Canada and until the early 1990s had limited access to visiting their ancestors' homeland. Hence many Canadian authors "attempt to locate Ukraine on the Canadian prairie as a substitute home-country" (Ledohowski "Canadian Cossacks" iii). The need to validate the "founding" status of pioneers was an important element in the Ukrainian Canadian post–Second World War identity formation; especially after the appearance of the bicultural Lester B. Pearson's Royal Commission on Bilingualism and Biculturalism (1963) which "[denounced] ... other ethnic groups to an inferior, 'non-founding' status and their cultures to eventual submersion in one of two 'official cultures'" (Bociurkiw 105). Several Ukrainian organizations and intellectuals "voiced their staunch disapproval of a bipartite model of nationhood [...] [and] played an active, if not central, role in lobbying for the institutionalization of multiculturalism" (Grekul "Re-Placing" 373–374). As Swyripa observes, "a founding fathers myth [was] erected on the peasant pioneers: in their backbreaking toil and sacrifice to introduce the prairie and parkland to the plough and to exploit mining and forest frontiers so that Canada could be great, lay Ukrainians' right to full partnership in Confederation" ("Wedded" 221). Hence promoting "the pioneer story, Ukrainian Canadians could write themselves into Canadian history as a 'third force' to counter the two founding nations' model that dominated those early discussions" (Ledohowski "Little Ukraine" 188). Notably, when multiculturalism was announced as Canada's official policy by Prime Minister Pierre Elliott Trudeau in 1971,[9] it happened at an assembly of the Ukrainian Canadian Congress (Hryniuk and Luciuk 3; Grekul "Re-Placing" 374).

The discourse of multiculturalism boosted the development of Ukrainian Canadian literature and culture as it "created audiences and funding for Ukrainian Canadian literary works, so Ukrainian Canadian writers were ostensibly able to acknowledge and explore their Ukrainian backgrounds for the first time with neither embarrassment nor shame" (Grekul "Re-Placing" 372). As Polish scholar Mirosława Buchholtz notes, Ukrainians were the first Canadian ethnic minority which in the 1970s participated in the practice of printing books from "cultures other than Anglophone, Francophone, and First Nations" (344). Despite these efforts, as Dagmara Drewniak observes in *Forgetful Recollections: Images of Central and Eastern Europe in Canadian Literature*, most authors of Central or Eastern European heritage, including Ukrainians, "have been recognized as separate entities rather than members of a large migrant group" (18).[10] Moreover, their representation in mainstream books on Canadian literature, such as Smaro Kamboureli's *Making a Difference: Canadian Multicultural Literature* (1996) or *Canadian Literature in English: Texts and Contexts* (2009), the anthology edited by Sugars and Laura Moss, is poor (Drewniak "Major Themes" 151).

While initially Ukrainian Canadians were pressured "to assimilate to Anglo-Canadian society," they managed to preserve "a distinct, unified cultural heritage," yet one which "often relies on folkloric expressions of ethnicity" (Grekul "Re-Placing" 378). Such folkloristic expressions of Ukrainian identity are present in Marguerite V. Burke's *The Ukrainian Canadians*, a didactic children's book about three generations of Ukrainian Canadians, which was published in the Multicultural Canada Series in 1978 – a decade before the implementation of The Canadian Multiculturalism Act (CMA). Burke urges the readers to cook *borscht*, write a *pysanka*, and read folktales and Kurelek's picturebooks. After encouraging the children to read more about *"assimilation, acculturation,* and *integration,"* Burke informs them that "Canada has been described as a 'salad bowl' and not as a 'melting pot.' This means that people from other cultures have been encouraged to keep their *folkways"* (39, 51; emphasis mine). Notably, the CMA passed in 1988 further encouraged "the preservation of *some* aspects of immigrant culture and communal life within the context of Canadian citizenship and political and economic integration into Canadian society" (Palmer 163; emphasis mine). CMA also promotes "the understanding that multiculturalism is a fundamental characteristic of the Canadian heritage and identity and that it provides an invaluable recourse in the shaping of Canada's future" (*The Canadian Multiculturalism Act* clause 3(1)b). Hence all Canadians are to "preserve, enhance and share their cultural heritage," which seems to be a palimpsestic picture (*The Canadian Multiculturalism Act* clause 3(1)a). CMA portrays "an official vision of Canada in which immigrants [...] are encouraged to retain their heritage languages and ethnocultural traditions" (Edwards and Satman 192). The policy of multiculturalism "deeply influenced Canadian children's literature" (Edwards and Satman 192), including Ukrainian Canadian historical fiction.

In her examination of books written by Canada's Ukrainians, Lisa Grekul notes that despite the ideological and social differences within the diaspora, Ukrainian Canadians "together turned their heritage into a commodity-like product," but because of it they "united for the first time by common symbols and expressions of their ethnicity [and] began to take public pride in their cultural heritage" ("Leaving Shadows" 54). Hence for many Ukrainian Canadians, being Ukrainian became synonymous with culinary and folkloristic dimensions represented by *baba, pysanky* (Easter eggs), *pyrohy,* embroidery, and dancing *hopak* dressed up as a Cossack – notably all featured extensively in children's literature, especially Marion Mutala's series of *Baba's Babushka* picturebooks discussed in Chapters 1 and 3. The old country many Ukrainian Canadians know does not evoke the diverse and transcultural post-Soviet Ukraine. Moreover, as Kulyk Keefer points out, also for many Anglo-Canadians, Ukraine is associated with "*borshch* and cabbage rolls, vast and shining wheat fields, and pretty girls with whirling ribbons and flashing red boots" ("Dark Ghost" 19). Thus in the Ukrainian Canadian cultural memory Ukraine is synonymous with the prairie and emerges as a pioneer myth, a simulacrum represented by the Cossack and the *baba*, which I explore in Chapters 1 and 3, respectively.

Despite the popularity of the folkloristic aspects of Ukrainian culture, including the *baba* who "functioned as part of a 'founding fathers' or 'peasant pioneer' myth to confirm her descendants in their Canadian birthright and to legitimize the Ukrainian group within Confederation" (Swyripa "Wedded" 26), in North American historical narratives Ukrainians tend to be depicted in a stereotypical, mostly negative way, which is the aftermath of the memory boom of the 1980s and the investigations of the alleged Nazi war criminals residing in Canada and the USA, often caused by KGB fabrications (cf. Zhuk). Considering Ukraine's complex history, it is not surprising that Ukrainian Canadians have been tangled in memory wars. As Rothberg notes, "those who understand memory as a form of competition see only winners and losers in the struggle for collective articulation and recognition" (5). Some accused Ukrainian Canadians of "whitewash[ing] Ukrainian atrocities against the Jews" – mostly those committed by the Waffen-SS Galizien, OUN, and UPA – and even "resort[ing] to a competitive victimology" by "exaggerat[ing] the death count associated with the Ukraine famine of 1932–33" (Ball and Rudling 35). Yet as Myrna Kostash, the influential author of *All of Baba's Children* (1977) and *Bloodlines: A Journey into Eastern Europe* (1993), notes, the position of Ukrainian Canadians has been continually questioned:

> [t]here is no getting around the psychological *insecurity* of a community that has periodically lived under a cloud in Canada as 'enemy aliens' in the Great War, 'Reds' in the 1930s, anti-communist extremists in the 1950s, and aging, anti-Semitic alleged pro-Nazi collaborators in the 1980s and 1990s.
> (qtd. in Grekul "Leaving Shadows" 197; emphasis in original)

In response to the aforementioned allegations, the diaspora popularized a narrative positioning Ukrainians as a nation starved by Stalin in the 1930s, trapped between two antagonistic regimes and fighting against both during the Second World War, and then openly opposing communism (cf. Chapter 5). This cultural memory, based on the simple categories of victims and oppressors, further contributed to tensions between various groups forming the Canadian mosaic. Accusations of Ukrainian Canadian anti-Semitism reappeared more recently before the opening of the Canadian Museum for Human Rights (CMHR) in September 2014 in Winnipeg, Manitoba, when the Ukrainian Canadian Civil Liberties Association (UCCLA) and the Ukrainian Canadian Congress (UCC) opposed the plans to inaugurate a separate and permanent gallery dedicated to the Holocaust (Ball and Rudling). After all, "how to think about the relationship between different social groups' histories of victimization" is "one of the most agonizing problems of contemporary multicultural societies" (Rothberg 2). The clashing visions of history do not seem surprising considering that "degrees of transparency and democratic memory construction determine the ultimate content of cultural and collective memory, and the transitions between various forms of memory invariably involve intergroup negotiations and contestations" (McConnell 332). Such conflicting versions of history appear in the novels I examine in Chapter 5.

Writing about the history of Eastern Europe, which he calls "bloodlands," Timothy Snyder fittingly argues that

> attention to any single persecuted group, no matter how well executed as history, will fail as an account of what happened in Europe between 1933 and 1945. [...] Often what happened to one group is intelligible only in the light of what happened to another.
>
> (xix)

However, until recently, in most historical novels for young readers set during the Second World War, Ukrainians were portrayed as perpetrators or collaborators.[11] The Ukrainian perspective has also been absent in literary criticism. Studying Anglophone Holocaust books, Kokkola mentions Ukraine only thrice – each time in the context of collaboration with the Nazis. Rachel Dean-Ruzicka, in her remarkable *Tolerance Discourse and Young Adult Holocaust Literature*, references Ukraine once: "mobile killing squads (Einsatzgruppen) were often the ones that decimated Jewish populations, particularly in the [sic!] Ukraine" (12). Notably, Dean-Ruzicka's book came out 14 years after Kokkola's *Representing the Holocaust*. At least six mainstream North American Ukrainian Second World War–themed books were published in the meantime, but they are not even briefly mentioned in *Tolerance Discourse*. Writing about the unrepresented victims of the Holocaust, Dean-Ruzicka lists "the Romani, the disabled, and homosexuals [...] black Europeans, Jehovah's Witnesses, and political dispensers" but does not reference non-Jewish Slavs (83). Yet in his *Lebensraum* project, Hitler wanted to exterminate 65% of Ukrainians and enslave all of the survivors (Schmuhl 334–348). The Nazi policies exterminated about three million Ukrainians, and two million were brought to Germany as slave labor. Incomparably more Ukrainians fell victim to the Nazis or fought against them than collaborated, but the Ukrainian perspective of the Second World War stayed essentially unfamiliar in North America because of Cold War politics (cf. Zhuk). Chapter 5 of *Next-Generation Memory* explores the roots of such stereotypical depiction of Ukrainians in North American culture and examines books where it is challenged.

In this project I write about the entangled social relations between Ukrainian Canadians, non-Canadian Ukrainians, and non-Ukrainian Canadians, including First Nations, and other immigrants from Eastern Europe, especially Poles, Germans, Mennonites, and Jews. Agreeing that cultural memory can become "the basis for the formation of culturally induced social relations and ties linking individuals or groups," in my analysis of children's literature, I consider its mnemonic and transcultural potential (Hałas 136). Moreover, I agree with Rothberg that instead of fighting memory wars and sticking to the simple victim oppressor binary, we should "consider memory as *multidirectional*: as subjects to ongoing negotiation, cross-referencing, and borrowing; as productive and not

16 *Introduction*

private" (3). Such an understanding of memory is especially productive in the transcultural contexts of both Ukraine and Canada.

Ukrainians and Canadian Literature

Perry Nodelman and Mavis Reimer argue that books for young readers "can make [children] conscious that there is more than one way of being normal" (149). In my exploration of Ukrainian and Ukrainian Canadian history and memory portrayed in contemporary fiction for young readers, I wonder if such narratives can show them that history is not one-dimensional without being misleading.[12] For my analysis, I have chosen texts published between 1991 and 2021. I attempted to locate all books authored by Ukrainian Canadians or devoted to Ukraine which were published in Canada, but it is possible that some titles were missed. To identify the texts I used the databases of the International Youth Library in Munich, the University of Florida, the University of Glasgow, all of the issues of *Resource Links* published since 1997, as well as 217 volumes of *Something About the Author*. Moreover, I consulted with publishers, educators, librarians, and authors. I compiled a corpus of 61 books (Appendix), with 41 fitting my criteria: authored by Canadians who are representatives of the next generations of immigrants from present-day Ukraine or have other links to Ukraine or dedicated to Ukrainian/ Ukrainian Canadian history and distributed in Canada. While several books were translated into other languages, including French, Korean, Portuguese, Spanish, and Chinese, none of them have been published in Ukraine.[13] Therefore *Next-Generation Memory* focuses only on the analysis of historical fiction listed in the Appendix. All of the books were written in English and published in North America; some were issued by major press or small independent publishers, while some were self-published; many won critical acclaim, but others went unnoticed. In my cross-sectional analysis, I showcase the importance of the growing number of Ukrainian Canadian children's books, but also point to the disadvantages of self-publishing and the importance of professionally published and widely circulated works. Some of the self-published books were reviewed in *Resource Links* and were nominated to local and national awards. Thus, most implied readers may not be aware that they were self-issued. However, I point to significant discrepancies between the literary quality of professionally and self-published books. This is particularly relevant in the context of historical accuracy and accessibility of fiction devoted to previously untold, hence little known, topics. Despite the variety of issues and historical periods covered, most of the texts portray Canada as the promised land, the only place Ukrainian customs and traditions can survive by becoming part of Canadian cultural memory.[14]

Ukrainian Canadian literature in English has been studied by numerous Canadian and international scholars, including, most recently,[15] Jars Balan (1998), Sonia Mycak (2001), Lisa Grekul (2004;

2005), Lindy Ledohowski (2007; 2008; 2013; 2015), Natalia Aponiuk (2015), Dagmara Drewniak (2014), Weronika Suchacka (2010; 2019), and others. Still, the status of Ukrainian Canadian literature and the scholarship about it is marginal.[16] For example, in *Canadian Literature and Cultural Memory*, the aforementioned volume edited by Sugars and Ty, the only time Ukraine is mentioned is in the context of Mennonite immigration. Additionally, works for younger readers have not been met with adequate scholarly recognition despite their popularity with readers and critics alike, relatively higher than the one the so-called mainstream Ukrainian Canadian books receive.[17] In her 2005 book *Leaving Shadows: Literature in English by Canada's Ukrainians*, Grekul writes that "the realization that keeping ethnic identity alive requires acts of will, courage, and above all, imagination" and emphasizes "the crucial role that literature plays in nurturing – imagining and re-imagining – ethnic identity" (xxiii). Hence the limited critical attention applied to Ukrainian Canadian children's literature seems surprising, especially considering that books for children have "played a special role in the process of nation-building" in Canada (Richter xiv).

In her *From Nursery Rhymes to Nationhood: Children's Literature and the Construction of Canadian Identity*, Elizabeth A. Galway shows that in Anglophone children's books published in the late nineteenth and early twentieth centuries, "[e]xploring national history became a key part of the process of developing national unity and identity" (13). She argues that in history authors "found a source of literary inspiration, and the tools needed to construct a Canadian identity" (13). Thus "[h]istorical narratives taught children about their nation's past, and groomed them for their role as contributors to its future" (13). Whereas between 1867 and 1914 Canadian children's literature played the role of "a powerful tool [...] used to help build the nation" (Galway 2), in the second half of the twentieth century books, including historical fiction, endorsed the image of Canada as a multicultural country formed by people of various ethnicities and cultural backgrounds.

The thriving popularity of Canadian children's literature, especially in the second half of the twentieth century, "has always had everything to do with Politics" (Davis 5). The first library programs for children were established by the Toronto Public Library under the supervision of Lillian H. Smith in the early 1910s and were a great success in the process of "civilizing" non-English immigrants, including "Galicians" (Richter 61–63). While the early library programs were aimed at instructing immigrants into (Anglo-)Canadians, initiatives involving a different, multicultural perspective were led by Lyn Cook right after the Second World War with the influx of new immigrants. Cook's local "standing-room only" story hours featured tales about children in other countries and foreign legends. Instead of civilizing, Cook was motivated by the need to preserve "the traditions of immigrants' home countries" and her initiative was met with great success (Richter 73). Later she was even offered a radio show called "Doorways to Fairytale," which proved to be popular nationwide (Richter 73–74). Such initiatives did not become mainstream until the 1970s, though. While until the 1960s the official policy was that of assimilation, it is "[f]or ideological reasons, official discourse has presented the concept of the multicultural mosaic as a feature of Canadian society from its very beginnings" (Richter 43). Only after Prime Minister Pierre Trudeau's White Paper and the introduction of multiculturalism as official policy, librarians nationwide started paying more attention to "discarding of children's books containing racial stereotyping" (Richter 75).

Ukrainians were among the first non-Anglo- and non-French Canadians represented in children's literature[18] long before the Canadian Multiculturalism Act was introduced in 1988 and a few years before Vera Lysenko's *Yellow Boots* (1954), widely regarded as the first Ukrainian Canadian novel in English, was published. Lyn Cooke's first best-selling multicultural children's novels, *The Bells on Finland Street* (1950) and *The Little Magic Fiddler* (1951), both include a variety of Ukrainian characters. *My Name Is Paula Popowich!* (1983), one of Monica Hughes' few non-science-fiction novels, portrays identity struggles of a teenage girl who learns that her father is Ukrainian. Notably, *My Name Is Paula Popowich!* is the first Anglo-Canadian children's book which openly mentions the existence of a distinctive "Ukrainian-Canadian" identity (127; cf. Richter 256). Cooke's and Hughes' three novels contributed to the visibility of Ukrainian Canadians, yet they were written by Anglo-Canadian authors with no Ukrainian background and are not free of ethnic stereotypes (cf. Richter).

The presence of Ukrainian Canadian voices in children's and young adult literature is of particular importance considering Grekul's claims – echoing Margaret Atwood's 1972 *Survival: A Thematic Guide to Canadian Literature* – that "[t]he Ukrainian Canadian literary tradition simply will not survive if it is not included in classroom syllabi and drawn into ongoing debates in Canadian literary studies" ("Leaving Shadows" 203). After all, writing approachable fiction for Canadian youth, authors like Skrypuch, Langston, or Warwaruk become "poet pedagogues"[19] who can have "a profound impact on the next generation" (Ledohowski "Introduction" 9). To further rephrase Atwood's influential *Survival*, it may be argued that writing, reading, and teaching Ukrainian Canadian literature is of great importance because "it's hard to find out who anyone else is until you have found out who *you* are" (16; cf. Ulanowicz 143–154).

In their introduction to *Cultural Grammars of Nation, Diaspora, and Indigeneity in Canada*, Christine Kim and Sophie McCall observe "that diaspora and nation are interdependent and mutually constituting, just as indigeneity and nation are reciprocally contingent and responsive" (2). Agreeing with Kim and McCall, in this book I point to the transcultural dimensions of historical children's books authored by those who identify as Ukrainian Canadians or have direct or indirect links with Ukraine. I concur with Grekul that "past definitions of the nation never pass away completely; on the contrary, they leave indelible traces of the social, political, and cultural landscape of the country" ("Leaving Shadows" 9). Yet I also believe that the present-day reality always shapes the way we read the past.

Chapter Outline and Corpus

This book consists of five chapters offering cross-sectional readings of 41 books identified as historical fiction from a corpus of 61 children's texts (see Appendix). The first three chapters focus on the experiences of the first two waves of Ukrainian immigration and the process of becoming Ukrainian *Canadian*. The last two chapters are devoted to the significance of the cultural memory of the Holodomor and the Second World War for *Ukrainian* Canadians. In the opening chapter titled "Land of All Colors and Races? Canadian Cossacks, Indigenous Peoples, and The Myth of the Founding Fathers of the Prairies," I examine books depicting the emigration from Western Ukraine to the Canadian prairie at the turn of the twentieth century – mainly Larry Warwaruk's *Andrei and the Snow Walker* (2002), its companion novel *Brovko's Amazing Journey* (2013), and Laura Langston's *Lesia's Dream* (2003). In my analysis I also point to other texts, most notably Marsha Forchuk Skrypuch's *Prisoners in the Promised Land: The Ukrainian Internment Diary of Anya Soloniuk* (2007) and Marion Mutala's *Kokhum's Babushka: A Magical Métis/Ukrainian Tale* (2017) illustrated by Donna Lee Dumont. I demonstrate how Andrei Bayda, the 12-year-old protagonist of Warwaruk's novels, and Langston's Lesia Magus, become the symbolic guardians of Ukrainian customs and traditions, represented by the Bible, Cossacks, Scythians, and *kobzars*. In my close reading of the books, I point to the way in which Warwaruk depicts the chronotope of the Canadian prairie as a multicultural simulacrum of Ukraine, a land inhabited by the English, Métis, and Ukrainian Canadians, where Ukrainian Canadians, just like Indigenous Peoples, are shown as having a special and natural connection to the prairie. While Warwaruk highlights the alleged similarities between Ukrainians and Indigenous Peoples, they are absent in *Lesia's Dream*.

Chapter 2, titled "'Unspeakable. Unacceptable. Then and Now' – The First World War and Canadian Internment Camps," focuses on books featuring the theme of Ukrainians as enemy aliens during the First World War and the Canadian First World War Internment. Skrypuch was the first children's author to publish a picturebook about the internment of Ukrainians, which was recognized by parliament almost 90 years later, provoking a discussion on the contemporary Canadian migration policy. *Silver Threads* (1996), illustrated by Michael Martchenko, came out nine years before the approval of Bill C-331 (Internment of Persons of Ukrainian Origin Recognition Act) in 2005. Examining several internment-themed texts, I point to the discursive changes in the place of the internment in Canadian children's literature *and* collective memory. In my cross-sectional close reading of multiple texts published between 1996 and 2021 – including *Silver Threads* (1996) by Skrypuch and Martchenko, Skrypuch's *Prisoners in the Promised Land: The Ukrainian Internment Diary of Anya Soloniuk* (2007), Glen Huser's *Firebird* (2020), Pam Clark's *Kalyna* (2016), and the graphic novel *Enemy Alien: A True Story of Life Behind Barbed Wire* (2020) by Kassandra Luciuk and nicole marie burton – I demonstrate that the official recognition and commemoration of the internment directly contributed to the popularization of this theme among Canadian authors, scholars, and readers, also those outside of the Ukrainian diaspora.

The last chapter in this cluster, titled "Canadian Pysanky and the Survival of the Seeds of Memory," is devoted to the examination of the themes of femininity, mothering, childbirth, and assimilation in books by Warwaruk, Langston, Skrypuch, and Gloria Kupchenko Frolick. Unlike *Lesia's Dream* and *Andrei and the Snow Walker*, Frolick's *Anna Veryha* (1992), a novella inspired by one of Kurelek's pictures, is set in the depression-era Canadian prairie. Close-reading the books, I showcase the various ways in which the authors approach the *baba* and *Nasha Meri* and *Katie* stereotypes. I argue that many Ukrainian Canadian narratives focus on the importance of birth and mothering in the survival of Ukrainian customs and traditions. Moreover, I show that girls and young women depicted in the books are surrounded by clashing visions of femininity performed by members of the protagonists' family and neighbors – first- and second-generation Ukrainian immigrants displaying conflicting approaches towards national identity, memory, traditions, and the role of women in society.

Studying books by authors of Ukrainian (Mutala, Gal, Skrypuch), Mennonite (Dueck), and German (Goldstone) heritage, in Chapter 4, titled " 'You filthy little *Zaraza*!' – Red Terror, Collectivization, and the Holodomor in Canadian Cultural Memory," I examine narratives depicting the experiences of immigrants from Ukraine who are *not* ethnic Ukrainians and point to aspects of Ukrainian history little known in North America, such as collectivization, the Bolshevik revolution, and the anarchist Makhno movement, previously one-sidedly portrayed by Barbara Smucker in the Canadian classic *Days of Terrors* (1979). In my analysis of Holodomor-themed books, I show that the Great Famine of 1932–1933 has become a fundamental part of Ukrainian Canadian memory politics, yet until recently it was of limited interest to the mainstream, as until 2022 only *Enough*, Skrypuch's 2000 picturebook illustrated by Michael Martchenko, was issued by a major publisher. Although authors investigated in this chapter focus on introducing the readers to little known facts from Eastern European history, in their books Canada emerges as the promised land similar to that found in other Canadian texts, including Holocaust novels.

The final chapter, titled "Survivors, Oppressors, Implicated Subjects, and Entangled Bystanders: The Second World War and the Holocaust," includes some of the most controversial aspects of contemporary Ukrainian Canadian history – Ukrainians in the context of the Second World War and the Holocaust. Agreeing with Kokkola that "[h]istorical inaccuracy, even in works of fiction, is morally unacceptable in writing about the Holocaust" (23), I compare Skrypuch's Second World War books with Kathy Kacer's *Louder than Words* (2020), a Canadian novel about a Ukrainian rescuer of Jews, and consider the potential risks of including oversimplifications, misinformation, historical inaccuracies, and infantilization in children's Holocaust fiction. I argue that by bringing attention to the traumatic experiences of many Ukrainians, who were "trapped in Hitler's web," in her seven Second World War–themed novels, Skrypuch attempts to put them on the landscape of Canadian collective and cultural memory and depicts them as "implicated subjects," to borrow Rothberg's term ("Implicated" 19–20). Exploring the *Lebensborn* program victims and child *Ostarbeiters* and portraying Canada as their new home, Skrypuch introduces a different perspective to Canadian Holocaust fiction in her early novel *Hope's War* (2001) and the two commercially successful trilogies published by Scholastic. By positioning Ukrainians as individuals risking their lives hiding their Jewish friends and neighbors, the novels challenge the anti-Semitic generalizations attributed to Ukrainians in North America without withholding information about the instances of collaboration from the reader or being overly didactic. All of the chapters demonstrate the entanglements of Ukrainian and Canadian history and point to the role Anglophone children's literature can play in preventing the symbolical seeds of memory from withering.

Notes

1 In my formulation of next-generation memory, I agree with Ulanowicz that children's literature, especially books representing the transgenerational memory transfer, are equally oriented towards presenting the present and the future and are not dominated by the narrations of the past.
2 Although similar in meaning, multiculturalism usually suggests embracing diversity and transculturalism, a more inclusive term, "signifies acceptance, exchange and dialogue between cultures" (Sojka 7; cf. Drewniak 15–26). Scholars like Ricard Zapata-Barrero argue that "multicultural policies in the past have missed an important point: interaction between people from different cultures and national backgrounds" and propose the use of the term interculturalism, which is a policy promoting "open spaces of interpersonal relations, to generate socialization effects [...and] a common public culture with stability, cohesion, and a developing sense of loyalty and belonging" (4,8).
3 I refer here to Roman Ingarden's understanding of active reading, a process in which the reader understands and "has a sort of intercourse" with the sentences they are reading (37–40).
4 See Chapter 1 footnote 3.

5   Throughout this book, I use my own translation of texts that have not been translated into English.
6   Furthermore, as they add, "[t]o speak of Canadian culture as a consciously constructed 'culture of memory' may be an accurate way of designating the tentativeness of the Canadian project since its foundations" (5–6).
7   To quote Peter Hollindale, "writers for children are transmitters not of themselves uniquely, but of the worlds they share" (15). Sometimes, these worlds can be problematic.
8   However, in the Appendix I also list Ukrainian-themed books available in French.
9   Trudeau declared that Canada is bilingual but not bicultural:

> [f]or altogether there are *two official languages*, there is *no official culture*, nor does any ethnic group take precedence over any other. *No citizen or group of citizens is other than Canadian*, and all should be treated fairly [...] National *unity*, if it is to mean anything in the deeply personal sense, must be founded on confidence in one's own individual identity; out of this can grow respect for that of others and a willingness to share ideas, attitudes and assumptions. A vigorous policy of multiculturalism will help create this initial confidence.
>
> (qtd. in Wilson 655; emphasis mine)

As V. Seymour Wilson notes, most critics focused on "three principal objectives derived from the 'multicultural assumptions': the promotion of intergroup contact and sharing; the promotion of the maintenance and development of cultural heritage; and the promotion of other-group acceptance and tolerance" (655; cf. Siemerling 1–18).

10 Waldemar Zacharasiewicz notes that

> [t]he belated recognition of the so-called heritage languages in Canada, which, through the ideology of the "mosaic," rather that of the "melting pot" as in the U.S.A., had nominally favored a more positive attitude towards the cultures of allophone immigrants, is reflected in the records of individual lives and life-writings and travelogues produced by the descendants of immigrants form Central, Eastern, and Southern Europe.
>
> (45)

11 For example, in Louis Begley's *Wartime Lies* (1991), they are Nazi collaborators who mostly rape women and act "like wild animals" (126; cf. Keefer "Honey and Ashes" 200–201). In Michael P. Spradlin's more recent *The Enemy Above* (2016), Christian Ukrainians are more sympathetic, yet they eventually hand over the location of the hiding Jews. Novels published in the 2020s challenge such one-dimensional depiction, for example *Traitor* (2021) and *The Silent Unseen* (2022) by Amanda McCrina and *Alias Anna: A True Story of Outwitting the Nazis* (2022) by Susan Hood and Greg Dawson.
12 Writing about this type of books, John Stephens notes that "[t]he audience for historical fiction begins at the upper primary years, and probably exists, in so far as it exists at all, most extensively among junior secondary school readers" (278).
13 Skrypuch's first Second World War trilogy was scheduled to be published in Ukraine in 2022, but because of the current war, its release has been postponed. While her two picturebooks illustrated by Michael Martchenko were translated into Ukrainian, they were published exclusively in Canada

by the Canadian Institute of Ukrainian Studies, University of Alberta as *Sribni nytky* (1996; *Silver Threads*) and *Dosyt'* (2000; *Enough*). Moreover, a Ukrainian version of "The Rings" can be downloaded from Skrypuch's official website. Three of Skrypuch's Second World War–themed books were reissued with new titles. My corpus contains both editions as I studied different versions of the texts to trace any possible changes.

14 In this context, it is worth mentioning that memory

> plays a crucial role within the contexts of migration, immigration, resettlement, and diasporas, for memory provides continuity to the dislocations of individual and social identity, particularly in a country like Canada, a nation in large part formed by migration and the memory of migrants.
>
> (Creet 3)

15 For a more detailed overview of scholarship on Ukrainian Canadian literature in English see Grekul 2005, xii–xiv; Ledohowski 2007; Suchacka 2019.

16 There are some notable exceptions, including the aforementioned Kurelek. Ukrainian Canadian novels which were met with mainstream recognition, include, among others, Ilia Kiriak's *Sons of the Soil* (1959) and Janice Kulyk Keefer's *The Green Library* (1996). Excerpts from the former were included in *Women in Canadian Literature* edited by M.G. Hesse. For a detailed analysis of these novels, as well as other Ukrainian Canadian texts, see Grekul (2005) and Suchacka (2019). While Keefer published *Anna's Goat* (2001; illustrated by Janet Wilson), a picturebook for children, it is a Second World War story about a Polish woman, Anna Kozicka Simon, who immigrated to Canada.

17 Notably, Jennifer Henderson (2013) and Ledohowski briefly examine Skrypuch's *Prisoners in the Promised Land* (2013; 2015) together with mainstream literature, without acknowledging the narrative practices typical of children's literature. Skrypuch is also the only children's author whose essay was included the award-winning collection *Unbound: Ukrainian Canadians Writing Home* edited by Ledohowski and Grekul. While Grekul (2005), Ledohowski (2007; 2008), and Suchacka (2019) acknowledge the existence of Kupchenko Frolick's *Anna Veryha*, they do not study it. Grekul's novel *Kalyna Song* (2003), initially titled *Sing for Me, Kalyna!*, has already been studied extensively by Ledohowski (2011; 2013; 2015) and Suchacka (2019). Despite the book's references to Ukrainian history, which I point to in the last chapter, it is not strictly a historical novel but a Bildungsroman about a young Canadian woman who explores her Ukrainian identity. While it was marketed as a crossover book, due to its complexity and length, it is difficult to call *Kalyna's Song* a children's or even YA narrative. I agree with Joan Marshall, who, in a review for *Resource Links*, writes that despite the book's high literary value, "today's teens will struggle to sustain their interest" as the novel is long and Grekul "falls prey to the mistake made by many beginning writers of historical fiction: to tell everything one knows" (35).

18 For a survey of mainstream Anglo-Canadian works featuring Ukrainian characters see Aponiuk 49–65.

19 Sneja Gunew uses the notion of "poet pedagogues" to describe "artists who are also teachers" and frequently "become the focus for creating and maintaining an intellectual community informed by the diasporic histories of its constituent members and enmeshed in contradictory relations with

the dominant cultural paradigms" (13). Ledohowski in the introduction to *Unbound* uses this term to describe Ukrainian Canadian authors: "There are many Ukrainian Canadian creative writers who also function as literary critics and ethnic theorists, as 'poet pedagogues' communicating their individual visions of how best to retain, or address the loss of, Ukrainian Canadian-ness" (cf. 3–22).

Works Cited

Ankersmit, Frank R. *Narrative Logic: A Semantic Analysis of the Historian's Language*. The Hague-Boston-London: Martinus Nijhoff, 1983, pp. 248–260.

Aponiuk, Natalia. "'...No Longer Quite Ukrainian but Not Quite Canadian Either...': The Ukrainian Immigrant in Canadian English-Language Literature." *Canadian Ethnic Studies*, vol. 47, no. 4–5, 2015, pp. 49–65.

Assmann, Aleida. "Transformations between History and Memory." *Social Research*, vol. 75, no. 1 (SPRING), 2008, pp. 49–72.

Assmann, Jan. "Collective Memory and Cultural Identity," translated by John Czaplicka. *New German Critique*, No. 65, Cultural History/Cultural Studies (Spring–Summer), 1995, pp. 125–133.

Atwood, Margaret. *Survival: A Thematic Guide to Canadian Literature*. Toronto: Anansi, 1972.

Balan, Jars. "Old World Forms, New World Settings: The Emergence of Ukrainian-Canadian Plays on North American Themes." *Cultural Identities in Canadian Literature: Identités culturelles dans la littérature canadienne*, edited by Bénédicte Mauguière. Peter Lang Publishing, 1998.

Ball, Karyn and Per Anders Rudling. "The Underbelly of Canadian Multiculturalism: Holocaust Obfuscation and Envy in the Debate about the Canadian Museum for Human Rights." *Holocaust Studies: A Journal of Culture and History*, vol. 20, no. 3, Winter 2014, pp. 33–80.

Begley, Louis. *Wartime Lies*. New York: Ivy Books, 1991.

Bellah, Robert N., Richard Madsen, William M. Sullibanm, Ann Swindler, and Steven M. Tipton. *Habits of the Heart: Individualism and Commitment in American Life*. University of California Press, 1985.

Bociurkiw, Bohdan. "The Federal Policy of Multiculturalism and the Ukrainian Canadian Community." *Ukrainian Canadians, Multiculturalism, and Separatism: An Assessment*, edited by Manoly Lupul. University of Alberta Press; Canadian Institute of Ukrainian Studies, 1978, pp. 98–128.

Bosmajian, Hamida. *Sparing the Child: Grief and the Unspeakable in Youth Literature about Nazism and the Holocaust*. Routledge, 2002.

Bradford, Clare. "Transformative Fictions: Postcolonial Encounters in Australian Texts." *Children's Literature Association Quarterly*, vol. 28, no. 4, 2003–2004, pp. 194–202.

Buchholtz, Mirosława. "O czerwonych liściach, młodych ludziach i ich książkach." *Państwo – naród – tożsamość w dyskursach kulturowych Kanady*, edited by Mirosława Buchholtz and Eugenia Sojka. Universitas, 2010, pp. 335–351.

Burke, Marguerite V. *The Ukrainian Canadians*. Van Nostrand Reinhold Company, 1978.

"The Canadian Multiculturalism Act (CMA)". *Justice Laws Website*. https://laws.justice.gc.ca/eng/acts/C-18.7/page-1.html

Carpenter, Carole Henderson. "William Kurelek: Teller of Tales." *The Lion and the Unicorn*, vol. 24, no. 2, 2000, pp. 260–278.
Corse, Sarah M. *Nationalism and Literature: The Politics of Culture in Canada and the United States*. Cambridge University Press, 1997.
Creet, Julia, "Introduction: The Migration of Memory and Memories of Migration." *Memory and Migration: Multidisciplinary Approaches to Memory Studies*, edited by Julia Creet and Andreas Kitzmann. University of Toronto Press, 2011, pp. 3–28.
Davis, Marie. "Editorial: Politics and Our Anniversary." *Canadian Children's Literature*, vol. 100–101, 1990, pp. 4–6.
Dean-Ruzicka, Rachel. *Tolerance Discourse and Young Adult Holocaust Literature: Engaging Difference and Identity*. Routledge, 2017.
Diakiw, Jerry. "Children's Literature and Canadian National Identity: A Revisionist Perspective." *Canadian Children's Literature*, vol. 87, 1997, pp. 42–43.
Drewniak, Dagmara. "'[They] would say she was betraying Poland already": Major Themes in Contemporary Canadian Literature by Writers of Polish Origins." *Anglica: An International Journal of English Studies*, vol. 27, no. 1, 2018, pp. 150–164.
Drewniak, Dagmara. *Forgetful Recollections: Images of Central and Eastern Europe in Canadian Literature*. Poznań: Adam Mickiewicz University Press, 2014.
Edwards, Gail and Judith Saltman. *Picturing Canada: A History of Children's Illustrated Books and Publishing*. University of Toronto Press, 2010.
Egoff, Sheila. "Canadian Historical Fiction for Children." *Canadian Literature*, vol. 27, 1966, p. 44.
Egoff, Sheila. "Children's Books: A Canadian's View of the Current American Scene." *Crosscurrents of Criticism: Horn Book Essays 1968–1977*, edited by Paul Heins. Boston: Horn Book, 1977, pp. 128–136.
Erll, Astrid. "Cultural Memory Studies: An Introduction." *Cultural Memory Studies: An International and Interdisciplinary Handbook*, edited by Astrid Erll and Ansgar Nünning, with Sara B. Young. Walter De Gruyter, 2008, pp. 1–15.
Erll, Astrid. "Literature as a Medium of Cultural Memory." *Memory in Culture*. Palgrave, 2011.
Erll, Astrid. "Travelling Memory." *Parallax*, vol. 17, no. 4, 2011, pp. 4–18.
Ewers, Hans Heino. "Children's Literature and the Traditional Art of Storytelling," *Poetics Today*. vol. 1, no. 1, 1992, pp.169–178.
Galway, Elizabeth A. *From Nursery Rhymes to Nationhood: Children's Literature and the Construction of Canadian Identity*. Routledge, 2008.
Gangi, Jane M. *Genocide in Contemporary Children's and Young Adult Literature: Cambodia to Darfur*. Routledge, 2017.
Goldie, Terry. *Fear and Temptation: The Image of the Indigene in Canadian, Australian, and New Zealand Literatures*. McGill-Queen's University Press, 1989.Grekul, Lisa. *Leaving Shadows: Literature in English by Canada's Ukrainians*, University of Alberta Press, 2005.
Grekul, Lisa. "Re-Placing Ethnicity: New Approaches to Ukrainian Canadian Literature." *Home-Work: Postcolonialism, Pedagogy, and Canadian Literature*, edited by Cynthia Sugars. Ottawa: University of Ottawa Press, 2004, pp. 369–384.

Grekul, Lisa and Lindy Ledohowski (eds.). *Unbound: Ukrainian Canadians Writing Home*. University of Toronto Press, 2016.
Gunew, Sneja. *Haunted Nations: The Colonial Dimensions of Multiculturalisms*. New York: Routledge, 2004.
Hałas, Elżbieta. *Przez pryzmat kultury. Dylematy badań nad współczesnością*. Warszawa: Wydawnictwo Uniwersytetu Warszawskiego, 2015.
Henderson, Jennifer. "The Camp, the School, and the Child: Discursive Exchanges and (Neo)liberal Axioms in the Culture of Redress." *Reconciling Canada: Critical Perspectives on the culture of Redress*, edited by Jennifer Henderson and Pauline Wakeham. University of Toronto Press, 2013, pp. 65–83.
Hesse, M.G. (ed.). *Women in Canadian Literature*. Borealis Press, 1976.
Himka, John-Paul. "The Background to Emigration: Ukrainians of Galicia and Bukovyna, 1848–1914." *A Heritage in Transition: Essays in the History of Ukrainians in Canada*, edited by Manoly R. Lupul. Toronto: McClelland and Stewart, 1982, 11–31.
Hirsch, Marianne. *Family Frames: Photography, Narrative, and Postmemory*. Harvard University Press, 1997.
Hirsch, Marianne. "The Generation of Postmemory." *Poetics Today*, vol. 29, no. 1, 2008, pp. 103–128.
Hollindale, Peter, "Ideology and the Children's Book." *Signal: Approaches to Children's Books* vol. 55, 1988, pp. 15.
Howard, Vivian. "Picturing Difference: Three Recent Picture Books Portray the Black Nova Scotian Community." *Bookbird*, vol. 51, no. 4, 2013, pp. 11–20.
Hryniuk, Stella and Lubomyr Luciuk (eds.). *Multiculturalism and Ukrainian Canadians: Identity, Homeland Ties, and the Community's Future*. Toronto: Multicultural Society of Ontario, 1993.
Hunt, Peter. *An Introduction to Children's Literature*. Oxford University Press, 1994.
Hutcheon, Lidia. "Introduction." *Other Solitudes: Multicultural Fiction and Interviews*, edited by Linda Hutcheon and Marion Richardson. Oxford University Press, 1991.
Ingarden, Roman. *The Cognition of the Literary Work of Art*, translated by Ruth Ann Crowley and Kenneth R. Olson. Evanston: Northwestern University Press, 1973.
Innocenti, Roberto, "The War Inside Books," translated by Luana Viaggi. *Bookbird*, vol. 47, no. 4, 2009, pp. 27–31.
Kaplita, Marek. "Autor, dzieło i czytelnik w świetle potrójnej mimesis Paula Ricoeura." W: *Estetyka i Krytyka*, vol. 2, no. 29, 2013, pp. 115–137.
Keefer, Janice Kulyk. *Anna's Goat*. Illustrated by Janet Wilson. Orca Book Publishers, 2001.
Keefer, Janice Kulyk. *Dark Ghost in the Corner: Imagining Ukrainian-Canadian Identity*. Saskatoon: Heritage Press, 2005.
Keefer, Janice Kulyk. "From Mosaic to Kaleidoscope: Out of the Multicultural Past Comes a Vision of a Transcultural Future." *Books in Canada*, vol. 20.6, Sept. 1991, pp. 13–16.
Keefer, Janice Kulyk. *Honey and Ashes: A Story of Family*. Harper Flamingo Canada, 1998.
Kertzer, Adrianne. *My Mother's Voice. Children, Literature, and the Holocaust*. Broadview Press, 2002.

Kidd, Kenneth B. (ed.). "T Is for Trauma: The Children's Literature of Atrocity." *Freud in Oz: At the Intersections of Psychoanalysis and Children's Literature.* University of Minnesota Press, 2011.

Kim, Christine and Sophie McCall. "Introduction." *Cultural Grammars of Nation, Diaspora, and Indigeneity in Canada*, edited by Christine Kim, Sophie McCall, and Melina Baum Singer. Wilfrid Laurier University Press, 2012, pp. 1–18.

Kokkola, Lydia. *Representing the Holocaust in Children's Literature.* Routledge, 2003.

Kordan, Bohdan S., *Enemy Aliens, Prisoners of War: Internment in Canada during the Great War.* McGill-Queen's University Press, 2002.

Kruk, Laurie. " 'Outsiders' and 'Insiders': Teaching Native/Canadian Literature as Meeting Place." *Home-Work: Postcolonialism, Pedagogy, and Canadian Literature*, edited by Cynthia Sugars. Ottawa: University of Ottawa Press, 2004, pp. 301–320.

Lachmann, Renate. "Mnemonic and Intertextual Aspects of Literature." *Cultural Memory Studies: An International and Interdisciplinary Handbook*, edited by Astrid Erll and Ansgar Nünning. Sara B. Young and Walter De Gruyter, 2008, pp. 301–310.

Landsberg, Alison. *Prosthetic Memory: The Transformation of American Remembrance in the Age of Mass Culture.* Columbia University Press, 2004.

Langston, Laura. *Lesia's Dream.* Harper Throphy Canada, 2003.

Lazarenko, Joseph M. (ed.). *The Ukrainian Pioneers in Alberta.* Edmonton: Ukrainian Pioneers Association in Edmonton, 1970.

Ledohowski, Lindy. "Becoming the Hyphen: The Evolution of English-Language Ukrainian-Canadian Literature." *Canadian Ethnic Studies*, vol. 39, no. 1–2, 2007, pp. 107–127.

Ledohowski, Lindy. *Canadian Cossacks: Finding Ukraine in Fifty Years of Ukrainian-Canadian.* 2008. University of Toronto, Ph.D. dissertation. https://tspace.library.utoronto.ca/bitstream/1807/16761/1/Ledohowski_Lindy_A_20 0811_PhD_thesis.pdf

Ledohowski, Lindy. "Introduction: Ukrainian Canadian Poet Pedagogues." *Unbound: Ukrainian Canadians Writing Home*, edited by Lisa Grekul and Lindy Ledohowski. University of Toronto Press, 2016, pp. 3–22.

Ledohowski, Lindy. "Little Ukraine on the Prairie: 'Baba' in English-language Ukrainian-Canadian Literature." *Place and Replace: Essays on Western Canada*, edited by Esyllt W. Jones, Adele Perry, and Leah Morton. University of Manitoba Press, 2013, pp. 186–206.

Ledohowski, Lindy. " 'The Compulsion to Tell Falls on the Next Generation': Ukrainian Canadian Literature in English and Victims of the Past." *Reconciling Canada: Critical Perspectives on the Culture of Redress*, edited by Jennifer Henderson and Pauline Wakeham. University of Toronto Press, 2013, pp. 198–214.

Ledohowski, Lindy. " 'White Settler Guilt': Contemporary Ukrainian Canadian Prairie Literature." *Canadian Ethnic Studies*, vol. 47, no. 4–5, 2015, pp. 67–83.

Marshall, Joan. "Grekul, Lisa—Kalyna's Song." *Resource Links*, vol. 12, no. 3, 2006, p. 35.

Martynowych, Orest T. "Sympathy for the Devil: The Attitude of Ukrainian War Veterans in Canada to Nazi Germany and the Jews, 1933–1939." *Re-imagining*

Ukrainian Canadians: History, Politics, and Identity, edited by Rhonda L. Hinther and Jim Mochoruk. University of Toronto Press, 2011, pp. 173–220.

McCall, Sophie. "Diaspora and Nation in Métis Writing." *Cultural Grammars of Nation, Diaspora, and Indigeneity in Canada*, edited by Christine Kim, Sophie McCall, and Melina Baum Singer. Wilfrid Laurier University Press, 2012, pp. 21–421

McConnell, Taylor. "Memory Abuse, Violence and the Dissolution of Yugoslavia: A Theoretical Framework for Understanding Memory in Conflict." *Innovation: The European Journal of Social Science Research*, vol. 32, no. 3, 2019, pp. 331–343.

Montgomery, Lucy Maud. *Anne of Avonlea*. L.C. Page & Co., 1909. www.pagebypagebooks.com/Lucy_Maud_Montgomery/Anne_Of_Avonlea/A_Golden_Picnic_p2.html

Mycak, Sonia. *Canuke Literature: Critical Essays on Canadian Ukrainian Writing*. Huntington: Nova Science, 2001.

Nodelman, Perry and Mavis Reimer. *The Pleasures of Children's Literature*. 1992; Boston: Allyn & Bacon, 3rd ed, 2003.

Plokhy, Serhii. *The Frontline—Essays on Ukraine's Past and Present*. Harvard University Press, 2021.

Richter, Miriam Verena. *Creating the National Mosaic: Multiculturalism in Canadian Children's Literature from 1950 to 1993*. Amsterdam-New York: Rodopi, 2011.

Rothberg, Michael. *Multidirectional Memory: Remembering the Holocaust in the Age of Decolonization*. Stanford University Press, 2009.

Rothberg, Michael. *The Implicated Subject: Beyond Victims and Perpetrators*. Stanford University Press, 2019.

Rudling, Per Anders. *The OUN, the UPA and the Holocaust: A Study in the Manufacturing of Historical Myths*. The Carl Beck Papers in Russian and East European Studies 2107. Pittsburgh: The Center for Russian and East European Studies at the University of Pittsburgh, 2011.

Saltman, Judith. "Once Upon a Time: Canadian Children's Picture Book Illustration." *Canadian Children's Literature*, vol. 51, 1988, pp. 51–65.

Satzewich, Vic. *The Ukrainian Diaspora*. Routledge, 2002.

Schmuhl, Hans-Walter. *The Kaiser Wilhelm Institute for Anthropology, Human Heredity and Eugenics, 1927–1945. Crossing Boundaries*. Netherlands: Springer, 2008.

Schwebel, Sara L. *Child-Sized History: Fictions of the Past in U.S. Classrooms*. Nashville: Verderbilt University Press, 2011.

Siemerling, Winfried. "Writing Ethnicity: Introduction." *Writing Ethnicity: Cross-Cultural Consciousness in Canadian and Québécois Literature*, edited by Winfried Siemerling. ECW Press, 1996.

Skrypuch, Marsha Forchuk. "Am I Ukrainian?" *Unbound: Ukrainian Canadians Writing Home*, edited by Lisa Grekul and Lindy Ledohowski. University of Toronto Press, 2016, pp. 65–68.

Skrypuch, Marsha Forchuk. (ed.). *Kobzar's Children: A Century of Untold Ukrainian Stories*. Fitzhenry & Whiteside, 2006.

Snyder, Timothy. *Bloodlands: Europe Between Hitler and Stalin*. Basic Books, 2010.

Sojka, Eugenia. "Contemplating otherness in the Transcultural Canadian Context. Introduction." *Embracing Otherness: Canadian Minority Discourses in Transcultural Perspectives*, edited by Eugenia Sojka and Tomasz Sikora. Toruń, Poland: Wydawnictwo Adam Marszałek, 2010.

Stephens, John. *Language and Ideology*. Language in Social Life Series. Longman, 1992.

Story, Norah. "Ukrainians." *The Oxford Companion to Canadian History and Literature*. Oxford University Press, 1967, pp. 807–808.

Suchacka, Weronika. *'Za Hranetsiu' – 'Beyond the Border': Constructions of Identities in Ukrainian-Canadian Literature*. Wissner-Verlag, 2019.

Sugars, Cynthia and Eleanor Ty. "Thinking beyond Nostalgia: Canadian Literature and Cultural Memory." *Canadian Literature and Cultural Memory*, edited by Cynthia Sugars and Eleanor Ty. Oxford University Press, 2014, pp. 1–19.

Swyripa, Frances. *Storied Landscapes: Ethno-Religious Identity and the Canadian Prairies*. University of Manitoba Press, 2010.

Swyripa, Frances. *Wedded to Ukrainian-Canadian Women and Ethnic Identity 1891–1991*. University of Toronto Press, 1993.

Trzeszczyńska, Patrycja. "Ukraińska diaspora w kanadyjskim Edmonton. Krajobraz etniczny miasta i prowincji a praktyki pamięci." *Etnografia Polska*, vol. LX, no. 1–2, 2016, pp. 82–104.

Trzeszczyńska, Patrycja. *Diaspora – pamięć – miejsca: Ukraińcy z Polski z lat 80. XX wieku w Kanadzie. Studium etnograficzne*. Wydawnictwo Uniwersytetu Jagiellońskiego, 2019.

Ulanowicz, Anastasia. *Second-Generation Memory and Contemporary Children's Literature: Ghost Images*. Routledge, 2013.

Vardanian, Maryna. *Svii – Chuzhyi v Ukrainskii Diaspornii Literaturi dlia Ditei ta Yunatstva: Natsionalna Kontseptosfera, Imaholohichni modeli*. Kryvyi Rih: Dionat, 2018.

Wilson, Seymour V. "The Tapestry Vision of Canadian Multiculturalism." *Canadian Journal of Political Science / Revue canadienne de science politique*, vol. 26, no. 4, December 1993, pp. 645–669.

Yekelchyk, Serhy. *Ukraine: What Everyone Needs to Know*, 2nd ed. Oxford University Press, 2020

Yokota, Junko. "Issues in Selecting Multicultural Children's Literature." *Language Arts*, vol. 70, 1993, pp. 156–167.

Zacharasiewicz, Waldemar. "Transatlantic Memories and Ethnic Encounters in Canadian Literature." *Mosaics of Words: Essays on the American and Canadian Literary Imagination in Memory of Professor Nancy Burke*, edited by Agata Preis-Smith, Ewa Łuczak, and Marek Paryż. Warsaw: Institute of English Studies, 2006, pp. 45–53.

Zapata-Barrero, Ricard. "Interculturalism: Main Hypothesis, Theories and Strands." *Interculturalism in Cities: Concept, Policy and Implementation*, edited by Ricard Zapata-Barrero. Northampton: Edward Elgar Publishing, 2015, pp. 3–19.

Zhuk, Sergei I. *KGB Operations against the USA and Canada in Soviet Ukraine, 1953–1991*. Routledge, 2022.

1 Land of All Colors and Races?
Canadian Cossacks, Indigenous Peoples, and the Myth of the Founding Fathers of the Prairies

> The old world is very lovely and very wonderful. But we have come back very well satisfied with our own land. Canada is the finest country in the world.
>
> (L.M. Montgomery, *Rainbow Valley*)

On one of the last pages of Larry Warwaruk's *Andrei and the Snow Walker* (2002),[1] set in 1900 in Saskatchewan, Danylo Skomar, the maternal grandfather (or *Dido*) of the eponymous protagonist, says:

> Here there are heroes other than Cossacks. *There can be heroes of all colours and races in a land of all colours and races.* Here it is not like in our old Ukraine, where our Cossacks had enemies in every directions ... Turks, Poles, Russians. And what did it get us? Great horsemen. Blood shew with sabres. Has that kept our Ukraine alive? No, Andrei, it is our poets who keep Ukraine alive [...] in Canada, it's only your old dido who's still a Cossack. *Here the people will be mixed together.*
>
> (190; emphasis mine)

This long quotation illustrates several problems connected to studying transcultural historical fiction. In 1900 the citizens of Canada were still considered British subjects; Saskatchewan did not become a province until 1905; the rights of the First Nations and the Métis were violated, with some of their most important traditions, like the Sun Dance and Potlatch banned until 1951; and the policy of multiculturalism began only in the 1970s as an effort to bring together and balance the various "'collective memories' of cultures" (Richter 38).[2] Moreover, legislations like the Indian Act passed in 1876 or Bill-C31, amending the Indian Act (1985), continued to pit various Indigenous groups against each other (cf. Lawrence). The Métis, prominent in Warwaruk's novels, and "non-status Indians," were granted the same constitutional rights as "status Indians" only in 2013. Yet in *Andrei and the Snow Walker* the chronotope[3] of the prairie emerges as diverse, inclusive, and peaceful. The Cree and the

Métis welcome and accept Ukrainians, presented here as the descendants of the ancients Scythians and Cossacks, treating them – unlike the English colonizers – as the rightful new owners of the land. To recall the words of Andrei's Dido, the world of Warwaruk's novel is inhabited by "heroes of all colours and races," because Canada emerges as "a land of all colours and races" (190). This world, however, is a literary creation, a simulacrum in Jean Baudrillard's understanding of the term.[4]

Similar to the poets who "keep Ukraine alive," Warwaruk attempts to keep alive the image of Ukrainians as the founding fathers of the Canadian prairies. According to this narrative, the descendants of the first Ukrainian settlers emerge as *indigenous* to the land (cf. Ledohowski "White" 68). Indigenization, as Terry Goldie observes writing about the pattern present in non-Indigenous fiction published in Australia, Canada, and New Zealand, is a process of trying to "become 'native,'" it is the "impossible necessity of becoming indigenous" (13). It is difficult not to agree with Lindy Ledohowski who notes that this "founding fathers" mythology is highly problematic due to its colonial nature ("White" 69). The last sentence of Dido's words seems to echo a common narrative trope used by non-Indigenous authors, one showing all Canadians as having "equal right to be here together in this place [they] all own" because they "are all non-Aboriginal together – and paradoxically, therefore, the rightful inheritors of the land" (Nodelman 115). Such an approach towards the history of colonization of the prairies positions Ukrainian Canadians as the land's rightful residents, not implicated subjects who "inhabit, inherit, or benefit from regimes of domination" without originating them (Rothberg 1).

In this chapter I examine Ukrainian Canadian books devoted to the so-called first wave of immigration to the prairies and study the various ways their authors attempt to transfer next-generation memory to present-day readers.[5] Reading Warwaruk's *Andrei and the Snow Walker* and its companion novel *Brovko's Amazing Journey* (2013), I juxtapose them with another settler narrative, Laura Langston's *Lesia's Dream* (2003). In my analysis I also point to other texts, most notably Marsha Forchuk Skrypuch's *Prisoners in the Promised Land: The Ukrainian Internment Diary of Anya Soloniuk* (2007) and Marion Mutala's *Kokhum's Babushka: A Magical Métis/Ukrainian Tale* (2017) illustrated by Donna Lee Dumont. The latter is one of the titles in the study set that moved through a process of self-publishing, hosted by an editing business, while the other titles were published by a professional publisher. Differences in publishing may have resulted in varying levels of supports for authors and illustrators, as with a standard publishing house, the work of a project editor, a copyeditor, a designer, and, if illustrated, an illustrator and usually an art director, are all part of the consultation team. While this study has not questioned to any depth what different systems might have meant for resulting books, it is significant to note that individual writers and artists have very likely had wider encouragement and advice related to accuracy and cultural consciousness than others, in traditional publishing, and that the analysis to follow is merely an adjudication of the content of various books rather than a directed critique of authors and illustrators themselves in connection to the projects they have championed. It would be interesting to analyze the appearance of tropes and stereotypes by choices in publishing, and this might be an intriguing subject for further research.[6]

Although I agree with Sophie McCall that the positions of diasporas and the Indigenous-sovereignty "share the desire to challenge settler nationalisms and expose the expulsions that have produced Canadian citizenship," in some of the books studied in this chapter the diasporic settlers try to *become* native to the land (22). I argue that by portraying Canada in the 1900s as a place where Ukrainians are building a better and bigger version of the old country – in the case of Warwaruk's novels with the help of the Cree and the Métis – the books consolidate the myth of Ukrainians as the founding fathers of the Canadian prairies. *Andrei and the Snow Walker* ends with unintentional aperture – the fate of Brovko, Andrei's dog who stays in Ukraine. Inspired by a student who asked what happened to the pet at a school reading, Warwaruk wrote a sequel titled *Brovko's Amazing Journey*, focalized mostly by the eponymous dog. This novel not only ends with full closure but also enhances the limited representation of Ukraine in the original book, which mainly focuses on the homesteading struggles of Andrei's family, their close relationship with the Cree and the Métis, and the process of turning the new country into home. Moreover, in the sequel, Warwaruk further reinforces the similarities between the old and new countries and indigenizes Ukrainian Canadians. Hence the novels not only echo the post–Second World War attempts of Ukrainian Canadians to promote the image of the first immigrants as the prairie's "founding fathers" but also resonate with the efforts to popularize Ukrainian culture and claim its ties to Canada's Indigenous Peoples.

Writing a historically accurate and culturally conscious novel for children without too many oversimplifications and inaccuracies is an arduous task. Warwaruk and Langston do it in a matter typical of some other children's authors who seem to look for means of constructing the Canadian prairie as a simulacrum, a substitute for Ukraine, the old country which was "lost and inaccessible" (Ledohowski "Little Ukraine" 187). Introducing magical elements and references to ancient Scythians, Cossacks, and also the Hutsuls in *Brovko's Amazing Journey*, Warwaruk highlights the alleged similarities between Indigenous Peoples and the Ukrainian pioneers, at the same time challenging the stereotypical depiction of Ukrainians as illiterate men in sheepskin coats. Langston's protagonist has to tame the prairie by learning to hunt and fish. However, before she eventually emerges as the founding *baba* of the prairie and the giver of the Ukrainian and Ukrainian Canadian "seeds of memory," she also needs to learn to read and write. While the narration in *Lesia's*

Dream is predominately third-person, the story is clipped by the first-person narrator, whose teenage self is the novel's focalizer. The prologue, last chapter, and parts of several other chapters are narrated by the eponymous Lesia Magus, who tells the story of her emigration from the Galician village of Shuparka to Manitoba, Canada to her 16-year-old great-granddaughter Laisha. By using such a narrative technique, Langston attempts to make the historically and geographically distant story more approachable and believable to the young reader. Although in Warwaruk's novels the prairie is ethnically diverse, in *Lesia's Dream* it is completely deprived of the presence of Indigenous Peoples. Yet it also fits what Mavis Reimer recognizes as "[t]he most valued story in English-Language Canadian children's literature," that is

> a narrative in which the central child character, pushed out of an original home by the decisions or behavior of powerful adults, journeys to an alien place and, after a series of vicissitudes that occupy most of the tale, chooses to claim the unfamiliar space as a new home.
> (Reimer 1)

Writing about Canadian and Australian texts, Clare Bradford observes that "[a]ny formulation of home incorporates a sense of who is included and who is excluded or marginal" ("The Homely Imaginary" 178). Eventually both Lesia and Andrei claim the prairie as their new home, yet Langston, unlike Warwaruk, who includes Cree and Métis characters, indigenizes her protagonist by excluding Indigenous characters.

Notably, both *Andrei and the Snow Walker* and *Lesia's Dream* were met with acclaim and were nominated to various awards, including the 2006 KOBZAR Award, which Langston won. Such a critical recognition of the novels by mainstream and Ukrainian Canadian specialists echoes Pierre Bourdieu's concept of "capital of consecration" mentioned by Perry Nodelman in the context of Canadian non-Indigenous fiction. This capital, as Bourdieu argues, happens when "a known, recognized name, a capital of consecration implying a power to consecrate objects (with a trademark or signature) or persons (through publication, exhibition, etc.) and therefore to give value, and to appropriate the profits from this operation" (75 qtd. in Nodelman 107). The critical acclaim the books received consecrates the status of Ukrainian Canadians as the founding fathers they convey. Moreover, it further boosts these novels' potential to become the media of next-generation memory.

Homesteaders, Cossacks, and Scythians

Andrei and the Snow Walker, Warwaruk's first book for young readers, was published in Coteau Books' "In the Same Boat" series.[7] The novel's third-person narrator tells the story focalized by the 12-year-old Andrei Bayda, who, together with his parents and grandfather, leave the village of Zabokruky near Horodenka, Galicia, for a homestead near Batoche, Saskatchewan. Unlike Langston and other Ukrainian Canadian authors of prairie books,[8] Warwaruk combines historical and speculative fiction genres by introducing magical elements, making the story not only potentially more interesting for young readers, but also more problematic. The first of the 22 chapters of *Andrei and the Snow Walker* is the only one set in Ukraine. After hearing that even "a poor Ukrainian peasant" can afford to buy a farm in Canada, Stefan Bayda, the protagonist's father, decides to sell his modest piece of land and move to the promised land where his family "will live like landlords" (9). This seems to refer to the program started by Minister Clifford Sifton in 1896 to attract Ukrainian farmers to come to Canada. As Myrna Kostash notes, in the poor Ukrainian peasants Sifton saw an unlimited source of excellent, hand-working laborers who "have been bred for generations to work from daylight to dark" and because they "have never done anything else [...] they never expect to do anything else" (7–8). Tempted with the prospects of buying 160 acres of land for ten dollars, Ukrainians began to come to Canada in large numbers, especially after the encouragement provoked by the two promotional pamphlets published in Lviv by Dr. Joseph Oleskiw/Osyp Oleskiv (cf. Swyripa "Ukrainian Canadians" 91; Swyripa "Storied" 25–26; Kaye and Swyripa 38; Petryshyn and Dzubak 22).

To keep the memory of the old country alive, Langton's Lesia, an elderly woman, has to share the metaphorical seeds of memory with Laisha, her granddaughter and the representative of the next generation of Ukrainian Canadians (cf. Chapter 3). As Aleida Assmann notes, when one dies, their individual memories and items of mnemonic importance are permanently lost (98). Yet some memories *can* be transferred. The symbolic transfer of the seeds of memory is reflected in the story of the emigration of the 15-year-old Lesia and her family to Canada in 1914. Together with her older brother Ivan, the girl saves money to persuade her family to go to "the land of milk and honey," about which they have received contradictory information from their former neighbors who had already left for Canada (5). Lesia's stubborn father, a direct opposite of Stefan Bayda, the father of Andrei in Warwaruk's novels, initially does not want to hear about the departure and states that "[t]he Magus family belongs in Ukraine just like the great Dnister [Dniester] crests its banks in spring" (5). Mr. Magus is reluctant to leave his land, despite the looming fear of the coming war. He is also worried about his wife's next pregnancy, as they have previously lost their youngest son Slavko. While Reimer notes in "Homing and Unhoming: The Ideological Work of Canadian Children's Literature" that typically the child's departure from home is caused by the actions of adults, it is Lesia who encourages her parents to leave Ukraine. In order for the journey to take place as soon as possible, Lesia, without her father's knowledge, borrows some money from the kind Polish Master Stryk, whose son Michal openly shows his aversion and calls Lesia "a dirty, uneducated peasant" who is "useless. Stupid.

Brainless," has "no substance" and is too "thin and frail" to make it in Canada (14). Lesia is indeed poor and illiterate, but she manages to get the money and promises to repay the debt.

Before leaving their village, the Baydas in Warwaruk's novel take many objects typically attributed to the first Ukrainian immigrants to North America, such as the stereotypical "sheepskins, woven blankets, [...] onions, garlic, horseradish" and "Holy pictures" (9–10). They travel to Lviv, then to Hamburg, and after 15 days, finally arrive in Canada. The transcontinental journey is long, but it is romanticized. Although neither Warwaruk nor Langston describe their character's appearance in detail, this lack is not surprising considering that the novels, like most children's books, are "plot oriented" (Nikolajeva 12). However, *Andrei and the Snow Walker* contains a few black and white illustrations depicting the protagonist in different situations and a colorful cover featuring Andrei wearing a present-day-looking hat and his Dido's sheepskin coat, the golden cup, and a big bear, presumably the Snow Walker. The illustration showing Andrei with his grandfather on the deck of the ship pointing in Canada's direction seems to further minimize the hardship of a typical passage of poor peasants to North America at the turn of the twentieth century.

In *Lesia's Dream* the two-week long journey to Canada is also portrayed briefly in the retrospective story told by the elderly protagonist. Unlike Andrei, Lesia recalls traveling in *"the stench of vomit and body odour. Of herrings and garlic and onions"* and witnessing the death of two people (21; emphasis in original). However, what she remembers the most is the feeling of hope that she *"would live rich, live free"* (22; emphasis in original). Yet upon the arrival to Canada Lesia's family is met with hatred from Anglo-Canadians, who cheat them and call "Dirty bohunks," "Filthy peasant scum," and "Ignorant foreigners" (24). In both *Lesia's Dream* and Skrypuch's *Prisoners in the Promised Land*, Canadians frequently call Ukrainians dirty. The stereotypical depiction of Eastern European immigrants as "dirty" was the consequence of the conditions in which most of them traveled to Canada. After two weeks without bathing, because there was not enough water on the ship, Ukrainians who stepped on the Canadian soil were greeted with aversion. Anya Soloniuk, the protagonist of *Prisoners in the Promised Land*, recalls that upon her arrival to Canada "one couple held their noses and made faces" (25). She does, however, boldly ask her diary – and the readers – "[h]ow would they like it if they had just been in the bottom of a ship for two weeks?" (25). This question further highlights the hardships of the transcontinental journey, which are absent in Warwaruk's *Andrei and the Snow Walker*.[9]

Mary Douglas argues that the "idea of dirt takes us straight into the field of symbolism and promises a link-up with more obviously symbolic systems of purity" (48). Hence the references to dirt in the novels can also be linked to the nativist discourse, the belief that immigrants embody "dirt, disgust, abjection and disorder in a variety of symbolic ways depending on the scale" (Kil 178). Assuming that dirt can be read as "a less hygienic concept and more an ontological one," we may argue that by calling immigrants dirty or filthy, Anglo-Canadians in Langston's and Skrypuch's novels embody what Sang Hea Kill has called "racist dirt fixations" (Kil 178). The racist aspect of expressions like "Dirty bohunks" becomes apparent considering that although Ukrainians are Caucasian, Slavic immigrants in the late nineteenth and early twentieth century were often called "Oriental" or "Asiatic" (Zecker 69–70). Hence Ukrainian immigrants are initially positioned as the non-white "pollutants" of the clean national body of Canada. This further problematizes their relationship with Indigenous Peoples.

When Lesia first sees the prairie, she notices that it looks nothing like the Galician landscapes and calls it *"a quilt of grey and brown – of snow and soil"* (24; emphasis in original). Warwaruk, on the other hand, pays more attention to the Baydas' train journey through Canada, which allows them to notice the similarities between the Canadian and Ukrainian wilderness. As the novel is set in 1900, it is worth recalling that at that time in Canada "grand, national monuments and buildings" were not common so "it was the natural environments that begun to concentrate the sympathy and constitute the identity of the nation" (Galway 146). On the one hand, identifying with nature was easier for Eastern European peasants coming from small Galician villages. On the other hand, as Nodelman notes, "writers again and again identify Aboriginal culture with what is natural and untainted" (126). Thus in his novels Warwaruk indigenizes the Ukrainian characters and shows the alleged similarities between the Baydas' old and new country.

Like Lesia in the opening and closing chapters of Langston's novel, in *Andrei and the Snow Walker* it is Dido who emerges as the elderly storyteller sharing cultural memory and knowledge with his grandson.[10] Though Andrei was taught about Canada at school, he wants Dido to tell him the stories about the new country (9). As Andrei's grandfather says: "Canada is on the other side of the world" and is a place where they "will wear gold watches, just like the landlords" (10). For Danylo Skomar it is also the land of the free, with "no *pahn* landlord to rob [them]," a place where he could finally own a horse, like the Cossacks he admires and tells Andrei about (3).

Before leaving Ukraine, Andrei's family passes the old graveyard "where Cossack warriors were buried three hundred years ago" (1). Although this may seem surprising considering that the Baydas live in Galicia and the Cossacks originated in Central and Eastern Ukraine, the Cossack became one of the key symbols of Ukrainian Canadian identity. Similar to the Vikings associated with Canada's Icelanders, the Cossacks were an "apolitical but also passive and static" symbol chosen and used "to win group legitimacy and respect in both the Canadian and western Canadian contexts," because they evoked such attributes as courage, originality, vigor, and flashiness (Swyripa "Storied" 161). In *Andrei and the Snow Walker* Dido emerges as a figure looking like an old Cossack with his "braid [which] snakes across his shoulder [and h]is shaved head" (11). Notably, he is also the one who tells Andrei that the Baydas are going to "some cowboy land" by "Saskatchewan River" (8). Explaining who a cowboy is, Dido compares him to a Cossack, further pointing to the alleged similarities between Ukraine and North America (8). Andrei asks if there are Cossacks in Canada, but Dido naively says that it is the land of cowboys and "Indians [who also] ride horses [but n]ot like Cossacks" (11). The mention of the cowboy does not seem accidental as Cossacks are the romanticized counterpart of the North American cowboys (Kornblatt 3; cf. Ulanowicz "Reassembling Sacred Relics" 414). In popular culture and literature, cowboys, the "civilized" tamers of the prairies, are juxtaposed with the "wild" Indigenous Peoples. By comparing Cossacks to cowboys, Dido seems to highlight the settler, hence colonial, position of the Canadian Cossacks. Yet when Andrei asks "[c]an farmers be Cossacks," Dido replies with a paraphrased question: "can Cossacks be farmers? Could they have ever wanted to be farmers when they could ride their horses across the steppes?" (12). Dido's words emphasize the free-spirited nature of the Cossacks, which positions them as closer to the novel's Indigenous Peoples. Thus the Cossack emerges as a peculiar hybrid of the colonizer *and* the colonized.

While some of Warwaruk's and Langston's narrative choices may not be historically accurate, they echo the attempts of the diaspora since the 1970s to popularize folkloristic – positive, universally recognized, and easily performed – symbols of Ukrainianness. While the Cossack is now unequivocally associated with Ukrainians, it is worth remembering that many ethnoreligious groups in Canada tried to find noble ancestors who would help them "compete with Canada's two charter peoples" and the values of freedom and democracy attributed to them (Swyripa "Storied" 166).[11] Marcia Ostachewski points to the parallels between the Cossacks, who "were originally farmers but sought freedom from serfdom by moving to the fertile region on the edge of the steppe near Kyiv," and Ukrainian Canadians seeking "freedom from the poverty and hardship [...] by immigrating to a more autonomous and prosperous life in a new, democratic Canadian land" (30; cf. Seaton 73–96). The Cossack's nobility mentioned by Dido has little connection to the Ukrainian peasants' past. Yet the role of the Cossack as a symbol of Canadian's Ukrainianness is "*not* an example of continuity, but purely a part of the production and performance of heritage" (Ostashewski 16; emphasis in original).

The Cossack has had a special significance in Ukrainian history, "becoming one of the most important factors in the formation of the modern Ukrainian nation" (Plokhy "Unmaking" 194). Whereas the figure of the military master of horsemanship is a part of Ukrainian *and* Russian history, its role in the national discourses of both countries was "profoundly different" (Plokhy "Unmaking" 194). Unlike in

Russian historiography, where the Cossacks function predominantly as a military formation used by the Tsar to protect the country's borders, in the Ukrainian historical discourse the Cossack symbolizes freedom and Ukraine's separateness from Russia. As historian Serhii Plokhy notes, since the eighteenth century, the Cossack mythology has been used to legitimize Ukraine's distinctive national identity. Plokhy maintains that although the image of the Cossack is frequently associated with Ukraine, it only became "an icon of Ukrainian historical identity in the early eighteenth century within the boundaries of the Hetmanate" ("Unmaking" 193). However, already in the late nineteenth century the Cossack became a vital symbol of Ukrainian identity (Ostashewski 16–17). Plokhy points to the publication of "a mysterious manuscript" after the Napoleonic wars, "a historical-treatise called the *History of the Rus'*, in which the term *Rus'* referred to the Ukrainian Cossacks" ("The Cossack Myth" loc. 147). The text of the *History of the Rus'* positions the Cossacks "as a nation separate from the Russians to the north" ("The Cossack Myth" loc. 147). Moreover, it points to the mistreatment of the Cossacks by the Russian tsar who even "t[ook] away their ancestral name of Rus' and appropriat[ed] it for themselves" ("The Cossack Myth" loc. 147). The manuscript "became one of the most influential [...] historical texts of the modern era" ("The Cossack Myth" loc. 154). Therefore, as Plokhy notes, in the Ukrainian context the Cossacks emerged as the defenders of "the national religious and cultural tradition against the attacks of foreign states, which culminated in the creation of a polity of their own" ("Unmaking" 194; cf. "The Cossack Myth").[12]

The entanglements of literature and the Ukrainian national movement further contributed to the popularization of the figure of the Cossack. Andrei's Dido in Warwaruk's novel is right when he highlights the role of Ukrainian poets in nation-building, as it was literature that helped to promote the "Cossack-related historical memory far beyond the boundaries of the Hetmanate" (Plokhy "Unmaking" 194). As Jaroslav Hrycak notes, "[i]n a situation where the overwhelming majority of Ukrainians could not form a normal political life and their language was forbidden, literature became the proof of the existence of Ukrainians" (268). Statelessness and the persecution of the Ukrainian language provoked "the Ukrainian imagination to become captured entirely by literature, and the Ukrainian national movement carried [...] a distinctly philological character" (268).

George G. Grabowicz observes that the Cossack trope "animates Ukrainian Romanticism and provides its most productive theme" ("Three Perspectives" 171). Moreover, "its impact is strongly felt beyond the bounds of Ukrainian literature," as it resonated in other literary traditions, most importantly Russian and Polish ("Three Perspectives" 171). The Cossack was romanticized by authors like Panteleimon Kulish, Nikolai Gogol, and most importantly, Taras Shevchenko, who is widely regarded as the spiritual father of Ukraine, and whose legacy is commemorated every March both in Ukraine, and Canada (cf. Swyripa "Storied" 135; Plokhy "The Cossack Myth" loc. 1185). As Oksana Zabuzhko argues in *Shevchenkiv mif Ukrainy: Sproba filosofs'koho analizu* (*Shevchenko's myth of Ukraine: An attempt at a philosophical analysis*), Shevchenko was also Ukraine's first national intellectual. He saw "the Ukrainians as a modern nation in the making, an 'imagined community' in Benedict Anderson's sense, held together by horizontal ties, not by dynastic or religious identification" (Chernetsky 262). However, as Zabuzhko notes, he can also be described as a poet-mythmaker (cf. Chernetsky 261–263).

While Shevchenko lived under the Russian rule and never visited Canada, his statue was unveiled there in 1961 to commemorate the seventieth anniversary of the Ukrainian Canadian migration from Western Ukraine (Swyripa "Storied" 168). In Shevchenko's poetry, the key features of the Cossack myth were circulated and provoked Ukrainians to awake "with the sense of a shared glorious past" (Plokhy "Unmaking" 194). The same poetry also helped the Ukrainian Canadian settler face the challenges of "the early days" (Swyripa "Storied" 168). Hence both Shevchenko and the figure of the Cossack played a vital role in forming modern Ukrainian and Ukrainian Canadian national identity (Plokhy "Unmaking" 194). Andrei's Dido shares with him a romanticized image of "a Cossack [who] can ride at full gallop, swing himself down and snatch a silk kerchief from the ground with his teeth" (11). This description is not unforeseen considering that "the Cossack trope mythologizes the Zaporozhetz – the unregistered freebooter who fought against the Poles, Turks and, later, the Muscovites" (Ostashewski 17). It is Zaporozhian Cossacks who are widely regarded as one of the most important sources of Ukrainian distinctive national identity.

In Shevchenko's verse "the Cossacks are both communitas and structure," meaning that at the same time they represent "the 'native' freedom, equality, and emotional spontaneity, and the 'foreign' of authority, hierarchy" (Grabowicz "Three Perspectives" 179). The Cossack's ambiguous position is one of the factors explaining his popularity in North America. Plokhy contends that the Cossack wars led Western writers to regard Cossackdom "as part of the general European wave of revolutions of the Christian struggle against the Ottomans" ("The Frontline" loc. 222). Since the late nineteenth century, the Cossack has been an important symbol in Ukrainian diaspora's cultural memory, "a revered and cherished figure from a proud nation, in spite of its complex, contested history" (Ostashewski 29). For example, William Paluk's 1943 collection, the first Ukrainian one in Canada written in English, titled *Canadian Cossacks: Essays, Articles and Stories on Ukrainian-Canadian Life*,[13] uses the Cossack as a transcultural trope. As Ostashewski notes, "when discrimination was more overt, the romantic ideal of the Cossack may have provided [Ukrainian peasants with] a sense of power and pride" (30). Moreover, with his quest for freedom, the Cossack echoed with North American ideas, especially the fascination with sovereignty (Klymasz

"Culture Maintenance" 174; cf. Klymasz "Cossacks and Indians" 359–361). Thus the Cossack and the values found in Shevchenko's poetry "firmly attached" Ukrainian Canadians to Canada (Swyripa "Storied" 170).

Dido in *Andrei and the Snow Walker* tells the protagonist that while the Baydas are peasants, their ancestors were brave Cossacks and Scythian warriors. According to a family story, Andrei's ancestors include Hetman Dmytro Vyshnevetsky, whose legendary nickname, Baida, sounds like Andrei's last name. The boy also remembers that his teacher talked in class about "the ancient battles against Turks and Poles," and "the Hetman Bayda-Vyshnevetsky with 35,000 Cossacks fighting on this hillside three hundred years ago" (12). While there is no evidence of such a battle in Western Ukraine, the mentions of school seem to validate Warwaruk's historical references. Plokhy notes that the image of Dmytro Vyshnevetsky was popularized by Mykhailo Hrushevsky, who wrote about him as "a true leader of emerging Cossackdom – above all, a forerunner of the Zaporozhian Host" (Plokhy "Unmaking" 204; cf. Plokhy "The Frontline" loc. 752). According to Hrushevsky, Vyshnevetsky "introduced Cossackdom to the world of international politics and made, or attempted to make, alliances with Muscovy, the Ottoman Empire, and Moldavia" (204). Hrushevsky also argued that Vyshnevetsky, under the name of Baida, was portrayed in one of Ukrainian *dumy* (epic songs)[14] (cf. Plokhy "Unmaking" 204). Interestingly, in Warwaruk's novel, it is Dido, Andrei's *maternal* grandfather, who "never can say enough about Cossacks" and tells his grandson about Vyshnevetsky, who "had started this brotherhood of Cossacks" (12).

At the beginning of his journey in the second novel, Brovko, Andrei's dog, meets a blind *kobzar* on the train and becomes "the *kobzar*'s eyes" until he gets to Lviv (41; emphasis in original). Notably, he understands "that a *kobzar* is a little bit like a hermit, except that a *kobzar* doesn't live in just one place" (40; emphasis in original). Brovko knows it because "Andrei's *dido* said so. He said that a *kobzar* moves around the countryside. He sings and plays and maybe writes a song. He stops at villagers and people pay him. He said that a *kobzar* is usually blind" (40; emphasis in original). This description seems correct, as the kobzar was a bard, frequently blind, who performed psalms and dumas, singing accompanied by a kobza or bandura (cf. Kononenko 45–90). This tradition was established in the sixteenth century, during the Hetmanate Era. However, *kobzars* were seen as a political threat and were allegedly murdered in Kharkiv in 1932 on the order of Stalin (Conquest 266; cf. Applebaum 135–136). *Kobzar* is also the title of Shevchenko's 1840 debut volume of poetry, which Hrycak has called the Bible of Ukrainian nationalism (268). Shevchenko himself is also often referred to as *kobzar* ("Kobzar" 302; cf. Grabowicz "The Poet as Mythmaker"; Zabuzhko "Shevchenkiv mif").[15] By spending time with the *kobzar*, Brovko, and more importantly, the implied readers, can learn more about Ukrainian culture. "The old *kobzar*, as if recalling a memory of a loved one, caresses the strings of his *bandura*" and sings songs by "Taras Shevchenko [...] The poet of Ukraine" (47–48). The old man tells Brovko that "[a]s long as his words are sung, so long will live the spirit of Ukraine" (47–48). The songs performed by the blind bard are those of "the Cossacks, the mounted warriors of Ukraine" (49). Although Brovko enjoys performing with the *kobzar*, he meets an old hermit – first introduced in *Andrei and the Snow Walker* – who informs the bard that Brovko has a mission to go to Canada (55). While the journey to Canada in *Andrei and the Snow Walker* is short, during his magical journey Brovko not only learns about Ukrainian history but also contemporary culture. Seeing Lviv, "the city of lions" (60) with many people and "church domes – gold, copper, silver, green," he introduces the readers to a different, urban character of Ukraine (62).

Considering the numerous references to Cossackdom and Ukrainian history in *Andrei and the Snow Walker*, what may come as a surprise is that in the second half of the novel Andrei starts calling Ukraine "the old country" and seems to have forgotten about Dido's stories. He even asks "[w]hat is a Hetman?," to which Danylo Skomar replies, "[t]he head man [...] Your ancestor Bayda-Vyshnevetsky!" (120). Then Andrei questions if Dido had met Vyshnevetsky, to which his grandfather answers, "[n]ot exactly. It was three hundred years ago when he ruled" (120). Andrei's oblivion can be explained either by Warwaruk's mistake or the need to show how easily Andrei can forget about his heritage when Dido's story is not repeated. Although "characters in children's fiction are not necessarily less complex," Maria Nikolajeva notes that "they must be comprehensible for young readers" because "they serve as ideological (or rather educational) vehicles" (x). The fact that Andrei forgets something so important may amaze the readers. Even though in Ukraine Andrei enjoyed listening to Dido's stories, in Canada he becomes more interested in spending time with his Métis friends and his horse Vityr. Instead of listening to stories about the Cossacks, he prefers to *perform* Cossackdom.

The image of a Cossack "brotherhood" is "a strongly masculine part of the Ukrainian cultural tradition" (Ostashewski 17). Because having a horse was an important element of being a Cossack, it can be argued that by spending time in a homosocial environment and learning how to ride a horse and take care of it, Andrei symbolically *becomes* a Ukrainian Canadian Cossack (cf. Kononenko 180). After all, as Dido says, "[a] Cossack is not a Cossack without a horse" (3). Whereas in Ukraine Andrei went to school, he does not in Canada, and it is his newfound Métis friends who teach him about horses and the traditions of the new country. When Andrei saves Mr. Kuzyk's mare, which is "bogged in a soap hole of slippery white mud" (128), he gets "the honour" to select the name for the mare's colt and calls him Vityr, the wind (132). Like a free warrior who knows how to communicate with his horse, Andrei seems to sense the feelings of Vityr, as the following quotation demonstrates:

"If Andrei didn't know better, he'd say that it [Vityr] knows the mare's in trouble, and that Andrei's trying to help" (130). At the end of the novel, after being saved by the Snow Walker, the eponymous Cree man, Andrei is given the horse by Mr. Kuzyk; in *Brovko's Amazing Journey*, the protagonist spends his days horse-riding on the prairies with his Métis friend Chi Pete.

After saying that Ukrainians "have the world's greatest horsemen" because they "were the first to take the horse" (11), Dido links the cultural myth of the Cossack with that of the Scythians: "[t]hree thousand years ago, *our Scythian warriors* rode far and wide across the grasslands of Ukraine. They introduced horses to the world. Horsemanship is in *our* blood" (11; emphasis mine). Despite Dido's insistence of the Scythians' links to contemporary Ukrainians, they were nomads of Iranian descent who traveled from Central Asia to present-day Russia and Ukraine in the eighth and seventh centuries BC and established a potent empire with the center in Crimea (cf. Rolle 7–10). Yet in *Andrei and the Snow Walker* they emerge as the *direct* ancestors of the Cossacks. Apart from portraying the Scythians as proto-Ukrainians, Dido is right as they were well-regarded for their fighting skills and horsemanship, and it is widely believed that they were one of the first peoples to master horse-riding. As Herodotus famously recorded:

> [h]aving neither cities nor forts, and carrying their dwellings with them wherever they go; accustomed, moreover, one and all of them, to shoot from horseback; and living not by husbandry but on their cattle, their wagons the only houses that they possess, how can they fail of being unconquerable, and unassailable even?
>
> (41)

Like the Baydas and other immigrants, the Scythians carried all of their belongings with them but were "unassailable." Notably, the Scythians were also known for their sophisticated culture and a class of wealthy nobles. In their graves, some opulently worked golden objects were found, often decorated with turquoise and amber. Many Scythian gold objects discovered in Ukraine in the last two decades of the twentieth century were presented at the exhibition *Gold of the Nomads: Scythian Treasures from Ancient Ukraine* (cf. Reeder).

In *Andrei and the Snow Walker* Ukrainians emerge as the descendants of the Cossacks *and* the Scythians. Furthermore, it is the Scythian magical golden cup which leads the Baydas' way to Canada and links them to Canada's Indigenous Peoples. Writing about double-focalized novels, Nodelman argues that they "represent a dynamic of multiculturalism – a way of allowing people of different backgrounds their differences while nevertheless sharing the same space, our home here in Canada" ("At Home" 114). Although Warwaruk uses different narrative techniques, both of his novels fit Nodelman's description. By focusing on Ukrainian history, Warwaruk makes the past taking place in a distant space meaningful but positions Ukraine as "the undesirable opposite of the desirable place," that is Canada ("At Home" 114). Such positioning is impossible in the context of Indigenous Peoples because, as Nodelman notes, "[t]heir history did not take place elsewhere. It occurred nowhere else" (114).

Ukrainian Founding Fathers and the First Nations

Unlike Warwaruk, who uses the trope of the Cossack, in *Lesia's Dream* Langston refers to Christian symbolism. Lesia gains wisdom which allows her to keep, and later plant, the metaphorical seeds of memory. She does so with the help of her family Bible and the traditional attributes of Saint Sophia – Faith, Hope, and Charity. Initially the whole Magus family is preparing to emigrate, yet at the last minute Nadia Chernetska, Lesia's grandmother, decides to stay in Ukraine, close to the grave of her husband and grandson. The woman gives Lesia her most precious treasure – her late husband's Bible, which she compares to her heart and tells the protagonist to keep close to her own, because it "will comfort [her]. It will help [her] keep the faith" (19). Nadia, or hope in Ukrainian, symbolizes this very virtue in the novel, thanks to which Lesia not only ultimately becomes the bearer of memory herself but is also able to survive all difficulties and become its giver to the next generations. While Lesia is illiterate and initially does not feel worthy of receiving the holy book, her grandmother states that "in God's eyes we are all worthy" (20).[16] Anticipating the problems that Lesia may face in the future, the woman tells her: "in the eyes of God, we are all equal. Peasants and landowners. Ukrainians and Canadians. The Bible will help you remember" (20). These are the words Lesia recalls when she is struggling with Anglo-Canadian hatred and the hardships of the prairie work. Lesia promises to take the Bible to Canada and learn to read, first Ukrainian and then English. The handing over of the Bible is connected with the symbolic marking of Lesia as the guardian of traditions, values, and memory. Passing over the symbols of memory is an important part of incorporating individual memories into collective and cultural memory. As Assmann explains, such memory

> relies on a pool of experiences and knowledge that has been released from its living carriers and *passes over into material media*. It is the way that memories can be stabilized over generational thresholds. While social memory repeatedly vanishes with the people that keep it going, cultural symbols and signs are more durable.
> (21; emphasis in original)

The past coincides with the present when Lesia becomes the rightful heir to the memory which her grandmother passes on to her without hesitation.

Canada emerges as Lesia's second home, and she becomes the second love of Andrew Korol, a young widower who came to Canada at the age of seven. Although he grew up in Canada, he still does not feel completely at home in the English-speaking community: "I've been here thirteen years and I still don't belong. Not like the Irish and the Scottish do" (184). Still, addressing the protagonist, he says: "remember, we've been outsiders in our own land for centuries. We still are. Give Canada a chance" (184). Andrew's words highlight the difficult situation of Ukrainians under Austro-Hungarian and Russian rule and the opportunities that Canada could give them. The man and his loved ones have been selflessly supporting Lesia from the beginning, helping her when the other men in her family first depart in search of work, leaving the heroine with her pregnant mother and a little sister, then when the men are sent to an internment camp (cf. Chapter 2). Desperately wanting to go back to "Shuparka [which] wasn't perfect, but it was better than Canada" (170), Lesia sells the Bible, her most valuable possession, to save money for the trip back home. She temporarily loses faith and doubts her grandmother's words, believing that "[t]here were no possibilities in Canada [...] Not unless you counted internment, discrimination and enough cold weather to freeze people's hearts" (174). Whereas in Warwaruk's novels Andrei has to lose the magical cup in order to become Ukrainian Canadian, the Bible returns to Lesia, because its place is in Canada. It is Andrew who redeems the Bible and the hope chest from the pawnshop. Not wanting Lesia to leave, he also buys her a cow which was to be slaughtered. Moved by the fate of the animal, whom Andrew calls Faith, Lesia decides to take care of her. The animal symbolizes Lesia's struggles in the new homeland – although she was sentenced to death because her owners did not believe she could give milk, the goodness and love of the eponymous protagonist make Faith turn out to be rich in milk. Milk and dairy, as well as the money earned from selling them, allow Lesia to regain her faith and the Magus family to survive the difficult period of the Great War. Hope, charity, and faith, symbolized in the novel by Grandmother Nadia, Andrew, and the cow, help Lesia eventually find happiness in Canada. In the last chapter Laisha receives the same Bible, a token of the symbolic seeds of memory, from her great-grandmother Lesia who says that her hard work paid off because the Canadian prairie gave birth to her anew and the land is marked with her blood, sweat, and tears.

What comes as a surprise in the chronotope of *Lesia's Dream* is the lack of any mention of Indigenous Peoples, present extensively in Warwaruk's novels. Whereas the absence of Indigenous Peoples in the prairie of 1914 seems unlikely, it allows Langston to position Lesia as the first inhabitant of the Canadian wilderness and the only Other facing discrimination and reluctance of English-speaking Canadians. This absence is not coincidental if we consider Linda Alcoff's words that "[w]ho is speaking, who is spoken of, and who listens is a result, as well as an act, of political struggle" (Alcoff 15). Referring to Alcoff, Nodelman observes that "speaking for others or *choosing not* to are equally political acts, equally prone therefore to re-inscribe the power relations of the context from which they emerge" (111; emphasis mine). By not including Indigenous characters, Langston on the one hand detaches her protagonist from the risk of cultural appropriation; on the other hand, however, she creates an image of Canada as an uninhibited wilderness tamed by the Ukrainian homesteaders – the founding fathers – "who were ploughing and cultivating *virgin* soil" while being ridiculed, shamed, and abused by Anglo-Canadians (Langston 142; emphasis mine). Therefore, even though Langston makes different narrative choices from Warwaruk, she also ultimately indigenizes Ukrainian Canadians.

Notably, in the late nineteenth and early twentieth centuries Ukrainian immigrants and Indigenous Peoples "were seen as similarly foreign occupants of the Canadian landscape" (Ledohowski "White" 69). It is also worth mentioning that "in North America [...] the European conquest and colonization are often denied, largely through the fantasy that North America was peacefully settled and not colonized" (Razack, 1–2). Warren Cariou observes that in the second half of the twentieth century some settlers struggled with "a widespread and perhaps growing anxiety" about "the legitimacy of their claims to belonging on what they call 'their' land" (727; cf. Ledohowski "White" 71). Ukrainian Canadians, Ledohowski notes, share this "growing anxiety," especially since they are "often seen as synonymous with the prairie" ("White" 71). The Ukrainian situation is complex because like the Cossack in Warwaruk's novels, the pioneers were "a strange hybrid" of the colonizer and the colonized ("White" 71). As Bradford argues, frequently "indigenous traditions become merely sites of abundance and meaningfulness that supply western consumers with that they lack, and in this way hybridity shades into neocolonial appropriation" ("Transformative Fictions" 195–196). Studying present-day Canadian novels, we may observe a specific type of fear "borne out of a desire to be indigenous to the land, but not complicit in the marginalization of those who were, in fact, indigenous to the land" (Ledohowski "White" 71).

Ledohowski argues that many Ukrainian Canadian texts about the early settlement do not portray "historical truths" connected to the first settlers' attitudes toward Indigenous Peoples ("White" 71). On the contrary, in a matter typical of historical fiction, they echo "the many varied and vexed feelings that the contemporary descendent may feel about that historical interaction between the non-Anglo European settler who [...] participated in a colonial marginalization and displacement of Aboriginal peoples" (71). Authors of historical fiction attempt to commemorate their ancestors who emigrated and faced difficulties, but at the same time distinguish "the colonial project into which those ancestors may well have been co-opted into participating" (69). While the early Ukrainian Canadians may not have been aware of their colonial position in the context of Indigenous Peoples, modern writers recognize "the complex currents swirling between the two groups – immigrant and Aboriginal – of the early Canadian prairie" and their own position as *implicated subjects* benefiting from the history of colonization without originating or controlling it (70; cf. Rothberg 1–2). As Michael Rothberg argues, the implicated subject is an umbrella term used to describe roles exceeding the fixed "conceptual space of victims, perpetrators, and bystanders" (13). Moreover, the implicated subject is dynamic and "is not an ontological identity that freezes us forever in proximity to power and privilege" (Rothberg 8; cf. Chapter 5).

Adapting Margery Fee's terminology, Ledohowski distinguishes between four types of attitudes towards Indigenous Peoples found in Ukrainian Canadian novels. One of them is "claim-by-identification," which she describes as a need to *soften* the "white-settler guilt," not avoid it ("White" 74). This can be accomplished by showing connections between Ukrainians and Indigenous Peoples "as a way of creating a symbolic legitimacy for the immigrant settler who participated in exploitation and colonization" (74). In literature this is done by "peopling non-Aboriginal texts with Aboriginal characters and themes to show *imagined connections* between the two groups to construct the settler as somehow indigenous to the colonized space" (74; emphasis mine). This approach is used by Warwaruk but also other Canadian writers, including Marsha Forchuk Skrypuch and Marion Mutala.

The links between Ukrainians, Cossacks, and Scythians allow Warwaruk to show the *imagined connections* between Ukrainians, the Cree, and the Métis. Like other authors, Warwaruk uses Indigenous Peoples to gift his Ukrainian protagonists "a kind of adopted Aboriginal status, thus distancing them from the colonial project and legitimizing their place in Canada" (Ledohowski "White" 74). Hence the first non-Ukrainians the Baydas befriend are not Anglo-Canadians but the Métis, people of mixed Indigenous and European heritage. When Andrei first sees Gabriel Desjarlais "wear[ing] a black hat with a high crown and a wide, flat brim," the boy notices that despite Gabriel's darker skin tone, he looks similar to Petrus Shumka, Andrei's Ukrainian friend and the boyfriend of his sister Marusia/Marie. Gabriel "has a sash tied around his waist *like a Ukrainian*," but he speaks French, which the protagonist instantly identifies as "different from that spoken by the officials on the train [English]" (31; emphasis mine). Gabriel not only looks like a Ukrainian of a darker skin tone and speaks a language Andrei does not associate with Anglo-Canada but also knows "broken Ukrainian" (31). That is why he can explain that he is Métis, an identity with which the Baydas are unfamiliar. When Dido says "[y]ou must be Indians," Gabriel once again explains "The Métis" (32). By listing the names of important political leaders Louis Riel and Gabriel Dumont and positioning them together with his Uncle Moise, who in Warwaruk's novel fought in the 1885 Battle at Batoche for "the freedom of our Métis people [...] For *our* land," Gabriel further distances himself from the colonial, Anglo-Canadian position (32; emphasis mine). Riel, under whom in 1870 a provisional Métis state was declared in the Red River Valley, was seen as a traitor of the Canadian government (Lawrence 34).[17] Dido promptly compares the Métis to "Cossacks [who] fought to save *our* land" (33; emphasis mine). While the "*our* land" they talk about is different, the one the Métis fought for is subsequently settled by Ukrainians. As Gabriel later informs the Baydas, his uncle and many other Métis want to move as "there are too many of your people [Ukrainians] coming to Fish Creek" and changing the prairie into a mirror image of Galicia (97).

Andrei straightaway befriends Gabriel and Chi Pete, who have horses named Raven and Crow. The boys take Andrei hunting and together they eat a Canadian bird and traditional Ukrainian dishes – the Baydas' first meal in Canada. Notably, Gabriel notices that the Ukrainian dish prepared by Paraska Bayda "looks and tastes like [his] mother's bannock" (37). For Andrei, Gabriel looks "almost" Ukrainian. When the protagonist sees Gabriel on his horse wearing a hat, he compares the man to a cowboy, further pointing to his similarity to the Cossack (54). Despite their growing friendship, Andrei still does not understand Gabriel's Métis identity, asking questions like: "Are you an Indian? [...] And you are a cowboy?" to which Gabriel replies: "I am Métis [...] Both Indian and French" (57). The identity of Gabriel and Chi Pete is something Andrei writes about in a letter sent to his Ukrainian neighbors, which is quoted in *Brovko's Amazing Journey*. He explains that his new friend is "an Indian, but also not an Indian. He's Métis. Both French and Indian" and his "older brother [...] owns the fastest horse in the district" ("Brovko" 28). By pointing to Gabriel's in-betweenness, Warwaruk seems to further highlight the imagined connections between Ukrainian Canadians and the Métis.

Teaching Andrei about the new country and its customs, Gabriel and Chi Pepe become his new male role models, gradually replacing his Ukrainian Dido. Andrei is stunned when he witnesses Gabriel hunting a moose. In the old country, as he notes, "such events were for the sports of the Polish landlords, not the people. Even the rich would never have hunted an animal this big" (60). Warwaruk's choice of the moose does not seem accidental, as "beavers, moose, and Canada geese [...] have come to serve as fields of [Canadian] identification" (Richter 31). As Elizabeth A. Galway notes, "[i]n addition to Canada's physical environment, the animals that share this space have also played a significant role in the developments of the country's national identity" (16). The process of dismembering the moose is described in detail, with Gabriel teaching the protagonist about the traditional meaning of each part, including the stomach, which in his family is called "the bible" (60–61). Gabriel also shares meat with the Baydas when Dido and Andrei's father go working for the Mennonites; this allows the family to survive the harsh winter.

Andrei and the Snow Walker challenges the typical trope found in novels authored by non-Indigenous writers. Nodelman notes that

> in order to move past prejudice and intolerance and/or to find redemption for the guilt of the theft of land and the mistreatment of indigenous peoples by their ancestors and/or contemporaries, the people of non-Aboriginal backgrounds in these novels can and must learn to think and act like Aboriginals – like those shaped by the land they live on.
>
> (115)

Whereas Warwaruk shows the imagined connections between Indigenous and non-Indigenous characters, in *Andrei* and *Brovko* it is also Indigenous characters who have to learn to think and act like Ukrainians. One of the most puzzling elements of the relationship between Andrei and his Métis friends is that they "speak Ukrainian so well" ("Andrei" 57). As Gabriel explains, it is because "Ukrainians come through nearly every day" and learning the difficult Slavic language was necessary (58). Gabriel's knowledge of the Ukrainian language seems so natural that Dido seems surprised that the young man's uncle does not speak it, as he knows "*just* French, Cree, and English" (32; emphasis mine). While at first it is only Gabriel who communicates with the Baydas in Ukrainian, Chi Pete also quickly learns it and "[h]is mastery of Ukrainian is remarkable" (83). The speed of Chi Pete's acquisition of Andrei's language comes as a surprise, especially considering the complex discussions the boys have and the proper English used by Warwaruk. Remarkably, the Baydas, including Andrei, do not even try to learn French, Cree, or English – it is the others who have to learn the language of the new settlers. Such depiction may imply that in the world created by Warwaruk, the "white settler guilt" does not exist as the Ukrainian "white settlers" become part of the inclusive imagined community built by the Indigenous Peoples *and* Ukrainians who appear to be "adopted into one indigenous family" (cf. Ledohowski "White" 76). Despite such a portrayal, as Goldie observes, "no matter how much the object of a writing subject approximates the self, the object cannot be turned into the subject"; hence, Indigenous Peoples in Warwaruk's novels emerge as what Goldie calls "a semiotic pawn on a chess board under the control of the white signmaker" (217, 10). As Andrei spends a lot of time with his new friends, he is surprised to hear that non-Ukrainian speaking Indigenous Peoples live at the Reserve.

Similar to Dido, Gabriel serves the role of the storyteller who introduces Andrei to the history of the Buffalo hunters and the causes of the poverty of the First Nations and the Métis (64–65). He also invites Andrei and his sister to a celebration at the church, which helps the protagonist see the similarities between the Métis and Ukrainians. Gabriel's uncle plays the fiddle, reminding Andrei of Dido, who plays the flute, and

[t]hough it's not Ukrainian, the procession seems to warm Andrei, seems to fill him with a sense of well-being. *The walk of the people reminds him of his lost homeland,* with its colours, and the smell of incense and candles burning ... Andrei *belonging* to the pageantry.

(104; emphasis mine)

The imagined links between Ukrainians and the Métis are strengthened when Gabriel agrees to take part in "a Ukrainian play" organized to celebrate the Baydas' first successful harvests in Canada (148). The performance takes place in the new Ukrainian church cofounded by Mr. Kuzyk, who agrees to play the role of the devil trying to tempt Marusia/Marie, "the maiden of bountiful harvest" (155). Gabriel stars as a buffalo hunter – and not a Cossack as the protagonist originally wanted – and Chi Pete is a Scythian warrior (150).[18] As Andrei believes, the play helps the local community to connect and allows his grandfather to "be Cossack for a day" (149). While playing instruments is not allowed by the Orthodox churches, "[t]he Holy pictures are put away" (152) and Dido can play the flute. After the performance, the Métis organize a dance for the entire community.

Although ultimately Andrei seems to forget that Gabriel is not Ukrainian and represents a different culture, he reminds the protagonist of it by saying: "I'm Métis [...] not a Cossack" (150). However, as we learn from *Brovko's Amazing Journey*, he does eventually become a member of the Bayda family after marrying Andrei's sister, Marusia/Marie who is the first one wanting to assimilate and become Canadian (cf. Chapter 3). Marie is not the only one, though, as in the second half of the novel, the protagonist starts thinking of Ukraine as "the old country" (127). Notwithstanding being friends with Petrus Shumka, his sister's former boyfriend, Andrei "likes Gabriel a whole lot, and even if he is of a different people, what difference should that make?" he wonders before adding that "Ukrainians have to change their ways here in Canada and not be so stubborn" (163). When Andrei sees Petrus for the first time in a year, he instantly recognizes him based on the "Old Country hat" he is wearing (185). Seeing his former best friend, Andrei is "holding back from laughing" (186). Surprised, Petrus says that "[i]t's the same hat [he] always wear[s]" (186). In reply, Andrei looks not at Petrus but at his Métis friend, and says, "[n]othing wrong with that hat, is there, Chi Pete?" (186). After only a few months spent in Canada with Gabriel and Chi Pete, "Petrus's floppy hat with its colourful band seems so strange" (186). This scene is significant as it shows Andrei's gradual detachment from "the Old Country" and his newfound status as a Canadian Cossack.

It is Gabriel who becomes Andrei's link between the old and the new world *and* the Scythian and Indigenous cultures. He is also the one to tell Andrei about the eponymous Snow Walker, "a spirit man who lives alone [...and] predicts the coming of bad weather" (58–59). The Snow Walker is "Cree of the One Arrow people" who "lives at the river by himself, as if watching out for the arrival of intruders" – and at first it is the Baydas who emerge as the intruders (59). According to the local people, he can also "turn himself into a bear," a fact both Andrei and his dog Brovko later experience (59). Interestingly, in some of the books examined by Galway, the bear and the "Indian" both function as symbols of Canadian landscapes (193).

The character of the Snow Walker puts Warwaruk in the category of writers who "identify Aboriginal culture with what is natural and untainted" (Nodelman 126). Yet in Warwaruk's novel the Cree man is also the Indigenous equivalent of the Ukrainian Holy one, the hermit who gives Dido the Scythian golden cup. Unaware of the power of the ancient object, Dido buries it under the rock which "[t]he Cree people, the people who were always here, see it [...] as a shrine. A place of retreat. A place where the Great Spirit lives" (186). When Andrei sees the Snow Walker for the first time, the man asks if Dido "left the bag as a gift, or as a curse to the spirits" and calls him Rope Head, referring to his Cossack hair, one who prays like "the French Black Robes" who brought havoc to the Cree land (88–89). The Snow Walker's similarity to the Ukrainian Holy one is further highlighted in the letter Andrei sends to his Ukrainian friends in *Brovko's Amazing Journey*:

> [m]y friend Chi Pete and I met up with an Indian *starets* in the woods. His name is Snow Walker, and he carries a rattle made from deer's dewclaws. He wears a cap of weasel skins with the heads still on.
> (29; emphasis in original)

The Snow Walker, a *starets* or an old man, is also compared to the Ukrainian hermit by the narrator, who says "[t]wo hermits helped Brovko in Ukraine, and now he has a Canadian hermit who feeds him" (138). After all, when Dido hears that the Snow Walker saved Andrei from drowning, he says that he did "as a Cossack would have done," and he did it for him to "grow into a man in this new land" (190).

The one-dimensional depiction of the Snow Walker recalls the Pikogan women in Skrypuch's *Prisoners in the Promised Land*. While the Soloniuks in the novel are positioned as unequivocally innocent victims of the internment (cf. Chapter 2), Ledohowski notes the problematic portrayal of the relationship between Ukrainian Canadians and Indigenous Peoples in the book. In Spirit Lake Anya Soloniuk, who is not a homesteader but an internee, befriends two Pigokan Indians, who help her family survive by bringing them wild berries. Like many characters in Warwaruk's novels, Skrypuch's protagonist sees a special connection between Ukrainians and Indigenous Peoples as both groups are treated unjustly by the Canadian government. Anya also notices that the beadwork the women do is similar to her own and even compares a Pigokan woman to "a long-lost relative" (Ledohowski "White Settler" 158). When an Aboriginal elder gives Anya a special bead, it is a symbolic "benediction, a gifting of the land from Aboriginal hands to Anya and people like her, who are, after all, just 'long lost relatives,' not imperial colonizers" (Henderson 75). This scene recalls Nodelman's words that "once non-Aboriginals have learned Aboriginality, they are understood to have become legitimate members of the group of Aboriginals with a claim to the land" ("At Home" 115). Although Anya is not a homesteader, she is still a settler. I concur with Jennifer Henderson who in her reading of the novel notes that

> The gift gives the immigrant child an affiliation with Indigeneity, but insofar as this affiliation with a Pikogan "relative" seems to be earned through the child's experiences of marginalization, confinement, and compensatory attachment to culture as traditional craft, that is given back to the Pikogan woman in the exchange would seem to be her reframing as a member of ethnocultural group, like the Ukrainian Canadians, determined to preserve her culture's distinctiveness.
> (75)

Hence in a matter similar to Warwaruk, Skrypuch signifies the alleged similarity between Ukrainian Canadians and Indigenous Peoples and their role as the Others in relation to colonial Anglo-Canada. The exchange of gifts suggests "a continued literary colonialism whereby the Aboriginal object serves the needs of the European subject" ("White Settler" 78).[19] The apparent similarity between Ukrainians and the Pikogan are further highlighted by a traditional vest, looking like a Ukrainian *kamizelka*, a sheepskin coat, which the lady gives Anya, an item analogous to the one given by Gabriel to Marusia/Marie in *Andrei and the Snow Walker*. For Anya it is beautiful, as she finds it similar to Ukrainian outfits, but for Anglo-Canadians it is a symbol of otherness. Notably, it is only when Anya gives the Pigokan lady a traditional, Ukrainian embroidered *rushnyk*, that she says that the woman looks "noble" and Anya "think[s] she is the spirit of the lake" (201). Henderson argues that while by the gift exchange Anya – and symbolically Ukrainians in Canada – receives legitimization, her recognition of the Pikogan woman "as a sister-embroiderer" is not of the same resonance to Indigenous Peoples (75).

Prisoners in the Promised Land echoes the problematic trope found in many Canadian non-Indigenous novels, where "Aboriginals consist of everyone in Canada who has learned to think and act in an appropriate Aboriginal manner" (Nodelman 115).[20] This also seems to be the case in *Kokhum's Babushka: A Magical Métis/Ukrainian Tale*, Mutala's picturebook illustrated by Donna Lee Dumont, a Métis artist known for *Peter Fidler and the Métis* (2012).[21] Picturebooks, as Peter Hunt notes, "are a polyphonic form that embodies many codes, styles, textual devices and intertextual references and which frequently pushes at the boundaries of convention" (128). In her examination of Canadian picturebooks about residential schools written by Indigenous and illustrated by settler authors, Roxanne Harde argues that settler illustrators "reinforce the story and emphasise particular episodes, and, in their representations, they suggest a settler acknowledgment of Indigenous experiences, an honouring of the truth of many decades of historical injustices" (276). In *Kokhum's Babushka* the authorial dynamic is reversed as the text was written by a settler author and the illustrations created by a Métis artist. Yet the picturebook is an interesting example of a different type of intercultural collaboration. Harde observes that "complementing and amplifying the words of the Indigenous writers, the settler illustrators suggest how Canadians might learn to listen and work to understand the historical wrongs of the residential school system" (286). In the case of *Kokhum's Babushka*, it is Mutala who suggests how Ukrainian Canadians might try to reconsider the myth of Ukrainians as the founding fathers of the uninhabited prairie by listening to Indigenous voices. Although I believe that Mutala only partially succeeds due to simplifications and her attempts to indigenize Ukrainians, Dumont's illustrations complement the text and highlight the relationship between the people and the natural environment, as the detailed landscapes are juxtaposed with very simple and one-dimensional characters. This may encourage the readers to rethink their own connection to the land and its people. After all, picturebooks can open a dialogue about the readers' relation "to Indigenous peoples, territory issues and living together on the land" (Korteweg, Gonzalez, and Guillet 331). *Kokhum's Babushka*, like Mutala's previous picturebooks, also highlights the importance of the intergenerational transfer of memory.

A year after the loss of her Baba (grandmother), Natalia, the young protagonist known from Mutala's *Baba's Babushka* picturebooks,[22] once again travels back in time with the use of a magical kerchief or babushka. Yet unlike in the case of the three volumes of *Baba's Babushka* where Natalia goes to Ukraine to connect with her Baba's homeland and experience first-hand traditional Christmas, Easter, and wedding celebrations, in *Kokhum's Babushka* the girl travels to "the middle of an open field surrounded by green grass, near a fire pit," which is later revealed to be Saskatchewan.[23] There she encounters an old Métis woman, a kohkum, telling her granddaughter a story in Michif. While Natalia does not speak the language, in her magical journey she understands everything. The woman is wearing a babushka, which instantly makes Natalia feel "comforted," as it reminds the girl of her own late grandmother. Surprisingly, the tale is that of the first wave of Ukrainian immigration and the first encounters between the Métis and Ukrainians, including women who "worked just as hard as the men." Introducing her readers to the history of homesteading, Mutala points to the hardships of Ukrainians and the role of "[t]he Métis and the First Nations [who] helped the immigrants, especially during the first few harsh winters." The image emerging from the story is idyllic and oversimplified because it positions the immigrants as people rightfully claiming the vast and unoccupied land, not as colonial settlers. Moreover, Dumont's naïve illustrations further highlight the textural depictions of transcultural collaboration between Ukrainian immigrants and Indigenous Peoples.

The kokhum focuses on a Ukrainian-Métis encounter taking place in 1911. Similar to Skrypuch's *Prisoners in the Promised Land*, also here two families exchange gifts and customs. In the picturebook Ukrainians and the Métis communicate with body language, share food, dance *kolomeyka* and "Red River Jig," traditional dances of the Ukrainian Hutsuls and the Métis. Unlike Warwaruk's characters, here both groups learn basic expressions in one another's language. Dumont's illustrations strengthen the resemblance between Ukrainians and the Métis, especially when it comes to their flashy outfits. The similarities between the families are highlighted by clothing, most notably the red sashes worn by many characters in the picturebook (and reminiscent of Warwaruk's portrayal of Gabriel), the eponymous kerchiefs, as well as Ukrainian embroidery and Métis beadwork. As the storyteller frequently notes, during their first meeting both Ukrainians and the Métis considered their customs and traditions "different but good," which further problematizes the portrayal of the imagined Ukrainian-Métis connections.

Kokhum's Babushka: A Magical Métis/Ukrainian Tale introduces the idea that the word "babushka," meaning a grandmother or an old woman in Russian but reclaimed in North America to describe headscarves worn by immigrant women from Eastern Europe, actually comes from the Michif word "pootishka," meaning "put it on." As Mutala notes in the author's note, she was introduced to this theory in 2010 by Kelly O'Kanee, an Indigenous man who "said he studied languages." Notably, Mutala notes that "the Ukrainian word for headscarf was actually '*fustka*' or '*khusta*,'" but she does not mention the Russian origins of the word babushka, which can be found in her previous picturebooks. This seems to legitimize the theory that babushka was unknown in Ukraine and materialized only in Canada.[24] In *Kokhum's Babushka* Ukrainian and Métis women exchange their colorful scarves and "[f]rom then on, kokhums and babas both called the headscarves, 'babushkas.'" Moreover, as the old storyteller notes, "[t]he generosity of our grandmothers and their exchange of words turned out to be something that made both women happy," as later Ukrainian and Métis old women "would meet, laugh, smile, and would point and trade their *babushkas*." The protagonist returns to present-day Canada learning that in Saskatchewan there are "[s]o many different people: '*different but good, very, very good, duzhe, duzhe dobre*'" (emphasis in original). As is the case in Skrypuch's *Prisoners in the Promised Land*, in *Kokhum's Babushka* the Ukrainian presence in Canada is legitimized as the women emerge as symbolical "sisters." Moreover, the headscarves position them as the Others in the context of Anglo-Canadians. In Skrypuch's novel it is Anya's grandmother's visual difference caused by her traditional kerchief which marks her as an outsider, leading to physical aggression when a man "ran up to Baba and grabbed her *babushka*" on her the way to church, trying to get rid of the woman's visual emblem of ethnic Otherness (98; emphasis in original). Anya's grandmother "held onto it and wouldn't let him pull it off her head," the man "knocked her to the ground, but she still wouldn't let go" (99). The bystanders "were laughing at Baba, telling her she should go back to where she came from" (99). While after the Second World War the romanticized Ukrainian *baba* and "the Ukrainian male pioneer" were recognized "as founding people of western Canada" (Swyripa 256), in the 1910s the female immigrant wearing a headscarf represented illiteracy, backwardness, and reluctance to assimilate (cf. Chapter 3).

In the books by Skrypuch and Mutala/Dumont the imagined connections between Ukrainians and Indigenous Peoples are linked to the exchange of traditional, feminine craft. In *Andrei* and *Brovko* Paraska, Andrei's mother, one of the novels' two major female characters, openly displays hostility and racism. Unlike her tolerant and open-minded son and husband, she is suspicious of the Indigenous Peoples, "wondering if the dark-skinned men at the ferry are Gypsies" she dislikes so much (32). Whereas whiteness is invisible "at least to whites themselves" (Fondrie 12), it "provides white characters status and privilege not accorded to other characters" (Fondrie 9). It is worth recalling that when multiculturalism was introduced by Trudeau, it was predominantly white as it included "Canadians of Ukrainian [...and other] similar descent[s] [who] challenged the right of Canadians of French descent to specific claim and statuary privilege, without, necessarily wishing to distinguish themselves from general Anglophone-Canadian culture" (Davey 105). Canada's whiteness was the consequence of immigration laws which encouraged the maintenance of the Anglo- and Franco-Canadian form of society and the lack of visibility of the Indigenous Peoples (cf. Richter 40). Surrounded only by other Ukrainian immigrants, Paraska Bayda does not encounter any discrimination on behalf of Anglo-Canadians. She is also not aware of her own relative privilege, which was typical of many Eastern European immigrants.[25] Although only Paraska openly expresses racism, all of Warwaruk's characters show superiority in their contact with Indigenous Peoples (cf. Richter 53).

The Bible and the Cup

Writing about how societies remember, Paul Connerton distinguishes between three types of memory: personal (memories produced by an individual), cognitive (what the individual has learned), and habit memory (35). Connerton notes that social habits help to build and strengthen collective memory because "the images of the past and recollected knowledge of the past [...] are conveyed and sustained by (more or less ritual) performances" (4). In Ukrainian Canadian children's fiction, especially in the books by Warwaruk and Langston, the role of rituals is to keep the memory of the old country alive and plant it in the new country's cultural memory. While the Scythian cup helps Andrei and Brovko get to Canada, it has to be eventually returned to Ukraine, where it belongs. This seems symbolical as the cup, just like Ukraine, no longer belongs to Andrei's present. What is sufficient is the memory of the old country, the rituals, customs, and traditions which can be cultivated in the new country. That is why at first the cup falls to "the bottom of the river" (189), but it does not belong to Canada, so in the second novel it has to be returned to Ukraine. Notably, both times with the help of the eponymous Snow Walker, the embodiment of Indigenous Peoples.

The magical cup, pictured on the cover of *Andrei and the Snow Walker*, is introduced at the beginning of the first novel when Andrei has a vision seeing "the shadow of a man approaching a cross" and "a golden halo [... with] a red sparkle" (2). It is the first vision which makes Andrei's "left temple twitch" and takes him to a different dimension, a place where the past, the present, and the future intertwine:

> he loses any sense of where he is. Slowly the fog lifts the halo around the cross reappears, rolls down the mound and then to the river. He's taken with it, transported at once to walk along the river to where his grandfather has netted fish. He doesn't know how long he's been walking, or if he walks at all, or is he being carried? The dark water below him transforms into a road of gold bricks. The brush along its edges hangs heavy with branches full of coins of silver and gold. On a rolling plain beyond the river's far bank, a herd of riderless Cossack horses runs in spirals like the wind [...] The vision's disappeared and he's back at the yard. The halo has returned to the cross and then a black figure takes it. Andrei reaches as if to grab a handful of coins from a willow branch, but instead he grasps a stick from the willow fence.
>
> (2)

The vision foresees the landscape of the Canadian wilderness and its alleged similarity to Ukraine. Andrei wonders if it is "a signal lighting his way to Canada [...] a promise of fortune" and if the vision is "meant for him alone" (2–3). As it later turns out, he is right.

Unlike Andrei, the Holy man who gifts Dido the cup is described in detail and looks like the shadow from Andrei's first vision. The man, the Ukrainian equivalent of the Snow Walker, is Dido's "Uncle Skomar." His "time ends," so before the Baydas head for Canada, Skomar wants to give Dido a goatskin bag with "[a] relic of the Scythians" (13–15). When Andrei meets him, "the twitch in his temple returns, like a seizure" and he once again has a vision, seeing "the willow branches [which] are laden again with coins and the river water's turned to a broad path of gold. A fog rises swirling in circles, and like Aladdin, Andrei's standing at the mouth of a cave" (14). The vision symbolizes prosperity and opportunities waiting for Andrei in Canada but also points to his encounter with the Snow Walker. Then he sees "two Scythian warriors stand guard, each with swords, shield, and gold helmet, each with a horse at this side; a white horse and a red horse" (14). The men first look like younger Dido and the Holy one, but then Andrei "recognizes *himself* on each face, himself a Scythian soldier, the earliest of Ukrainians" (14; emphasis mine). This scene is of great significance as it implies Andrei's connection to his family, heritage, and the land. The vision features the ornamented cup that is inside the bag and the images of Andrei's future combined with his ancestors' past. While in the novel's chronotope it is Ukrainians who are the descendants of the Scythians, Dido tells Andrei that "two hundred years ago a Skomar ran off with a [Romani] woman [...whose] people had carried this with them for centuries" (16). Still, Dido states that despite being a Cossack, there is also "Skomar blood in [Andrei]" and says that the Holy one, the protagonist's great-uncle, handed Dido "a talisman [...] that came from somewhere deep inside a Scythian burial mound" and "will reveal messages for lives yet unborn who will struggle far off in a new land" (16). Andrei realizes that the halo he saw "was guarded by the ghosts of Scythian warriors" and its "power's been assigned to Andrei himself, and it might give him the strength of a Scythian warrior" (17). That is why "the secret of this magic" has to be taken to Canada (17). Notably, it is only Andrei, allegedly the descendant of *both* Cossacks and Scythians, who has the visions.

Because the cup is supposed to "reveal its wants" in Canada, the novel's promised land (20), the Baydas see it only after settling down in Saskatchewan. The cup is described in detail and echoes the one from Andrei's visions:

> It's an ornate work of art, a treasure piece of crafted gold. The body of the cup is a circle of six horses, their heads reined in to the centre, the animals appearing to be running anti-clockwise as if in the frenzy of a whirlwind. A ruby the size of a walnut is set at the bottom of the cup, holding the reins.
>
> (41)

The description is that of a typical example of Scythian art. Seeing it in Canada, Andrei once again has a vision, this time one which takes him back to Ukraine and "Brovko [who] runs back and forth from Martha to the girls, barking in a frenzy" (43). Hence the object becomes a link between the two countries. Dido decides to hide the cup in the forest, near the holy rock of the Cree. When Andrei once again has a vision, he realizes that "Dido should never have buried the cup there. It is not the place for Scythian warriors" (115). He also understands that "[h]e should have told Dido about Snow Walker" and the message the Cree man had (121).

Notably, it is only much later when Dido tells Andrei about the visions of "perils and destruction [...] coming to the lands of Ukraine" that Uncle

Skomar shared with him, ones recalling the many twentieth-century atrocities, including the Holodomor and the two world wars (121). Moreover, as Dido adds, the Holy man: "said that some of the people should leave, that I, Danylo Skomar, with my grandson, Andrei, should take the goatskin bag and leave. [...] The Holy one vowed that in the bag are the keys to the future" (121). Hence Canada appears as the place where Ukrainians and their culture, including the legacy of the Cossacks and the Scythians, can survive. Canada is the future and Ukraine is the past. Yet when the Baydas get settled and rebuild their old Ukrainian community in Canada, the cup has to return to protect the people left in the old country. Once Andrei's grandfather falls into the river through the ice and gets seriously sick, he tells his grandson that Uncle Skomar "directed that [they] pass the secrets of the past, the secrets of the old world, to the new generation in the new world" and that Andrei is "the new generation" (122). When they go together to the woods to take back the cup, Dido "takes on the appearance of a boy whispering to a boy" because they "are about to witness the unknown, and Dido's age counts for nothing" (124). It is worth noting that this description is not negative as some "[c]hildren's books with a romantic vein [...] cast the young as empowered, intelligent, and sensitive beings and suggest that the equation with childhood is the biggest compliment an adult can receive" (Joosen 193). Moreover, such books "do not base their comparison between children and old people on their perceived weaknesses, but on their supposed strengths – creativity, fantasy, curiosity" (Joosen 193). Hence it is curiosity and strength that link Dido and Andrei. Remarkably, as Dido says, "the talisman fascinates anyone who beholds it [...because] it captures souls"; that is why the Holy one "warned that the cup can sometimes give you back only your own thought, only your own dreams and nightmares, that you imagine predict the future" (124). Andrei once again has a vision, but this time he sees Ukraine and Brovko asking him to return home. Moreover, Andrei notices horseriders who look like Cossacks but who are racing at Batoche. Thus, this vision is another reference to the alleged similarities between Ukrainians and the Métis.

When Dido asks Andrei to take the cup from the rock, he gets lost in the blizzard. After opening the magical object, Andrei sees that "[a] black feather rests on the ruby jewel at the centre" signifying that someone, probably the Snow Walker, put it there (175). Yet Andrei knows that the non-Ukrainian feather "can't belong" and "pulls it out and drops it in the snow" (175). This scene is of great importance as the protagonist appears to be separating the Scythian and Indigenous talismans and putting them back, signifying that they both belong to the past, not to "the land of all colors and races." The cup guided Andrei, but the boy becomes indigenized and no longer needs it. Only when Andrei removes the feather, "a golden halo of light rises from the cup, the spray of red glowing at its centre, rising form the ruby jewel. The six golden horse heads twirl in a circle" (175). Andrei knows that being in a blizzard, he should not "allow himself to be drawn to magic" because he may freeze and has to reject the vision (175). The cup seems to be calling him, and Andrei sees "[a] miniature Scythian warrior, *the very picture of Andrei*, clings to the ruby, his arms extended, holding the lines of the six horses from the cup" (176; emphasis mine). In this vision Andrei emerges as the warrior, the symbolical new keeper of customs and tradition, yet one representing the new, Ukrainian *Canadian* generation.

Margaret Atwood argues that

> [t]he Canadian's author's two favourite 'natural' methods for dispatching his victims are drowning and freezing, drowning being preferred by poets – probably because it can be used as a metaphor for a descent into the unconscious – and freezing by prose writers.
> (55)

Andrei almost drowns and freezes as he falls through the ice and reaches for the cup, seeing it for what it is for the first time, just "a circle of reined-in horses, spinning as if in a whirlwind, the ruby in its eye," yet quickly his temple starts to twitch again and "[t]he vision grows as the Scythian warrior rises from his horse into the sky" (179). This time Andrei rejects the vision and throws the cup away. Then he drowns and "falls into a calming sleep" (180). He does not die, though, as he is saved by a bear – the Snow Walker. He does, however, lose the cup, his link to the old country. The medicine man brings Andrei to his hut where he takes care of the boy, gives him tea, food, and medicine. Andrei comes back home fully healed and realizes that the Snow Walker is "a Cree medicine man" (184). Grateful for being saved, Andrei gives him Dido's "Cossack pipe," which "is of glazed white clay. The design of a poppy flower is carved on each side of the bowl. Dido never uses this pipe [...] [it] is more like a treasure to him, and he has promised it to Andrei" (11). Importantly, the pipe is a sacred object to many Indigenous Peoples, as historically it was an element "used to open negotiations between different nations as a way for good talk to take place" (Asikinack). Such a "ceremony was also regarded as the way by which participants would be truthful, respectful and abide by the decisions and agreements that were made during the meeting time" (Asikinack). By giving the Snow Walker the pipe, Andrei unwittingly promises to be respectful and truthful. The man accepts the gift and says something "in Cree [...] skyward, the Cossack pipe raised toward the ceiling" (183).

In *Brovko's Amazing Journey*, the eponymous dog manages to get to Canada with the help of a magical Scythian "collar made of goatskin and cloth" embroidered with "six golden horses" (32) given to him by the same Holy one who now, when the Baydas are settled, wants the cup to return to Ukraine. After the Baydas' journey to Canada, Brovko, who was left with Petrus, meets the Holy one, who talks to the dog as if he were human:

[y]ou remember the golden cup I gave Andrei's *dido*. The cup of wisdom [...] I'm worried about the cup. I can't tell where it is, but I think it might be lost. So if you are going, maybe you can find it for me?

(32)

The Holy one adds that the cup "belongs to Ukraine" (32). Brovko survives the turbulent journey with the help of Ukrainian immigrants, a *kobzar*, and eventually the Snow Walker, but mostly due to his wit and the ability to hunt in the Canadian wilderness. The Holy one tells him "[h]ow you get there will be solely up to you, with the Lord's help" (33). As the narrator eventually says, Brovko "[i]s a Ukrainian dog with the courage of a *Cossack* to fight on to his last breath" (156).

Atwood argues that "Canadians as a whole do not trust Nature, they are always suspecting some dirty trick. An often-encountered sentiment is that Nature has betrayed expectations, it was supposed to be different" (49). Yet "it was Canada's natural environment that increasingly let the nation to realise just how distinct it was from its European motherland, and from its continental neighbours" (Galway 16). Ukrainian Canadian scholar Jerry Diawik lists several categories most Canadians – knowingly or unknowingly – identify with Canadianness, including the beauty of the nature's wilderness (32). When Brovko eventually gets to Canada and continues to look for Andrei, he feels "this place called Canada is strange and foreign" (121). Yet this initial feeling changes. Unlike Buck, the dog protagonist of Jack London's *The Call of the Wild* (1903)[26] who experiences Canadian landscapes as significantly different from the American ones, Brovko, a Ukrainian dog, gradually notices similarities between the nature of Canada and Ukraine, such as the fact that "the bank has no trees, just like Ukraine's Bald Mountain near Lviv" (126), and the presence of animals he can hunt, like fish, rabbits, gophers, and ducks.

The Snow Walker saves both Andrei and Brovko, healing the dog with the use of traditional medicine, which Brovko refers to as made of "Ukraine's *kalyna* bush" (111). Andrei does not understand the man, but Brovko does. The Snow Walker speaks Cree, but "[d]ogs just know – no matter what the language" (138). Before meeting him, Brovko sees Indigenous People whom he mistakes for *viy*, the "chief of the gnomes" a character unknown in Ukrainian folklore but attributed to it after being introduced by Nikolai Gogol in the 1835 horror novella "Viy" (124). Despite his initial fear, in one of the novel's most problematic scenes, Brovko witnesses a ceremony and confuses Indigenous Peoples for "demons," but realizes that they are "people like the ones who fished near the Kopko homestead' who only "dance to the beat of a drum" (124). As the narrator notes, "Brovko's fear of the Canadian unknown has done crazy things to his judgement. A Ukrainian dog? And he doesn't recognize *dance*?" (124; emphasis in original). Although the "Canadian unknown" Brovko is afraid of is synonymous with "Indigenous," it becomes another alleged imagined connection between Ukrainians and Indigenous Peoples. Whereas the Indigenous People are known for their ceremonies, Brovko compares them to the traditional Ukrainian dance, which became one of the crucial elements of Ukrainian Canadian identity in the second half of the twentieth century.

Conclusion

Initially Canada seems nothing like the promised land Langston's Lesia expects it to be whilst dreaming about emigrating. Although the Magus family follows values such as honesty and diligence, in Canada they are positioned as the Others, met with suspicion and discrimination similar to that which Lesia experienced from Michal. In the new country Lesia, a young female pioneer, has to work even harder than in Ukraine, grubbing up the tree-lined land with men and fighting every day to get food for her family, especially when her father and brother are labeled as enemy aliens and interned (cf. Chapter 2). Although in Warwaruk's novels "[a]ll tasks in Canada are ten times larger, the land ten times bigger" (53), after a year the Baydas, like Lesia and her family, are also settled and happy. This is not surprising since "[t]he Canadian wilderness, which held the potential for prosperity and freedom, was quite literally a beacon of salvation for those seeking to better their lot in life" (Galway 159). As the narrator in *Andrei and the Snow Walker* says, "they have been luckier than most people, to have a proper house built so they won't have to hunch down in a *buda* like bears their first winter" (145). Moreover, just like Lesia, they have a garden, a milk cow, and hens. When in *Brovko's Amazing Journey* the Baydas' former neighbors arrive in Canada, they want them to see that it "is not a place only for back-breaking work," as in a year they have managed to build a strong local community (117). The Holochuks are their last Ukrainian close neighbors who come to Saskatchewan and inform the Baydas that the old hermit wants the cup back because it "belongs to Ukraine – for good, or for evil" (158). Although the ancient cup has to return to Ukraine, the old country, in Warwaruk's and Langston's novels the memory of Ukrainian history, customs, and traditions belong to Canada.

Like for many descendants of the first wave of Ukrainian immigrants, the real Ukraine in the novels remains a fading memory replaced by the prairie, its new, improved version. As Dido, the elderly storyteller says to Andrei before leaving the country: "[r]emember the pictures, my boy. Some day you will be Dido, and you will tell your grandson about the very last things you saw leaving your homeland" ("Andrei" 8). Throughout the novel, Andrei, just like the eponymous Leisa, *becomes* Canadian. Langston creates a narrative that has the potential to initiate the transfer of next-generation memory, both individual and collective. As a result,

Lesia's Dream appears to be a text that can promote the memory of the Ukrainian diaspora in its youngest representatives, people who do not know the country of their ancestors. It may also help to incorporate the experience of the first wave of Ukrainian immigration into Canadian cultural memory. To maintain a sense of unity and continuity, the diaspora community must continue to feed on the memories of its own past, especially those of its near-death, thus avoiding the hypothetical threat of losing a separate identity.

Renée Hulan argues that "instead of raiding the spiritual and cultural material of First Nations, in effect 'going Native,' Euro-Canadians should look to their own traditions before joining the circle to listen to and learn about First Nations" (215; qtd. in Kruk 309). With the numerous references to Cossacks, Scythians, and Ukrainian culture, Warwaruk attempts to look to his own traditions, but by doing so, he does not seem to want to learn about Indigenous Peoples, who in his books emerge as foil characters used only to indigenize Ukrainian immigrants. Yet both Warwaruk and Langston recreate the myth of "Ukrainian founding fathers" and challenge the stereotypical image of Ukrainians as uneducated peasants by showing their shadow in the form of a strong sense of a distinctive national identity and heritage represented by the Scythians and Cossacks. What is most frequently associated with Canada is its "status as a country of immigrants [which] is generally considered to be the outstanding national property, a foundational myth" (Richter 34). This myth, which is echoed in Dido's words about the land of all colors and races, marginalizes the role of Indigenous Peoples in Canadian history and culture. In his 1943 collection, Paluk writes that

> the Canadian Cossack found that [...l]ike a shadow, each newcomer brought with him his racial experiences, his language. And he found that he couldn't deny this shadow, that it had followed him across the ocean, that it was part of him.
>
> (11)

Hence in the novels examined in this chapter the Canadian prairie emerges not as a land claimed and transformed by the settlers but as a vast promised land, a simulacrum of Ukraine where Ukrainian Canadian Cossacks can finally be free.

Notes

1 Warwaruk (1943–2017) published two novels for children and a few books for adults. His last work, *To Find Myhailo*, was published posthumously in 2022.
2 Gaining independence from the United Kingdom was a long process, and a separate Canadian citizenship was introduced only in 1947. While Canada has strong colonial ties with the United Kingdom, it has two founding nations, and is also regionally divided (Richter 27–29). Anglo-Canada, Québec, and

Indigenous Peoples represent Canadian three "sociological nations" but despite the internal differences, representatives of these three groups "belong to and identify with the pan-Canadian community with differing degrees of enthusiasm" (Cairns 185–186).

3   In this study I understand the chronotope ("time space") as "the intrinsic connectedness of temporal and spatial relationships that are artistically expressed in literature" (Bakhtin 84). This notion was introduced to literary studies by Russian scholar Mikhail Bakhtin, who argued that time and space in literature are interrelated: "Time, as it were, thickens, takes on flesh, becomes artistically visible; likewise, space becomes charged and responsive to the movements of time, plot and history. This intersection of axes and fusion of indicators characterizes the artistic chronotope" (Bakhtin 84–85). Moreover, as Bakhtin claimed: "[t]he chronotope as a formally constitutive category determines to a significant degree the image of man in literature as well. The image of man is always intrinsically chronotopic" (Bakhtin 84–85).

4   In "The Precession of Simulacra," Baudrillard argues that

> [s]imulation is no longer that of a territory, a referential being, or a substance. It is the generation by models of a real without origin or reality: a hyperreal [...] It is no longer a question of imitation, nor duplication, nor even parody. It is a question of substituting the signs of the real for the real.
>
> (1–2)

5   It is worth noting that the depiction of an Indigenous character in Gloria Kupchenko Frolick's *Anna Veryha* (1992), a novella set in 1942, differs radically from the relationships between Ukrainians and Indigenous Peoples portrayed in the books investigated in this chapter. The brief appearance of an Indigenous woman seems to further problematize the romanticized character of the pioneer narrative told to the novella's protagonist by her grandmother Julia (cf. Chapter 3). On their way to borrow some sugar from the Melnyks, Dotsia and Anna, the novella's protagonists, encounter a woman wearing ragged clothes, which later turn out to have been given to her by the Melnyks, in "the strangest [...] horse-drawn buggy" (45). Despite speaking almost no English, she offers them a ride. Anna feels grateful and tries to talk with the woman about the weather, which annoys Dotsia. The ravenous horse is too tired to carry three people. Because the woman keeps on whipping the animal, it eventually "veered and headed straight for the fence, with the wild-eyed woman pulling back hard on the reins" (48). While the girls manage to jump off the buggy, Anna feels guilty that they did not thank the woman for trying to help them. Dotsia does not share her sister's sentiment. When they arrive at their neighbors', Mr. Melnyk tells the girl the woman is known as "crazy Mary" (51) and explains that "[s]he's from the Good Fish Lake reserve. A few years back she lost all her children in a house fire – seven or eight kids" (51). Notably, Anna, the story's focalizer does not mention the woman's ethnicity during their encounter. Mrs. Melnyk seems uncomfortable with the mention of "crazy Mary" and tells the girls that the woman, whom they sometimes give food and old clothing, kidnaps children, but "Indians, like everyone else, want boys" (55). The meeting with "crazy Mary" haunts Anna. The presence of the Indigenous woman in *Anna Veryha* disrupts the colonial Ukrainian Canadian "founding fathers" mythology. Anna, who is

not as wealthy as her neighbors, is the only character in *Anna Veryha* who sympathizes with the Indigenous woman and even dreams of their *imagined* connection: "[t]he Indian woman beckoned to her, said she'd like Anna for a daughter because Anna was so beautiful [...] soon she was living with the Indian woman, until Tony rescued her" (81). While in the dream Anna willingly agrees to take the woman's hand and becomes her imagined daughter, the use of the expression *rescue* suggests how strong Anna's familiarity with captivity narratives is. Remarkably, the imagined connection Anna feels with "crazy Mary" is different from the ones depicted in other Ukrainian Canadian books for young readers. Here, it is not connected to the imagined similarities between the Ukrainians and Canada's First Nations, but the feeling of loss. Whereas the Indigenous woman lost her children, Anna is afraid of her mother's possible death at childbirth. Anna also fears losing Dotsia. Hence "crazy Mary," whose name may be a reference to the mother of Jesus, can be read as the embodiment of all of Anna's anxieties discussed in Chapter 3 of *Next-Generation Memory*. While Mary's children died in a fire, their loss can also symbolize the death of millions of Canada's Indigenous Peoples.

6 I want to thank one of the reviewers for pointing out the importance of the differences between various types of publishing.

7 All of the books in the series explore the cultures of Canada's ethnic minorities (cf. Alter 171–172).

8 For example Pam Clark in *Kalyna* (2016) and Shandi Mitchell in *Under This Unbroken Sky* (2003).

9 In Skrypuch's *Silver Threads* – studied in Chapter 2 – Michael Martchenko's illustrations also romanticize the journey to Canada, showing Anna and Ivan, the protagonists, hopefully looking at the ocean. In *Prisoners in the Promised Land* Anya's passage lasts for two weeks, with some people almost dying of fatigue and food poisoning, recalling the reference to Lesia's journey in Langston's novel and the first two chapters of Clark's *Kalyna*.

10 The notion of the elderly bard has a long history in literature and is usually used to initiate an intergenerational dialogue and provoke the transfer of knowledge, memory, and experience (cf. Joosen 195). This seems to be the case in both novels. Notably, as Justyna Deszcz-Tryhubczak and Zoe Jaques note, the depiction of intergenerational solidarity "may hone readers' generational intelligence" as they "not only depict instances of solidaristic endeavors but also constitute vital elements of broader intergenerational ventures" (xxiii).

11 It is worth noting that the portrayal of the Cossacks in Warwaruk's novels echoes a long tradition in Ukrainian literature. For example, the Cossack appeared in Andriy Chaikovsky's *Za Sestroyu* (1907), one of the most popular Ukrainian children's novels of the twentieth century. Notably, in the early 1940s the book was translated into English and serialized in the US-based *The Ukrainian Weekly*. The novel, as Ulanowicz argues, "[draws] on the mythologized figure of the steppe-dwelling Kozak in order to allegorize a nascent nation's bid to wrest itself from both Polish and Russian occupation"; moreover, as she notes, its translation "appealed to young readers who were gradually assimilating to the dominant American culture; moreover, it symbolically performed and reinforced the Second World War–era diasporic community's claims to American allegiance that at that time were being subjected to both popular and state scrutiny" ("Reassembling Sacred Relics" 413).

12 Hrushevsky was an eminent Ukrainian historian who played an important part "in the demise of the old imperial Russian narrative and the forging of the new Ukrainian paradigm" (Plokhy "Unmaking" 5). As Plokhy argues, "Hrushevsky not only moved from one empire to another but also developed a nonimperial intellectual framework to create a historical narrative for the Ukrainian nation" ("The Frontline" loc. 237). Moreover, Anne Applebaum observes that similar to Taras Shevchenko, who "had linked 'Ukrainianness' to the peasants' struggle against oppression," in his texts Hrushevsky highlighted "the role of the 'people' in the political history of Ukraine" while underlining the significance "of their resistance to various forms of tyranny" (12). It is worth noting that out of the various regiments of Cossacks, only the Ukrainian one welcomed Jews. However, the growing animosities between Polish nobility and the Cossacks led to tensions between Jews – who were Poles' tax-farmers – and Cossacks, eventually culminating in the attracts during the uprising of 1648–1658 (cf. Rosenthal).
13 Ledohowski took inspiration from Paluk for the title of her remarkable 2008 dissertation *Canadian Cossacks: Finding Ukraine in Fifty Years of Ukrainian-Canadian*.
14 In this epic tale Baida is

> a valiant fighter who is offered the sultan's daughter in marriage and the high position that would go with such a union. The offer is made on the basis of Baida's military prowess and his reputation for unparalleled courage and daring. But Baida refuses the offer, an act which the sultan finds insulting and which leads him to order the Kozak's torture. Baida is suspended from a meat hook inserted under his ribs and thus made to suffer a slow and painful death. He endures his agony for three days, but eventually convinces his servant to give him his bow and arrow which he uses to kill the Turkish ruler and his family, this exacting revenge just moment before he himself dies.
>
> (Kononenko 110)

Ukrainian *dumy* were translated into English by Yuri Tarnawsky and Patricia Kilina (penname of Patricia Nell Warren) and published in 1979 by the Canadian Institute of Ukrainian Studies.
15 Unlike Warwaruk, who directly mentions Shevchenko, Langston indirectly refers to a different important figure in Ukrainian history. Although the name of Lesia's great-granddaughter, Laisha, is a tribute to the novel's protagonist and her Ukrainian origin, as Lesia herself points out, despite the apparent similarity, the names are clearly unlike, which symbolically represents the difference in experience between the great-granddaughter and her great-grandmother. Lesia states in the prologue that Laisha "*is not [her] name*" (x; emphasis in original). She does, however, add that the name Laisha "*is beautiful. It is all that is good from [her] and [her] time, sprung forth into all that is new and wonderful in your time*" (x; emphasis in original). In Ukrainian Lesia (Lesya) is a diminutive of the name Olesia (Olesya), which is itself a diminutive of Oleksandra. It also has the status of a separate given name. Laisha, on the other hand, is a form of the Arabic name Aisha, common in Canada. Despite the separate etymology, the pronunciation of the two names in English is very similar, which may suggest that Laisha's parents mistakenly assumed that it was the same name as Lesia, or decided to anglicize it. It is worth recalling that Larysa Kosach-Kvitka (1871–1913), a Ukrainian writer,

Land of All Colors and Races? 65

poet, translator, and literary critic, widely regarded as the most important figure in Ukrainian literature and culture next to Taras Shevchenko and Ivan Franko, used the pseudonym Lesia (Lesya) Ukrainka (cf. Zabuzhko "Notre"). Ukrainka was an important figure for both progressives and nationalists in the diaspora as her "works became a catalyst to uncompromising struggle for freedom, truth and justice" (Swyripa "Wedded" 128). Swyripa also notes that Lesia Ukrainka's statue at the University of Saskatchewan was "the most conspicuous progressive symbol of the relationship between the pioneer woman in Canada and her predecessors in Ukraine" ("Wedded" 234). Hence Langston's choice of the protagonist's name does not seem accidental as she echoes the Ukrainian Canadian pioneer woman, the baba-storyteller, and Lesia Ukrainka, the symbol of the old country's culture. The importance of Ukrainka's poetry is also shown in Skrypuch's *Trapped in Hitler's Web*. Maria, the teenage protagonist, uses quotes from Ukrainka's poetry in her secret communication with UPA (cf. Chapter 5).

16 In Skrypuch's *Prisoners in the Promised Land* Anya knows how to read and write in the native tongue only because of her rebellious late brother Volodymyr. Irena, Anya's friend, like most Ukrainian girls, becomes literate only in Canada. Because of her literacy, Anya can exchange letters with Halyna, her friend from Horoshova and Volodymyr's girlfriend. As Natalia Khanenko-Friesen notes, letters from the homeland were important in the process of keeping the links between the old and new country and in the development of the Canadian diaspora in general (106–111).

17 Gabriel introduces the Baydas to the 1885 Battle of Batoche, the last major fight of the North-West Rebellion, in which more than 40 people were killed. After the rebellion Riel was convicted of high treason and hanged in Regina (Conrad 161). The execution of Riel was met with condemnation in Quebec, leading to mass protests in Montreal (Conrad 164). It significantly marginalized the political position of the Métis (Conrad 6). Moreover, as Bonita Lawrence demonstrates, The Rebellion "broke the long Cree resistance to Canada's westward expansion and shattered Métis resistance entirely" (34).

18 In *Brovko's Amazing Journey*, Andrei compares Chi Pete to "a Cossack warrior on that horse" (106).

19 Interestingly, while talking about the experience of his father, Marshall Forchuk compares the "invisible loss" of identity to the situation of Indigenous children in residential schools (Semchuk 181). In the context of the Ukrainian Canadian books analyzed in this chapter it is not coincidental that the exchange of gifts happens between white children and Indigenous adults. As Bradford observes in her analysis of Australian narratives of survival, "[t]he figure of the child" was of great significance in British colonialism. First, the colonies and their citizens were seen as the children of mother Britain. Second, Indigenous Peoples in Australia, Canada, New Zealand, and the USA were considered "as incapable of the higher-order reasoning of Europeans and hence in need of supervision and discipline, like children dependent on adult guidance" ("The Stolen Generations" 242; cf. Wesseling and Reimer 231).

20 This trope also appears in Skrypuch's *Dance of the Banished* where Ali, one of the novel's protagonists, befriends Nadie, a Cree woman, who hunts in the Kapuskasing woods where the internment camp is located (cf. Chapter 2). Ali,

an Alevi Kurd, struggles with cutting down trees due to his spiritual beliefs, at first does not understand why Nadie kills animals, he tells him that the Cree "are one with nature" and they "take what [they] need to survive, but no more" (130). She is "the first non-Alevi [Ali] had ever met who seemed to understand" his relationship with nature. "Our cultures were vastly different yet we had so much in common," Ali says (131). While Nadie wants to help him escape from the camp, Ali realizes that despite these similarities with the Cree, what he really wants is to become Canadian and – like his Ukrainian friend Bohdan – fit in with the Anglo-Canadian majority.

21 Interestingly in the context of Métis literature, McCall argues that "a diasporic-Indigenous-sovereigntist critical approach may be best suited to address Métis writing, which paradoxically enacts national (i.e., The Métis nation) and diasporic (i.e., Métissage) identifications" (21).

22 *Baba's Babushka: A Magical Ukrainian Christmas* (2010) and *Baba's Babushka: A Magical Ukrainian Easter* (2012) were illustrated by Wendy Siemens, *Baba's Babushka: A Magical Ukrainian Wedding* (2013) by Amber Rees, and *Baba's Babushka: A Magical Ukrainian Journey* (2020) by Olha Tkachenko. The last story was only published in an anniversary edition of *Baba's Babushka*. Dumont's illustrations differ significantly from Rees' and Tkachenko's, yet the way she depicts the characters is reminiscent of the first two books illustrated by Siemens. The main difference is Dumont's attention to portraying sophisticated landscapes and nature.

23 This picturebook is not paginated.

24 In the author's notes to the previous three picturebooks Mutala writes that "Ukrainian people first came to Canada during the late 1800s. Babushka is the Russian word for 'old woman' often used to describe the headscarves worn by those early immigrants" ("A Magical Ukrainian Christmas"; "A Magical Ukrainian Easter"; "A Magical Ukrainian Wedding"). Interestingly, in Carola Schmidt's picturebooks *Tell Me a Story, Babushka* (2019) and *Babushka is Homesick* (2020), the word "babushka" stands for a grandmother, further problematizing Mutala's theory. Notably, in her 1980 hit song "Babooshka," the first single off the bestselling *Never for Ever* album, English singer–songwriter Kate Bush uses the eponymous word as the pen name of a woman testing her husband's loyalty. At that time Bush was not aware of the Russian meaning of "babooshka."

25 In her 2004 essay "The Shock of White Cognition" Myrna Kostash writes – "I discovered that, in the new terms of the discourse, I was white. I was a member of a privileged *majority*" (135). Her statement illustrates the discursive changes happening to the position of Canada's white minorities, as well as the growing anxiety of losing ethnic distinctiveness.

26 Notably, as Galway notes, "[a]ided in large part by the children's writing from the late nineteenth and early twentieth centuries, the natural environment came to be envisioned as an integral part of the Canadian national identity" (171).

Works Cited

Achilli, Alessandro, Serhy Yekelchyk, and Dmytro Yesypenko. *Cossacks in Jamaica, Ukraine at the Antipodes: Essays in Honor of Marko Pavlyshyn*. Academic Studies Press, 2020.

Alcoff, Linda. "The Problem of Speaking for Others." *Cultural Critique*, vol. 20, Winter 1991–1992, pp. 5–32.
Alter, Grit. *Inter- and Transcultural Learning in the Context of Canadian Young Adult Fiction.* Verlag Münster, 2015.
Applebaum, Anne. *Red Famine: Stalin's War on Ukraine.* Allen Lane, 2017.
Asikinack, William. "Pipe Ceremony." *Indigenous Saskatchewan Encyclopedia* https://teaching.usask.ca/indigenoussk/import/pipe_ceremony.php
Assmann, Aleida. "Canon and Archive." *Media and Cultural Memory*, edited by Astrid Erll and Ansgar Nünning. Berlin-New York: Walter de Gruyter, 2008, pp. 9–108.
Atwood, Margaret. *Survival.* Anansi Toronto, 1972.
Bakhtin, Mikhail Mikhailovich. "Forms of Time and of the Chronotope in the Novel: Notes toward a Historical Poetics." *The Dialogic Imagination: Four Essays.* Slavic Series, no. 1, edited by Michael Holquist, translated by Caryl Emerson, Michael Holquist, University of Texas Press, 2020 [1981], pp. 84–85.
Baudrillard, Jean. "The Precession of Simulacra." *Cultural Theory and Popular Culture: A Reader* (4th ed.), edited by John Storey. Harlow: Pearson, 2009, pp. 409–415.
Bourdieu, Pierre. *The Field of Cultural Production*, edited by Randal Johnson. New York: Columbia University Press, 1993.
Bradford, Clare. "The Homely Imaginary: Fantasies of Nationhood in Australian and Canadian Texts." *Home-Words: Discourses of Children's Literature in Canada*, edited by Mavis Reimer, Wilfrid Laurier University Press. 2008, pp. 177–193.
Bradford, Clare. "The Stolen Generations of Australia: Narratives of Loss and Survival." *International Research in Children's Literature*, vol. 13, no. 2, 2020, pp. 242–258.
Bradford, Clare. "Transformative Fictions: Postcolonial Encounters in Australian Texts." *Children's Literature Association Quarterly*, vol. 28, no. 4, 2003–2004, pp. 194–202.
Cairns, Alan C. "The Fragmentation of Canadian Citizenship." *Belonging: The Meaning and Future of Canadian Citizenship*, edited by William Kaplan. McGill-Queen's University Press, 1993, pp. 181–220.
Chernetsky, Vitaly. *Mapping Postcommunist Cultures: Russia and Ukraine in the Context of Globalization.* McGill-Queen's University Press, 2007.
Connerton, Paul. *How Societies Remember.* Cambridge University Press, 1989.
Conquest, Robert. *The Harvest of Sorrow: Soviet Collectivization and the Terror-Famine.* Oxford University Press, 1986.
Conrad, Margaret. *A Concise History of Canada.* Cambridge University Press, 2012.
Deszcz-Tryhubczak, Justyna and Zoe Jaques. "Introduction." *Intergenerational Solidarity in Children's Literature and Film*, edited by Justyna Deszcz-Tryhubczak and Zoe Jaques. Jackson: University Press of Mississippi, 2021, pp. i–xxviii.
Douglas, Mary. *Purity and Danger: An Analysis of Concepts of Pollution and Taboo.* Penguin, 1966.
Fee, Margery. "Romantic Nationalism and the Image of Native People in Contemporary English-Canadian Literature." *The Native in Literature*, edited by Thomas King, Cheryl Calver, and Helen Hoy. Toronto: ECW Press, 1987, pp. 15–33.

Fondrie, Suzanne. "'Gentle Doses of Racism': Whiteness and Children's Literature." *Journal of Children's Literature*, vol. 27.2, 2001, pp. 9–13.

Galway, Elizabeth A. *From Nursery Rhymes to Nationhood: Children's Literature and the Construction of Canadian Identity.* Routledge, 2008.

Goldie, Terry. *Fear and Temptation: The Image of the Indigene in Canadian, Australian, and New Zealand Literatures.* McGill-Queen's University Press, 1989.

Grabowicz, George G. *The Poet as Mythmaker: A Study of Symbolic Meaning in Taras Ševčenko.* Harvard University Press, 1982.

Grabowicz, George G. "Three Perspectives on the Cossack Past: Gogol', Ševčenko, Kuliš." *Harvard Ukrainian Studies*, vol. 5, no. 2, June 1981, pp. 171–194.

Harde, Roxanne. "Talking Back to History in Indigenous Picturebooks." *International Research in Children's Literature*, vol. 13, no. 2, 2020, pp. 274–288.

Herodotus. *The Histories of Herodotus*, a New English Version, vol. 3, translated and edited by George Rawlinson, Sir Henry Rawlinson, and John Gardner Wilkinson. London: John Murray, 1859.

Hinther, Rhonda L. and Jim Mochoruk (ed.). *Re-Imagining Ukrainian Canadians: History, Politics, and Identity.* University of Toronto Press, 2011.

Hrycak, Jarosław. *Ukraina. Przewodnik Krytyki Politycznej. Z Jarosławem Hrycakiem rozmawia Iza Chruślińska.* Warszawa–Gdańsk: Krytyka Polityczna, 2009.

Hunt, Peter. *Understanding Children's Literature.* Routledge, 2005.

Joosen, Vanessa. *Adulthood in Children's Literature.* Bloomsbury, 2018.

Kaye (Kysilewsky), Vladimir J. and Frances Swyripa. "Settlement and Colonization." *A Heritage in Transition: Essays in the History of Ukrainians in Canada*, edited by Manoly R. Lupul. Toronto: McClelland and Stewards, 1982, pp. 32–58.

Khanenko-Friesen, Natalie. *Ukrainian Otherland: Diaspora, Homeland, and Folk Imagination in the Twentieth Century.* Madison: Wisconsin, 2015.

Kil, Sang Hea. "A Diseased Body Politic." *Cultural Studies*, vol. 28, no. 2, pp. 177–198.

Klymasz, Robert B. "Cossacks and Indians? Métissage in Action." *Canadian Ethnic Studies Journal*, vol. 47, no. 4–5, 2015, pp. 359–361.

Klymasz, Robert B. "Culture Maintenance and the Ukrainian Experience in Western Canada." *New Soil—Old Roots: The Ukrainian Experience in Canada*, edited by Jaroslav Rozumnyj. Winnipeg: Ukrainian Academy of Arts and Sciences in Canada, 1983, pp. 173–182.

"Kobzar." *Shevchenkivs'kij slovnik, Institut literaturi imeni T. G. Shevchenka Akademiï Nauk URSR*, vol. I, 1978.

Kononenko, Natalie. *Ukrainian Epic and Historical Song: Folklore in Context.* University of Toronto Press, 2019.

Kornblatt, Judith D. *The Cossack Hero in Russian Literature: A Study in Cultural Mythology.* Madison: University of Wisconsin Press, 1992.

Korteweg, Lisa, Ismel Gonzalez, and Jojo Guillet. "The Stories Are the People and the Land: Three Educators Respond to Environmental Teachings in Indigenous Children's Literature." *Environmental Education Research*, vol. 16, no. 3–4, 2012, pp. 331–350.

Kostash, Myrna. *All of Baba's Children.* [1977]. Edmonton: NeWest, 1992.

Kostash, Myrna. "The Shock of White Cognition." *Postcolonial Subjects: Canadian and Australian Perspectives*, edited by Mirosława Buchholtz. Toruń: Wydawnictwo Uniwersytetu Mikołaja Kopernika, 2004, pp. 133–136.
Kruk, Laurie. "'Outsiders' and 'Insiders': Teaching Native/Canadian Literature as Meeting Place." *Home-Work: Postcolonialism, Pedagogy, and Canadian Literature*, edited by Cynthia Sugars. Ottawa: University of Ottawa Press, 2004, pp. 301–320.
Kupchenko Frolick, Gloria. *Anna Veryha*. Maxwell Macmillan, 1992.
Langston, Laura. *Lesia's Dream*. HarperTrophy Canada, 2003.
Lawrence, Bonita. *"Real" Indians and Others: Mixed-Blood Urban Native Peoples and Indigenous Nationhood*. University of Nebraska Press, 2004.
Ledohowski, Lindy. *Canadian Cossacks: Finding Ukraine in Fifty Years of Ukrainian-Canadian*. 2008. University of Toronto, Ph.D. dissertation. https://tspace.library.utoronto.ca/bitstream/1807/16761/1/Ledohowski_Lindy_A_20 0811_PhD_thesis.pdf
Ledohowski, Lindy. "Little Ukraine on the Prairie. 'Baba' in English-Language Ukrainian-Canadian Literature." *Place and Replace: Essays on Western Canada*, edited by Adele Perry, Esyllt W. Jones, and Leah Morton. University of Manitoba Press, 2013, pp. 186–206.
Ledohowski, Lindy. "White Settler Guilt": Contemporary Ukrainian Canadian Prairie Literature." *Canadian Ethnic Studies*, vol. 47, no. 4–5, 2015, pp. 67–83.
McCall, Sophie. "Diaspora and Nation in Métis Writing." *Cultural Grammars of Nation, Diaspora, and Indigeneity in Canada*, edited by Christine Kim, Sophie McCall, and Melina Baum Singer. Wilfrid Laurier University Press, 2012, pp. 21–421.
Montgomery, Lucy Maud. *Rainbow Valley*. McClelland & Steward, 1919. Accessed from www.gutenberg.org/files/5343/5343-h/5343-h.htm#chap35
Mutala, Marion. *Baba's Babushka: A Magical Ukrainian Christmas*. Illustrated by Wendy Siemens. Regina: Your Nickel's Worth Publishing, 2010.
Mutala, Marion. *Baba's Babushka: A Magical Ukrainian Easter*. Illustrated by Wendy Siemens. Regina: Your Nickel's Worth Publishing, 2012.
Mutala, Marion. *Baba's Babushka: A Magical Ukrainian Wedding*. Illustrated by Amber Rees. Regina: Your Nickel's Worth Publishing, 2013.
Mutala, Marion. *Baba's Babushka: Magical Ukrainian Adventures*. Illustrated by Wendy Siemens, Amber Rees, and Olha Tkachenko. Regina: Your Nickel's Worth Publishing, 2020.
Mutala, Marion. *Kokhum's Babushka: A Magical Métis/Ukrainian Tale*. Illustrated by Donna Lee Dumont. Saskatoon: Gabriel Dumont Institute Press, 2017.
Nikolajeva, Maria. *The Rhetoric of Character in Children's Literature*. The Scarecrow Press, 2002.
Nodelman, Perry. "At Home on Native Land: A Non-Aboriginal Canadian Scholar Discusses Aboriginality and Property in Canadian Double-Focalized Novels for Young Adults." *Home-Words: Discourses of Children's Literature in Canada*, edited by Mavis Reimer. Wilfrid Laurier University Press, 2008, pp. 107–128.
Ostashewski, Marcia. "A Song and Dance of Hypermasculinity: Performing Ukrainian Cossacks in Canada." *The World of Music*, vol. 3, no. 2, 2014, Music, Movement, and Masculinities, pp. 15–38.

Palmer, Howard. "Mosaic Verses Melting Pot? Immigration and Ethnicity in Canada and the United States." *A Passion for Identity: An Introduction to Canadian Studies*, edited by Davis Taras, Beverly Rasporich, and Eli Mandel. Scarborough: Nelson Canada, 2nd ed., 1993, pp. 162–174.

Paluk, William. *Canadian Cossacks: Essays, Articles and Stories on Ukrainian-Canadian Life*. Winnipeg: Canadian Ukrainian Review Publishing, 1943.

Petryshyn, Jaroslav and Luba Dzubak. *Peasants in the Promised Land: Canada and the Ukrainians, 1891–1914*. Toronto: JamesLorimer, 1985.

Plokhy, Serhii. *The Cossack Myth: History and Nationhood in the Age of Empires*. Cambridge University Press, 2012.

Plokhy, Serhii. *The Frontline: Essays on Ukraine's Past and Present*. Harvard University Press, 2021.

Plokhy, Serhii. *Unmaking Imperial Russia: Mykhailo Hrushevsky and the Writing of Ukrainian History*. University of Toronto Press, 2005.

Razack, Sherene. *Race, Space, and the Law: Unmapping a White Settler Society*. Toronto: Between the Lines, 2002.

Reeder, Ellen D. (ed.). *Scythian Gold: Treasures from Ancient Ukraine*. New York: Harry Abrams in association with the Walters Art Gallery and the San Antonio Museum of Art, 1999.

Reimer, Mavis. "Homing and Unhoming: The Ideological Work of Canadian Children's Literature." *Home Words: Discourses of Children's Literature in Canada*, edited by Mavis Reimer. Wilfrid Laurier University Press, 2008, pp. 107–128.

Richter, Miriam Verena. *Creating the National Mosaic: Multiculturalism in Canadian Children's Literature from 1950 to 1993*. Amsterdam-New York: Rodopi, 2011.

Rolle, Renate. *The World of the Scythians*, translated by Gayna Walls. London: B.T. Batsford, 1989.

Rosenthal, Herman. "Cossacks' Uprising." *Jewish Encyclopedia*. www.jewishencyclopedia.com/articles/4685-cossacks-uprising#anchor5 Accessed May 28, 2021.

Rothberg, Michael. *The Implicated Subject: Beyond Victims and Perpetrators*. Stanford University Press, 2019.

Seaton, Albert. *The Horsemen of the Steppe: The Story of the Cossacks*. New York: Hippocrene Books, 1985.

Semchuk, Sandra. *The Stories Were Not Told: Canada's First World War Internment Camps*. University of Alberta Press, 2018.

Skrypuch, Marsha Forchuk. *Dance of the Banished*. Pajama Press, 2014.

Skrypuch, Marsha Forchuk. *Prisoners in the Promised Land. The Ukrainian Internment Diary of Anya Soloniuk*. Scholastic Canada, 2007.

Story, Norah. "Ukrainians." *The Oxford Companion to Canadian History and Literature*. Oxford University Press, 1967, pp. 807–808.

Swyripa, Frances. *Storied Landscapes: Ethno-Religious Identity and the Canadian Prairies*. University of Manitoba Press, 2010.

Swyripa, Frances. *Ukrainian Canadians: A Survey of their Portrayal in English-language Works*. University of Alberta Press, 1978.

Swyripa, Frances. *Wedded to the Cause: Ukrainian-Canadian Women and Ethnic Identity 1891–1991*. University of Toronto Press, 1993.

Ulanowicz, Anastasia. "Reassembling Sacred Relics: Translation, Diaspora, and Andriy Chaikovsky's *Za Sestroyu*." *Children's Literature Association Quarterly*, vol. 43, no. 4, Winter 2018, pp. 412–433.

Warwaruk, Larry. *Andrei and the Snow Walker*. Regina: Coteau Books, 2002.

Warwaruk, Larry. *Brovko's Amazing Journey*. Regina: Coteau Books, 2013.

Wesseling, Elizabeth and Mavis Reimer. "Introduction: Child Separation Projects as a Strategy of Colonisation." *International Research in Children's Literature*, vol. 13, no. 2, 2020, pp. 231–241.

Zabuzhko, Oksana. *Notre Dame d'Ukraine: Ukraiinka v konflikti mifolohiy*. Kyiv: Fakt, 2007.

Zabuzhko, Oksana. *Shevchenkiv mif Ukraïny. Sproba filosofs'koho analizu*. Kyiv: Abrys, 1997.

Zecker, Robert M. "'A Slav Can Live in Dirt That Would Kill a White Man': Race and the European 'Other'." *Race and America's Immigrant Press: How the Slovaks were Taught to Think Like White People*. London: Bloomsbury Academic, 2011, pp. 68–102.

2 "Unspeakable. Unacceptable. Then and Now"[1]
The First World War and Canadian Internment Camps

> "Before this war is over," he said – or something said through his lips – "every man and woman and child in Canada will feel it – you, Mary, will feel it – feel it to your heart's core. You will weep tears of blood over it. The Piper has come – and he will pipe until every corner of the world has heard his awful and irresistible music. It will be years before the dance of death is over – years, Mary. And in those years millions of hearts will break.
> (L.M. Montgomery, Rilla of Ingleside)

In the chronotope[2] of L.M. Montgomery's *Rilla of Ingleside* (1921), chronologically the last novel[3] featuring Anne Shirley, who is widely regarded as "one of literature's most distinctly Canadian figures," all Canadians eventually feel the toll of the Great War (Galway 9). Although the First World War was "the event that forged a nation from a colony," in *Rilla of Ingleside* the nation is clearly monoethnic and deprived of immigrants other than those from England (Reimer 15; cf. Leden; Tector). The heroism and patriotism of Montgomery's characters, both on the home front on the idyllic Prince Edward Island and in the trenches, echo the belief in the moral righteousness of the Allied powers' fight against the Axis present in numerous other Canadian books (cf. Webb; Johnston and Paul). Women in *Rilla of Ingleside* read the news about the courageous Canadian men fighting first in the foreign and mysterious territory of Eastern Europe with cities of names "far from being decent," ones they cannot pronounce, including Premysl (Przemyśl), "a conundrum which nobody seems to have solved yet" (37). While the brave Canadian and British soldiers fight "the Huns" together with non-Anglo allies, these are described as no more than: "Foreigners – Foreigners […] Russians or Rumanians or whatever they may be, *they are foreigners and you cannot tie to them*" (86; emphasis mine). No sooner does the fighting move to the Western front than the inhabitants of Montgomery's Avonlea start considering the seriousness of the Great War, which can lead to the destruction of places they are familiar with, including Paris and London.

DOI: 10.4324/9781003367918-3

The hatred towards "the Huns," that is, the citizens of Germany and Austria-Hungary, depicted in *Rilla of Ingleside* and the quite dismissive – and othering – mentions of Eastern Europe are representative of most one-dimensional and overly patriotic Canadian texts about the Great War, especially those published between 1915 and 1921 (cf. Webb). Many present-day Canadian books, however, challenge "the national metanarrative of sacrifice" by presenting the previously untold perspectives and portraying the traumatic influence "the war to end all wars" had on various marginalized groups, including Ukrainian Canadians (cf. Branach-Kallas "Trauma Plots" 47). Until the late twentieth century the "unspeakable" and "unacceptable" story of the internment of 8,579 Austro-Hungarian immigrants – mostly Ukrainians – under the War Measures Act (1914) and the deprivation of 144,000 Canadians of Ukrainian origin of their electoral rights under the War Times Election Act (1917) remained largely untold. Formally not recognized and commemorated, the internment functioned only in the recollections of its survivors and direct witnesses who often stayed silent and repressed the traumatic memories (cf. Luciuk "Ukrainians," "In Fear"; Luciuk and Kordan; Kordan; Kordan and Mahovsky). Yet the predicament of Ukrainians during the Great War is significant to contemporary Canadians of Ukrainian origin who see it "as part of their mythology and birthright as Ukrainian Canadians" (Swyripa "The Politics of Redress" 370). After all, memories of various important events appear, disappear, and reappear in the public consciousness, at time "tak[ing] on a surprising importance long after the materiality of the events remembered has faded from view," as is the case in this context (Rothberg 17).

One of the reasons for the decades-long silence regarding the internment was connected to the assimilation policy, which dominated in Canada until the late 1960s and is depicted in some of the books investigated in this chapter (cf. Kostash "Baba Was a Bohunk" 33–38). Second, the traumatic First World War experience was not as important in the identity formation of Ukrainian Canadians as the prairie homesteading, which gave them the more positive "founding fathers" status (Swyripa "The Politics of Redress" 360; cf. Chapter 1). Hence for decades, the internment seemed to be practically erased from the Canadian mnemonic discourse and public consciousness.[4] While such acts of erasure and forgetting, as Aleida Assmann notes, "are a necessary and constructive part of internal social transformations," they are "violently destructive when directed at an alien culture or a persecuted minority" ("Canon and Archive" 97).

Historical books have contributed to the popularization of the internment in the mainstream Canadian discourse on the First World War. Ukrainian Canadian authors introduce young readers to the internment through narratives crafted with the use of stories shared by their families, fragmented memories of the survivors, witnesses, and their children, as well as the few remaining written documents. Literature for young readers, which combines aesthetic and educational values, serves as a particularly useful tool in the transfer of next-generation memory of the internment, which happened more than 100 years ago and until the early 2000s was not officially recognized. In my cross-sectional examination of internment-themed literature published before and after the implementation of the Act C-331 Internment of Persons of the Ukrainian Origin Recognition Act (Bill-C331), in this chapter, I concur with Assmann, who notes that "to transform ephemeral social memory into long-term collective memory that can be transmitted from generation to generation, it has to be elaborated and organized in various forms" ("Transformations" 55–56; cf. "Canon and Archive" 98). Children's literature can be one of the most effective of such transformers, and historical books can transmit next-generation memory of the internment to children born more than 100 years after the end of the Great War. Moreover, such narratives introduce young readers to the problematic aspects of Canadian history during the First World War, such as the negative attitudes toward immigrants from Eastern Europe and the forced assimilation policy. In my close reading of texts published between 1996 and 2020, I show how the official recognition and commemoration of the internment directly contributed to the gradual shift of the imprisonment of "enemy aliens" from the margins to the mainstream of Canadian children's literature. I argue that while in their narratives authors like Marsha Forchuk Skrypuch, Glen Huser, and Laura Langston point to the fact that both the internees and the families left behind fell victim to the War Measures Act (1914), they pay no attention to the War Times Election Act (1917) and describe cultural assimilation as a necessary step in the process of becoming Ukrainian *Canadian*. Although all of the books point to the importance of keeping the memory of the internment alive, I show that most of them promote forgiveness and reconciliation.

Representations of the Internment before Bill C-331

The internment of Ukrainians during the First World War was brought up to public awareness by Ukrainian Canadian historians only in the late 1970s. Frances Swyripa argues that after the implementation of the multicultural policy, in the following decades, it "became a symbolic focal point for Ukrainian Canadians as *Canadians*, still grappling with a legacy of prejudice, discrimination, suspect loyalty, and marginalization" ("The Politics of Redress" 355; emphasis in original). Furthermore, what is of great importance in the context of children's texts examined in *Next-Generation Memory*, the internment was used in the fight against the allegations that "as *Ukrainians*, [Ukrainian Canadians] had been guilty of war crimes in Nazi-occupied Europe," a theme investigated further in the last chapter (Swyripa "The Politics of Redress" 356; emphasis in original). As Swyripa argues, "in seeking redress for wartime wrongs," Ukrainian Canadian activists focused on "the emotionally powerful issue of internment" instead of "the less sensational issue of disenfranchisement" ("The Politics of Redress" 264). Moreover, after the accusations against post–Second World War displaced persons as "Nazi collaborators," the analogies between the Holocaust and the internment were "psychologically more satisfying" ("The Politics of Redress" 264).

Although the redress campaign in the late 1980s paid little attention to the war disenfranchisement of Ukrainian Canadians, it brought the internment into the general awareness (Swyripa "The Politics of Redress" 371). Still, Canadian authorities did not officially acknowledge the existence of the 24 labor camps until 2005 when, after eight years of efforts by Inky Mark, the Act C-331 Internment of Persons of the Ukrainian Origin Recognition Act (Bill C-331) was approved. The Canadian First World War Internment Recognition Fund was established three years later to maintain Canadian internment memory. The official process of filling the blank spots in collective memory began. It has been challenging, though, because a century after the end of the Great War, the survivors and witnesses are no longer alive. Hence the mnemonic narrative is fragmented and reconstructed based on the postmemory of the descendants of the survivors and witnesses (cf. Semchuk 179–209).

The first Canadian children's author who published a book about the Canadian First World War Internment of Ukrainians was Marsha Forchuk Skrypuch, whose grandfather Yuri (George Forchuk) was interned at Jasper, Alberta.[5] As she clarifies in the preface to *Kobzar's Children: A Century of Untold Ukrainian Stories* (2006), she "write[s] stories that capture real experiences that have been suppressed or lost" because "[w]hen you don't write your own stories, someone else will write their version for you" (vi–vii).[6] Skrypuch's words recall Margaret Atwood's famous statement that "[i]f you read only the work of dead foreigners you will certainly reinforce the notion that literature can be written only by dead foreigners" and point to the importance of introducing various perspectives and discourses into Canadian literature (15). Writing about the First World War experiences of Ukrainian Canadians, Skrypuch attempted to challenge the typical portrayal of the Great War found in the majority of Anglophone children's books. Her first internment-themed work was *Silver Threads* (1996), a picturebook illustrated by Michael Martchenko, which was initially published nine years before the approval of Bill C-331 and led to the popularization of the topic among Canadian educators and librarians. Skrypuch later returned to the internment in three other texts: *Prisoners in the Promised Land: The Ukrainian Internment Diary of Anya Soloniuk* (2007), a novel published in the popular *Dear Canada* series, its companion Christmas story "An Unexpected Visitor" (2009), and the young adult novel *Dance of the Banished* (2015).[7]

In an essay published in the KOBZAR Award-winning collection *Unbound*, "Ukrainian Canadians Writing Home" (2016), Skrypuch notes that her grandfather's traumatic experience of internment indirectly triggered a sense of shame and a strong desire to assimilate and suppress all traits of Ukrainianness in her grandfather's family ("Am I Ukrainian?" 66). Skrypuch's father fell victim to the assimilation policy: "[he] had the Ukrainian beaten out of him at elementary school in Alberta and his teachers changed his name from Myroslav to Marshall" ("Am I Ukrainian?" 65). Young Skrypuch's knowledge of Ukraine was folkloristic, reduced to *pyrohy* and *pysanky* (traditional Easter eggs), because she "couldn't find stories about the Ukrainian experience" in the local libraries ("Am I Ukrainian?" 65). She also did not learn the Ukrainian language as her assimilated father "vowed that his kids wouldn't suffer like he did" ("Am I Ukrainian?" 65). Although Skrypuch became interested in Ukrainian culture and history only in college, she had always felt a strong connection to the country of her ancestors. However, what she was familiar with since childhood was the sense of being the other, handed down from generation to generation ("Am I Ukrainian?" 66). It was only during her librarian studies that she learned more about Ukraine and began writing her first short stories about the history of Ukrainians and Ukrainian Canadians.

The genre of *Silver Threads* (1996), Skrypuch's first Ukrainian-themed book, seems not accidental, as picturebooks are narratives developing the visual and verbal thinking of the young readers, at the same time enabling adults to familiarize children with problematic topics in a safe environment.[8] Picturebooks may also invite the readers to "cross borders between artistic genres, languages and cultures" (Arizpe, Colomer, Martin-Roldan et al. 3) and initiate an intergenerational – and transcultural – dialogue between children and adults, one exceeding the textual and visual narrative. Hence picturebooks can stimulate discussions on transculturalism and difficult subjects, such as war or death, further ensuring the transfer of next-generation memory (cf. Coulthard 164–189; McGonigal and Arizpe; Evans; Kiefer; Świetlicki "*Oh, What a Waste*", "Mój tato"; Kachak; Howard). As Gail Edwards and Judith Saltman note in their influential study on Canadian children's literature, picturebooks "are a particularly rich source for the exploration of national identity formation in which the hegemonic commonplaces and myths about history, ethnocultural identity, landscape and region, and definitions of community are articulated and contested" (193). Notably, of all forms of children's books, it is the picturebook that can offer the most surprising narrative on trauma, as it is associated with the youngest, thus most innocent, readers (cf. Kidd 196).

At the suggestion of the publisher, Skrypuch chose the picturebook format for *Silver Threads* and persuaded Michael Martchenko, a Ukrainian Canadian artist known for his collaboration with Robert Munsch, to illustrate it.[9] In *Silver Threads* Skrypuch and Martchenko combine the history of Ukrainian immigration to Canada and the internment with the elements of an Eastern European folktale about the Christmas spider which brings luck to the poor and hardworking. The picturebook was marketed as suitable for children aged 9–12 (grades 4–6) – an unusual application of the picturebook form. However, like many other contemporary books for children, it is dual audience and not age limited. *Silver Threads* tells the story of Ivan and Anna, a young Ukrainian couple living in Bukovyna, part of the Austro-Hungarian Empire, before the outbreak of the First World War. The difficult political and economic situation forces them to leave their village for Canada. Not wanting to fight for the unnamed "foreign emperor," Ivan and Anna take the advice of an old lady who tells them about the poster she saw endorsing Canada as a "land of milk and honey, with plenty of black soil but not enough farmers to plough it. One hundred and sixty acres are waiting for anyone brave enough to claim them."[10] Before leaving for Canada, Ivan and Anna take their most precious belonging – the hinges from the door and a pane of window glass. The last thing Ivan does at home is to feed a black spider with breadcrumbs and ask him for "good luck."

Skrypuch and Martchenko point to the homesteading struggles of the first Ukrainian immigrants before the First World War. When Anna and Ivan finally arrive in Canada, they realize that there is "no land for newcomers" in this part of the country. Hence they have to travel west for days before claiming their homestead. Although the promised land is fertile, it is overgrown with numerous large trees; there is no equipment necessary for grubbing and ploughing, and "winters [are] so cold, a flask of water could freeze before it reached the lips." This does not discourage the young couple, as together they manage to obtain their first harvest and survive the harsh winter. Eventually Anna and Ivan start appreciating Canada, feeling happy in their new home, with Ivan feeding "a tiny black spider nestled in a corner, spinning its threads of silver," similar to the one at home. Gradually, the prairie becomes the mirror reflection, or simulacrum, of their home in Ukraine.

The outbreak of the war encourages Ivan to prove his loyalty to both Canada and Ukraine by enlisting. After all, in the Austro-Hungarian Empire he sees a common enemy of his new and old homeland. However, unlike the courageous Anglo-Canadian young men in novels like Montgomery's *Rilla of Ingleside*, Ivan cannot prove his heroism and patriotism by fighting in the trenches. "I want to fight for Canada. For *my country*," he says to the recruiter, but is ridiculed by the "barrel-bellied" officer who says: "[y]ou don't sound like a Canadian" (emphasis mine). Eventually, Ivan is arrested and recognized by his new country as an enemy alien because of his Ukrainian background: "Bukovyna is part of the Emperor's land. You are an enemy of Canada," he hears from the recruiter. Ivan is then taken "where other prisoners were chained."[11]

Skrypuch's text is complemented by Martchenko's illustrations, which add additional meaning to *Silver Threads*. One of the double spreads includes the British flag and a portrait of King George V, highlighting the Anglo-Canadian heritage of the recruiter and the fact that Canada fought in the First World War because of its ties to Britain.[12] Usually in picturebooks "the story depends on the interaction between written text and image" as they "both have been created with a conscious aesthetic intention" (Nikolajeva and Scott 22). Hence it is Martchenko's illustration featuring dozens of men standing behind a barbed wire and three armed soldiers watching them, which indicates that Ivan is imprisoned in an internment camp. Notably, as Perry Nodelman observes, most adults assume that "pictures communicate more naturally and more directly than words, and thus help young readers make sense of the texts they accompany" ("Illustration" 111). However, Martchenko's illustration cannot be read easily without a certain level of visual literacy and contextual knowledge. Considering Skrypuch's historical note and the fact that the plot is loosely based on the story of her grandfather who escaped from an internment camp, it may be assumed that Ivan is interned at Jasper, Alberta. When at the end of *Silver Threads* Ivan is finally reunited with Anna, he confirms to have "escaped from the internment camp" and "hid in the woods"; these words are the only textual reference to the camps.

Silver Threads positions women who stayed at the homesteads as direct victims of men's internment. During Ivan's absence, Anna struggles to take care of the land, because, as Ivan says throughout the story, it "takes two of [them] ... one to push the plough and one to pull." After a few years the recruiter comes to Anna's homestead and threatens to take the land away from her because the "agreement says that [Ukrainian Canadian farmers] must clear some land each year." He also informs her that the war is over and Ivan must be dead. Here Skrypuch refers to the policy of taking land away from interned Ukrainians, such as her own grandfather, who lost his homestead. Feeling sorry for Anna, the official gives her more time to clear the land.

The happy ending in *Silver Threads* is possible only because of the fairytale element. Despite her poverty, Anna keeps on feeding the spider, which reminds her of Ivan and Ukraine. The spider is the only one Anna talks to, so cleaning the house she remembers "not to disturb the spider's web." Her kindness is rewarded. Not losing hope that her husband is alive, Anna prepares a Christmas Eve dinner consisting of improvised variations of the traditional Ukrainian dishes. Unexpectedly, the next morning, Ivan returns home. The spider, which Ivan, and later Anna, feed with breadcrumbs, even when they have little for themselves, repays for their selfless kindness and decorates Anna's Christmas tree with magical silver threads. The brightness of the tree helps Ivan find his way back home: "I was lost in the dark, then I noticed something sparkling in the distance. If it weren't for those silver threads, I might still be searching for home," he says.

The original publication of *Silver Threads* by Viking (Penguin Books Canada) in 1996 was co-financed by the Ukrainian Canadian Taras Shevchenko Foundation and was received positively by most Canadian and Ukrainian Canadian reviewers, gaining a nomination for the

Amelia Frances-Howard Gibbon Award. In 2004 it was translated into Ukrainian but published only in Canada. Historian Lubomyr Luciuk in a review for Kingston-Whig Standard wrote that "[t]his is a book that every Canadian grade school library should own." Yet some Ukrainian Canadians accused Skrypuch, who does not speak fluent Ukrainian, of having "no right to this story" and being not "a 'real' Ukrainian" ("Am I Ukrainian?" 68). Others, on the other hand, considered the traumatic and previously untold matter of internment camps to be shameful and inappropriate, particularly given that until 2005 their existence was not officially recognized by the Canadian Parliament. In a review issued in *CCL/LCJ: Canadian Children's Literature/Littérature canadienne pour la jeunesse*, Laura Macleod argues that "many people, especially non-Ukrainian-Canadians, will be uncomfortable with the book" because "it resurrects a lost episode from Canada's past" (119). Macleod further notes that "[t]here is another side to the internment story, one not presented here, which raises the question: is it appropriate to treat such a complex issue with a simplistic good vs. evil story" (119). Some criticism was caused by Martchenko's illustrations, "in particular the 'Soviet' hat on Ivan's head, despite the fact that the era was pre-Soviet and the hat had been drawn from archival photos" ("Am I Ukrainian?" 68).

In 2004 *Silver Threads* was reissued by Fitzhenry & Whiteside in hardback and paperback with a few notable changes.[13] The new edition, which is about 300 words shorter than the original and features sharper illustrations, contains an altered author's note, showing the train and fields also used for the title page, with a list of additional materials that may allow the readers to learn more about the historical context. The inclusion of books and multimedia links shows the growing visibility of the internment in Canadian collective memory. Skrypuch does, however, highlight that as of 2004, the Canadian authorities had still not officially recognized the existence of the internment camps. The illustration showing Ivan feeding the spider was used as *Silver Threads*' original 1996 cover. The endpapers and back cover also include drawings of spiderwebs, the eponymous silver threads. The second edition uses plain yellow endpapers and has an additional title double spread showing a train going through the yellow fields of the prairie, initially used as an illustration depicting the protagonists' journey through Canada. Unlike the original landscape layout, the 2004 printing contains white frames, in many cases cutting the original illustrations. This is most notably seen in the illustration depicting the modest Christmas Eve dinner Anna prepares when Ivan is interned. Here the frame cuts the Christmas tree and the window showing a spiderweb. The cover and back cover of the 2004 edition are also different, portraying the protagonists standing on a field, with Anna hopefully pointing in the direction of something. Anna and Ivan are surrounded by sunflowers, the national flowers of Ukraine, which are native to North America. While the images from the pastoral cover and back cover illustrate the protagonists' life in Ukraine, they also recall the traditional depictions of the Canadian prairie discussed in Chapter 1. Unlike the original cover, based on the Western Ukrainian legend about the spider, which may not be familiar to many North American children, the 2004 one seems to better resonate with Canadian readers' knowledge and the imagery of the "founding fathers" of the prairie and the idyllic books of William Kurelek.

Interestingly in the context of *Silver Threads*' alleged limited mainstream potential mentioned by Macleod, the picturebook was also published in South Korea (2016). This seems to reflect Michael Rothberg's words that even seemingly local memories can be of transcultural potential because they "are not owned by groups – nor are groups 'owned' by" them (5). On the contrary, as he notes, "the borders of memory and identity are jagged" (5). In 2013 *Silver Threads* was included in Ingrid Johnson and Joyce Bainbridge's study *Reading Diversity through Canadian Picture Books* as an example of a Canadian picturebook that can be effectively used in teaching about diversity and multiculturalism. As Lynne Wiltse notes, most participants of the research conducted by Canadian teacher educators and researchers were not familiar with the Canadian Internment. Yet several teacher candidates saw *Silver Threads* "as a way to expose students to this little-known topic" (65). One of the participants quoted by Wiltse observes "that students should be shown the progress that Canada has gone through in terms of the way immigrants are treated" (65). This statement differs significantly from Macleod's 1996 review and shows the growing visibility of non–Anglo-Canadian voices and the educational potential of *Silver Threads*.

The theme of internment is also addressed in Laura Langston's *Lesia's Dream* (2003; 2nd edition 2006). Published two years before the Canadian government officially recognized the existence of the internment camps, yet at a time when the awareness was significantly higher, the novel was met with critical acclaim and positive reader response, being shortlisted for the Rocky Mountain Book Award, the Snow Willow Award, and the Manitoba Young Readers' Choice Award. Moreover, the second edition won the 2006 KOBZAR Literary Award. The novel's cover was changed from a picture of a young woman wearing a Ukrainian headscarf, and looking like Lesia Ukrainka (cf. Chapter 1), to a more ambiguous one showing a field of wheat and a blurry part of a woman's face. In the novel Langston demonstrates the consequences the war propaganda had on the Anglo-Canadians' treatment of Ukrainians as foreigners during and after the war and points to the importance of reconciliation. As I have previously argued, Lesia becomes the bearer of the memory of the events without which the youngest generations of the Ukrainian diaspora represented in the novel by Laisha, Lesia's great-granddaughter, would not exist. In the novel's final chapter, the eponymous protagonist says:

There were still Canadians who disliked us, who still used words like bohunk and honky... There are still those who do it today. You think I do not hear. I do. But I accept. Because accepting brings me peace.
(206; emphasis in original)

This quotation highlights the need to commemorate the internment *and* forgive the Canadian government for the war operations, themes which are further explored in the books examined in the following section.

Assmann argues that a characteristic feature of cultural memory is forgetting. Such forgetting may be active, insofar as it involves the deliberate destruction, or erasure, of memories of events (e.g., by means of censorship); moreover, it may be passive, inasmuch as it can be connected with the loss of discourses or carriers of memory. She emphasizes that due to the tensions between remembering and forgetting, both of which can be "conscious and unconscious, visible and hidden," cultural memory "is incomparably more complex and capable of transformation (but also more fragile and problematic than collective memory ("Vier Formen" 183–190). In the prologue to *Lesia's Dream*, the protagonist says: "*I am old. My eyes are failing. My legs are weak. But my memories are strong. And they have been silent for too long*" (x; emphasis in original). The last sentence can be read as a reference to active forgetting, the absence of the experiences of the Ukrainian diaspora in the collective and cultural memory of Canadians, and the erasure of traumatic memories by the survivors of the internment and discrimination during the Great War from the sociopolitical discourse. Moreover, by using "silent" – an adjective – instead of "silenced," a verb, Langston points to Lesia's decision not to share her memories with anyone. The decision may have been connected to the protagonist's need to assimilate and repress the difficult past and the position of an enemy alien. As Lesia recalls in the last chapter of the novel, many internees lost their homesteads and were kept in the camps longer than her father and brother, who were *"never quite the same after"* and displayed symptoms typical of PTSD (207; emphasis in original).

Langston only briefly depicts Lesia's visit to the camp where her father and brother are interned and, similar to Skrypuch in *Silver Threads*, she focuses on showing that the victims of the internment were also women and children left behind. Hence the experiences of the wives, mothers, and sisters of the interned men emerge as comparable to those of Canadian women in *Rilla of Ingleside*, whose dear ones fight in Europe. Ukrainian women in *Lesia's Dream* have to take care of the family's survival in an unfavorable socioeconomic situation, preserve traditions and the memory of their homeland, as well as cultivate the homestead. Thus, they are forced to perform both traditionally feminine and masculine roles, such as childbirth and hunting (cf. Chapter 3). Lesia gets letters from her interned father and brother which, although censored, show the camp as a terrible and dehumanizing place. However, when the girl visits them, she sees that the conditions in which the interned men live are actually *better* than those faced by their families at the homestead.[14]

Representations of the Internment after Bill C-331

Two years after the first publication of Langston's *Lesia's Dream* and a year before the novel's second, award-winning edition, the mainstream relevance of the Canadian Internment of Ukrainians and the experiences of first Eastern European immigrants grew significantly due to the implementation of Bill C-331. The Canadian First World War Internment Recognition Fund established in 2008 has supported the commemoration of the memory of the survivors, for instance, in the form of the publication of new multimodal narratives, most notably Sandra Semchuk's *The Stories Were Not Told: Canada's First World War Internment Camps* (2018). The release of such books is directly connected to the attempts to incorporate the internment and its impact on Ukrainian Canadians into Canadian cultural memory of the First World War. Hence children's and young adult books examined in this chapter have not only an epistemological function but also transmit next-generation memory and play the role of "a cognitive disposition, a cultural medium, a generator of identity patterns and a praxis of learning about the world" (Łebkowska 190). After 2008 the theme of the internment proved to be appealing to various Canadian authors, appearing in Sylvie Brien's francophone *Spirit Lake* (2008),[15] Pam Clark's crossover novel *Kalyna* (2016),[16] and most recently in Glen Huser's *Firebird* (2020) and the graphic novel *Enemy Alien: A True Story of Life Behind Barbed Wire* (2020) written by Kassandra Luciuk and illustrated by nicole marie burton.

Eleven years after the publication of the first edition of *Silver Threads*, also Skrypuch returned to the First World War predicament of Ukrainian Canadians. However, it happened in a significantly different sociopolitical situation. *Prisoners in the Promised Land: The Ukrainian Internment Diary of Anya Soloniuk*, a novel with a title echoing Jaroslav Petryshyn's influential *Peasants in the Promised Land* (1985), was issued in Scholastic's popular *Dear Canada* series (the equivalent of *Dear America*), and was met with critical praise. In a review for *Resource Links* Claire Hazzard writes that "Skrypuch has tackled a difficult topic with ease" and ranks the novel as excellent, calling it "[a]n essential purchase for every elementary school library, this is a book you can recommend to both *Dear Canada* fans and historical fiction fans without hesitation" (35). *Prisoners in the Promised Land* was named one of the best books of 2007 by *Resource Links*.

Written in the form of a diary of a girl named Anya Soloniuk, the novel shows the readers the changing attitudes towards Ukrainians represented by the government and common Canadians in Montreal. This is important in the context of both Canadian and Ukrainian history, as the book tells the story of the first wave of immigration and the attempts at assimilation

The First World War and Canadian Internment Camps   83

while cultivating traditions and customs. Besides, since Anya is concerned about the situation in her homeland and is surprised by the lack of interest in Central and Eastern Europe in Canadian frontal combat messages, the reader can get a different perspective on the Great War, one absent from Anglo-Canadian novels like *Rilla of Ingleside*. With the inclusion of *Prisoners in the Promised Land* in the *Dear Canada* series, the experience of the internment and immigration of Ukrainian Canadians was finally included in the mainstream Canadian literary discourse. On her way to Montreal, Anya befriends Irena, whose father set out earlier and already has a farm in Canada. Thanks to the correspondence between the girls, Yuri Feschuk, Irena's neighbor, a character based on Skrypuch's grandfather, appears in Anya's diary. Feschuk, just like George Forchuk and Ivan in *Silver Threads*, is interned but escapes from the camp. Due to the internment he loses his homestead; there is no fairytale element in *Prisoners in the Promised Land* that would allow him to return home magically.

Launched in 2001, *Dear Canada* consists of novels written by eminent authors such as Jean Little, Perry Nodelman, and Janet Lunn. The series is aimed at school-age children and can be found in most Canadian libraries in two language versions, English and French. The books are focalized by girls experiencing important but sometimes forgotten events in Canadian history. The formula of each volume is similar: it is a diary written by a girl, with no name of the author on the cover, just the title featuring the name of the protagonist, her picture, date, and place (Bell 163). The young first-person narrator is a participant in many events and a direct witness to others. The adult voice appears only in the epilogue in the form of a third-person narrator who introduces the readers to the future fate of the main protagonists. All books in the series are accompanied by paratexts: maps, photographs, and informative historical notes investigated thoroughly by eminent historians, making it easier for readers to understand the complex historical background. The inclusion of photographs helps to identify with the protagonist and her experiences. As the novels feature both fictional and historical characters, the pictures can help envision the protagonist's journey as a fictional representation of real people.

Prisoners in the Promised Land contains several paratexts, including a glossary with Ukrainian, German and Irish terms used in the novel, which may be incomprehensible to most readers, and a poster issued by the Canadian Department of Immigration promoting settlement in the Canadian West (221). Moreover, the readers can find two photographs showing Galician immigrants arriving in 1905, wearing traditional clothes and appearing visibly different from typical Canadians, juxtaposed with a group of Ukrainian children in Alberta in 1920. In the second picture, the *Canadianized* children no longer differ from typical Canadian children from the period. As Jennifer Henderson argues, the inclusion of a picture of a Pikogan tribe

is supposed to document something more than an accidental proximity [...] It provides evidence for the text's implicit argument that Ukrainian immigrants and First Nations shared a condition of unrecognized, marginalized cultural distinctiveness within a Canadian nation which had not yet embraced the values of multiculturalism.
(74; cf. Chapter 1)

The book also includes two maps: one of Europe in 1914, with borders of contemporary Ukraine highlighted (234), and the other with all 24 Canadian internment camps (235); documents (227–229); photographs of the Spirit Lake camp from 1914, featuring children, adults, soldiers (223–227), and tents of the Pikogan community (229); and a picture of a contemporary monument commemorating the victims of the internment (231). The detailed historical note was vetted by the aforementioned historian Frances Swyripa, the author of several books on Ukrainian Canadians and the First World War internment, which legitimizes the version of history Skrypuch presents.

The cover of *Prisoners in the Promised Land* is red and features the title and a photo of a young, dark-haired Galician girl taken in 1905. On the title page there is information that the journal belongs to the 12-year-old Anya Soloniuk from the village of Horoshova in the Crownland of Galicia in the Austro-Hungarian Empire, dated April 13, 1914. The first entry is preceded by a letter from Anya's father, who is already in Montreal and sends his daughter name-day greetings and a journal to help her write down the memories of leaving the village and traveling to Canada. As most of Anya's entries begin with an apostrophe to the journal, the reader can feel closer to the heroine and the story she tells. The pages of Anya's diary also contain several drawings, unfinished entries, as well as crossed-out and corrected sentences, further highlighting its status as a "real diary." Lindy Ledohowski argues that the name of the protagonist of *Prisoners in the Promised Land* "echoes Anne Frank and her diary" and "the allusions to Anne Frank offer Anya as a sympathetic alternative image of the war criminal," yet *Anya*, a diminutive form of *Anna*, also seems to unequivocally recall Montgomery's eponymous *Anne of Green Gables*, one of the best-known Canadian literary figures (cf. "The Compulsion to Tell" 208; cf. Chapter 3).

Skrypuch's Anya Soloniuk, unlike the protagonists of other internment-themed books examined in this chapter, immigrates to Montreal, a big city significantly different from her Ukrainian village. Thus she struggles with both the experience of emigration from Ukraine to Canada as well as migration from the countryside to the city. Hence Anya's later enchantment with the unspoiled nature of Spirit Lake may be explained by the similarities she sees between the Ukrainian and Canadian landscapes. Unlike Montreal, Spirit Lake does not seem so distant. Anya leaves Horoshova with her mother, grandmother, and brother, but before leaving, she writes down the people and things she will miss, as well as the expectations she has about Canada, the eponymous promised land. As Anya later explains, her father was robbed and could not set off in search of his 160 acres of land. Instead, he found work in a factory. Before leaving Horoshova, Anya paints an image of Canada as the promised land of plenty, especially after seeing a photograph showing her father's house on Grand Truck street. The protagonist is not aware that life in a Canadian city is so different from that she is used to. Several other families live in the building on Grand Truck street where there is a severe problem with rats, and there is no vegetable garden.

The first 120 pages of *Prisoners in the Promised Land* depict Anya's assimilation, the process of becoming *Canadian* by adjusting to the Canadian lifestyle but also becoming *Ukrainian* in a matter more equivocal than in Warwaruk's and Langston's novels studied in Chapter 1. As Vic Satzewich notes, immigrants' "consciousness of themselves as 'Ukrainian' did not develop until they were *in* the diaspora and was not part of the baggage that they *brought to* the diaspora" (27; emphasis in original). To understand the complexity of the Ukrainian situation, it is necessary to recall that at that time, present-day Ukraine was split between two empires, Austria-Hungary and Russia, and in 1900 95% of Ukrainians in Galicia and Bukovyna were mostly illiterate peasants (Satzewich 27). Writing about an "imagined political community," Benedict Anderson famously highlights the importance of various peoples in nation-building. He argues that such a community "is *imagined* because the members of even the smallest nation will never know most of their fellow-members, meet them or even hear of them, yet in the minds of each lives the image of their communion" (6). When Anya and her mother are supposed to go to "the Association of Ukrainians, which is at 481 Wellington Street" or "the Ukrainian Society on the corner of Centre Street and Ropery Street" (30), they are surprised to learn that "both of these places had 'Ukrainian' in their names and not 'Galician'" (31). Their new neighbor explains that "Galicia was just one area where people share [their] language and customs. There's also Bukovyna, the Crimea, the Carpathian Mountains and even parts of Russia and Poland" (31). Anya, like most Ukrainians who at that time emigrated to Canada, has a stronger connection to her village of Horoshova, a place she knows, than Ukraine, an "imagined political community." Hence it is only in Canada where she symbolically becomes Ukrainian.

The issue of belonging is surprisingly absent from Glen Huser's novel *Firebird* (2020). While immigrants from Austria-Hungary are described here by various Anglo-Canadian characters as Galicians, Ruthenians, or Ukrainians, the differences between these terms are never explained in the text or the paratexts. Published 13 years after Skrypuch's *Prisoners in the Promised Land*, *Firebird* is Huser's first Ukrainian-themed book. The novel tells the story of Alex Kaminsky, a 14-year-old boy who comes to Canada from Lviv with his brother Marco three years earlier.[17] Like most other immigrants in texts studied in this chapter, Alex's family decides to move to Canada for economic reasons, believing that it is "a new world of golden grain fields, happiness and prosperity" (82). However, unlike the parents of Anya Soloniuk, Lesia Magus, or Ivan and Anna, who are all farmers, Alex's father was a baker and his mother was a governess "teaching the landowner's children" (24). As Alex remembers, the woman spoke four languages and taught him English: the boy "would read aloud to her from a book of English stories and, if she wasn't too tired, they would practice simple exchanges of English conversations" (Huser 24). Despite Alex's mother's efforts and the fact that the boy started going to school in Canada at the age of 11 and understands almost everything Anglo-Canadians say, throughout the novel, Huser highlights how poor Alex's English is. Notably, all non–Anglo-Canadians in *Firebird* use very simple vocabulary and make serious grammatical mistakes, including Karl, a Norwegian man who has lived in Canada for 16 years. One of the protagonist's teachers even says that "[i]t'll take a genius to teach [Alex] the English language," and this genius turns out to be Aunt Mathilde, the boy's future guardian (169). Alex and Marco arrive in Canada together but are quickly separated. At first, Alex lives with his Uncle Andrew, an antiwar socialist and an alcoholic, because on their way to Canada the boys' parents died of "the sickness" in Hamburg, where they were buried (Huser 24). Marco, who is a talented painter, tells Alex that they "will be a force in this new land," yet his words are not prophetic (Huser 26). Marco works at a farm near Vegreville for an Anglo-Canadian man named Granger, who later accuses him of theft and has him imprisoned. Granger, an abusive old man, beats his young Ukrainian wife because she has an affair with Marco, by whom she later turns out to be pregnant. When Marco is gone, Alex survives a house fire, which kills their uncle, and leaves the protagonist with burns on his face and hands.

The fire changes Alex as he gradually distances himself from his Ukrainian heritage and assimilates. Surprisingly, unlike the female characters in the books by Langston and Skrypuch, Alex is a more passive character, and most of his actions are caused by the decisions and choices of adults. Alex wants to be reunited with his brother, who later in a letter calls the protagonist: "*a firebird* [...] *Alive out of Ashes*" (138; emphasis in original). When Alex's late uncle's homestead is taken away by his Anglo-Canadian neighbor, the boy embarks on a turbulent journey to be reconnected with Marco. He stays with different people, has to use two different identities – Alex Arneson and Alex Stephenson – and pretend to be Norwegian to avoid potential imprisonment. Eventually, with the help of various people, Alex finds Marco, who dies of tuberculosis but lives long enough to see the birth of his and Stella's son, named Stephen Marco. Because Alex loses all of the photographs and objects reminding him of his family, the sketchbook he gets from Marco becomes the only material marker of his past and link to Ukraine.

Huser is not Ukrainian Canadian and has no direct links to Ukraine; hence, it is not surprising that his focus is not on keeping the memory of the old county alive but on showing the protagonist's assimilation to

Anglo-Canada. Alex watches Charlie Chaplin's films, listens to Frederic Weatherly's "Danny Boy," and learns about authors like Elizabeth Barrett Browning, John Keats, and Charles Dickens. Although the descriptions of Canada in 1915–1916 and the internment in *Firebird* are accurate, Huser's choice of the Ukrainian characters' names – especially Alex and Stella – is questionable, particularly considering the true-to-custom names of the Arnesons, the Norwegian family which Alex meets. Alex's full name is Alexander, the English version of its Ukrainian variation Oleksandr, but his brother calls him Lexie, an atypical diminutive form, which sounds more similar to Alexiy, a common Russian name. Huser's decision may be explained by his attempt to make it easier for the Canadian readers to connect with the protagonist – who learns English and becomes Canadian – or a sign of his limited knowledge of Ukrainian culture.

In Skrypuch's *Prisoners in the Promised Land*, Anya Soloniuk also changes. First, she begins to understand her cultural distinctiveness as a Ukrainian. Second, she gradually becomes Canadian. Anya is culturally in-between, as her family continues cultivating their own traditions, but gradually tries to assimilate, especially because of the increasing hostility and discrimination they face. Just like the family of Lesia Magus in the prairie, the Soloniuks in Montreal are met with "racist dirt fixations" (Kil 178), being split at and called "Dirty-bohunk" long before the start of the First World War (31; cf. Chapter 1).[18] Notably, Anya learns that despite her low social status, she is nevertheless relatively privileged because she is a white girl, and whiteness makes it possible for her to assimilate. In *Prisoners in the Promised Land*, Skrypuch shows how culturally distant the category of whiteness was for Eastern European immigrants at that time: "[t]he only white people I have ever seen are those ladies with too much powder on their faces," she initially says (63–64). Anya's teacher Miss Boyko explains that "'white' means different things in different cities and provinces and that it is all very confusing" (64). Skrypuch's references to whiteness reflect a more recent awareness of the complex racial dynamics in North America. While Anya has just arrived to Canada, Skrypuch depicts her as being closer to present-day Canadian values than the Anglo- and French-Canadian adults in the novel, symbolically representing the importance of immigrants in the formation of Canada's future more inclusive transcultural society.

Anya Soloniuk's transformation from a Galician peasant into a Ukrainian Canadian white girl begins with a change of clothes, which "symbolized an assimilation with Anglo-Canadian attitudes and ideals" (Swyripa "Wedded" 92). When the Soloniuks arrive in Canada, Anya observes that people dress differently, as "women don't have scarves on their heads. Instead, they wear odd hats ... And they don't braid their hair. It is somehow puffed or curled and it looks ugly" (24–25). For Ukrainian women braids and headscarves were essential attributes of femininity. A similar portrayal of Canadians is found in Langston's *Lesia's Dream*, where "women looked like fancy birds with their long, sweeping skirts, fitted white blouses and high" (25). Also here the different and dirty outfits of the new immigrants, the "unpreferred Continentals," position them as the others (25). The readers of *Prisoners in the Promised Land* can compare Anya's description of typical Canadians with the picture showing Galician immigrants in 1905 (222). In Langston's novel Lesia wears the same old Ukrainian outfit, but in the Association of Ukrainians Skrypuch's Anya instantly gets new boots, stockings, a plain long-sleeved blouse with a collar, and a dark-blue jumper. She does not like "this ugly *thing* called a jumper," and believes the shirt to be "indecent" (33; emphasis in original). At first, Anya does not understand why Canadians do not wear embroidery. She does, however, appreciate the new "smooth black leather" boots with "a little heel" (35). Gradually, however, she grows to like Canadian fashion and starts dreaming of a ribbon like the ones other girls at Notre-Dame-des-Anges wear. The importance of clothes in the performance of Canadianness is highlighted in the epilogue, where the adult narrator informs the readers that after the war, Anya spent "four months' wages" to buy a suit for her brother before his graduation (208). Although Mykola graduates from the University of Toronto with a degree in engineering, his sister knows how important it is for him not to look like an outsider in order to be accepted and appreciated. Looking like "the prime minister" in the new, expensive suit, Mykola gets his first job "with the Canadian National Railway" (208), symbolizing his successful assimilation.

Assimilation into white and middle-class Canadianness is seen as a value by many Ukrainian characters in *Prisoners in the Promised Land*, who reject Ukrainian clothes and food and learn English. When Anya meets Stefan, she believes him to be "the meanest, ugliest boy," and calls him in her diary "pimply" and "mean" (37). This is caused by the fact that Stefan laughs at her traditional Ukrainian clothes, saying that she looks "like a 'dirty-bohunk,'" explaining that "that's what Canadians call Ukrainians because they don't wash" (38). Moreover, speaking English and French, and having lived in Canada for a longer time, Stefan distances himself from the newer immigrants, saying: "[e]ven after you wash, *you* stink like garlic" (38; emphasis mine). Notably, the distinctiveness of Ukrainian culture in Skrypuch's *Prisoners in the Promised Land* is also represented by food, which positions Ukrainians as the ethnic others. "Food is more than a matter of physical sustenance," argue John Radzilowski and Ann Hetzel Gunkel: "[i]t is also a system of communication, a type of language through which we express identities and relationships, including gender, ethnicity, nationality, festivity, and sacrality" (136; cf. Niewiadomska-Flis; Gunkel). In Skrypuch's novel Anya has to learn a new system of communication. When she gets "rye bread spread with chicken fat and sliced onion" with "a jar of sour milk" for lunch on her first day of school, Stefan says "[y]ou really are a dirtybohunk" and trades lunches with her, giving Anya "a white bread sandwich with butter and brown sugar and a jar of tea" (41-42)[19]. Hence, he saves the protagonist from embarrassment which previously happened to Mary, who brought a garlic sandwich on her first day, and probably also an experience no one saved Stefan from.[20]

Education and the ability to speak English are other important elements in the process of becoming Canadian showcased in the novels. Lesia in Langton's book has to learn to read and write in Ukrainian and English on her own; these skills help her gain the respect of the local community. Skrypuch's Anya Soloniuk and Huser's Alex Kaminsky do it at school, where they also learn about Canadian customs and traditions. Without having access to education at the prairie, Lesia Magus has no opportunity to learn about Anglo-Canadian history and culture. Unlike her, Anya and Alex learn about the essential elements of Anglo-Canadian cultural memory, which makes it easier for them to understand the new country and assimilate. As Assmann notes, this type of remembering is "based on institutions [...] of education and the arts as well as ceremonies and commemorative dates and practices" ("Transformations" 56). Anya finds history and geography interesting because her teacher talks about both Canada and Ukraine. Notably, one of the first things Anya learns there is to sing "God Save the King" (55) and paint the Red Ensign (56). Because Alex Kaminsky comes from an educated family, he started learning English from his late mother. Yet the boy's knowledge of English is limited, and even after spending three years in a Canadian school, he only uses basic present tenses for most of the book. He does, however, write longs letters in English, even to his brother, and rarely uses any Ukrainian words. With the help of supportive teachers, Mrs. Anderson, who teaches him "God Save the King" and does not let him use Ukrainian in class, Mr. Dallaine, who introduces him to poetry and helps him hide, and Mr. Dallaine's Aunt Mathilde Lafontaine, who teaches him about literature and culture, throughout the novel Alex gradually improves his knowledge of the English language and reads books like Charles Dickens' *Oliver Twist*. He does not, however, learn anything about Ukrainian culture. Aunt Mathilde, a progressive widow, who becomes his guardian, tells him, "[o]ne of the best ways for [him] to develop a feel for the language [...] is to read from the masters" (Huser 185). The progress in Alex's skills is noticeable as he finally starts using more complex grammatical structures and sophisticated vocabulary in the novel's last few chapters.

Skrypuch and Huser point to the similarities between various marginalized groups in Canada.[21] Anya Soloniuk witnesses the bullying of a poor girl named Slava, who speaks no English, by Canadian girls who call her "a dirty little animal" (49). The protagonist befriends Slava and is surprised to see the conditions her friend lives in: "Even the poorest person in Horoshova lives better than this," Anya believes (51). Seeing Slava's home, Anya starts doubting the sense of her family's, and other Ukrainians', immigration to the eponymous promised land. The Soloniuks also have to struggle with mice and smelly outhouses of their neighbors. Anya regularly compares the crowded and dirty Montreal to her clean and neat village in Galicia. Notably, Skrypuch shows that poverty was not only attributed to Eastern European immigrants. Maureen, Anya's Irish-Canadian friend, who is also picked on by the mean girls, lives in similar conditions. Maureen's house also "smells like cabbage," but instead of "cabbage rolls," her family eats "cabbage potatoes" (76). Huser, on the other hand, introduces a family of Norwegian immigrants who, despite their difficult material status, help Alex survive and later stay in touch with the boy. As Karl Arneson, the head of the family, says: "Not Ukrainian, true. I'm from Norvay [sic!]. But what it is to be new to this country, that I know" (106–107).

Skrypuch and Huser demythologize Canada as the land of plenty, the eponymous promised land. Still, unlike Langston, who focuses on showing the Anglo-Canadian discrimination of Ukrainians, they also include numerous sympathetic Anglo-Canadian characters. In addition to rejection and hatred, Anya Soloniuk meets with sympathy and support. Apart from everyday discrimination by Canadian girls and the indifference of the teachers, at school she also encounters kindness and befriends many children. She and Mykola, just like all other young Canadians, get milk from the government, at that time a treat unheard of in Ukraine. When Anya's family assimilates and starts calling Canada home, the First World War breaks out and the Warfare Act is introduced. Anya's parents lose their jobs, but are assured that they are good workers and must be dismissed for "patriotic" reasons only. Alex Kaminsky in *Firebird* faces discrimination on behalf of Ukrainian and not Anglo-Canadian children. The only boy who makes fun of him after the fire is Orest Potchak, who says that his father believes Uncle Andrew "was crazy" and "the fire was God's breath breathing on a heathen" (64). When Alex goes to a different school, he is met with sympathy, even though "he was a couple of years older than most of them, fitting awkwardly into the desk" (133). While some children keep away from him, he is not bullied and plays with other boys. Alex even goes to see Charlie Chaplin's new film with Eric Richards, his closest friend, whose father has the protagonist expelled when he realizes the boy is not Norwegian, a fact Eric does not believe to be of any importance (145). Explaining his decision to expel the boy, the headmaster says that Canadians are "fighting for decency and freedom" in Europe (158). However, the words of Mr. Dallaine, a different teacher: "[m]en fighting their little wars whenever they have a chance," show that not all Anglo-Canadian have such a negative approach towards enemy aliens (158, 167).

Firebird depicts the various ways in which Ukrainians were treated by Canadians during the First World War. When Alex and Marco are finally reunited, the protagonist says: "I have no answer. Why some people are good, like Mr. Bayles, Karl and Mr. Dallaine and his aunt – and other people would like to beat you down. Like Liz Eddy and Mr. Richars and Granger" (223). In this sentence, Alex mentions all of the people who help him get better after the fire, and those, who do not treat him with kindness. It is worth mentioning that Liz Eddy, a girl Marco's age, is the daughter of the Anglo-Canadian family who initially take care of Alex. She is the first one who uses the word "Hun," and when Alex is put in her brother's room, Liz tells him not to touch anything, or he will be "really sorry, that [he] didn't stay back in Hun country where [he] belong[s]" (16). Robin, Liz's older brother, is a soldier about whose death the family hears from Mr. Bayles at Christmas. Seeing Alex wearing her late brother's old clothes, Liz says "[t]hey've killed him. Those bloody Huns have killed him," as in her eyes the boy embodies the enemy, the cause of her brother's death (46). Consequently, her negative attitude towards Alex can be explained as a direct reaction to the loss of her brother. Mr. Richards, the father of Eric, who looks like King George V, represents the British Empire, and Granger, an old man who wears a hook instead of a hand, is a direct referent to Captain Hook, the arch-enemy of Peter Pan from J.M. Barrie's 1904 *Peter Pan; or, the Boy Who Wouldn't Grow Up*, a villain most readers will be familiar with due to the numerous film adaptations of the play. Granger, who steals money from Ukrainians, hypocritically accuses them of theft and says that he "never met a bohunk yet [who] wouldn't dip his fingers in your bankroll [...] it's just part of their nature" (86).

Huser portrays characters who express hatred towards enemy aliens but show Alex kindness: for example, Mrs. Eddy, who takes care of him after the fire and gives him a Christmas gift, and Jim Hainstock, who gives Alex a ride to the train station. On the way there, Jim says he has "never seen anyone work like them Ruthenians" (74). However, when he is buying Alex a ticket to Edmonton and hears the seller say that Canadian soldiers are fighting in Europe and "these Austro-Huns [are] staying behind and reaping the profits" (75), he replies "we wouldn't want them in the forces. We don't need to be giving no enemy aliens rifles and bayonets. Might as well shoot yourself and get it over with" (75). Although Alex stands next to them, the men ignore his presence. Yet right after hearing these words, the protagonist meets a kind Canadian soldier. Notably, every time Huser introduces a hateful adult, he juxtaposes them with a sympathetic one. A character probably most sympathetic towards the Ukrainian cause in *Firebird* is Aunt Mathilde. She is the one who calls the internment camps "ridiculous" and "scandalous" (188) and believes that enemy aliens "did everything they could to get away from places of oppression and injustice and poverty. That's why they came to Canada" (180–181). Although Mathilde helps Alex the most, she makes sure that he learns English and assimilates as fast as possible.

The internment of Ukrainians appears in adults' conversations throughout Huser's novel, which seems to show that despite their absence from Canadian cultural memory and books published before 1996, at that time, the existence of the camps was not a secret. Granger, who has Marco interned, tells Alex that the government is "settling up [camps] for enemy aliens, that's the ones they don't shop back to Hun-country where they should have stayed in the first place" (87). Ivan, a Ukrainian man who wants to escape to the USA but is caught and interned together with Marco, says: "you might find yourself on the way to *concentration camp*. I hear there's one in Lethbridge in the south" (97; emphasis mine). The problematic use of the expression *concentration* instead of *internment* does not seem coincidental, as it highlights the brutality and inhumanity of the camps, provoking the young readers to associate them with the Nazi camps. Notably, as Swyripa notes, the "emotionally charged term 'concentration camps' evoking Nazi atrocities" points to the alleged similarities between the Shoah and the Canadian internment of enemy aliens and has been used by redress campaigners since the publication of Michael Marunchak's *The Ukrainian Canadians: A History* in 1970 ("The Politics of Redress" 374). This is not the only reference to Holocaust imagery in *Firebird*. When Alex wants Marco to hide at Aunt Mathilde's place, the woman says "there might be very serious consequences for anyone harbouring an escapee," which may be read as a reference to the risk some Europeans would take to save Jews during the Second World War (207; cf. Chapter 5).

Huser and Skrypuch are the only authors mentioning the internment of women and children. In *Firebird* sympathetic adult characters, Karl and Aunt Mathilde, warn Alex to be careful, as there are camps for Ukrainians across Canada, and in some of them children are also imprisoned (129, 204). In reality, Spirit Lake in Quebec and Vernon in British Columbia were the only camps where women and children joined men. As Swyripa notes, "81 women and 156 children of all nationalities joined their menfolk" there ("The Politics of Redress" 363). Due to the character of the *Dear Canada* series, which is aimed at young readers, the camp where the Soloniuks in Skrypuch's *Prisoners in the Promised Land* are interned is Spirit Lake. It is worth noting that Mary Manko Haskett, an internee who was one of Skrypuch's inspirations, became "the unofficial spokesperson for the Ukrainian Canadian campaign for acknowledgment and redress," as at the time of the internment she was "a six-year-old girl who watched her two-year-old sister, Nellie, die of pneumonia in the camp" (Henderson 74). Swyripa notes that being interned as a child, Haskett "legitimized the continued use in the redress rhetoric of terms as 'interned Canadians' and 'women and children'" in the redress campaign in the late 1980s and early 1990s ("The Politics of Redress" 365). After the arrest of Anya's father in *Prisoners*, the rest of the girl's family, as well as their neighbors and Anya's closest friend Stefan, are sent to Spirit Lake. Anya's first reaction to the news of the internment is to ask her diary: "What did we do to deserve this? Didn't they ask us to come here? If the Canadian government didn't want us, why did they encourage us to come?" (124). Similar questions appear in Clark's *Kalyna* and Huser's *Firebird*. *Kalyna*'s two major male characters, Wasyl and Ivan, are interned. Wasyl Fedorchuk, the husband of Katja, the protagonist of the three parts of *Kalyna*, is an exemplary immigrant who, unlike Ivan, does not want to escape the camp or rebel against the authorities. The eponymous Kalyna, who is the central character of the last part of the novel, is the daughter of Katja and Dr. Edward Smith, an Englishman who raped Katja when Wasyl was still interned. After going to law school, Kalyna learns about her biological father's identity and Wasyl's internment. She meets and rejects Dr. Smith, now a professor, and decides to fight to bring justice to the survivors of the internment.[22] After the internment of her husband, Katja asks: *"what is their crime? [...] That they came to Canada and wanted a better life for their families?"* (114; emphasis in original). Alex in *Firebird* wonders: *"What had they* [Ukrainians] *done to the world to deserve this?"* (90; emphasis in original). The questions asked by children and women in the books remain unanswered but may provoke the readers to read the paratexts or additional sources.

Although all of the novels point to the numerous instances of discrimination of Ukrainians by Anglo-Canadians, they all demonstrate the beauty of the landscapes and point to the similarities between the old country and the Canadian hinterlands. The Soloniuks travel to Spirit Lake on a train with "bog windows" and "comfortable benches" (130). Much like Andrei in Warwaruk's novel, they admire Canadian landscapes with deer and moose; "the most beautiful sights" (131) remind Anya of "the birch forests in Horoshova" (132). Moreover, as in *Andrei and the Snow Walker* and *Brovko's Amazing Journey*, the Canadian wilderness in this text also appears not as distant but as similar to Ukraine. The references to the beauty of Canadian landscapes also appear in *Kalyna* where Wasyl, Kalyna Fedorchuk's adoptive father, in a letter to his wife Katja writes that *"the mountains here are enormous and beautiful, in a fierce way"* (120; emphasis in original). Marco, the interned brother of Alex in *Firebird*, also mentions *"the beautiful mountain town of Banff"* where the Cave and Basin camp is located (155; emphasis in original). Anya, the child focalizer in *Prisoners...*, is impressed with the beauty of Spirit Lake when she says: "If I pretend there is no guardhouse in our camp and no barber wire around the single prisoners' camp, Spirit Lake is beautiful" (136). As she later adds: "if we hadn't come to Canada, I never would have seen Spirit Lake. It is sad that this is a jail ... because it is one of the most beautiful places in the whole world" (145–146). Such romanticized depiction of the eponymous prison camp is quite problematic.

The portrayals of the camp in *Prisoners in the Promised Land* and *Kalyna* significantly differ from those in *Firebird* and *Enemy Alien: A Graphic History of Internment in Canada During the First World War* (2020), a crossover graphic novel based on a recently found anonymous diary by a Ukrainian internee in Kapuskasing between 1914 and 1917, written retrospectively in 1945. The account of Wasyl in Clark's novel contradicts the one in *Firebird*, where the "[a]lmost freezing" internees sleep in tents and are "half-starved" with "no boots" while working "on the golf course below the Banff Springs Hotel" (Huser 180, 277). Despite the natural beauty and cleanliness, Spirit Lake and Cave and Basin are still prisons, and the weather conditions are harsh. Men are forced to work hard, cutting down trees, and some of the internees, including children in the latter, die of exhaustion, illnesses, or, in the case of *Kalyna*, suicide. When the Duke and Duchess of Connaught visit the camp in *Kalyna*, Wasyl feels *"like a caged animal in a zoo on view"* but is *"glad they saw [them] working so hard for [their] country"* (194; emphasis in original). This type of enthusiasm is nowhere to be found in *Firebird*, where tourists "look at them [the prisoners] as if they were animals in a zoo," or *Enemy Alien*, the only text written entirely from the perspective of a male internee (Huser 189). As Luciuk notes in the introduction, it is "the only comprehensible account of First World War internment written by an internee" (vii). The diary is anonymous, probably because "[l]eaving one's name off of one's own memoir is telling of the ongoing fear of repression that was so clearly prominent in the author's life" (x). After all, "even after their incarceration, Ukrainians long remained in fear of the barber wire fence" (x). John Boychuk, the "equivalent of John Smith," a name Luciuk chose to represent "the average Ukrainian internee," the novel's adult focalizer, struggles with hard physical labor, harsh weather, emotional and physical abuse but also anxiety and fear which haunt him long after the internment (xi). In Boychuk's diary there is no place for sympathetic officers, like in the texts by Clark or Skrypuch, and descriptions of the beauty of the Canadian landscapes. Moreover, burton's black and white illustrations with only hints of light green further make it difficult to find beauty behind barbed wire.

Enemy Alien and *Firebird* demonstrate the Anglo-Canadian exploitation of the internees during and after the war. Boychuk and other men imprisoned at Kapuskasing are ridiculed and beaten by the Anglo-Canadian officers. In *Firebird*, the guards are shown in an unequivocally negative way, with one of them calling an internee a "[s]tupid bohunk" (199), comparing guarding prisoners to watching cattle, and wishing he were "where the action is, where you can actually shoot the buggers" (209). While many adults in *Firebird* describe the camp as a place safer than the trenches, the internment is a prison that leads to Alex's brother's death. When Marco gets sick, he is forced to work and tied to a tree. The man is rebellious and fights with a guard, who then puts him in solitary confinement. Marco, whose "collar bones and ... ribs were so apparent beneath his pale skin," eventually escapes from the camp (220). However, he contracts tuberculosis and soon after dies.

Skrypuch and Clark, on the other hand, focus on depicting individual acts of kindness in the camp and point to the importance of reconciliation and forgiveness. In *Kalyna*, some of the guards are shown as sympathetic, most notably Captain Davis, who respects Wasyl and treats him with kindness because they "were all forced to be there and [they] made the best of it" (274). At the novel's end, Kalyna, now a lawyer trying to bring public attention to the internment, meets Davis. The man, who has lost sight, gives her a diary with "details nobody knew unless they were there at Castle" (274). While doing so, Davis asks her to "understand and forgive" (274–275). Anya in Skrypuch's *Prisoners* meets with good officers, most importantly Private Palmer, who takes pictures of the children and talks with the internees, showing them kindness. Others openly display hostility, especially after hearing about the allies' defeats. Notably, one of the guards in the camp turns out to be Howard Smythe, the poor Canadian neighbor of the Soloniuks, a Ukrainophobe who openly shows resentment from the beginning of their stay in Canada. He frequently spits at Anya and calls her names. In Spirit Lake, he abuses the authority he is given to show his aversion to his former neighbors. For instance, he accuses Anya of stealing eggs because she and the other girls make hollow *pysanky* (Easter eggs) for sale in the nearby town of Amos, where some of the internees work. The protagonist explains to the commander that *pysanky* are decorated empty shells. Intrigued by Anya's manual skills, he believes her and asks to make embroidered kerchiefs for his wife. Smythe is then transferred to another camp. In the epilogue, we learn that after the war, Smythe and Anya's father worked together, with the former being made manager. When the workers went on strike, Anya's father "was elected union steward," Smythe "handled the whole situation so poorly that [...] he was fired," and Mr. Soloniuk was offered Smythe's position (207).

Skrypuch returns once more to Smythe in "An Unexpected Visitor," a festive short story published in *A Christmas to Remember: Tales of Comfort and Joy* (2009), a *Dear Canada* anthology. Set after the war, it is written as Anya's letter to her friend Irena, in which she focuses on forgiveness and reconciliation. When Smyth loses his job, he struggles with poverty and hunger, becoming a beggar. In the meantime, Anya gets promoted and works in good conditions, as her supervisor brings her fish and chips and "that lovely Coca Cola" (43). Regardless of Smyth's earlier actions, Anya feels sorry and brings him food. Mr. Soloniuk shares his daughter's sentiment and invites Smythe to spend Christmas Eve with the family as "it is traditional to invite strangers to share our meal on this night" (46). Smythe apologizes for his hateful behavior, saying: "I am sorry for what I did to you" (46). Unemployed and homeless, he finally understands the Soloniuk's predicament: "I know now that it was hard for you when you came to this country [...] Back then, I just thought of you all as dirty foreigners" (46–47). Smythe also thanks Anya for her kindness. This fairytale-like ending, also reminiscent of Dickens' *A Christmas Carol* (1843), fits in well with the hopeful character of the *Dear Canada* series.

Internment camps where enemy aliens, primarily Ukrainians, are forced into slave labor, some of them die, and most leave traumatized appear in all of the texts examined in this chapter. Yet their authors never put the blame on Anglo-Canadians and point to the opportunities awaiting their characters in Canada after the war. Moreover, war imprisonment in present-day historical novels emerges as the foreigners' opportunity to prove their loyalty to the state by sacrificing their freedom. While Aunt Mathilde in Huser's *Firebird* says that the "whole government" is responsible, she also adds that "[p]eople can be so blind and stupid and uncaring during a war," which points to the effectiveness of war propaganda (Huser 272). The former employers of Anya Soloniuk's parents are overwhelmed with guilt and send letters asking the government for her release. Anya also receives messages from her Canadian friends, and after being released from the camp in Montreal, she and her parents have jobs waiting for them. However, they do not get their confiscated valuable possessions back, and some, like Slava, lose their close ones and are traumatized. Even when Anya Soloniuk is a prisoner at the Spirit Lake Internment Camp, she tells her diary that she is still grateful to be alive – in her bombed village she would not have a chance to survive. Moreover, she tries to focus on the positive aspects of Canada: "There are no lords, and in the future maybe we will own land and maybe we will be free to live like other Canadians" (145). After all, as she believes, it is possible to "have a good life in Canada" (146).[23]

Ukrainian Canadian historical fiction points to the long absence of any formal commemoration of the internment which complicates the transmission of next-generation memory. In the epilogue to Skrypuch's *Prisoners in the Promised Land*, the third-person adult narrator says that the children of Anya and Stefan did not believe in their parents' stories, treating them as fairy tales because they could not understand how a country as tolerant as Canada could have had internment camps. Their disbelief echoes the case of Mary Manko Haskett, who was born in Canada and, at the age of six, was interned with her parents and siblings, and whose children "had refused to believe her story" (Swyripa "The Politics of Redress" 369). Skrypuch writes that when Anya and Stefan's children were teenagers, their parents took them to Spirit Late, the place of memory that was turned into "a government experimental farm" (210). The doubt of second-generation Ukrainian Canadians does not seem surprising considering the long-term absence of the internment in history textbooks, collective consciousness, and popular culture. The lack of commemoration is also depicted in the last chapters of *Enemy Alien*. When John Boychuk visits Kapuskasing in 1945, the camp no longer exists and is erased from the local memory. In the town, which was built on the hinterlands the internees had made fertile by cutting down trees, the local inhabitants are unaware of Ukrainians, who during the First World War were "fed on sauerkraut and rotten liver" and "cleared hundreds of acres of forest" in the territory once stolen from the Cree and the Moose Cree (74). While the town is thriving, no one visits the cemetery where lay some of the internees who are "forgotten by the world as if they were made by another God" (78).

The importance of telling the world about the camps and introducing their existence into Canadian cultural memory is reflected in all internment-themed books, most notably in *Enemy Alien*, which ends with the words: "[w]e were going to tell the world about how we were tortured ... and it would become a part of history" (79), and in Clark's *Kalyna*. After finding out about her Ukrainian father's internment, the eponymous heroine, introduced only in the last part of the book, which takes place between 1935 and 1956, wonders: "[a]ll his life, her father had reiterated what a gift it was to be born Canadian and professed his love for this country which gave him freedom ... Had her father really believed what he said?" (245). This quotation demonstrates that in the case of the role of the internment of Ukrainians in Canada in the twentieth century, we can talk about displacement, a generational nonmemory. Kalyna eventually learns that the man she knew as her father raised her, but her biological father was an Englishman called Edward Smith who raped her mother, which can also be read as a symbolical rape committed on people called enemy aliens. Kalyna's landlady tells the young woman: "Ukrainians don't speak of this time because the older generation still lives in fear of the barbed wire fence" (247). Kalyna, who symbolizes the new generation of Ukrainian Canadians, does not share this fear. Many years after the novel's action finishes, the descendants of the survivors have managed to destigmatize the internment and share its memory with the next generations of Canadians.

Conclusion

When Gilbert Blythe in Montgomery's *Rilla of Ingleside* tells Susan Baker: "We are told to love our enemies," the woman replies: "Yes, our enemies, but not King George's enemies" (Montgomery 37). The First World War resulted in radical discursive changes, epistemological and worldview crises, transcultural and transnational trauma, but also the Canadian shift from colony to nation (cf. Branach-Kallas "Szok Wielkiej Wojny", "Trauma Plots"; Reimer). After the Great War, King George's political "enemies" were no longer synonymous with the enemies of Canada. Internment-themed books examined in this chapter promote forgiveness and reconciliation between Anglo-Canadians and Ukrainian Canadians and point to the need to commemorate the past. This need is reflected in the words of Kalyna's mother in Clark's novel, who says: "[i]f your father could forgive the government for imprisonment, surely you can forgive what has happened" and encourages her daughter to "change things" (253). Authors of historical fiction for young readers attempt to change things. Their mnemonic narratives are, to recall Astrid Erll's words, "memory reflexive" but can also be "memory productive," especially in the context of producing next-generation memory.

Although we usually refer to victories while discussing collective memory designed by state authorities and institutions, after a while even dishonorable events can be seen as ones strengthening the sense of national identity and the memory of a community, forming its collective and then cultural memory, which "serves to pass on experience and knowledge beyond the borders of generations, thus producing long-term social memory" (Assmann "Transformations" 55). It is precisely this memory that is a storehouse of knowledge about the identity of a given community, and its carriers can be various media products, such as children's books. The internment of Ukrainians in Canada was recognized by parliament almost 90 years later, provoking a discussion on the changes in the immigration policy of the country and its history. More than a 100 years after the outbreak of the Great War and the events described in the texts analyzed in this chapter, the subject of internment is no longer a taboo among the next generations of the ancestors of the War Measures Act survivors – victims, perpetrators, and bystanders alike.

Notes

1 The quotation in the title comes from Laura Langston's *Lesia's Dream* (101).
2 See Chapter 1 note 3.
3 Although *The Blythes Are Quoted* (2009) is the last book featuring Anne Blythe, it is not a novel.
4 While the Wartime Election Act is briefly discussed in the entry devoted to Ukrainians in Norah Story's *The Oxford Companion to Canadian History and Literature* (1967), the internment and the War Measures Act are not mentioned (807–808). This lack is of great significance but does not seem surprising as most official internment documentation was destroyed in 1954. The internment is also often omitted or only briefly mentioned in mainstream Canadian history textbooks. For instance, Margaret Conrad in *A Concise History of Canada,* published in 2012 by Cambridge University Press, writes about the internment of "half a million people in Canada who traced their origin to enemy countries," but she does not mention that most of them were Ukrainians and omits the War Measures Act (199).
5 While Skrypuch claims her grandfather's name to be Yuri Feschuk or George Forchuk, Marshall Forchuk, acknowledges that his father started using a different name after the internment because of fear:

> What did he change his name to? Dad lost more than five years. He lost more than his homestead and the horses and the cattle that he had. He lost his identity. He had to become someone else because, even when he relocated later, in civilization he could not be the same person because he did not know who his enemies were. He had to be a frightened man. I don't know, to this day. I don't know for sure what Dad's original name was. I don't even know – and I suppose it isn't if my name Forchuk is the name he came over with.
>
> (qtd. in Semchuk 134)

6 The volume includes Skrypuch's two short-stories "The Red Boots" and "The Ring" (cf. Chapter 4).
7 The novel is a love story about Zeynep and Ali, a betrothed couple of Kurds of Anatolia who come to Canada during the First World War. Zeynep's first-hand experiences the Armenian Genocide in Turkey, while Ali is interned in Canada in a camp with other enemy aliens, including Ukrainians. Skrypuch manages to show the similarities in the treatment of both minority groups.

The First World War and Canadian Internment Camps   99

Dance of the Banished was included in The White Ravens catalog by the International Youth Library in 2015.

8   The potential of the picturebook as a multimodal treasure trove of interpretations has been studied by seminal scholars like Barbara Bader (1976), Perry Nodelman (1988), Maria Nikolajeva and Carole Scott (2001), David Lewis (2001), and Evelyn Arizpe and Morag Styles (2003).

9   "I was also surprised to see that the illustrator for *The Paperbag Princess* had a Ukrainian name. It was the first time I had seen a Ukrainian name on a commercially published book," writes Skrypuch in "Am I Ukrainian?" (65). Martchenko was included in Alison Gertridge's list of Canada's most important children's authors and illustrators alongside L.M. Montgomery, Lyn Cook, Monica Hughes, Jean Little, and Barbara Smucker (74–75).

10   *Silver Threads* is not paginated.

11   Books published after the official recognition by the internment by the Canadian government point to the fact that some assimilated Ukrainian Canadians who spoke good English enlisted under false names. This motif appears in Skrypuch's *Prisoners in the Promised Land*, Huser's *Firebird*, and Clark's *Kalyna*. In *Kalyna*, Wasyl mentions Pascal, a Ukrainian Canadian boy who wanted to enlist, but was interned and committed suicide. Alex, the protagonist of *Firebird*, meets a sympathetic Canadian soldier on the train, who tells him about a friend who changed his name from Starsychyn to Smith and enlisted, which was a common practice among those Ukrainians who wanted to voluntarily join the Canadian army (Luciuk "In Fear" 33). The man also adds that "[a]ll this stuff about allegiance to the kaiser's a load of crap if you ask me," hence shows attitude different from the anti-Ukrainian ones expressed by some Anglo-Canadians in the novel (Huser 77).

12   Notably, in Huser's *Firebird*, published 24 years after *Silver Threads*, one of the Anglo-Canadian antagonists is also described as looking similar to King George (149).

13   The third edition will be published in 2023.

14   In Skrypuch's *Prisoners in the Promised Land* and Clark's *Kalyna*, the camps are portrayed in a similar way. Unlike in the Soloniuks' dirty building in Montreal, their new bunkhouse in Spirit Lake is clean and spacious, and the "water closets smell of pine needles and soap" (136). Wasyl in *Kalyna* describes the Cave and Basin camp in a similar manner: "*there is a hot spring here that we can use for bathing, The hot water feels like heaven in these cold temperatures. We now sleep in barracks with a stove in the middle,*" he writes in a letter to his wife (158; emphasis in original).

15   As of 2022, the novel has not been translated into English.

16   *Kalyna* is a crossover historical novel about the Canadian prairies set in the early 1910s. First published as a mainstream novel, *Kalyna* was also marketed as a YA book. However, Angela Thompson in her *Resource Links* review calls "a niche novel at best" which "will not appear to the majority of teen readers" (24).

17   Both *Firebird* and *Prisoners in the Promised Land* share several similarities with Brien's Francophone *Spirit Lake*. *Spirit Lake* is set in 1915 in the eponymous camp and Brien's protagonists are male teenagers who have to "clear and grub five hundred acres of cultivable land" ("les prisonniers défrichent et essouchent cinq cents acres de terre cultivable" 237). Peter Gaganovitch, who is 14-year-old, and Iwan Nikolaiczuk, his five years older

adoptive brother, are new immigrants from Lviv forced to face the harsh reality of Spirit Lake right after their arrival to Canada. Because unlike *Firebird* and *Prisoners in the Promised Land* the book is directed at slightly older readers, the narration is more complex: for example, Brien uses several flashbacks introducing the protagonists' lives before the internment and the novel's ending is more ambiguous.

18 In the book Skrypuch refers to the controversy surrounding a pastoral letter by Bishop Nicetas Budka read on January 27, 1914. In the letter Budka encouraged Ukrainians to return to Galicia and fight for Austria. "Budka, who had come to the northwest from Galicia in 1912, was not aware that this flock regarded the Austrian empire as an oppressor" (Story 807). This fact is also mentioned in Clark's *Kalyna*.

19 In Skrypuch's Second World War novel *Stolen Child*, the encounter with Canada's white sliced bread, Wonder Bread, provokes the protagonist to ask if it is bread at all, and if it is "the only kind of bread [she] could eat in Canada" ("Stolen" 7). Nadia/Larissa does not understand why Wonder Bread is called bread, because unlike the traditional Ukrainian bread, it has no taste. Throughout the novel the girl goes to school, learns about Canadian customs, and tries other Anglo-Canadian dishes, such as Campbell's tomato soup and grilled cheese. While she does not like the plain dishes, she is "grateful – as always – for any food" ("Stolen" 22). References to white bread also appear in Skrypuch's *The Hunger* (1999). Paula, the novel's protagonist, suffers from an eating disorder and, as Anastasia Ulanowicz argues, she "is conflicted by her simultaneous desire for and rejection of the 'white store-bought stuff' " that her grandmother associates with Canada (148). In addition to the othering function of food, it can also bring people together. This is portrayed in *Lesia's Dream*. Minnie, the niece of Lesia's future husband Andrew, makes fun of the protagonist's ethnicity and calls her "dirty," replicating the slurs she hears from Anglo-Canadians (30; cf. Chapters 1 and 3). Minnie's attempts at distancing herself from Lesia do not change the fact that they are both considered enemy aliens by the novel's Anglo-Canadians. The traditional Ukrainian bread and butter that the girls need to sell at the market in one of the novel's last chapters are initially met with Anglo-Canadians' suspicion. When Lesia saves Amy Scott, a Canadian child, she breaks the bread into small pieces and shares them with the people who witness her heroic deed. No sooner does Lesia save the child and share bread – a symbol of peace, friendship, and friendliness – with those who previously ridiculed her than she gains the respect she desperately wants (cf. Chapters 1 and 3).

20 He also introduces Anya to other typical Canadian things, such as street hokey. Eventually the boy becomes Anya's best friend, and, as we learn from the epilogue, husband.

21 However, non-Ukrainians are absent from the monoethnic chronotope of Langston's prairie, where the protagonist's family is the only one struggling with poverty and discrimination.

22 Despite being a historical novel, *Kalyna* contains several factual mistakes, especially considering Ukrainian customs, traditions, and names. With numerous plot-holes and time shifts, at times it may be difficult to follow for young readers.

23 This sentiment is also found in Skrypuch's young adult novel *Dance of the Banished*, where Ali says: "[i]f I had come to this place as a free man instead

of a prisoner, I could grow to love it" (106). Ali decides not to escape from Kapuskasing with the help of a Cree woman. He rejects her offer to live with her as he "would never be allowed to be a Canadian citizen" (138). When he returns to the solitary confinement after leaving it for some time, he tells the novel's sympathetic guard: "My dream is to become a Canadian" (192). The officer adds: "It's good that you can think into the future" (192). Thinking about his predicaments, Ali believes that "[t]his place was a prison camp, but it was also [his] refuge" (193). Notably, it is Bohdan, Ali's Ukrainian friend, who tells him: "[t]hink of this as your sacrifice to Canada's war efforts" (197). The belief that the internment is a sacrifice gives the men hope that they will survive and become part of the Canadian mosaic.

Works Cited

Arizpe, Evelyn and Morag Styles. *Children Reading Pictures: Interpreting Visual Texts*. Routledge, 2003.

Arizpe, Evelyn, Teresa Colomer, and Carmen Martínez-Roldán et al. *Visual Journeys through Wordless Narratives: An International Inquiry with Immigrant Children and "The Arrival."* Bloomsbury, 2014.

Assmann, Aleida. "Canon and Archive." *Media and Cultural Memory*, edited by Astrid Erll and Ansgar Nünning. Berlin-New York: Walter de Gruyter, 2008.

Assmann, Aleida. "Transformations between History and Memory." *Social Research*, vol. 75, no. 1, *Collective Memory and Collective Identity* (SPRING 2008), pp. 49–72.

Assmann, Aleida. "Vier Formen des Gedächtnissesm." *Erwägen –Wissen –Ethik*, no. 13, 2002, pp. 183–190.

Atwood, Margaret. *Survival: A Thematic Guide to Canadian Literature*. Toronto: Anansi, 1972.

Bader, Barbara. *American Picture Books: From Noah's Ark to the Beast Within*. Macmillan, 1976.

Bell, Katherine, "Behind the Blackout Curtains: Female Focalization of Atlantic Canada in the *Dear Canada* Series of Historical Fiction." *Children's Literature in Education*, vol. 49, 2018, pp. 161–179.

Branach-Kallas, Anna. "Szok Wielkiej Wojny – o traumie indywidualnej, traumie kulturowej oraz portretach gueules cassées we współczesnej literaturze brytyjskiej i francuskiej." *Teksty Drugie*, vol. 4, 2018, pp. 12–36.

Branach-Kallas, Anna. "Trauma Plots: Reading Contemporary Canadian First World War Fiction in a Comparative Perspective." *Canadian Literature*, vol. 238, 2019, pp. 47–64.

Brien, Sylvie. *Spirit Lake*. Paris: Gallimard Jeunesse, 2008.

Clark, Pam. *Kalyna*. Stonehouse Publishing, 2016. E-book.

Conrad, Margaret. *A Concise History of Canada*. Cambridge University Press, 2012.

Coulthard, Kathy. "The Words to Say It: Young Bilingual Learners Responding to Visual Texts." *Children Reading Pictures*, edited by Evelyn Arizpe and Morag Styles. Routledge, 2003, pp. 164–189.

Edwards, Gail and Judith Saltman. *Picturing Canada: A History of Children's Illustrated Books and Publishing*. University of Toronto Press, 2010.

Erll, Astrid. *Kultura pamięci: wprowadzenie*. Warszawa: Wydawnictwo Uniwersytetu Warszawskiego, 2018.

Evans, Janet (ed.). *Talking Beyond the Page: Reading and Responding to Picturebooks*. Routledge, 2009.

Fee, Margery. "Romantic Nationalism and the Child in Canadian Writing." *Canadian Children's Literature*, vol. 18–19, 1980, p. 46.

Galway, Elizabeth A. *From Nursery Rhymes to Nationhood: Children's Literature and the Construction of Canadian Identity*. Routledge, 2008.

Gertridge, Alison. *Meet Canadian Authors and Illustrators*. Scholastic Canada, 1994.

Gunkel, Ann Hetzel. "Of Polka, Pierogi and Ethnic Identity: Toward a Polish American Cultural Studies." *Polish American Studies*, vol. 62, no. 1, Spring, 2005, pp. 29–42.

Hazzard, Claire. "Skrypuch, Marsha Forchuk – Prisoners in the Promised Land." *Resource Links*, 2007.

Henderson, Jennifer. "The Camp, the School, and the Child: Discursive Exchanges and (Neo)liberal Axioms in the Culture of Redress." *Reconciling Canada: Historical Injustices and the Contemporary Culture of Redress*, edited by Jennifer Henderson and Pauline Wakeham. University of Toronto Press, 2012, pp. 65–83.

Howard, Vivian. "Picturing Difference: Three Recent Picture Books Portray the Black Nova Scotian Community." *Bookbird*, vol. 51, no. 4, 2013, pp. 11–20.

Huser, Glen. *Firebird*. Ronsdale, 2020.

Janes, Daniela. "'The Clock Is Dead': Temporality and Trauma in *Rilla of Ingleside*." *Canadian Literature*, vol. 244, 2021, pp. 125–143.

Johnson, Ingrid and Joyce Bainbridge (eds.). *Reading Diversity through Canadian Picture Books: Preservice Teachers Explore Issues of Identity, Ideology, and Pedagogy*. University of Toronto Press, 2013.

Johnston, Rosemary Ross and Lissa Paul. "Approaching War: Australian and Canadian Children's Culture and the First World War." *Childhood in the Past*, vol. 7, no. 1, 2014, pp. 3–13.

Kachak, Tetiana. "Tanatychni motyvy u suchasnij ukrainskij prozi dlja ditej ta junactva." *Slavica Wratislaviensia*, vol. 168, 2019, pp. 207–217.

Kidd, Kenneth B. "T is for Trauma: The Children's Literature of Atrocity.". *Freud in Oz: At the Intersections of Psychoanalysis and Children's Literature*, edited by Kenneth B. Kidd. University of Minnesota Press, 2011.

Kiefer, Barbara Z. *The Potential of Picturebooks: From Visual Literacy to Aesthetic Understanding*. New Jersey: Prentice-Hall, 1995.

Kil, Sang Hea. "A Diseased Body Politic." *Cultural Studies*, vol. 28, no. 2, 2014, pp. 177–198.

Kordan, Bohdan S. *Enemy Aliens, Prisoners of War: Internment in Canada during the Great War*. Montréal: McGill-Queen's University Press, 2002.

Kordan, Bohdan S. and Craig Mahovsky. *A Bare and Impolitic Right: Internment and Ukrainian-Canadian Redress*. Montreal: McGill-Queen's University Press, 2004.

Kostash, Myrna. *All of Baba's Children*. [1977]. Edmonton: NeWest, 1992.

Kostash, Myrna. "Baba Was a Bohunk." *Saturday Night*, October 1976, pp. 33–39.

Langston, Laura. *Lesia's Dream*. HarperThrophy Canada, 2003.
Łebkowska, Anna. "Narracja." *Kulturowa Teoria Literatury*, edited by Michał Paweł Markowski and Ryszard Nycz. Kraków: Universitas, 2012, p. 190.
Leden, Laura. "L. M. Montgomery Censored? Canadian War Commentary in *Rilla of Ingleside* Adapted for Nordic Audiences." *The Lion and the Unicorn*, vol. 41, 2017, pp. 143–166.
Ledohowski, Lindy. "*Becoming the Hyphen: The Evolution of English-Language Ukrainian-Canadian Literature.*" *Canadian Ethnic Studies*, vol. 39, no. 1–2, 2007, pp. 107–127.
Ledohowski, Lindy. "'The Compulsion to Tell Falls on the Next Generation': Ukrainian Canadian Literature in English and Victims of the Past." *Reconciling Canada: Critical Perspectives on the culture of Redress*, edited by Jennifer Henderson and Pauline Wakeham. University of Toronto Press, 2013, pp. 198–214.
Lewis, David. *Reading Contemporary Picturebooks*. London: Routledge Falmer, 2001.
Luciuk, Kassandra and natalie marie burton. *Enemy Alien: A Graphic History of Internment in Canada During the First World War*. Toronto: Between the Lines, 2020.
Luciuk, Lubomyr Y. *In Fear of the Barbed Wire Fence: Canada's First National Internment Operations and the Ukrainian Canadians, 1914–1920*. Kashtan Press, 2001.
Luciuk, Lubomyr Y. *Ukrainians in the Making: Their Kingston Story*. Kingston: Limestone, 1980.
Luciuk, Lubomyr Y. and Bohdan S. Kordan. *Creating a Landscape: A Geography of Ukrainians in Canada*. University of Toronto Press, 1989.
McGonigal, James and Evelyn Arizpe. *Learning to Read a New Culture: How Immigrant and Asylum Seeking Children Experience Scottish Identity through Classroom Books* (Final Report). Edinburgh: Scottish Government, 2007.
Montgomery, Lucy Maud. *Rilla of Ingleside* [1921]. Prabhat Prakashan, 2017.
Niewiadomska-Flis, Urszula. *Live and Let Di(n)e: Food and Race in the Texts of the American South*. Wydawnictwo KUL, 2017.
Nikolajeva, Maria and Carole Scott. *How Picture Books Work*. New York: Routledge, 2001.
Nodelman, Perry. "Illustration and Picture Books." *International Companion Encyclopedia of Children's Literature*, edited by Peter Hunt. Routledge, 1996, p. 111–155.
Nodelman, Perry. *Words about Pictures: The Narrative Art of Children's Picture Books*. University of Georgia Press, 1988.
Petryshyn, Jaroslav and Luba Dzubak. *Peasants in the Promised Land: Canada and the Ukrainians, 1891–1914*. Toronto: JamesLorimer, 1985.
Radzilowski John and Ann Hetzel Gunkel. *Poles in Illinois*. Southern Illinois University Press, 2020.
Reimer, Mavis. "Homing and Unhoming: The Ideological Work of Canadian Children's Literature." *Home Words: Discourses of Children's Literature in Canada*, edited by Mavis Reimer. Wilfried Laurier University Press, 2008, pp. 107–128.
Rothberg, Michael. *Multidirectional Memory: Remembering the Holocaust in the Age of Decolonization*. Stanford University Press, 2009.

Satzewich, Vic. *The Ukrainian Diaspora*. Routledge, 2002.
Semchuk, Sandra. *The Stories Were Not Told: Canada's First World War Internment Camps*. University of Alberta Press, 2018.
Skrypuch, Marsha Forchuk. "Am I Ukrainian?" *Unbound: Ukrainian Canadians Writing Home*, edited by Lisa Grekul and Lindy Ledohowski. University of Toronto Press, 2016, pp. 65–72.
Skrypuch, Marsha Forchuk. "An Unexpected Visitor." *A Christmas to Remember: Tales of Comfort and Joy*. Scholastic Canada, 2009.
Skrypuch, Marsha Forchuk. *Dance of the Banished*. Pajama Press, 2014.
Skrypuch, Marsha Forchuk (ed.). *Kobzar's Children: A Century of Untold Ukrainian Stories*. Fitzhenry & Whiteside, 2006.
Skrypuch, Marsha Forchuk. *Prisoners in the Promised Land. The Ukrainian Internment Diary of Anya Soloniuk*. Scholastic Canada, 2007.
Skrypuch, Marsha Forchuk. *Silver Threads*. Illustrated by Michael Martchenko. Toronto: Fitzhenry & Whiteside, 2004.
Skrypuch, Marsha Forchuk. *Silver Threads*. Illustrated by Michael Martchenko. Toronto: Viking (Penguin Books Canada), 1996.
Skrypuch, Marsha Forchuk. *Stolen Child*. Scholastic Canada, 2010.
Story, Norah. "Ukrainians." *The Oxford Companion to Canadian History and Literature*. Oxford University Press, 1967, pp. 807–808.
Świetlicki, Mateusz. "Mój tato został gwiazdą. Tanatos w ukraińskiej książce obrazkowej." *Slavica Wratislaviensia*, vol. 168, 2019, pp. 197–206.
Świetlicki, Mateusz. "*Oh, What a Waste of Army Dreamers...*: The Revolution of Dignity and War in Contemporary Ukrainian Picturebooks." *Filoteknos*, vol. 8, 2018, pp. 118–129.
Swyripa. Frances. "The Politics of Redress: The Contemporary Ukrainian-Canadian Campaign." *Enemies Within: Italian and Other Internees in Canada and Abroad*, edited by Angelo Principle. University of Toronto Press, 2000, pp. 355–378.
Tector, Amy. "A Righteous War?: L.M. Montgomery's Depiction of the First World War in *Rilla of Ingleside*." *Canadian Literature*, vol. 179, 2003, pp. 72–86.
Thompson, Angela. "*Clark, Pam – Kalyna*." *Resource Links*, vol. 21, no. 1, 2015, pp. 24.
Ulanowicz, Anastasia. *Second-Generation Memory and Contemporary Children's Literature: Ghost Images*. Routledge, 2013.
Webb, Peter. "'A Righteous Cause': War Propaganda and Canadian Fiction, 1915–1921." *British Journal of Canadian Studies*, vol. 24, no. 1, pp. 31–48.
Wiltse, Lynne. "Historical and Contemporary Perspectives on Cultural, Social, and Political Issues in the Canadian West." *Reading Diversity through Canadian Picture Books: Preservice Teachers Explore Issues of Identity, Ideology, and Pedagogy*, edited by Ingrid Johnson and Joyce Bainbridge. University of Toronto Press, 2013, pp. 56–77.

3 Canadian Pysanky and the Survival of the Seeds of Memory

Thus faith, superstition, and incredulity strove together amongst us, as in all history.

(L.M. Montgomery, *The Story Girl*)

On Easter Saturday Anna Veryha, the eponymous heroine of Gloria Kupchenko Frolick's[1] novella published in 1992, receives a gift from her pregnant mother's godmother. Mrs. Anastasia Bidniak gives Anna a *pysanka*, a traditional ornamented Easter egg onto which designs are written with beeswax, saying: "I made it special for you because you have a good soul" (91). This scene, just like the numerous references to eggs, birth, and motherhood in *Anna Veryha*, has a symbolical meaning that goes beyond the textual frames of the book. Gifting a *pysanka*, a symbol of fertility and an emblem of Ukrainianness,[2] appears in other texts for young readers, such as Marsha Forchuk Skrypuch's *Hope's War* (2001)[3] and *Prisoners in the Promised Land: The Ukrainian Internment Diary of Anya Soloniuk* (2007), Marion Mutala's *Baba's Babushka: A Magical Ukrainian Easter* (2012), and Lisa Grekul's crossover novel *Kalyna's Song* (2003). Using Marusya Bociurkiw's observations that "*in Ukrainian, the word for writing is* pysaty *and ... the word for Easter Egg is* pysanka: *literally, written object*" (qtd. in Grekul 203; emphasis original), Grekul maintains that *pysanka* can be seen "as a tribute to [Ukrainian] literary past and as a guiding light for the future of Ukrainian Canadian literature" (204). With their references to Ukrainian traditions and Canadian popular culture, the heavily gendered texts cross-sectionally examined in this chapter, set between 1900 and 1942 in Canada, seem to echo the role of women – grandmothers, mothers, and daughters – in the symbolical transfer of the seeds of memory to the next generations. However, they also illustrate more complex issues typical of women's diasporic writing, namely negotiations with "identity, belonging, loss, guilt, powerlessness, patriarchal oppression, and objectification" (Kozaczka 10). These themes, as Grażyna J. Kozaczka notes in her analysis of Polish American fiction, are crucial for "ethnic women existing in a liminal space between

DOI: 10.4324/9781003367918-4

different cultural constructs," female characters "constructing self from the opposite pulls of disparate cultures" (Kozaczka 10, 3).

Although cultural memory is multifaceted and fragile, including new narratives may lead to changes in its scope. The elderly storyteller in Laura Langston's *Lesia's Dream* compares memory to the seeds without which the soil is barren and says to Laisha that she gives them to her to "*pass them along so they may grow and ripen and nourish*" the subsequent generations of Ukrainian Canadian women (xi; emphasis in original). This metaphor is central in the context of the role women play in the literal and metaphorical survival of nonvisible ethnic diasporas.[4] Writing about the intergenerational transfer of memory portrayed in children's literature, Anastasia Ulanowicz observes that it depends on a person's interposition within a specific genealogy. The recipient of memory has to acknowledge how her present circumstances have been formed by the older family members' "recollections and habit memories" (141). Next-generation memory transmitted by children's literature is not only anticipatory but also relational. The author's intentions and the subject position of the reader influence whether the seeds of memory can sprout or wither.

While in *Anna Veryha* Kupchenko Frolick "employs no particular stylistic tricks," as Myrna Kostash notes, "there is something nudging at her folksy material which makes it more interesting than we might expect" (254). Set at an Alberta farm on the Easter weekend of 1942, the novella portrays an episode from the life of Anna, a sensitive nine-year-old tomboy who seems anxious because her 37-year-old mother is about to give birth to a son her father so desperately wants. Aware that her mother almost died when Anna was born, the protagonist is afraid of losing her. Anna also struggles with the feeling of loneliness, as her 16-year-old sister Dotsia has recently become emotionally withdrawn. Unlike Anna, Dotsia is at odds with their strict and patriarchal father and wants to leave the hardships of the family farm for university. In her attempts to detach herself from her ethnic and class background, Dotsia aspires to perform a different version of femininity than the one represented by her submissive mother and neighbors. She looks for role models in popular culture, most notably actress Deanne Durbin and Anne Shirley, the protagonist of L.M. Montgomery's 1908 *Anne of Green Gables* and its sequels.[5]

Similarly to Langston's *Lesia's Dream, Anna Veryha* is built around the themes of death, birth, and motherhood.[6] Reading both novels I investigate how their authors depict the role of women as carriers of the seeds of memory, whose bodies emerge as symbolical *pysanky* on which cultural practices inscribe different meanings. The protagonists of the books grow up in patriarchal communities, but they negotiate with traditional gender norms.[7] Kupchenko Frolick's protagonist is surrounded by various visions of femininity performed by first- and second-generation Ukrainian Canadian women, who display conflicting approaches towards the role of women and girls in Canada, both in the diasporic and mainstream – Anglo-Canadian – frameworks. While in the context of nation and nationalism women are usually "constructed as the symbolic bearers of the nation," they "are denied any direct relation to national agency," contends Anne McClintock (252). Men, on the other hand, are "contiguous with each other and with the national whole" because they "represent the progressive agent of national modernity" (McClintock 254, 359). As I argue in this chapter, in Ukrainian Canadian children's historical fiction these dynamics tend to be questioned since it is young women who emerge as not only bearers of the nation, but also progressive agents.

In *Women and the Nation-State* (1989) Floya Anthias and Nira Yuval-Davis identify the five most common roles women play "in ethnic and national processes and in relation to state practices" (7; cf. Federici). First, as mothers they emerge as "biological reproducers of members of ethnic collectives" (7). Second, when they marry, they become the "reproducers of the boundaries of ethnic/national groups" (7). Third, as keepers of traditions, they play a crucial role "in the ideological reproduction of the collectivity and as transmitters of its culture" (7). Fourth, women are symbolical "signifiers of ethnic/national differences," which can be "used in the construction, reproduction and transformation of ethnic/national categories." Finally, they can be active "participants in national, economic, political and military struggles" (7). In most cases women perform various roles, sometimes more than one at time. Although girls and women in the novels examined in this chapter are mostly expected to become mother and bearers of memory – hence biological and symbolical reproducers of Ukrainianness – I would like to argue that they are not static and the lines between the roles they perform are blurred and overlap. Instead of reproducing the same cultural *pysanka*, characters like Lesia Magus and Anna Veryha write its new versions while questioning objectification, patriarchal oppression,[8] and negotiating with traditional and progressive types of femininity.

It is typical of Ukrainian Canadian writers to construct "young, female protagonists engaged in complex cultural and personal negotiations with their babas" (Ledohowski "Little Ukraine" 191). Yet while both Anna and Lesia negotiate with their grandmothers, who embody conservative values of continuity, in *Lesia's Dream* the eponymous protagonist not only eventually *becomes* a *baba*, the custodian of Ukrainian customs and cultural memory, but also emerges as an open-minded agent of national, Ukrainian *Canadian*, modernity. Importantly, Anna and Lesia also negotiate with characters representing the stereotype of *Nasha Meri* (Our Mary) and *Katie*. The figure of *Katie*, a young Ukrainian woman trying to assimilate and detach herself from all things Ukrainian, was used in Ukrainian Canadian press already in the 1910s. *Nasha Meri* was a satirical comic character introduced in 1930 by Jacob Maydanyk, a cartoonist known for *Uncle Shtif (Steve) Tabachniuk*, and quickly became popular among the diaspora. Frances Swyripa has argued that *Nasha Meri* and

Katie describe assimilated young women – both new immigrants and those born in Canada – "testing the freedoms and attractions of the new country," hence separating themselves from their Ukrainian roots ("Wedded to the Cause" 64). Writing about the figures of *baba* and *Nasha Meri*, I also point to the ways they are portrayed in other texts, most notably Larry Warwaruk's novels, where intermarriage further leads to the indigenization of Ukrainian Canadians, and Skrypuch's *Prisoners in the Promised Land*. Skrypuch, as I contend, introduces the reader not only to the history of Ukrainian immigration to Canada and the topic of internment, but also to the struggles of women and minorities in the early twentieth century (cf. Chapter 2).

I agree with Anthias and Yuval-Davis that "the roles that women play" in the context of the nation/state "are not merely imposed upon them" (11). On the contrary, they "actively participate in the process of reproducing and modifying their roles as well as being actively involved in controlling other women" (Anthias and Yuval-Davis 11). Hence in my close reading of the books, I examine the convergences and divergences between women representing different generations and versions of femininity. I argue that by juxtaposing their protagonists with both older women – traditional *babas* – and other, more assimilated female characters, Kupchenko Frolick and Langston create girls who negotiate between the role of future mothers and bearers of next-generation memory, and more progressive, but potentially, less Ukrainian, independent women.

Negotiating with *Babas* and Patriarchal Oppression

The focalizer of Kupchenko Frolick's *Anna Veryha* is the eponymous Anna, whose name is similar to Montgomery's Anne, yet spelled with an "a," symbolically positioning her as Ukrainian *and* Canadian. She feels excluded when Dotsia instantly connects with Victoria, their wealthy and successful older cousin from Edmonton, who pays them a visit together with the girls' grandmother, Julia. As Ledohowski notes in the introduction to *Unbound: Ukrainian Canadians Writing Home*, a volume featuring contributions by Ukrainian Canadian women writers, "Ukrainian Canadian literature regularly focuses on female characters" and "*babas* and their descendants – have long featured prominently in Ukrainian Canadian literature in English" (15). Moreover, many diasporic authors, including those of children's fiction, portray female characters who perform *gendered* ethnicity shaped by social, political, religious, and racial tensions. Anna's grandmother Julia Veryha, who comes to help her daughter-in-law with the newborn, represents the first generation of Ukrainian Canadian immigrants. The only woman in the Veryha family who truly cares about keeping customs and traditions, Julia Veryha symbolizes the Ukrainian Canadian *baba*, who emerged in the post–Second World War Canada as a "beloved figure" and a "collective myth"

(Swyripa "Wedded to the Cause" 250, 24, 255).[9] As Swyripa argues, "If Ukrainian Canadians possess a Great Woman, or indeed boast a general mythic figure, she is the peasant immigrant pioneer in western Canada in the opening decades of the twentieth century" ("Wedded to the Cause" 215). Interestingly, Ledohowski observes that in Canadian literature *baba* "elicits feelings of both nostalgia and frustration" because she epitomizes "the desire to belong as much as feelings of non-belonging, particularly in her relationship with her Canadian-born granddaughters" ("Little Ukraine" 190). This is reflected in Kupchenko Frolick's novella. Despite having some health problems, Julia Veryha stays all night cleaning the Veryhas' house, sewing a dress for Anna, and rearranging her daughter-in-law's kitchen. She cooks Ukrainian dishes and takes pride in bringing to church the most beautiful Easter basket. Hence Julia emerges as the *baba*, "the custodian of traditions" (Swyripa "Wedded to the Cause" 217). Cooking, going to church, and talking about the past with her granddaughters seem to be Julia Veryha's means of transferring Ukrainian traditions to women of the younger generations. After all, as Swyripa notes, preserving "the quality of Ukrainian-Canadian life and commitment of future generations to things Ukrainian" was the responsibility of the mothers and grandmothers ("Wedded" 1991, 242).

Julia Veryha is her granddaughters' only tangible link to the family's pioneer heritage, another typical feature of the *baba* figure (Swyripa "Wedded to the Cause" 216). At the beginning of the novella, Anna recalls her grandmother's story of coming to Canada as a teenager and quickly getting married: "[t]hree months after I come to Canada, I am a married woman. Seventeen years old! A child! Believe me – a child [...] But when I look back now, I think to myself, those were good years!" (8). Instead of talking about the hardships of immigration and settlement, or the experience of being the ethnic other in Canada, Julia Veryha romanticizes the homesteading past, reinforcing her role of the *baba*, a narrative strategy present in several more recent Ukrainian Canadian books for the young readers, most notably Warwaruk's *Andrei and the Snow Walker*, Langston's *Lesia's Dream*, and Pam Clark's *Kalyna*.

Julia Veryha, the original owner of the Veryhas' farm, moved to the city after the death of her husband. However, she feels a strong connection to the land and is critical of her daughter-in-law's housekeeping. "Grandmother probably wouldn't even notice all the hard work they'd done," as she "would notice only what they hadn't done," thinks the protagonist before her Baba's[10] arrival (15). Julia is critical of her son's wife Vera, who replaced her as the lady of the house. While Anna's mother is an obedient and hardworking woman who "never said a word" and "never talked back" (39), her mother-in-law disapproves of her. This attitude can be explained by the fact that Vera represents the in-between second-generation Ukrainian Canadian femininity: she cooks plain Canadian dishes, such as porridge, and does not keep the house as clean as Julia used to. The older woman's attitude changes only when Vera Veryha gets pregnant. As Weronika Suchacka, agreeing with Swyripa, notes "it was the potential aspect of [Ukrainian Canadian women's] femaleness, namely the motherhood, that was so highly valued as their contribution" (203). The grandmother symbolically starts to value Anna's mother only when she is about to give birth to a boy, a child who can ensure the continuity of the Ukrainian family name.

Julia Veryha is the only person the readers are introduced to who sometimes uses Ukrainian words and has a heavy accent, making her "ashamed to speak in English in front of people" (122). Her accent positions her as the Other in Anglo-Canada. Anna notices that unlike the accent French Canadians speak with, which English speakers, including the members of her community, find "cute" (112), the Ukrainian way of speaking is seen as something less desirable. Julia, the only Ukrainian Canadian woman in the Veryha family born in Ukraine, is the symbolic guardian of cultural memory and traditional gender roles. Yet she is a complex character who defies the *baba* stereotype. Although Julia sees marriage as the most important aspiration for girls and young women, her own widowhood provides her with independence and social respect unreachable to married or single women. Hence widowhood can be read as another link between *Anna Veryha* and the *Anne of Green Gables* series (cf. Gubar). Kupchenko Frolick's choice of Julia Veryha's headpiece, a "pot-style hat decorated with ribbon and purple pansies" (77) instead of a traditional Ukrainian headscarf associated with the *baba* figure, further problematizes her gender role. Swyripa notes that "in their preference for hats Nasha Meri and Katie were making a statement of freedom and independence, perhaps they were also rejecting women's traditional status and roles that the headscarf symbolized" ("Wedded to the Cause" 93). Here the statement of independence is made by the *baba*, Julia Veryha, the guardian of Ukrainian customs and traditions but also a widow living on her own in the city, who comes to the farm carrying an Easter basket, yet arrives in a car driven by Victoria, the novel's symbolical *Katie*.

"The role of women as ideological reproducers is very often related to women being seen as the 'cultural carriers' of the ethnic group," argue Anthias and Yuval-Davis (9). In Langston's *Lesia's Dream* the only link between the present-day teenager Laisha and her Ukrainian heritage turns out to be her great-grandmother, who says: "*You are Canadian, you tell them* [the teachers]. *Born here. Just as your mother and grandmother [...] You do not know of heritage. You know only of me*" (ix; emphasis in original). Laisha's limited knowledge does not seem surprising considering the role the assimilation policy has had on the second-, third- and fourth-generation Ukrainian Canadians. It is not coincidental that she learns about her heritage from Lesia, her great-grandmother who came to Canada in 1914 at the age of 15. As we learn throughout the novel, without Lesia's homesteading struggles there would be no Laisha, and without those of the early Ukrainian immigrants, no Ukrainian Canadians:

Ach, sixteen. Back then, I carried within me the egg that would become your grandmother, the egg that would become your mother and the one that would become you. Yes, I carried generation in my loins. And even then I carried memories,

says Lesia in her prologue highlighting the role of femininity and motherhood in the survival of Ukrainian Canadians (x; emphasis in original). In the last chapter Lesia again turns to her great-granddaughter, highlighting the similarities and differences between Lesia's and Laisha's experiences. Then, speaking of herself, Lesia states: "*I am more than Canadian. I am more than Ukrainian. Those are my roots, yet, but I am more than roots. I carry within me memories, and now I scatter these memory seeds upon you*" (208; emphasis in original). With these words, the protagonist marks her great-granddaughter as another carrier and potential giver of memory, passing onto her the function she has had since her grandmother died. By emphasizing the role of the intergenerational transfer of memory and traditions, Langston shows the dynamics according to which the interest in the past is shown by third- or fourth-generation members of the diaspora, brought up by their more future-oriented and assimilated parents. Thanks to this narrative form, the story of Lesia can be read as one whose aim is to transfer memory, both individual and cultural, to the next generation – symbolically represented in the novel by Laisha.

As Anthias and Yuval-Davis observe, it is women who are usually "required to transmit the rich heritage of ethnic symbols and ways of life to the other members of the ethnic group, especially the young" (9). The role of grandmothers as givers of cultural memory is reflected in Marion Mutala's *Baba's Babushka* series and Skrypuch's *Prisoners in the Promised Land*. While the eponymous grandmother in Mutala's picturebooks is dead, her spirit looks after Natalia from heaven as the picturebooks contain double spreads showing Baba's face on a cloud. In every picturebook Baba sends Natalia a *babushka* or headscarf, which transfers the girl to Ukraine (cf. Chapter 1). Wearing her grandmother's scarves, Natalia travels in time and space and witnesses first-hand Ukrainian Christmas, Easter, and wedding traditions in the old country. She also meets her ancestors and watches the departure of her Baba and grandfather to Canada. While all of the picturebooks end with Natalia waking up, her travels are not oneiric because she brings material objects from Ukraine. In *Baba's Babushka: A Magical Ukrainian Wedding* (2013, illustrated by Amber Rees), she takes the wedding icon her grandparents forgot to pack. Moreover, she also directly influences the past. The *pysanka*, which Baba gave to her future husband when she was still in her teens, turns out to be the one Natalia makes at the beginning of *Baba's Babushka: A Magical Ukrainian Easter* (2012, illustrated by Wendy Siemens) and later magically brings from Canada. Hence Natalia's journey in time and space to Ukraine turns out to be necessary for the survival of her family and provokes her to think: "What would have happened if I hadn't been there to help?". Without the help of Natalia, the Canadian granddaughter, who gives the *pysanka* to her teenage grandmother, Baba would never have gifted it to her future husband, married him, and moved to Canada, where she escaped the First World War, the Holodomor, and the Second World War.

Anya's Baba in Skrypuch's novel moves to Canada, but unlike other *babas* discussed in this chapter, she does it at an old age; therefore, she finds it difficult to adjust to the new circumstances. Baba tries not to leave her new home, where she cooks traditional Ukrainian dishes like *pyrohy*. The kitchen becomes her haven and substitute for the old country. Despite the Soloniuks' poverty, she manages to prepare the traditional 12 Christmas Eve dishes. This encourages Anya to write down their names in her diary and explain some of the Ukrainian customs to the readers. Later, it is the grandmother who initiates the preparation of a traditional Christmas Eve dinner in the Spirit Lake camp (193; cf. Chapter 2). However, in a manner dissimilar from the other Ukrainian Canadian novels, *Prisoners in the Promised Land* does not portray a special bond between the protagonist and her Baba. Anya's grandmother is not a "wise old mentor" or an "elderly storyteller"; she is the only one who stays at home, as even Mykola, Anya's younger brother, eventually goes to school. She also has problems with assimilating and adapting to the new Canadian lifestyle. As we learn from the epilogue, Anya's Baba fails to learn basic English or French. While in Langston's novel Lesia's heritage helps her survive in Canada, Anya symbolically detaches herself from the old country by distancing herself from her grandmother and performing a more progressive type of femininity.

Because *Dear Canada* is a series directed mainly at girl readers, Anya in Skrypuch's *Prisoners* also learns about British and Canadian Suffragettes and sympathizes with them.[11] Observing politicians and other men making dubious decisions, and comparing them with the intelligent women she knows, at first only educated ones[12] but later also her own mother, Anya starts believing that all women, not only "white women with property," should have voting rights (63). "Why are those Suffragettes just interested in giving the vote to women like themselves? What about all the other people?" Anya wonders in a surprisingly open-minded way (63). Hastening the enfranchisement of women seems a necessity for Anya who witnesses women and girls who support their families when men lose their jobs, are arrested, or interned. Unexpectedly, Anya also becomes the sole breadwinner of the family, because against her father's will, she gains employment at the local clothes factory where most of her Ukrainian classmates also work. Her employment is possible not only because of the sewing skills her mother taught her, but also because of a parents' note Stefan helps her to forge. After all, at the age of 12, Anya is too young to legally work and Canadian children are expected to attend school. By rebelling against her father, Anya rejects the role of a housekeeper and patriciates in the economic struggles of her family. She does, however, become the keeper of the internment memory discussed in Chapter 2, yet one who significantly differs from her Ukrainian grandmother.

Before Lesia Magus becomes a heroic pioneer, reminiscent of John Weaver's statue *Madonna of the Wheat* erected in Edmonton, and then a *baba*, she also negotiates with her own Ukrainian grandmother. Before her death, the grandmother sends Lesia a letter and a parcel: a chest made by the protagonist's late grandfather, containing embroidery tools and scarves, which are attributes of traditional femininity, and a jar of honey, representing hard work and the effects it brings. On the day when the girl learns about her grandmother's death, her mother starts giving birth. Confused, Lesia does not know what to do, but she hears in her head her grandmother's voice telling her how to help deliver a baby. The woman appears in the novel like a Jungian archetype of the Great Mother, who cares about cultivating the richness of the matriarchal tradition (cf. Jung). Thanks to the symbolic help of her grandmother's spirit, Lesia manages to help with the birth of her brother, whom the mother calls Adam in honor of her own grandfather. The name can also be read as a symbol of a new beginning, as the child is the first in the Magus family born in Canada and is both Ukrainian and Canadian. To quote Margery Fee, "the child seems a natural symbol to represent the land, or the nation" (46). It is no coincidence that for most of the novel Lesia is a young woman, as gender plays an important role in mnemonic diasporic narratives. The protagonist's mother, suffering from anemia, may lose her child at any time, and because of hunger, both Lesia and her younger sister may stop the future reproductive cycle, leading to the symbolic death of the diaspora. Lesia's mother gives birth to Adam. Lesia, as we learn from the epilogue, not only becomes a valued member of the community but soon gives birth to another Canadian child. Her fertility metaphorically shows the potential of the diaspora for survival and auto-reproduction (cf. Ulanowicz 139–142).[13]

The theme of childbirth is also of great importance in *Anna Veryha*. Grandmother Veryha often criticizes the protagonist's thin body saying: "Eat, Anna, eat – you're like a little stick [...] Girls should be plump and round. Men don't care for bony women" (101). When they are trying on their best church clothes, the woman also comments on Anna's lack of hips, although Victoria, a trained nurse comments that this is typical for children her age (83). It is no accident that all of Baba's comments are connected to her granddaughter's fertility because Anna's role as the future guardian of the Ukrainian Canadian hearth is hinted at throughout the novella. The cover of the book, a painting by William Kurelek personally selected by Kupchenko Frolick, features a nest with three blue eggs, symbols of new life and the three children of the Veryhas.[14] Birth and death are recurring themes in *Anna Veryha*, set during Easter, the celebration of the death and resurrection of Jesus Christ. It starts with the death of a mouse for whom Anna sings a lullaby and buries in her secret cemetery, and ends with Anna going to the cemetery to see the grave of her brother at the time when her mother is about to give birth to another son. At the beginning, Gregory Veryha[15] screams at his apologetic and obedient daughter who wants to show kindness and pay respect to the mouse, but at the end, after she promises to help with the baby, the man says "[t]hat's my Anna!" and gives her an orange, a biblical emblem of prosperity, love, and happiness (129). In the past Anna used to bury animals in the secret cemetery with Dotsia. Together they paid respect to a bluebird, the symbol of the male child of the Sun in the Cochiti tribe, a spirit in the Navajo folklore, and hope in Slavic fairytales. For the first time, Anna has to do it alone, as her teenage sister has metaphorically flown away. While burying animals by children in the countryside can be read as a form of play, it is also an important means of acting-out traditional rituals. Anna prays for the mouse and even considers putting a little cross on its grave, yet decides not to, being too afraid of her despotic father. On Easter Sunday, Anna secretly goes to pray at the grave of the brother she and Dotsia never met, yet whose memory haunts their family. Her prayers are answered as on Easter Sunday Vera Veryha gives birth to a healthy boy, their "Easter miracle," whom Anna decides to name Gregory Victor, in honor of her father and godfather (128).

Except for Warwaruk's novels, all fathers in the texts examined in this chapter disregard their wives and daughters regardless of their aspirations and the type of femininity they perform. Gregory Veryha discredits the work of his wife. Saying "I'm running this farm all by myself," he fails to acknowledge that his wife works as hard as he does, a fact Anna struggles to understand (34).[16] The father of Anya Soloniuk in Skrypuch's *Prisoners in the Promised Land* does not even want to let his wife maintain religious traditions, believing that "religion should be left in the old country" (36). This causes his wife's strong opposition because in the Soloniuk family, like in the Magus' or the Veryhas', it is the women who are responsible for passing on the customs and cultural memory, with religion being one of its key elements. The role of the keeper of traditions was typical of other immigrant Slavic women, as it was "the Mother, who held the two places together, just as she held her family together" (Kurelek and Engelhart 35).

In *Lesia's Dream* it is mainly thanks to the protagonist's efforts that her mother, who is suffering from anemia, can maintain the pregnancy after her husband and son have left looking for work. Not only does Lesia grub up the land and cultivate the garden, but she also learns to hunt and makes a hole in the dam on the lake, which was installed by her Ukrainian-hating Anglo-Canadian neighbor, thus fruitfully restricting the Magus family's access to fish. Importantly, Lesia's absent father forbids the girl to borrow money because pride is more important to him than the survival of his family. The man neglects Lesia's situation, his wife's pregnancy, and his younger daughter's health. Lesia's father's indifference and his blindness to his daughter's perspective symbolize not only a patriarchal sense of superiority but also the conviction that apart from pride, he has nothing. Motivated by honor, he immediately sends a large sum of money to Master Stryk, after which he is accused of collaborating with Austro-Hungary and sent to an internment camp (cf. Chapter 2). Even after being interned, he cannot understand another perspective, clinging to his pride. The only thing Lesia gets from her father are shoes that are too large for her, which he passes on to the girl during her visit to the camp at the insistence of his son. The shoes become a symbol of the magnitude of the problems that Lesia has been struggling with since the beginning of the novel, *de facto* acting as the head of the Magus family and the main breadwinner. However, by remembering about the traditions and values handed down to her by her grandmother *and* performing stereotypical male tasks, she is able to survive and maintain the survival of the seeds of memory. Using sewing tools which she receives from her Ukrainian grandmother, Lesia creates traditional belts, similar to the ones made by Anya in Skrypuch's *Prisoners in the Promised Land*, which she sells to the local women.[17] Lesia, who was once a beekeeper, regrets that there are still no bees in her garden. However, the honey sent from Ukraine at least temporarily evokes the belief that Lesia's dream will come true and she will be respected, literate, and her family will never starve again. As we learn from the last chapter of the novel, after all of Lesia's struggles and sacrifices, bees eventually appear in her garden. Soon after the arrival of bees, the symbols of life and hope, Lesia marries Andrew and becomes pregnant with her first child.

Negotiating with More Progressive Versions of Femininity

Theodosia, known as Dotsia, is Anna's 16-year-old sister, named after their late older brother Theodosius. The use of this name may signify that for her parents the girl was to be a replacement of the son who died in infancy. Considering Kupchenko Frolick's numerous textual references to Christianity, it is worth mentioning that Saint Theodosia of Tyre was a 17-year-old martyr who refused to reject her beliefs. Similar to her patron saint, Dotsia is resistant to conformity. She does not want to replicate the patriarchal old world values and is eager to assimilate. Although she is girlish, Dotsia performs a significantly different type of femininity than the one represented by other women in her community. She is nothing like her obedient mother, representative of the first generation of Ukrainian Canadians born in Canada, and grandmother, the guardian of traditions and patriarchy. Unlike Vera and Anna, Dotsia frequently argues with her hard-working father and disapproves of his angry and ill-mannered behavior, for instance, the way he eats. Enchanted with Anglo-Canadian culture, she calls him "pops," making Gregory Veryha even more furious. While criticizing his daughter's behavior, the man says "Dotsia – you're a school girl – not some Kickata-Katie" (28). The use of this name does not seem coincidental as Dotsia and her cousin Victoria seem to echo the stereotypes of *Nasha Meri* and *Katie*. Dotsia's behavior echoes Swyripa's words that "Nasha Meri and Katie personified female rebellion against traditional demanding and subservient roles, parental expectations, and community directive in the name of the larger good" ("Wedded to the Cause" 65). Anna's sister, whom grandmother Veryha calls "the smart one" (78), rebels not only against the societal expectations put upon women of older generations, but also has dissimilar aspirations to her sister and friend Odarka, who love listening to her stories.

Dotsia dreams of "a better house" and Anna "kn[ows] by heart every room of her sister's imaginary house. It would be white with green shutters on the windows," similar to the one in *Anne of Green Gables* (41–42). As Paige Gray notes in her analysis of Montgomery's novel, "[i]magination in *Anne of Green Gables* serves not only as a source of pleasure for Anne, but also as a source of survival, motivation, and power" (169). Moreover, Janet Wesselius argues that "Anne's reading is part of learning to negotiate that tension between her imagination and the shared world of her body with its freckled and red hair" (34). A similar thing can be said about Dotsia. The fantasies of Anne, "a poor, clever girl with no family and few options in early twentieth-century Canada," give her comfort and "mentally create safe havens and luminous spaces" (Gray 169). Dotsia, disappointed with her harsh life on the farm, and afraid of becoming like her obedient mother, visualizes a different world and her imaginative capacity allows her to believe that she has other options. Similar to *Anne of Green Gables*, in which, as Gray observes, "imagination serves as a means to achieve liberation [...] a process of breaking from conventional gender expectations, in thought and action – a realization of the imagined" (170), in *Anna Veryha* imagination allows Dotsia to escape from her ordinary reality. While Anne "creates her own visionary reality [...] through her reconstruction of the world in terms of medieval romance and classical beauty," Dotsia seeks for inspiration in literature and popular culture (Gray 170). In this context it is worth noting that although Anne is a worldwide pop-cultural phenomenon whose status has been further boosted in the last four decades by numerous film adaptations and merchandising,[18] she is also the quintessential symbol of Anglo-Canadian girlhood (cf. Galway 9). Less than two decades after the publication of Montgomery's novel, critics already argued that it is "a text that is in a process of building a particular kind of imagined community in English Canada" (Devereux 21). Hence it is not surprising that references to Anne and her unrestricted imagination have appeared in numerous Canadian books for young readers, which "played a special role in the process of [Canadian] nation-building" (Richter xiv).[19] Laura Robinson maintains that the redhead Anne Shirley is an outsider "who achieves acceptance in a new cultural space," hence the novel reflects the importance of accepting differences (20). However, Cecily Devereux argues that while Anne is initially positioned as the Other, her integration to the local community can be read "within a white settler mythology of 'Canadianness,'" because despite her "marginalized, disempowered, impoverished" position, she is an "Anglo-Celtic" girl "who comes in, makes good and 'wins through'" (24).

Although Dotsia is not Anglo-Celtic, she like Anne also benefits from the privileges of white invisibility (cf. Frankenberg 1–2). She believes that her intellect and academic aspirations may help her leave the farm and "win through." Education provided Ukrainian Canadian women with the opportunity to climb the social ladder and assimilate "to Anglo-Canadian ideas and attitudes" and risk the loss of the seeds of memory (Swyripa "Wedded to the Cause" 79).[20] Dotsia dreams of studying at university and sees that escaping the farm is possible, as her idol Deanna Durbin (1921–2013) "a Winnipeg-born girl who got away from Winnipeg" (17) managed to make it in Hollywood. This Canadian actress and singer starred alongside Judy Garland in *Every Sunday* (1936) and in the late 1930s played the ideal teenage daughter in a number of hugely successful films, including *Three Smart Girls* (1938). Like the actress, whose name sounds like a combination of both Anna and Dotsia *and* Anna and Diana – the kindred spirits in *Anne of Green Gables* – Dotsia is traditionally beautiful. Because of her looks and imagination, she is also the most popular girl at school. Unlike Durbin, she has "no dreams of Hollywood," but hopes "[t]o escape from her harsh life on the farm" (17). As Swyripa notes, for young Ukrainian Canadians "the city represented material amenities and North American popular culture" ("Wedded to the Cause" 91). While moving to the city meant "freedom from often circumscribed and isolated life on the homestead," it could also mean "financial independence," and most importantly in the context of Dotsia, "escape from unwanted filial obligations, female roles, and parental authority" (Swyripa "Wedded to the Cause" 91). Looking at the picture of Durbin "makes [Dotsia] think that there's a place [...] where the sun is always shining" (17). For her, that place is Edmonton, the city where her cousin Victoria lives.

Like the stereotypical *Nasha Meri*, Dotsia wants to rebel against the role of a submissive and virtuous daughter that Ukrainian women were traditionally expected to perform. Moreover, women living on the prairie, unlike their relatives in the city, had to combine the role of guardians of traditions and patriarchy with work as hard as their husbands'. Therefore, by moving to Edmonton, the teenage Dotsia wishes to escape all of her filial obligations. Literary teenage characters, as Lydia Kokkola argues, are "a means by which adults can express their hopes, beliefs and fears about what teenagers could and might be like, and what the wider social implications of this might be" (11). Hence it can be argued that Dotsia represents the hopes and fears associated with the assimilation of young Ukrainian Canadian women and the possible loss of new generations of guardians of traditions.

The Ukrainian Canadian community Kupchenko Frolick portrays is even more patriarchal than those depicted in texts set 30 or 40 years earlier, such as *Lesia's Dream* or *Andrei and the Snow Walker*. Although Lesia and Marusia/Marie in the novels improve their situation by marrying, for Dotsia this is only an alternative plan. Dotsia's desire to make Tony Melnyk, a local womanizer, notice her, can be linked to her quest for independence. In the possibility of marrying a wealthy man, Dotsia seems to see an option to escape the hardships of the farm. To impress Tony, Dotsia puts on a "dark red lipstick [...] called Persian Red" and wears her hair in a similar way to Deanna Durbin, yet, as her sister notes, she "needed a lot more practice with this new and glamorous hairstyle" (43). Seeing her fascination with Tony, Mr. Lesyk, a friend of Gregory Veryha, warns Dotsia: "you watch those Melnyks [...] if I had a girl, I wouldn't let any one of them Melnyks near her with a ten-foot pole, and that includes their old man!" (67). This quotation illustrates a pattern in *Anna Veryha*: all men objectify Dotsia. They either openly flirt with her (Elias, Tony, Mr. Melnyk) or want to protect her chastity (Gregory Veryha, Mr. Lesyk, Victor). Most disturbingly, Mr. Melnyk, the father of Tony and Odarka, "a tiny, wind-burned man with deep creases around his mouth and eyes," who, like other men in the novella, "seemed attractive to Anna," openly flirts with Dotsia (50). When Anna and Dotsia visit their farm, he asks, "how do you like my kovbassa" and adds, "[n]othing but finest meat here," while looking only at the older Veryha sister (50–51). Anna, the child focalizer of the story, sees the flirt but is unaware of the highly inappropriate sexual overtones in Mr. Melnyk's question about the sausage, an obvious phallic symbol, which the younger readers may also miss. Even though Dotsia seems fascinated with Durbin and Anne Shirley, she has another role model, Mahatma Gandhi, the Indian lawyer and political ethicist who inspired nonviolent movements for civil rights across the world. Dotsia wishes he were her grandfather because of his nice and calm face, different from the hypermasculine men she is surrounded by. While Dotsia tries to rebel against her father and the social expectations embodied by her grandmother, she also seems persistent but peaceful in her actions.

Dotsia's fascination with Anglo-Canadian girlhood and disapproval of the traditional Ukrainian gender dynamics and class status are further displayed by her appearance and her fascination with cousin Victoria. The woman represents not only the new independent woman but also a Ukrainian Canadian one who has managed to make it in the Anglo-Canadian city of Edmonton. When Dotsia and Anna finally meet their wealthy 26-year-old cousin, who lives in the city, they are both enchanted. While Dotsia is impressed by Victoria's independence, Anna admires her clothes[21] and beauty as "she'd never seen anyone look so... shining clean" (78). Victoria's cleanliness is contrasted with Anna's dirty clothes and signifies her outsider status in the novella's chronotope. Victoria shows Dotsia and Anna that there are opportunities other than getting married. When the girls go to church with their grandmother, wearing their best clothes, everyone focuses on Victoria, whose white outfit symbolizes purity and assimilation with Anglo-Canadian ideas, indicating her outsider position. A local doctor living with his dominating mother, another man described as a seducer, who usually ignores the Veryhas, tries to ask Victoria on a date. Feeling her lack of interest in the man, Anna helps her by coming up with a story that she is engaged, making their grandmother furious.

Julia Veryha does not share the sentiments of her granddaughters and says that "Victoria was so fussy about choosing a husband that she'd be a sour old maid if she waited too long" (78). Anna's Baba seems not to care about Victoria's successful career; her value is reduced to her marriageability. Education provided young women with more independence but also allowed to "postpone marriage or to create viable alternatives" (Swyripa "Wedded to the Cause" 69). It is worth noting that the struggle for self-determination of ethnic, non-Anglo-Canadian women was linked to their dual role in local communities and in Canadian society (Swyripa "Wedded" 1991, 240). Women like Victoria and Dotsia were faced with another problem. As Swyripa notes, they had "to improve their position in an Anglo-dominated society (as women and as non–Anglo-Canadians) while simultaneously addressing their position (as women) within their group" ("Wedded" 1991, 240). Social mobility of Ukrainian Canadian women was difficult because of their gender and ethnicity. Next to the generally "low immigrant entrance status," women also had to face "the nativism shared by Anglo-Canadian men and women alike, and Canadian attitudes to women's roles in both public and private spheres" ("Wedded" 1991, 241). Victoria, as her name implies, meaning victory, but also an obvious reference to the British Queen Victoria, has managed to improve her social position, not only in the eyes of the Veryhas. She is "a nursing supervisor at the Edmonton General Hospital" who quickly bonds with Dotsia and tells the older Veryha sister that she can live with her when she decides to go to university. Her profession is indeed remarkable, as the gender gap in education before the Second World War was especially high for Slavs, and only "1.5 per cent of the Ukrainian female labour force" consisted of nurses (Swyripa "Wedded to the Cause" 72; cf. Kozaczka 14). The situation of women living in the city significantly differed from that of rural women. Unlike their relatives from the countryside, women like Victoria could study and earn money, becoming more independent, which Dotsia desires. Yet independence could also lead to assimilation and the loss of future bearers and givers of memory. Remarkably, it is Victoria who tells Dotsia "you'll be at university next year" and assures her that "there are a thousand Tonys out there [...] he's not for you" (99). By saying so, she symbolically renounces their role as future mothers and guardians of Ukrainian customs and traditions – one that Anna is destined to perform.

Throughout Kupchenko Frolick's novella, the readers see Anna's fascination with domesticity that distinguishes her from her sister Dotsia, who dreams of escaping from the farm and assimilating. Anna looks up to Dotsia and often picks up her vocabulary and ways of conduct, but she does not act in a traditionally feminine way. Yet she is the one who represents the future guardian of customs and traditions. After all, writing about American literature Sharon O'Brien observes that tomboyism is often seen as "a very common phase through which little girls would pass on their way to the safe harbor of domestic femininity" (354). While *Anna Veryha* reflects more conservative social norms from the 1940s, it is worth noting that in many contemporary children's books, the ideals of gender and sexuality are more diverse, with the boundaries between genders and what is considered "normal" behavior frequently blurred. *"Please dear God let my mother have a baby boy so my father will be happy,"* Anna prays obediently, knowing that the birth of another daughter would make her father furious (104; emphasis in original). Her sister, on the other hand, is anxious, knowing that having to take care of a sibling can force her to give up on her dreams. Notably, after the death of Matthew near the end of *Anne of Green Gables*, the eponymous protagonist decides to postpone her dreams of going to university and stays in Avonlea to take care of Marilla and Green Gables. Anna does not want her sister to back out, and agrees to take care of the baby, whose name she is asked to choose: "Anna promised Dotsia that she'd take over. 'Don't worry, Dotsia. I'll take care of the baby. When you're studying, I'll take it out for long walks in my old carriage. Don't worry'," she reassures her older sister (29). On Easter Sunday, Anna repeats the promise, this time to their father. By embracing the symbolical role of the mother, Anna not only allows her sister to follow her dreams but also embodies femininity that is not as distant as the one Dotsia wants to perform and not as patriarchal as the one represented by adult women from her grandmother's and mother's generations. While Anne Shirley wins through on her own, it takes the sacrifice of Anna for Dotsia to do so.

In Langston's *Lesia's Dream* the eponymous carrier and giver of memory is juxtaposed with another Ukrainian Canadian girl, Minnie. The first child in the Korol family born in Canada, three days after their arrival at the homestead, Minnie represents the *Nasha Meri* and *Katie* stereotype. From the very beginning, the girl, who is the niece of Andrew, Lesia's future partner, shows an open dislike for the protagonist. Like Anglo-Canadians and previously Michal, the son of the Polish master, she calls Lesia stupid, poor, and dirty. It is also through her denunciation that the authorities find out that the Magus family comes from Austria-Hungary, which in turn leads to the internment of Lesia's father (cf. Chapter 2). Minnie does not accept Lesia's traditional dress and hairstyle, her ethnic signifiers, or her musculature suggesting her hard physical work.[22] Lesia represents everything from which girls like Minnie and Dotsia in *Anna Veryha* want to escape. Unlike Dotsia, who is portrayed as a sympathetic character, Minnie emerges as the novel's villain, who eventually changes because of Lesia. At first Minnie ridicules the Magus' house, although she was born in a similar one. Even when she falls in love with Wasyl, a poor Ukrainian man, and when her father, despite his Canadian citizenship, is interned, Minnie does not change her attitude towards Lesia. In the final, symbolic scene, both Lesia and Minnie go to the marketplace to trade fresh bread, butter, and eggs. Although from the first meeting Minnie considers herself better than the protagonist, in the eyes of most Canadians, the girls are no different – both are Ukrainian. When Lesia reads an English inscription on a riverbank that says "danger," Minnie is shocked and says "[y]ou're not so dumb after all," to which Lesia answers: "Ukrainians, like *us*, are smart people" (192; emphasis in original). After a few hours, the protagonist is still unable to convince the crowds present at the market to buy their products. They constantly hear that bread and butter are either too expensive, cheap, or spoiled. Only when Lesia saves Amy Scott, a Canadian girl who falls into the river, do people start to perceive the Ukrainian teenagers differently and buy all their products. Unlike Lesia, who is proud of her heritage and accepts all of the hardships, Minnie wants to assimilate at the cost of breaking away from the traditions connected to the old country. Although Minnie is the only character who openly aspires to be like Anglo-Canadians and positions new immigrants as the Others, her family also justify the xenophobic behavior of their neighbors and other inhabitants of the province. Andrew, Lesia's future husband, emphasizes the need to believe in Canadian democracy and the importance of participating in civic life, as well as the pursuit of economic prosperity, which he, like the novel's other characters, identifies as the only way to gain social – that is Anglo-Canadian – acceptance.

Minnie is juxtaposed with Lesia, who remembers her grandmother's words about the equality of all people, the value of hard work, and the importance of faith. Seeing an Anglo-Canadian child in danger of drowning, the protagonist realizes that "[s]he wasn't worthless or useless or stupid. She wasn't dirty or scrawny, a liar of a thief. She was Lesia Magus, beloved daughter, beloved sister. Keeper of traditions, steward of the land" (196). Moreover, "she was a Ukrainian with a clear sense of right and wrong" (196). It is not assimilation but traditional values which provoke Lesia to risk drowning by trying to save the Anglo-Canadian child. Although the protagonist's heroic act eventually helps her and Minnie sell all of the bread and butter, Jack Scott, the father of Amy, the saved child, is unable to show gratitude. However, Lesia does not care about the man's behavior because, as she says, "[s]he had the approval of someone far more important. Herself" (198). After saving the child, she not only gains the confidence and respect she wanted but also finally connects with Minnie, symbolically saving a future mother and guardian of Ukrainian traditions from full assimilation into the Anglo-Canadian community at the expense of her heritage.

The role of women as reproducers of the boundaries of ethnic groups is common in many cultures. The reluctance to let women marry non-Ukrainian men can be explained by the belief that "the group suffered when it lost its future mothers to a rival culture" (Swyripa "Wedded to the Cause" 97). Hence it also risked losing the guardians and future givers of the seeds of Ukrainian cultural memory. The issues of assimilation and marrying outside of the diaspora are explored in Warwaruk's *Andrei and the Snow Walker* and *Brovko's Amazing Journey*, where Andrei's sister Marusia changes her name and marries a non-Ukrainian man. Before Marusia becomes Marie, she rejects a wealthy Ukrainian Canadian man *and* her former Ukrainian boyfriend. When Wasyl Kuzyk, a wealthy single man in his forties, living with his overprotective mother, comes to his new neighbors, the Baydas, with welcome gifts, a hen and a cow, he instantly notices Marusia, who is a teenager. The man asks if she "know[s] that here in Canada they would [call her] *Mary?*" (50; emphasis in original). Marusia refuses both the Anglo-Canadian name Mary and Kuzyk, who is much older. Kuzyk courts Marusia not because he falls in love, but because "a man should have a wife," and in Andrei's sister he sees a potential future mother of his children and the keeper of Ukrainian traditions (70). Considering that "a wife [was] an important asset on the Ukrainian farm," Kuzyk wants to get a wife and a laborer in one ("Wedded to the Cause" 88). When Andrei and Marusia/Marie[23] start working for Kuzyk, his mother feeds them traditional Ukrainian borscht and scrutinizes the way the girl cleans and cooks, evaluating their potential as a future wife and housekeeper. The old woman treats Marusia/Marie like an object, saying to Paraska, Andrei's mother, that her teenage "daughter isn't getting any younger" (81). Nevertheless, Marusia/Marie rejects Mr. Kuzyk's marriage proposal as for her "[m]oney isn't everything" (77). When Marusia/Marie receives a letter from Petrus, her old Ukrainian boyfriend, in which he says that he is coming to Canada before Christmas, she is thrilled as she sees being with Petrus as a better option than marrying Kuzyk. Yet Marusia/Marie does not want to marry either of them.

Marusia/Marie quickly rejects the Anglo-Canadian name *Mary* introduced by Kuzyk, but her reaction is different when Gabriel, a young and handsome Métis man, tells her that Marusia "is *Marie*, in the French language," which the Métis use (31). Appalled by the possibility of marrying the old Kuzyk, Marusia changes her name; "call me *Marie*," she tells Andrei, adding that they are "in Canada. No more *Marusia*" (73). By changing her name, the girl symbolically detaches herself from Ukrainianness *and* Anglo-Canadian culture mentioned by Kuzyk; thus, she also dissociates herself from the stereotypical *Nasha Meri* (cf. Swyripa "Wedded to the Cause" 64). First Andrei disregards Marie's decision, but since his sister insists on being called by the new name, he accepts it, later explaining to their father that "[s]he changed her name [...] to be more Canadian," which in Warwaruk's novels means not Anglo-Canadian, but Métis (92; cf. Chapter 1). Whereas Marie rejects Kuzyk, for whom marriage is just a transaction, she immediately connects with Gabriel, and as Andrei quickly realizes, it is Gabriel she wants to marry, not Petrus.

As I argue in Chapter 1, Andrei sees Gabriel as "almost Ukrainian." In the non-Ukrainian community Marie emerges as "almost Métis" (106). While her traditional outfit "stand[s] out, as the [Métis] women's dresses are either white or black," the beadwork and embroidered flowers on their outfits echo typical Ukrainian patterns worn by Marie (106; cf. Chapter 1). She also wears traditional moccasins made by Gabriel's mother, a token of acceptance and a symbol of indigenization. Andrei notices that while Gabriel becomes more "Ukrainian," Marie learns "to be Canadian," here synonymous with Métis. Watching Gabriel with his sister, Andrei sees Marie's "eyes sparkle" in a way being with Petrus never did (109). At the dance, the couple connect even more, and Gabriel gives Marie "the branch of red cranberries," similar to the Ukrainian *kalyna*, another symbol of the alleged similarities between Ukrainians and the Métis (156). During one of their subsequent secret meetings, Gabriel also gives Marie a vest, another emblem of the links between the immigrants and Indigenous Peoples. Seeing Marie sneak home at night, Paraska is upset. "*Oi*, Marusia [...] You are leaving us, Marusia?," she says, to which her daughter replies: "Marie, my name is Marie, and if you have to know, I was at a dance [...] At Fish Creek" (160). The mother is devastated because she wants Marie to marry "a nice Ukrainian boy" and tells her, once again ignoring her chosen name, "[y]ou have your family, Marusia. Don't turn your back on your family" (161). The attitudes expressed by Paraska Bayda in *Andrei and the Snow Walker* and Julia Veryha in Kupchenko Frolick's novella are not surprising considering that Ukrainian teenagers and young women were seen as "tomorrow's mothers and homemakers, and," as Swyripa observes, "this role would determine not only the level at which the next generation integrated into Canadian society but also the quality of its Ukrainianness" (Swyripa "Wedded to the Cause" 65). Hence Paraska's[24] words reflect the anxieties connected to the assimilation of young women, which was associated with the symbolical death of Ukrainianness.

Although marrying men from outside of the diaspora could have been "a stepping stone to wealth or acceptance" in Anglo-Canada, Swyripa argues that "it was also the harbinger of national suicide, beginning with the family unit" ("Wedded to the Cause" 97). While Warwaruk's Marusia/Marie embraces a different, Métis name and rebels against her mother's expectations, in *Brovko's Amazing Journey* it turns out that unlike a typical *Nasha Meri*, she does not marry an Anglo-Canadian, but a Métis man, yet one who speaks Ukrainian and participates in the life of the Ukrainian Canadian community. Her nuptial to Gabriel further strengthens the alleged ties between Ukrainian Canadians and Indigenous Peoples, discussed in Chapter 1, and distances both groups from Anglo-Canada. Marrying outside of her ethnic group, Marie risks not passing the Ukrainian customs and cultural memory to the next generations, but the alleged ties between Ukrainians and the Métis make her union with Gabriel acceptable for her family. Despite having "been away from home long enough to prefer being called the *Métis* name," in *Brovko's Amazing Journey* she does not forget about her roots and "still knows how to decorate bread" in a traditional Ukrainian way (151; emphasis in original).

Unlike his sister, Andrei, who also befriends Indigenous Peoples, is destined to marry Natasha, a Ukrainian girl, whose Hutsul mother is believed to possess magic. Warwaruk's brief description of Hutsuls, highlanders from the Carpathian Mountains, of whom "half the people in Ukraine are afraid," recalls the questionable way he depicts the Cree in both novels (30). Despite the interethnic relationship of Marie and Gabriel, in *Brovko's Amazing Journey* Warwaruk informs the readers about two other marriages: between Petrus and Tekla and Mr. Kuzyk and Petrus's sister, Martha (92). Matching the remaining characters into heteronormative[25] and monoethnic couples, Warwaruk prevents them from marrying outside of the diaspora, assimilating, thus committing "national suicide."

Conclusion

In the introduction to the second edition of *Sisters or Strangers? Immigrant, Ethnic, and Racialized Women in Canadian History*, Marlene Epp and Franca Iacovetta observe that "diaspora is an emotional and psychological state of existence as much as it is indicative of physical movement" (13). Hence they argue that "[a] diasporic identity might reflect the dual or multiple sites on which one's migration experiences occurred as well as one's ties to kin" (13). The Ukrainian Canadian children's texts analyzed in this chapter portray first- and second-generation Ukrainian Canadian girls in the first half of the twentieth century who reflect such multiplicity and negotiate with their *babas* and assimilated women representing the *Nasha Meri* stereotype. They also reflect the entanglements between the roles women usually are expected to perform in relation to the nation-state.

Lesia Magus, Anna Veryha, and Anya Soloniuk eventually become the new bearers of the seeds of memory, yet they do not simply reproduce the symbolical Ukrainian pysanka; rather, they create new, Ukrainian Canadian patterns, by writing Ukrainianness into Canadianness. Most girls and young women I have discussed in this chapter do not simply replicate the patterns of behavior performed by their mothers and grandmother; instead, they question both the patriarchal and more progressive versions of femininity and actively participate in their families' economic struggles. As I demonstrate in Chapters 4 and 5, the sociopolitical agency of girls and young women who survive traumatic events and emerge as the givers of memory are also prominent in books devoted to the Holodomor and the Second World War, which next to the pioneer experience, have become the central themes in the Ukrainian Canadian mnemonic discourse.

Notes

1. While both Lisa Grekul and Lindy Ledohowski mention Kupchenko Frolick in their extensive studies of Ukrainian Canadian literature, they do not analyze her texts. Myrna Kostash writes that Kupchenko Frolick is a "transitional figure, as one who is still concerned with the data of rural ethnic experience but who has caught them at the moment of their shift to the modern" (254). As we can read in a short note published in *Land of Silent Sundays*, Kupchenko Frolick "was born in Alberta, third of seven children born to the late Dr. Volodymyr and Anne Perich Kupchenko, long time Alberta school teachers. Actress, model, short story writer she began writing when the youngest of her four children left for university" (Hnatiw, Frolick, and Palij 29). Kupchenko Frolick published a collection of short stories, *The Green Tomato Years* (1985), and two short novels/novellas *The Chicken Man* (1989) and *Anna Veryha* (1992). While child characters appear in all of them, only the latter is intended for younger readers. Interestingly, the eponymous protagonist of *Anna Veryha* remembers stealing tomatoes with her sister from the yard of Mr. Babich, the protagonist of *The Chicken Man*. In the 1989 book also Babich recalls the incident. Notably, all of Kupchenko Frolick's books were illustrated by William Kurelek, a renowned Ukrainian Canadian painter and author of several commercially successful and critically acclaimed picturebooks. As Jars Balan notes,

    > Kurelek even had a hand in shaping the content of this impressionistic novella, persuading the author to change the cause of a pivotal death in the story from a botched abortion to a miscarriage, because he was anxious that his art not be used to lend support for something that he fiercely opposed.
    >
    > (12)

    Still, abortion is mentioned in *The Chicken Man* by Babich's mother-in-law. Since Elizabeth, the protagonist's late wife, was an educated woman who wanted to postpone having children, her death symbolically echoes the anxieties connected to assimilation and the possible loss of a distinct Ukrainian Canadian identity. In his investigation of Kulerek's art, Balan mentions Kupchenko Frolick's fiction and rightly states that she "died of cancer the following year [after the publication of *Anna Veryha*], before she was able to gain the critical recognition that her writing arguably deserves" (13).
2. The tradition of decorating eggs using wax in Slavic cultures predates the Christian era. Decorated eggs were later appropriated by Christianity. The oldest known Ukrainian *pysanka* dates to the fifteenth or sixteenth century. In 1974 the Vegreville egg, a gigantic metal Easter egg was erected to commemorate the centennial of the Royal Canadian Police and has become one of the best-recognized Ukrainian Canadian symbols.
3. The protagonist's late grandmother was the one who shared the seeds of memory with her daughter and granddaughters. She taught them customs

and traditions, including writing *pysanky* and preparing Ukrainian dishes. Baba also shared her experience as an *Ostarbeiter* and a DP (cf. Chapter 5).
4 The theme of intergenerational transfer of memory is a common trope in other diasporic children's and young adult texts, for example, those by Canadian Mennonites (cf. Chapter 4).
5 Anne Shirley, the protagonist of one of the best-selling Anglo-Canadian novels of all time, is "a discursive site for what can be understood in ideological terms as the interrelation of national identity" (Devereux 12). Kupchenko Frolick's *Anna Veryha* is an example of a text where Anne Shirley appears as a symbol of both otherness and assimilation.
6 The theme of mothering is also of great importance in Kupchenko Frolick's *The Green Tomato Years*, *The Chicken Man*, and poetry published in *Land of Silent Sundays*, a volume Kupchenko Frolick coedited with Chrystia Hnatiw and Lydia Palij.
7 As Vitaly Chernetsky demonstrates, unlike in Russia, the Ukrainian social structure has traditionally been more egalitarian and matriarchal, and the increase of patriarchal tendencies can be contributed to the growing Russian influences (237–238).
8 In her examination of Polish American children's fiction, Grażyna J. Kozaczka notes:

> [t]he working-class patriarchy, strongly endorsed by the Catholic Church, predicates that girling of the children promotes the gender construct that assigns women and girls roles subservient to the male, confines them within the domestic sphere, and advocates self-fulfillment through motherhood and service.
>
> (201)

While Ukrainian Canadian communities in the texts analyzed in this chapter are also patriarchal, I argue that most of the young female characters negotiate with traditional gender roles.
9 Swyripa argues that *baba* became "the spiritual and physical link to peasant pioneer heritage" helping new generations to "understood themselves as both Canadians and Ukrainians" ("Wedded to the Cause" 216). For many artists *baba*, a grassroot phenomenon, "possessed an inviolable dignity that deserved respect and admiration" (Swyripa "Storied" 175).
10 In this chapter, the word *baba* is italicized only when it stands for the symbolical figure. In other cases, it is capitalized (Baba) and refers to the protagonists' grandmothers.
11 While feminist ideas are not explicitly mentioned in Langston's *Lesia's Dream*, in Clark's *Kalyna* the main protagonist recalls her mother's fascination with suffragettes. Still, in her own retrospective observations she juxtaposes the accomplishments of the women's rights movement with the shameful internment of "enemy aliens" – "1917 may have been the year for Louise McKinney and women's rights, but it was also a stain on Alberta's history of human rights, one that had never been spoken of in her home or village. 1917, the year she was born and the year Papa was imprisoned and released" (Clark 249).
12 Mrs. Haggarty, for whom Anya's mother worked, is an example of a clever woman who uses sophisticated vocabulary in her letters to avoid censorship at the internment camp.

13 Examining Skrypuch's Armenian-themed novel *The Hunger* (1999), Ulanowicz argues that the "bodily health" of Paula, the novel's protagonist, who is fighting anorexia, "is implicitly an index of her capacity for biological reproduction; likewise, the relative health of a diasporic community is measured against its potential for future survival or self-reproduction" (142). Moreover, Ulanowicz notes that "Paula's body might just as well be read as an expression of mid-twentieth-century anxieties concerning the Canadian body politic as it is a call to preserve the constituent communities within this federal body" (143). Although the major female characters in the novels studied in this chapter do not suffer from any illnesses, their "capacity for biological reproduction" is directly connected to the survival of the seeds of memory.

14 Interestingly, Balan notes that *Anna Veryha* was

> directly inspired by the Kurelek painting which graces its attractive dust jacket. The image of a bluebird's nest served as the kernel from which the author developed this lyrical tale based on recollections of her own childhood in the Ukrainian bloc settlement northeast of Edmonton.
>
> (13)

15 Despite being sorry for her mother, Anna is an obedient daughter who tries to explain her hard-working father's behavior. The narrator explains that Gregory Veryha was

> acting out a role. That even this latest outburst was an act. That her father felt that as a man he had to be taken seriously. That his respect was earned by the number of reprimands he handed out daily to 'his' three women.
>
> (29)

Hence Gregory Veryha's behavior towards his wife and daughters is part of his attempts at performing hegemonic masculinity (cf. Connell and Messerchmidt). As the novella is focalized by Anna but not narrated by her, this description can be read as Kupchenko Frolick's contemporary, retrospective, and adult way of understanding Ukrainian Canadian patriarchy in the early 1940s. Odarka tells the protagonist a secret her own parents shared with her: Gregory Veryha cried and got drunk when his second daughter was born, "[h]e had cried because [Anna] were a girl, and not a boy" (120). Despite the fact that his wife previously almost died in childbirth, Gregory is excited about the pregnancy because he is desperate to have a son. The aforementioned disregard for his wife and criticism of Dotsia are embedded in patriarchal ideals, present in all novels examined in this chapter. The man's dominance in the household is already displayed in the novella's first chapter. Anna contemplates on the source of his anger, but, unlike her older sister, she never questions his words and later even prays for forgiveness, feeling guilty for making him mad. The protagonist sympathizes with her hardworking "bony father" and "want[s] to go up to him and hug him and try to calm him down" (21). Yet she is too afraid of his reaction. The man explains his anger by being surrounded by women. He does not accept the fact that he lost his only son and has two daughters. Interestingly, the only woman whom he treats with respect is his mother, the novella's *baba*. As Anna notes, "[t]he only really good thing about her grandmother's visits was her father's behaviour. He was different when his mother was over. He hardly spoke at all, complimented his mother's cooking, her successes and even her failures" (39). Moreover, Gregory represents the second-generation of Ukrainian Canadians. While at first glance he is a typical Ukrainian farmer, he is not very religious, and does not follow all traditions and customs, as he curses and eats meat during Lent. Gregory's anger disappears at the end of the novel when his wife finally gives birth to a son.

16   In one short flashback, Vera demonstrates that her husband was different when they were younger, as he "was a wonderful dancer" (33). Yet she remembers that when they went on a date and came home late, her father was furious and threatened to beat Gregory. Instead, the man hit his daughter who "was so ashamed and hurt in front of [Gregory]" (33). Hearing this story, "Anna's heart broke," and she decides that "[h]er mother needed her, she'd *never* leave her mother" (33; emphasis in original). Although *Anna Veryha* is directed at young readers, more experienced ones will notice the Veryhas' poverty and the local community's imperfections, most notably the patriarchal treatment of women.

17   Sewing is also portrayed as a lifesaving skill in Skrypuch's two Second World War trilogies. Lida, the protagonist of *Making Bombs for Hitler*, and Maria, the protagonist of *Trapped in Hitler's Web*, are both *Ostarbeiters* (Eastern workers) whose sewing skills help them survive the war (cf. Chapter 5).

18   Since the release of the first film adaptation of the novel in 1919 (directed by William Desmond Taylor), *Anne of Green Gables* and its numerous sequels have been adapted for radio, stage, screen, and TV. *Anne with and E*, the novel's most recent loose adaptation, was produced by Moira Walley-Beckett and Miranda de Pencie (2017–2019). For more about the worldwide phenomenon of *Anne of Green Gables*, see Ledwell and Mitchell (181–244).

19   For example, in Lillian Boraks-Nemetz's award-winning *The Old Brown Suitcase* (1994), the Polish translation of *Anne of Green Gables* is one of the two books Slava/Elizabeth, the teenage protagonist, brings to Canada after the Second World War. At the end of the novel, after learning English and successfully assimilating, Slava/Elizabeth wins a school competition and is awarded another copy of *Anne of Green Gables*, this time in English. Notably, the first translation of *Anne of Green Gables* into Polish by R. (Rozalia or Rachela) Bernsztajnowa was issued in 1911. *Anne* has never been out of circulation and at least 15 different translations of the book have been published. The novel quickly became a cultural phenomenon and, as some scholars argue, "emerged as an unlikely symbol of resistance to Nazism and the Soviet Union during World War Two" (Bowlby). Considering the book's popularity in Poland, it is worth noting that *Anne of Green Gables* was translated into Ukrainian by Anna Vovchenko only in 2012.

20   Interestingly, in Clark's *Kalyna* education allows the eponymous character, the daughter of a Ukrainian pioneer woman and an Anglo-Canadian doctor who raped her, to learn about the 1914 internment and bring it to the mainstream attention (cf. Chapter 2).

21   Clothes play an important role in *Anna Veryha*. While Anna is criticized for her boyish outfits, Odarka, whose mother forces her to wear dresses, is criticized by Anna's grandmother: "[s]he's a big girl with breasts and yet her mother dresses her like a child" (101). The protagonist does not understand her Baba's comments, as she likes her friend's dress. Anna gets sick because she does not want to wear an uncomfortable coat to church, which

"made [her] look like she had a humpback" (87). When Dotsia and Anna meet Elias, he gives them the Eaton catalog – another symbol of Anglo-Canadian femininity – and says that it is what women like. Published each fall and spring from 1884 to 1976, it was "one of the first to be distributed by a Canadian retail store" becoming the source of dreams for generations of Canadian girls. Selling mostly clothes and later other products, the catalog was known and the "Homesteader's Bible" and symbol of English Canada in Western Canada. Notably, "clothing symbolized an assimilation with Anglo-Canadian attitudes and ideals" (Swyripa "Wedded to the Cause" 92). Canadian children and immigrants learned to read with the catalog, girls and boys played with it, and finally, just like in *Anna Veryha*, it was used as reading material and toilet paper in outhouses ("Canadian Mail Order").

22 While in *Lesia's Dream* it is the protagonist's traditional outfit and musculature which visually distinguish her from Minnie, in Kupchenko Frolick's novella it is the hairstyles which represent the differences between the symbolical roles of the Veryha sisters. Despite their relative poverty, Dotsia, fascinated with Durbin, "took great care with her hair," washing it with rainwater and vinegar, and "[w]hen she saved enough money she'd buy a bottle of Drene shampoo and hoard it like a miser" (16). As Judith Butler famously argued, "gender is the repeated stylization of the body, a set of repeated acts within a highly rigid regulatory frame" ("Gender Trouble" 33), it is "a kind of doing, an incessant activity performed" ("Undoing Gender" 1). By styling her hair, Dotsia attempts to express what she believes to be more progressive, Anglo-Canadian version femininity. Unlike her, Anna is a tomboy whose hair is "short and fine and of no particular colour [...] no one ever noticed her hair" (16). While the protagonist, who looks just like her father, is not jealous of her sister's beauty, she does feel underappreciated. Interestingly, Dotsia's hair makes Gregory Veryha even more critical of her. He makes fun of the way she wears it and makes "scissor motions" (28). The girl also has to hide from him the fact that she wears lipstick. As Swyripa notes, women "were crucial to the future of the Ukrainian-Canadian group in a way to which men could not aspire, and when they renounced their own membership in the Ukrainian nation, they renounced that of the next generation too" ("Wedded to the Cause" 100). For Gregory Veryha, his older daughter's hair and lipstick symbolize her rejection of the traditional role of a daughter/wife/mother. The man is also dissatisfied with Dotsia's decision to study as "no man will want her. She's becoming mouthy. No decent man wants a woman like that" (120). His words highlight the patriarchal expectations he has towards Dotsia, whom in conversations with Vera he always calls *her* daughter.

23 While the narrator instantly starts using the girl's chosen name, in *Brovko's Amazing Journey* he obstinately refers to Marie as Marusia.

24 In Ukraine Andrei's mother Paraska Bayda was an important member of the local community and upon leaving she promises to write letters to her neighbors. Unlike most female peasants at that time, including Lesia in Langston's novel, she is literate as "[f]or four years, as often as she could, she'd follow [Andrei] to the reading hall, and she would stay a while to learn something herself" (6). Despite her literacy, Paraska is depicted as a stereotypical and devout woman desperate to find her daughter a wealthy Ukrainian husband. Unlike Anna Veryha or Lesia Magus, Marie has a troubled relationship with her mother, the guardian of traditions and patriarchy. While

Paraska believes that marrying Kuzyk is Marie's only opportunity to become a *"phania"* (a lady) and climb the social ladder, Stefan Bayda does not share his wife's sentiments and tells her that "Canada has all sorts" (93, 163).
25 Furthermore, in the original novel Mr. Kuzyk gives Andrei a dog the boy also calls Brovko. While throughout the book the dog is a male, in a letter sent to Ukraine in *Brovko's Amazing Journey*, Andrei claims that the new dog is *"not nearly as smart as Brovko"* (28) and while the pets look alike, "[t]*he only difference is that the dog is a female. She's a big bundle of fluffy white fur just like Brovko*" (29; emphasis in original). Hence the Canadian Brovko becomes Brovka, a female. Unsurprisingly, upon his arrival to Canada Brovko falls in love with Brovka.

Works Cited

Balan, Jars. "With Pictures and Words: The Role Played by Writing and Literature in William Kurelek's Art." *Australasian Canadian Studies*, vol. 26, no. 2, 2008, pp. 7–25.
Bowlby, Ewan. "Banning Anne: Why the Soviets Were Afraid of Anne of Green Gables." *Transpositions*, 13 May 2022, www.transpositions.co.uk/banning-anne-why-the-soviets-were-afraid-of-anne-of-green-gables/#_ftn3. Accessed 13 May 2022.
Butler, Judith. *Gender Trouble: Feminism and the Subversion of Identity*. Routledge, 1990.
Butler, Judith. *Undoing Gender*. Routledge, 2004.
"Canadian Mail Order Catalogues – History." *Bibliothèque et Archives Canada/ Library and Archives Canada*, 30 December 2019, www.bac-lac.gc.ca/eng/discover/postal-heritage-philately/canadian-mail-order-catalogues/Pages/catalogues-history.aspx. Accessed 14 May 2021.
Chernetsky, Vitaly. *Mapping Postcommunist Cultures: Russia and Ukraine in the Context of Globalization*, McGill-Queen's University Press, 2007.
Clark, Pam. *Kalyna*. Stonehouse Publishing, 2016. E-book.
Connell, R.W. (Raewyn) and James W. Messerchmidt. "Hegemonic Masculinity: Rethinking the Concept." *Gender & Society*, vol. 19, no. 6, 2005, pp. 829–859.
Davey, Frank. "The Literary Politics of Canadian Multiculturalism." *Multiculturalism in North America and Europe: Social Practices, Literary Visions*, edited by Hans Braun and Wolfgang Kloos. Trier: WVP, 1994, pp. 103–114.
Devereux, Cecily. "'Canadian Classic' and 'Commodity Export': The Nationalism of 'Our' Anne of Green Gables." *Journal of Canadian Studies*, vol. 36, no. 1, 2001, pp. 11–28.
Epp, Marlene and Franca Iacovetta. "Introduction." *Sisters or Strangers? Immigrant, Ethnic, and Racialized Women in Canadian History*, edited by Marlene Epp and Franca Iacovetta, 2nd ed. University of Toronto Press, 2016, pp. 3–18.
Federici, Silvia. *Wages against Housework*. Bristol: The Power of Women Collective and the Falling Wall Press, 1975.
Fee, Margery. "Romantic Nationalism and the Image of Native People in Contemporary English-Canadian Literature." *The Native in Literature*, edited by Thomas King, Cheryl Calver, and Helen Hoy. Toronto: ECW Press, 1987, pp. 15–33.

Frankenberg, Ruth. *White Women, Race Matters*. University of Minnesota Press, 1993.
Galway, Elizabeth A. *From Nursery Rhymes to Nationhood: Children's Literature and the Construction of Canadian Identity*. Routledge, 2008.
Gray, Paige. "'Bloom in the Moonshine': Imagination as Liberation in *Anne of Green Gables*." *Children's Literature*, vol. 42, 2014, pp. 169–196.
Grekul, Lisa. *Leaving Shadows: Literature in English by Canada's Ukrainians*. University of Alberta Press, 2005.
Gubar, Marah. "'Where Is the Boy?': The Pleasures of Postponement in the *Anne of Green Gables* Series." *The Lion and the Unicorn*, vol. 25, no. 1, 2001, pp. 47–69.
Hnatiw, Chrystia, Gloria Kupchenko Frolick, and Ludia Palij. *Land of Silent Sundays*. Willaims-Wallace Publishers, 1988.
Jung, Carl Gustaw. *The Archetypes and the Collective Unconscious*, translated by R. F. C. Hull. Princeton University Press, 1990.
Kokkola, Lydia. *Fictions of Adolescent Carnality*. John Benjamins Publishing Company, 2013.
Kostash, Myrna. "Gloria Kupchenko Frolick 'Anna Veryha' (Book Review)." *Journal of Ukrainian Studies*; Summer 1991, pp. 253–255.
Kozaczka, Grażyna J. *Writing the Polish American Women in Postwar Ethnic Fiction*. Ohio University Press, 2019.
Kupchenko Frolick, Gloria. *Anna Veryha*. Maxwell Macmillan, 1992.
Kurelek, William and Margaret S. Engelhart. *They Sought a New World: The Story of European Immigration to North America*. Montreal: Tundra Books, 1985.
Ledohowski, Lindy. "Introduction: Ukrainian Canadian Poet Pedagogues." *Unbound: Ukrainian Canadians Writing Home*, edited by Lisa Grekul and Lindy Ledohowski. University of Toronto Press, 2016, pp. 3–22.
Ledohowski, Lindy. "Little Ukraine on the Prairie. 'Baba' in English-Language Ukrainian-Canadian Literature." *Place and Replace: Essays on Western Canada*, edited by Adele Perry, Esyllt W. Jones, and Leah Morton. University of Manitoba Press, 2013.
Ledwell, Jane and Jean Mitchell (eds.). *Anne around the World: L.M. Montgomery and Her Classic*. McGill-Queen's University Press, 2013.
McClintock, Anne. *Imperial Leather: Race, Gender and Sexuality in the Colonial Context*. Routledge, 1992.
Montgomery, Lucy Maud. *The Story Girl*. L.C. Page & Co., 1913. www.gutenberg.org/files/5342/5342-h/5342-h.htm
Mutala, Marion. *Baba's Babushka: A Magical Ukrainian Christmas*. Illustrated by Wendy Siemens. Regina: Your Nickel's Worth Publishing, 2010.
Mutala, Marion. *Baba's Babushka: A Magical Ukrainian Easter*. Illustrated by Wendy Siemens. Regina: Your Nickel's Worth Publishing, 2012.
Mutala, Marion. *Baba's Babushka: A Magical Ukrainian Wedding*. Illustrated by Amber Rees. Regina: Your Nickel's Worth Publishing, 2013.
O'Brien, Sharon. "Tomboyism and Adolescent Conflict: Three Nineteenth-Century Case Studies." *Woman's Being, Woman's Place: Female Identity and Vocation in American History*, edited by Mary Kelley. G. K. Hall and Co., 1979, pp. 351–372.
Richter, Miriam Verena. *Creating the National Mosaic: Multiculturalism in Canadian Children's Literature from 1950 to 1993*. Rodopi, 2011.

Robinson, Laura M. "'A Born Canadian': The Bonds of Communal Identity in *Anne of Green Gables* and *A Tangled Web*." *L.M. Montgomery and Canadian Culture*, edited by Irene Gammel and Elizabeth Epperly. University of Toronto Press, 1999, pp. 19–30.

Skrypuch, Marsha Forchuk. *Prisoners in the Promised Land. The Ukrainian Internment Diary of Anya Soloniuk*. Scholastic Canada, 2007.

Story, Norah. "Ukrainians." *The Oxford Companion to Canadian History and Literature*. Oxford University Press, 1967, pp. 807–808.

Suchacka, Weronika. *'Za Hranetsiu' – 'Beyond the Border': Constructions of Identities in Ukrainian-Canadian Literature*. Wissner-Verlag, 2019.

Swyripa, Frances. *Storied Landscapes: Ethno-Religious Identity and the Canadian Prairies*. University of Manitoba Press, 2010.

Swyripa, Frances. "Wedded to the Cause: Ukrainian-Canadian Women." *Canada's Ukrainians: Negotiating an Identity*, edited by Lubomyr Y. Luciuk and Stella Hryniuk. University of Toronto Press, 1991, pp. 238–253.

Swyripa, Frances. *Wedded to the Cause: Ukrainian-Canadian Women and Ethnic Identity 1891–1991*. University of Toronto Press, 1993.

Ulanowicz, Anastasia. *Second-Generation Memory and Contemporary Children's Literature: Ghost Images*. Routledge, 2013.

Warwaruk, Larry. *Andrei and the Snow Walker*. Regina: Coteau Books, 2002.

Warwaruk, Larry. *Brovko's Amazing Journey*. Regina: Coteau Books, 2013.

Wesselius, Janet. "Anne's Body Has a Hind (and Soul) of Its Own: Embodiment and the Cartesian Legacy in *Anne of Green Gables*." *The Embodied Child: Readings in Children's Literature and Culture*, edited by Roxanne Harde and Lydia Kokkola. Routledge, 2018, pp. 21–36.

4 "You filthy little *Zaraza*!"
Red Terror, Collectivization, and the Holodomor in Canadian Cultural Memory

> *Star, ask yourself how many hearts ached—and broke—to make those crimson and purple pages in history that you find so enthralling.*
> (L.M. Montgomery, *Emily of New Moon*)

Pandemics happen when there is an outbreak of contagious disease occurring in many places at the same time. Although anyone can fall victim to a plague, as Susan Sontag notes in *Illness as Metaphor and AIDS and Its Metaphors*, epidemics are often used as metaphors and tools of symbolic violence in public discourse. This type of violence is often directed at entire social groups, as was the case with Ukrainian peasants who fell victim to the Great Famine of 1932–1933. For example, when Vera Philipovna,[1] the eponymous child protagonist of Valentina Gal's 2019 novel escapes from her village to an orphanage in the nearby city, after months of starvation she is greeted with the words: "[y]ou filthy little *Zaraza* [Plague]" (198). The words of the city woman to the peasant child reflect Sontag's observation that one of the traits "of the usual script for plague" is usually "the need to make a dreaded disease foreign" (47). Hence it is not only plagues which have deadly consequences but also the stigmatizing "metaphors and myths" which often put the blame on the victims (14). In this chapter I understand *the plague* both literally, as an infectious illness caused by malnutrition and no access to health care, and metaphorically, as a spreading ideology stigmatizing the victims of Lenin's so-called Red Terror, Stalin's collectivization, and most importantly, the Holodomor, the Great Famine of 1932–1933. The aforementioned quotation from *Philipovna: Daughter of Sorrow* also echoes Anne Applebaum's words that in Stalin's propaganda the victims of the Holodomor were not considered victims but perpetrators: "[t]hey were not sufferers; they were responsible for their terrible fate. They had caused the famine, and therefore they deserved to die" (300). Although currently in Ukraine the Great Famine "is mourned officially as the greatest national tragedy, an act of ideologically motivated mass murder," writing about in, and commemorating its victims, was forbidden in Soviet Ukraine (Yekelchyk 112; cf. Shkandrij 55; Marples 35). In my considerations I point to the

DOI: 10.4324/9781003367918-5

fact that during and after the Holodomor, the victims and survivors were blamed and shamed by the Soviet propaganda, which openly denied the occurrence of the famine.

The Holodomor became the center of the mnemonic politics of the Ukrainian diaspora in the 1940s and its memory survived in oral history, diasporic publications written in English and Ukrainian,[2] art (William Kurelek's *Famine 1933*, 1977), and places of memory, such as the monuments erected in Edmonton and Winnipeg in 1983 and 1984, respectively (Satzewich 178; cf. Cipko). Ukrainians living in the West agreed "that the attacks on Ukrainization and the famine were linked" because "Stalin was determined to destroy the roots of Ukrainian resistance to the regime, which lay in the countryside" (Shkandrij 56). After all, the countryside which Stalin attempted to destroy in the 1930s was the basis of Ukrainian Canadian identity, as I have demonstrated in the previous chapters of *Next-Generation Memory*.

This chapter consists of four major sections. In the first one, I introduce the historical background of the Holodomor and explain the place of the Great Famine in Ukrainian Canadian collective memory. Agreeing with Applebaum that understanding the 1932–1933 famine is not possible without considering what happened before it, in the following two sections, I briefly introduce the history of the Red Terror and Stalin's collectivization and study how Ukraine and Ukrainians are represented in books written by authors who are not Ukrainian Canadians, but Canadians whose ancestors come from present-day Ukraine. I argue that in texts like Adele Dueck's *Nettie's Journey* and Gabriele Goldstone's *The Kulak's Daughter/Red Stone* series, Ukraine emerges as a multiethnic country where Ukrainians are positioned as a minority. Analyzing these narratives will help me point to the destruction of the Ukrainian countryside between 1917 and 1931. In the last section, I examine the literary representations of the Holodomor in Canadian historical fiction published between 2000 and 2019, pointing to the fact that for many years Marsha Forchuk Skrypuch's books were the only Anglophone texts explicitly about the Great Famine. While the Holodomor still does not enjoy the same popularity as the subject of the Second World War investigated in Chapter 5, the number of publications about it began to grew after 2019, with the appearance of new narratives, including those by Marion Mutala and Valentina Gal. Throughout the chapter, I study the mnemonic potential of these books, showing that only some of them are likely to become the source of next-generation memory for the young readers.

The Role of the Holodomor in Ukrainian Canadian Cultural Memory

The term Holodomor is derived from the Ukrainian words "морити голодом," meaning "to kill by starvation." Victoria A. Malko argues that "*holodomor*, spelled with small-h, has been in use to refer to mass deaths as in a plague since 1889" (xvi; emphasis in original). The capitalized word was first used in the context of the famine of 1932–1933 in diasporic publications published in Czechoslovakia in the 1930s but was popularized in North America by author and politician Ivan Drach (cf. Ulanowicz "We *Are* the People" 49; cf. Malko xvi).[3] Writing about the number of people deliberately starved by Stalin in Soviet Ukraine, Applebaum states that the majority of contemporary historians and demographers agree that there were about "3.9 million excess deaths, or direct losses, and 0.6 million lost births, or indirect losses," meaning that at least 4.5 million Ukrainians died in the famine, that is "13 per cent of the Ukrainian population at that time" (285; cf. Yefimenko).[4] A few years after the Holodomor the Soviet Union changed death records to conceal the real numbers of casualties in Ukraine (cf. Applebaum 284; cf. Bertelsen 203–240). The lack of data about the 1932–1933 famine contributed to the belief that the Ukrainian claims about the Holodomor were overstated (cf. Applebaum 339).

The Holodomor, unlike most famines, such as the one which occurred in the Soviet Union in 1921, was man-made and resulted from Stalin's "Five-Year Plan." Instead of helping the starving peasants, Stalin deliberately set unrealistic quotas for grain requisition and "began using stark language about Ukraine as well as the North Caucasus, the Russian province that was heavily Ukrainian" (Applebaum 192). In addition to wheat, requisitioners confiscated fruit, vegetables, seeds, dairy, meat, honey, and other edible products. Hence according to the definition coined by Raphael Lemkin, the Great Famine of 1932–1933 was a genocide (cf. Gangi 8–10; cf. Malko xv–xxiv). While the Holodomor has been recognized as a genocide by Ukraine and 15 other countries, the application of this term in the UN understanding is sometimes questioned because in the context of the Nuremberg trials and the consequent legal disputes genocide was defined as "the physical elimination of an *entire* ethnic group, in a manner similar to Holocaust" (Applebaum 356–357; emphasis mine). However, as Applebaum notes, Soviet authorities contributed to the form of the language used in the legal documents to prevent their own actions from being categorized as "genocides" (cf. 357). In *The Ukrainian Intelligentsia and Genocide: The Struggle for History, Language, and Culture in the 1920s and 1930s* (2021), Malko argues that the Holodomor was Stalin's attempt at ethnic cleansing of Ukrainians. This was to be accomplished in four steps: killing "intelligentsia (the 'brain' of the nation), [...] clergy (the 'soul' of the nation), [...] farmers ([...] the 'national spirit')," and finally "change the demographic composition of the population in Ukraine by resettling Red Army veterans and Russian loyalists together with their families into areas depopulated by the genocidal famine" (xvii). Although Stalin failed to kill all Ukrainians and destroy Ukrainian culture, the Great Famine devastated "the Ukrainian peasantry as a social force capable of resisting the authorities" and accelerated the russification of Soviet

Ukraine (Yekelchyk 103). Hence the Holodomor further contributed to the destruction of the multiethnic Ukrainian countryside, which started during the Red Terror and Stalin's collectivization.

Unlike the subject of the Second World War, in the Soviet Union known as the Great Patriotic War, the history of the Great Famine was not taught in Ukraine until 1991. Moreover, the USSR simply denied the sole occurrence of the 1932–1933 famine (cf. Applebaum 22). The scarcity of domestic pre-1991 publications devoted to the deadly effects of collectivization and the Holodomor is not surprising because while the USSR existed, writing a complete history of the Soviet repressions and the Great Famine was not possible (cf. Applebaum 22). The Soviet denial of the Holodomor was effective because it also influenced many Western journalists and historians. Consequently, the suppression of the famine in Soviet Ukraine weakened the position of the Ukrainian diaspora in North America. As sociologist Vic Satzewich argues, the transcultural importance of the famine in the diaspora goes beyond the Soviet oppression of Ukrainians (178). Some North American Ukrainians felt victimized in their new homelands (178). The feeling of victimization is connected to the fact that for many decades of the Cold War, the authorities in countries like Canada or the USA – as well as the USSR and Soviet Ukraine – did not acknowledge the existence of the Great Famine and Stalin's persecution of Ukrainians. "Pressure for good relations," notes Shkandrij, "was being put on governments by businesses who saw the potential for trade and who preferred to believe that reports of famine were exaggerated" (56). Hence the occurrence of the Holodomor was questioned abroad, including Canada, where the government did not want the diplomatic relationships with USSR to deteriorate (Petryshyn 230). This began to change only in the late 1980s with the broadcast of a documentary titled *Harvest of Despair* on Canadian television in 1985 and the publication of British historian Robert Conquest's *The Harvest of Sorrow: Soviet Collectivization and the Terror-Famine* (1986), which was reviewed in major press and the subsequent year followed by Douglas Tottle's *Fraud, Famine and Fascism: The Ukrainian Genocide Myth from Hitler to Harvard*, "a classic of Soviet disinformation" (Shkandrij 61; cf. Zhuk). What contributed to the further recognition of the Holodomor was undoubtedly the aftermath of the 1986 Chernobyl disaster and the collapse of communism.

Many Western commentators argued that the Ukrainian discussions about the Great Famine were simply "a Cold War, anti-communist tactic" (Shkandrij 60). Even after the collapse of the Soviet Union some governments were reluctant to "recognize the famine as a form of genocide" and to treat the Holodomor as "the Ukrainian Holocaust" comparable to "the Jewish Holocaust" (Satzewich 178).[5] The comparison of the Holodomor to the Holocaust is not incidental. Michael Rothberg notes that the global spread of Holocaust-related memory politics "has contributed to the articulation of other histories – some of them predating the Nazi genocide" (6). Yet given the history of Ukrainian–Jewish relations in Ukraine and North America, the reference to the Holocaust in many Holodomor-themed publications seems deliberate. While most pre–Second World War immigrants to Canada came from Western Ukraine,[6] the famine, which happened in Southern Ukraine, became the "defining catastrophe" for the diaspora, equivalent to the role the Holocaust plays in the collective memory of North American Jews (Satzewich 182). The Holodomor gives the post–Second World War refugees "a sense of legitimacy" as it indicates that Ukrainians had to leave their country not because of economic reasons but rather "because of political and cultural persecution" (Satzewich 178). As Rothberg argues in the examination of what he calls multidirectional memory, comparing various historical traumatic memories can be beneficial, but only when it forms "new objects and new lines of sight" (19). On the one hand the comparison of the Holodomor to the Holocaust may be productive, but on the other hand, it can cause further disagreements and lead to memory wars between diasporic communities.

Considering the complex Ukrainian–Jewish relations discussed in detail in Chapter 5, it is worth noting that the memory of the Holodomor has been used by some diasporic organizations to defy "the allegations that Ukrainians are 'inherently' anti-Semitic and that they were overrepresented in the ranks of Hitler's executioners" (Satzewich 178). Because according to some diasporic Jews Ukrainians performed a "disproportionate role in the Nazi Holocaust," Ukrainians confront such claims by highlighting "a disproportionate role" the Jews played "in the victimization of Ukrainians by the Soviets" (Satzewich 178; cf. Marples 61–64). However, this seems to be the aftermath of the Nazi propaganda which blamed the famine on the local Jews (cf. Applebaum 332).

The alleged Jewish persecution of Ukrainians during the Red Terror, collectivization, and the Holodomor "is used, in part, to explain why some Ukrainians participated in pogroms against the Jews during World War II," a theme I examine in Chapter 5 (Satzewich 178). Notably, and quite problematically, diasporic organizations tend to use similar "imagery and terminology [as the one] used to describe the Jewish Holocaust," for example by quoting 6 million, or more, as the death toll of the Great Famine, a number similar to that of Jews who were murdered by the Nazis (Satzewich 182; cf. Yefimenko). This is hardly surprising as the Holodomor "provides Ukrainians with a common object of concern, and symbolizes the historical suffering of the Ukrainian people" (Satzewich 189). Victimization and survival "help to solidify group boundaries" within the diaspora (Satzewich 188) but also reflect what Margaret Atwood famously called "[t]he central symbol of Canada [...] Survival, *la Survivance*" (31). In her 1972 *Survival* she argues that "Canadians are forever taking the national pulse like doctors at the sickbed: the aim is not to see whether the patient will live well but simply whether he will live at all" (33). Keeping the memory of the Holodomor alive seems to symbolize the Ukrainian diaspora's attempts to cultivate a separate ethnic identity of a white, nonvisible minority, to keep it alive but also plant it in the Canadian mainstream collective memory. This can be done with the use of popular culture and historical fiction which has the potential to transfer next-generation memory of historically and geographically distant events to present-day young readers.

Studying the role of historical books in American schools, Sara L. Schwebel notices that fiction always reflects the current context of its authors and the state of their own world. Hence even books about past wars, plagues, and disasters echo the "knowledge, politics, and worldview of authors at a particular moment in time" (3). Reading about Soviet atrocities and the history of Canadians of Eastern-European heritage can help young readers appreciate their present reality and become more sympathetic towards the victims of genocides and other atrocities, including the ones happening right now. Comparing wars, plagues, or genocides is irrefutably problematic, but I bring these connections here to make an argument about the importance of narrating and mediating difficult and traumatic past to young generations. I believe that the reproduction of memory in children's literature allows more complex understandings of past events and how they may shape and inspire different futures. Indeed, as scholars like Astrid Erll note, the mnemonic potential of literature is immeasurable.

Before investigating books about the Holodomor, I want to point to the way Ukrainians are portrayed in children's historical fiction devoted to the events of 1917–1931. First, I agree with Applebaum that "[t]he Sovietization of Ukraine did not begin with famine and did not end with famine" (21). Second, collectivization, the famine of 1921, and emigration from Ukrainian territories in the 1920s appeared in Anglophone children's literature before the Holodomor in the mnemonic narratives of German and Mennonite minorities. Hence, for decades such books were the main ones forming the young readers' perception of Ukrainian history.

Ukraine and the Red Terror in Canadian Historical Fiction

In connection to the complex Ukrainian–Mennonite and Ukrainian–Jewish relations explored in this section, it is necessary to recall two things. First, the 1917–1921 events destroyed the traditional Ukrainian countryside and formed new ethnic and social disagreements that in the future had lethal consequences (cf. Chapter 5). Second, they also changed the Soviet view of Ukraine, which emerged "as potentially dangerous and explosive, and Ukrainian peasants and intellectuals as threats to Soviet power" (Applebaum 54). A few years later, these changes contributed to the Soviet treatment of Ukrainians during collectivization and the famine of 1932–1933.[7]

Between 1917 and 1921 Ukraine was a battlefield of three armies, the Red (Bolshevik), the White (Tsarist), and the Black, led by Nestor

Makhno, an anarchist characterized by exceptional cruelty. Writing about Makhno, whom she calls "the most powerful and probably the post charismatic of the Ukrainian peasant leaders who arose out of the chaos of 1919," Applebaum notices that his supporters, known as Makhnovites, "identified the Mennonite landowners of eastern Ukraine as 'German' exploiters who deserved to be stripped of their property" (41–42). Yet they desired to demolish the country, *not* make it independent, hence they should not be identified with the Ukrainian nationalist movement. All local armies were attempting to occupy Ukraine, but they also fought "Ukrainian nationalists, Ukrainian nationalism and even Ukrainian language along with Ukrainian land" (Applebaum 15). In the context of the representation of Ukrainians in the novels analyzed in this section, it is worth noting that the Red Army recruited "the least successful, least productive, most opportunistic peasants" and "offer[ed] them power, privileges, and land confiscated from their [wealthier] neighbours," mostly Jews and Mennonites (Applebaum 36). Such collaborators were supposed to find and seize the "grain surpluses" of their neighbors (Applebaum 36). Notably, in their attempts to discredit Ukraine's nationalism, Soviet propagandists frequently referred to the Ukrainian pogroms against Jews from this period. In their version of history, Soviet scholars branded Ukrainian politician Symon Petliura as an anti-Semite and refuted "the Bolsheviks role in pogroms" by equaling "Ukrainian nationalism to looting, killing and above all pogroms" (Applebaum 53–54).

During the 1921 famine, Southern Ukraine was among "the worst-hit regions in the whole of the USSR," with between 250,000 and 500,000 casualties (Applebaum 67–68). The American Relief Administration (ARA) was the main source of help as it "was already operating in Europe in the spring of 1921" (Applebaum 63). However, like during the Great Famine the following decade, also in 1921 the Soviet authorities, including Lenin, openly dismissed the occurrence of the famine in Ukraine. At first, Americans, including ARA, were not even informed about starvation there. Consequently, by delaying the arrival of the American aid, the authorities contributed to the deaths of thousands of Ukrainians. Interestingly, some scholars argue that the Soviet reluctance to inform the ARA about Ukraine's position "was politically inspired" as the famine might have been used "instrumentally, as [it] would in 1932, to put an end to the Ukrainian rebellion" (Applebaum 67).

In her now classic[8] novel *Days of Terror*, originally published in 1979 but reissued many times over the years, Barbara Smucker introduced the aforementioned issues to Canadian children's literature by highlighting the role of North American humanitarian aid in fighting the first Soviet famine, which severely impacted most Russian Mennonites.[9] The Mennonites in what is now Southern Ukraine "built a remarkable network of agricultural, religious, educational, and economic institutions sometimes referred to as the 'Mennonite Commonwealth,' which collapsed in the chaos that followed the Russian Revolution" (Zacharias

"Learning Sauerkraut" 105). Unlike the Holodomor, the famine of 1921 was not man-made and was not denied by the authorities, who eventually accepted the help of Western humanitarian organizations. Although *Days of Terror* is set in Southern Ukraine, both Smucker and scholars writing about it seem not to be bothered with Ukraine's cultural distinctiveness; then again, the book's protagonists are mostly German-speaking Mennonites whose ancestors were brought to Russia by Catherine the Great and who eventually immigrate to Canada.

Mennonite immigration to Canada began in 1874, but, as Robert Zacharias notes, emigration from the Soviet Union in the 1920s is the most common theme in Canadian Mennonite writing as it prompted a mass migration of 25,000 Mennonites (cf. Zacharias "Rewriting"; Swyripa "Storied" 16; Epp 416). This theme is also present in more recent Mennonite historical fiction for children. For example, Adele Dueck's 2005 novel *Nettie's Journey*, based on the story of the author's mother-in-law's immigration to Canada, explores similar issues to those found in *Days of Terror*. In the prologue of the novel, whose narrative structure is similar to Laura Langston's *Lesia's Dream*, teenage Lisa is baking zwieback, traditional Mennonite buns with her grandmother Nettie. Dueck's culinary choice is of great importance as "zwieback was first of all a sign of migration and preparedness against hunger" and frequently appears in Mennonite migrant narratives (Epp 422). Marlene Epp notes that if prepared correctly, this type of bun can stay fresh for a few months; hence, it is not surprising that it became a symbol of better future and hope in North America (Epp 422). In Dueck's novel spending time with the elderly Nettie prompts her granddaughter to ask: "[d]id you make buns like these when you lived in Russia?" (1). The first question leads to another: "[t]ell me more about when you were young" (2), "[w]hat was it like in Russia? Why did you leave? Why did you come to Saskatchewan? How old were you when you came?" (2).

Although the word Ukraine is not used in the questions, the Russia Nettie talks about in her story while baking zwieback is Southern Ukraine, specifically the Mennonite-inhabited village of Gruenfeld near Zaporizhzhia, which Nettie's family eventually leave for Canada. As is the case in *Days of Terror*, here also immigration to North America, the promised land, is depicted as the best decision the protagonist's father ever made. After hearing the story, Lisa says in the epilogue, "[i]f you hadn't left Russia, I wouldn't be in Canada" (191), and hears that "North America is full of descendants of people who were brave enough to leave their homes and move far away [...] We were full of hopes and dreams [...] That's what brought us here" (191). Just like Laisha in *Lesia's Dream*, Lisa, whose name is a tribute to Nettie's older sister Liese, hears a story of hope and dreams, which is supposed to become a seed of next-generation memory for both the girl and the readers.

Yet Ukraine depicted in *Nettie's Journey* differs from the one shown in *Lesia's Dream* or Larry Warwaruk's novels. Dueck, in a manner similar to Smucker, presents Ukraine as a country in turmoil, a place of constant struggles for power, the victims of which are ordinary people, in this case not Ukrainians, but mostly Mennonites. As in *Days of Terror*, in Dueck's novel Ukraine is a battlefield of three armies. After several years of struggling with collectivization and starvation – from which the Mennonite and Ukrainian peasants are saved by food parcels from North America – Nettie and her family leave for Canada in 1923. Notably, Mennonites who did not leave Ukraine for Canada or South America in the 1920s were among the victims of Stalin's man-made famine a decade later (Epp 416).

The portrayal of Ukrainians in *Nettie's Journey* is questionable. Interestingly, Dueck shows that in the late 1910s and early 1920s, the Communist government gave the land to "the Ukrainian peasants" (104); thus, she creates a vision of Ukrainians as direct beneficiaries of collectivization. Except for the controversial anarchist Nestor Makhno, none of the Ukrainians mentioned in the novel are referred to by name. Ukrainians in *Nettie's Journey* are milkmaids, herdsmen, peasants, or bandits. It is the bandits who speak the Ukrainian language that Nettie does not understand. Even the woman who saves the life of Nettie's brother is only called a "peasant woman" (Dueck 118). Unlike Smucker, however, Dueck does mention the exploitation of Ukrainian peasants by wealthy Mennonite landowners, a category the protagonist's family does not represent. Nettie's family is poor and nothing like the "rich Mennonites [who] thought they were better than the poor Mennonites" (24). Nettie's father, a humble teacher who eventually manages to emigrate with his family to Canada, does not deny that rich farmers treated peasants as objects. This is especially visible when he says that "the Ukrainian peasants [...] were jealous that those things belonged to the Wiebes and not to the Ukrainians. And some [...] and *many* Mennonite people have not been kind to the peasants. They treated them like ani-[mals]" (45). Although Dueck does not negate the exploitation of Ukrainians, she also points to the alleged Ukrainian jealousy, and in her novel Ukrainians emerge only as nameless peasants and anarchist bandits.

While Ukrainians never emerge as fully-formed characters in Mennonite children's fiction, Mennonite and Jewish immigrants from Ukraine are also "rarely mentioned in accounts of Ukrainian Canadian History" (Grekul 7). They only briefly appear in Ukrainian Canadian children's books, for instance in Warwaruk's *Andrei and the Snow Walker*. Although no Mennonite characters are directly introduced there, in Warwaruk's novel the Canadian prairie in the early twentieth century emerges as a simulacrum, not a mirror reflection, of Ukraine's social structure at the time (cf. Chapter 1). Right after arriving in Canada, Andrei's family meets their former Jewish neighbor, Sam Zitchka, who immigrated two years earlier. Zitchka offers to sell the Baydas everything they need on credit, saying: "If I can't trust *a fellow countryman*, who can I trust?" (27; emphasis mine). By referring to Stefan Bayda as "a fellow countryman," Zitchka dismisses the possible old country differences and positions each other as equals. In Canada they are both immigrants from Eastern Europe and, as Frances Swyripa notes in *Storied Landscapes*, "emigration and the peculiarities of frontier settlement forced a wide range of new constellations and identities onto individuals and groups for whom an equally complex mix of old-world constellations and identities no longer sufficed" (8). The presence of Sam Zitchka is not surprising as at that time half of the population of the nearby city of Horodenka where the Baydas come from consisted of Jews, most of whom were killed by the Nazis between 1941 and 1942, with only a dozen surviving (Altman 229–239).[10] Unlike Christian Slavs, Jews were not recruited by the Canadian governments. Like them, though, they were met with hostility on behalf of Anglo-Canadians (Swyripa "Storied" 17). It is also Sam Zitchka who tells Stefan about the Mennonites who "hire men to work on their farm" (28) and because of whom the Baydas can earn enough money to eventually start their own farm.

Dekulakization and Collectivization in Canadian Historical Fiction

Although the first attempts at collectivization were not successful, ten years later Stalin used the same discourse based on deepening divisions and ressentiments. Stalin's first "Five-Year Plan," which was adopted in 1928, promised a significant increase in production after the introduction of a seven-day working week "and a new ethic of workplace competition" (Applebaum 89–90). All farms were to be collectivized, as Stalin believed that this type of farming was key for fast production growth. Applebaum argues that "Stalin's ideology would not let him conclude that successful farmers should be allowed to accumulate more land and build up major estates, as had happened in every other society in history" (Applebaum 89). However, collectivization was disastrous and it further devastated "the ethical structure of the countryside as well as the economic order" already damaged during the Red Terror (Applebaum 139). Traditional country values like "respect for property, for dignity, for human life" were replaced by the Bolshevik "rudiments of an ideology that was about to become lethal" (Applebaum 139). This destruction of traditional values appears in all novels examined in the following two sections.

At first collectivization was assumed to be voluntary, but most farmers, referred to as *kulaks*, tried to resist. They were intimidated, "rounded up, stripped to their underclothes, black-mailed out of their possessions, mocked and humiliated, and sometimes shot" (Applebaum 53). The category of a *kulak*, a wealthy peasant, was first introduced during the Red Terror. Already then the Bolsheviks presented "three categories of peasants: *kulaks*, or wealthy peasants; *serendniaks*, or middle peasants; and *bedniaks*, or poor peasants" (Applebaum 36–37). Notably, the new government tried "to define who would be the victims of their revolution and who would be the beneficiaries" (36–37). This artificial division was supposed to promote "an ideological struggle against the 'kulaks,'" shown as individuals contaminating the Soviet Union (36–37). While this notion was practically unknown in Ukraine before, with the help of the Bolshevik propaganda, "the kulaks became one of the most important Bolshevik scapegoats," frequently being blamed "for the failure of Bolshevik agriculture and food distribution" (36). Soviet propaganda depicted *kulaks* as "parasites" feeding on the healthy body of the countryside.

The *kulak* category was stretchable and quite quickly a new subcategory of *podkulachniki* "the 'under-kulaks'" was introduced to signify people who were "under the influence of a kulak relative" (Applebaum 125). Yet the Soviets labeled some farmers *kulaks* only because they did not want to join the *kolkhoz*, that is a collective farm. Soon the notion of the *kulak* was used to refer to "the smaller ethnic groups who lived in the USSR, including Poles and Germans, both of whom had a distinct presence in Ukraine" (126). In the context of the novels investigated in this section, it is worth noting that "many Ukrainian officials believed that all of the ethnic Germans in Ukraine, who had been there since the eighteenth century, should be classified as kulaks" (126). Hence ethnic Germans were "de-kulakized and deported at about three times the rate of ethnic Ukrainians"; they were also treated with more violence (126). Being labeled a *kulak* had severe consequence as it was synonymous with being "a traitor, an enemy and a non-citizen" and led to the loss of property, work, and legal rights (127). While at first propaganda was used to promote collectivization, quickly the Soviets turned to intimidation and torture, leading some farmers to escape to the city (129–131).[11]

Gabriele Goldstone's *The Kulak's Daughter* (2009) portrays Ukraine as a multiethnic country where people of various backgrounds have to struggle with Stalinism and his plan to liquidate, that is get rid of, all *kulaks*. The importance of *The Kulak's Daughter* and its sequels in the context of the Holodomor is indisputable as collectivization directly led to the famine of 1932–1933. While Goldstone is a second-generation Canadian writer of German origin, her debut novel *The Kulak's Daughter* was listed in Lisa Grekul and Lindy Ledohowski's KOBZAR award winning collection *Unbound: Ukrainian Canadians Writing Home* (2016) next to books by Langston, Marsha Forchuk Skrypuch, or Warwaruk as an example of a Ukrainian Canadian text for young readers. Goldstone's historical middle grade novel is also the only Canadian children's book focused on depicting life in the Ukrainian countryside right before the Holodomor, being set between 1929 and 1931 in Fedorovka, Ukraine. However, these events are also partially covered by Gal in her semibiographical novel *Philipovna: Daughter of Sorrow* examined in the last part of this chapter.

The Kulak's Daughter is loosely based on the story of Goldstone's family. During Stalin's collectivization her mother's father, a windmill owner from Ukraine, was labeled a *kulak*. The grandfather was imprisoned by the OGPU, the secret police. His land was confiscated and Goldstone's grandmother and her children were exiled to Yaya, Siberia. Although the man lived through the Holodomor, he was killed during Stalin's Great Terror. It is worth noting that in the first three years of the 1930s more than 2 million people were displaced to underpopulated parts of the Soviet Union, most notably Siberia (cf. Applebaum 132). These banishments were "the most chaotic" ones in the Soviet history, as the exiled were provided with no food and no shelter; thus a significant number of them did not even survive the journey or the first harsh Siberian winter (Bougai 5–22; Applebaum 132–133). However, as some of those who managed to survive later claimed, this inhumane "exile saved them from the famine of 1932-3" (Applebaum 134). Although it does save Olga, the protagonist of *The Kulak's Daughter*, who is 12 in 1932, and her three younger siblings, it directly causes the death of their baby brother Emil, whose "warm body becomes cold" on the train to Yaya, where he dies "on the dirty, rough wooden floor of the smelly freight train" (*"Kulak's Daughter"* 88–89). The loss of the child has severe consequences on Olga's mother's psyche: "[i]t's like she's fallen into a deep, dark hole, and we can't get her out" (119). Eventually the woman dies of typhus in the camp and it is Olga who becomes responsible for the survival of her family.

The character of Olga is based on Goldstone's mother, Else, whose photograph appears on the book's original cover. The back cover features an additional family picture showing the girl with her father and four siblings. The protagonist finds a similar picture, taken after her father's first arrest, among her mother's personal belongings. Looking at it she notices that "Mama's face is full of worry [...they] all look worried" (144). After the Second World War, the real Else immigrated to Canada with her two sisters. Goldstone was the first member of her family born in North America. As she writes in the novel's author's note, only there her family "finally found peace, freedom, and new homes" (n.p.). The initial response to *The Kulak's Daughter* was positive. Next to the good reader reviews, it was shortlisted for the 2010 McNally Robinson Book of the Year Award for Children and won the Silver Moonbeam Award. In her CM Review, Ruth Latta describes it as "a dramatic and disturbing novel about a family caught up in tumultuous changes in the Soviet Union" ("Reviews"). Unfortunately, because it was issued by an independent publishing house that shut down a year later, *The Kulak's Daughter* received limited promotion and by 2011 was out of print. Four years later, it was revised and reissued as *Red Stone* by Rebelight Publishing, together with a sequel titled *Broken Stone*. In the new version, Olga's name was surprisingly changed to Katya,[12] and the mention of Canada disappeared from the author's note – probably so as not to spoil the planned sequels. While the new title, inspired by the red granite from Katya's father's windmill, is more universal and makes the novel easier to market, the story's plot is generally the same.

Another important change between these two editions of Goldstone's first book is that instead of Else's photograph, the cover of *Red Stone* features a stork silhouette in a nest and barbed wire. The cover, just like the title, seems more modern and commercially appealing, hence this version of the novel is more likely to be read. *Red Stone* received additional critical praise by readers on Goodreads and similar platforms. Published a few months later, *Broken Stone* was shortlisted for the McNally Robinson Book of the Year Award for Children (2016). Both books were positively reviewed by *Resource Links*. Unluckily, Rebelight also folded; hence the novels, despite their high literary value, received little attention. While as of 2021, all three books are long out of print, the third volume in Goldstone's family tetralogy, titled *Tainted Amber*, was published by Ronsdale Press, another minor Canadian publisher, yet unlike Rebelight and Tire Swing Books, one with a long history and a stable catalog.[13] The fourth volume, *Crow Stone*, is scheduled for a late 2022 release. Although in both *Broken Stone* and *Tainted Amber* Katya recalls the Great Famine, the probable cause of the death of her father, the books focus on the protagonist's experiences in East Prussia, where she manages to escape from Stalinist repressions along with her siblings, but has to face another deadly regime, Nazism. Notably, all of the novels end with aperture.

The Kulak's Daughter shows that Stalin's collectivization in the late 1920s was met with resistance in Ukraine. Franz Halter, the father of Olga, initially seems optimistic and refuses to emigrate to Canada like one of his neighbors, the father of Olga's classmate Peter. Although Franz tells other farmers that he is "staying for the children" because his land is "their future," he eventually loses the land and his family (*"Kulak's Daughter"* 25). Initially he wants to be obedient, but Franz quickly discovers that mutual cooperation is not something Stalin expects. Although the 10-year-old Olga seems to notice that there is no escape from collectivization, her father believes that the Soviets will let him keep his windmill as long as he is obedient. Yet his resistance and attempts to follow the rules do not change the fact that for the authorities he is a *kulak* who should be liquidated.[14]

In *Red Stone* Goldstone introduces some important changes, especially in the representation of the protagonist's parents, the Bolshevik uncle, and Natasha, their milkmaid. In *The Kulak's Daughter* Olga's politically engaged Uncle Leo, the husband of Aunt Helena, is juxtaposed with Franz Halter. When Leo is first introduced, he argues that "[w]ith Josef Stalin as our leader, this country is destined for great things [... because] Stalin has a vision" (7). Although the man is a devoted communist, at first he emerges as a sympathetic character, bringing Olga and her siblings gifts like dolls, chocolate, and toy automobiles. Hence he appears to be a typical boogeyman who, as Martina Warner notes, "can charm at the same time as he repulses" (167). Later it turns out that Leo is a member of the OGPU. He drives "the black bird, 'der schwarze Vogel'" (50; in *Red Stone* more accurately called "the Black Raven" 53)[15] and eventually arrests Franz. Only then Olga realizes that "Uncle Leo is a traitor" (51). However, at the end of the novel, it is Leo, not Franz, who saves Olga and her siblings, whom he calls "kulak parasites," from going to an orphanage in Moscow or the Gulag (188).

In *Red Stone* Leo turns out to be a Slav and his depiction is more negative. From the very first scene Katya does not trust the man who kicks her dog. She also detaches herself from him by questioning his marriage to Aunt Helena, her mother's sister. Leo is called "a rooster of a man" by Olga's mother, an expression Katya uses years later to describe a Nazi soldier in *Tainted Amber* ("Red Stone" 4; "Tainted" 87). From the very first encounter, Leo's relationship with Katya's family is more formal; for example, he calls her father "Comrade Franz Halter" ("Red Stone" 9). He is also the Soviet official who comes to the protagonist's school.[16] Upon seeing Leo, Katya calls him Uncle, but he replies: "[m]y name is Comrade Bonkowski, you little twit," and tells the teacher to "teach these children to respect their leaders" (41). Leo's Slavic last name is not mentioned in *The Kulak's Daughter*, but in *Red Stone* it is clear that he must be Ukrainian, Polish, or Russian. In *Broken Stone* Leo prohibits Helena from taking Katya and her siblings to East Prussia, which eventually leads to the children's separation and the further deterioration of the Halters' family ties.

Whereas Olga's attachment to her absent and stubborn father may seem surprising in *The Kulak's Daughter*, in *Red Stone* Katya spends significantly more time with the man in the windmill. It is also Franz who tells the girl about Siberia "where rats run over people's faces while they sleep" ("Red Stone" 14). It turns out that before Katya's birth Franz Halter was exiled there during the First World War. The inclusion of this reference helps to explain some of Franz's surprising actions and his attempts to protect his windmill, the symbol of peace and wellbeing "built on a mound of red granite boulders" which "stays the same – arms reaching out to the wind, to the sky" (1). While Franz is "not going to let them [the Soviets] send [him] to Siberia," his stubbornness indirectly leads to his family's exile to Yaya (64). In both novels Olga/Katya and her siblings believe that their father will eventually save them. She treats her father as a symbolic windmill whose "arms [...] make her feel safe" (33). However, both the actual windmill and Franz Halter are destroyed by the Soviet regime. When the protagonist briefly meets her father in *Broken Stone*, he is in disguise. Katya asks him: "[w]hy didn't you find us sooner? Where were you? Why didn't you help us?" (12). While she understands that it was impossible for Franz to save them, she is disappointed that she cannot be reunited with the man as he has to stay in hiding. In *Tainted Amber*, which takes place a few years later, teenaged Katya recalls never seeing him again and the feeling of "[a]nger toward a father who broke his promise, a father who never came to rescue his children" (19). After the meeting in *Broken Stone*, she realizes that there is no one she can depend on.

However, the most significant difference between *The Kulak's Daughter* and *Red Stone* is the way Ukrainians are portrayed. First, in the revised edition Goldstone uses the terms Russian German and Russian but rarely refers to the fact that the novel is set in Ukraine. Second, the Halters' milkmaid Natasha, who is described as "a gypsy orphan" in the original novel, becomes a Ukrainian in *Red Stone* ("*Kulak's Daughter*" 27). In *The Kulak's Daughter* the 11-year-old cheerful girl pierces Olga's ears. Natasha disappears before the Halters are exiled, yet the golden earrings she lends Olga make it possible for the protagonist to exchange them for a stamp and send a letter to Aunt Helena asking for help. Because Olga does not know Natasha's last name, the letter is addressed to "*Natasha Village of Fedorofka, near Zhitomir in Ukraine. Please forward to Helena, wife of Leo*" (151). Natasha gets the letter and gives it to Helena; because of her, Olga and her siblings are saved.

In *Red Stone* Natasha becomes a Ukrainian orphan who is the Halters' clumsy, "dirty," and lazy servant (4). Despite being of similar age, Katya and Natasha are not friends and as the protagonist herself notices, she has "never thought of Natasha as a person" (21). Most importantly, in *Red Stone* it is Natasha who quickly starts believing Stalin's propaganda and joins the collective. She does not disappear but joins the collective "because she no longer has to work for kulaks" (57). In *Broken Stone* it turns out that Natasha lives in Katya's old house, which she shares with a few other families. When Katya briefly returns to Fedorofka at the beginning of the novel, she is shocked to see Natasha with "a red pioneer tie over [her] best dress, the green velvet one with the white lace collar," which her own mother sewed ("Broken Stone" 19–20).

Although in *Red Stone* Natasha is depicted in a one-dimensional and negative way, in *Broken Stone* she emerges as a more complex character disappointed with the collective and the new order. Seeing Katya, Natasha decides to take a risk and share food with her, including strawberries from the protagonist's mother's old garden, saying that the woman "was always good to [her]" ("Broken Stone" 23). During one of their following meetings, Natasha apologizes "for the way things are turning out" (24). By making Natasha a Ukrainian adolescent enchanted and then disenchanted with Stalinism, Goldstone shows the power of Soviet propaganda and further highlights the devastation of the Ukrainian countryside. She does not, however, villainize the girl and gives her more agency that Dueck or Smucker offer their Ukrainian characters.

By writing and introducing young Canadians, the implied readers of their books, to the little-known aspects of Ukrainian and Soviet history, the authors of the books examined in this chapter seem to anticipate that the memory of the survivors of the Red Terror, dekulakization, and the Holodomor may fall into oblivion if it is not commemorated and shared with the next generations. As Goldstone notes on her website, she writes stories she wanted to read as a child: "As the self-conscious first-born daughter of immigrants, I looked for my reflection in books.

Disappointed, I escaped into *Nancy Drew* mysteries and longed to be a detective" ("About Me"). With their combination of complex family and class dynamics with history little known in North America, *The Kulak's Daughter/Red Stone* and its sequels at times indeed read like mystery stories. Writing about her mother's traumatic childhood, Goldstone explores her own heritage and works through posttrauma (cf. Bezo and Maggi). Her parents came to Canada as refugees and "[w]riting memoirs wasn't on the top of their to-do list either. They had a language to learn and travel debts to pay off," Goldstone notes in a recent blog entry ("Brotlose Kunst"). Like many immigrants at that time, even William Kurelek's father, they believed that art, including literature, was "'brotlose kunst' (bread-less art)" ("Brotlose Kunst"). However, this type of art prevented the experiences of Stalin's victim from falling into oblivion.

The Holodomor in Canadian and Ukrainian Canadian Historical Fiction

Stalin's policies in the late 1920s and 1930s led to the destruction of the traditional social structures in the Ukrainian countryside and the appearance of another famine in the Soviet Union (Applebaum 193; cf. Yekelchyk 110–112). During the 1921 famine addressed in *Days of Terror* and *Nettie's Journey*, the state eventually agreed to help starving Ukrainians. However, in 1932–1933 Stalin propelled "a famine within the famine," which was "specifically targeted at Ukraine and Ukrainians" (Applebaum 193). The famine changed the people; empathy disappeared and neighbors were no longer jovial and kind. Such emotions were replaced with fear, distrust, and betrayal. As one of the survivors quoted in Applebaum's *Red Famine* admits: "[t]he warm traditional hospitality of the villagers had disappeared, to be replaced by mistrust and suspicion" (Miron Dolot qtd. in Applebaum 250). The destruction of Ukrainian social structures is echoed in the narratives examined in the following section.

In the last two decades the Holodomor has been mentioned vaguely in Canadian literature for young readers, for example, in Heather Kirk's *A Drop of Rain*. Also Goldstone openly refers to the Holodomor in *Broken Stone* and *Tainted Amber*, the sequels to *The Kulak's Daughter/Red Stone*.[17] After hearing rumors about another famine in the USSR, in *Broken Stone* Katya wonders if her father is really starving. However, remembering typical Ukrainian harvests and knowing about the good crops in Prussia, she asks: "[w]hy would people starve? Did they have a bad harvest? Early frost? Hail? Was there a drought? What else can destroy a crop?" ("Broken Stone" 135). Her questions highlight the artificial and implausible genesis of the Holodomor. Goldstone mentions Gareth Jones and articles in German newspapers with headlines like "'*Hungersnot in Russland.*' Famine in Russia" (135; emphasis in original). Understanding the power of Stalin's propaganda, Katya believes that "no other foreign correspondents are allowed into the countryside" because probably "things are so bad they don't want anyone to see" (135). Eventually Katya receives letters from her father who writes that *"Things are very bad here. There's no food. Death is everywhere,"* and asks his daughter for money (138; emphasis in original). In another letter he adds that: *"[t]hings are still very bad. No seed for planting. Please send more money"* (138; emphasis in original). The letters eventually stop coming and in *Tainted Amber* Katya recalls that in the last one her father "wrote about the famine," but she has "no idea where he is now, or if he even survived," suggesting that he may have been one of the victims of the Holodomor (53).[18]

The Holodomor in Ukrainian Canadian Historical Fiction before 2019

The first Canadian children's book in English unequivocally devoted to the Holodomor was *Enough* (2000), a picturebook by Marsha Forchuk Skrypuch and Michael Martchenko.[19] Moreover, for almost two decades Skrypuch's *Enough* and "The Rings," a short story published in *Kobzar's Children: A Century of Untold Ukrainian Stories*, a volume of Ukrainian Canadian fiction and nonfiction which Skrypuch edited in 2006, remained the only children's English-language texts on the Holodomor. "The Rings" was originally written as a chapter of an early draft of *Hope's War*, Skrypuch's first Ukrainian-themed novel discussed in Chapter 5. The protagonist of "The Rings" is Danylo, a boy who loses his entire family to the famine but manages to survive and escapes to Western Ukraine. This didactic[20] short story includes direct references to the Soviet atrocities and the propaganda used by the regime to convince Western journalists that the famine is not real as Ukrainians live in prosperity.

In her detailed analysis of *Enough*, Anastasia Ulanowicz argues that this multimodal narrative written in the form of a folk-inspired tale "offers particular insight into the role of traumatic collective memory in diasporic communities [...] and implicitly proposes collective, not just individual, strategies for working through such trauma" ("We Are the People" 52). *Enough* tells the story of a girl named Marusia who magically travels to Canada on a giant stork. There she is given enough food for her village to survive the famine. To trick the requisitioners – people taking all of the food from Ukrainian peasants – Marusia decides to bury the wheat at a local cemetery. Ulanowicz argues that by setting part of the picturebook in Canada instead of an unknown magical land, Skrypuch and Martchenko echo "anxieties and concerns that structure diasporic cultural memory of the Holodomor" (53). Moreover, this seems to further strengthen the alleged links between the Ukrainian countryside and the Canadian prairies I discuss in Chapter 1.

The Holodomor in Ukrainian Canadian Historical Fiction after 2019: Mutala

In 2019, two years after Anne Applebaum published her influential *Red Famine* and the year of the release of Agnieszka Holland's film *Mr. Jones* about the aforementioned Gareth Jones, a Welsh journalist who tried to inform the West of the Great Famine, new narratives appeared on the Canadian books market. Marion Mutala, an author known for *Baba's Babushka*, an ethnic-themed series of picturebooks which I examine in Chapters 1 and 3, published a short epistolary novel entitled *My Dearest Dido: The Holodomor Story*. Clearly didactic in character, the book is accompanied by numerous paratexts: a bibliography and a list of sources (147–158); a glossary of Ukrainian words (135–137); a timeline of the famine (139–140); a list of questions asking readers to research other genocides in the Ottoman Empire, Nazi Germany, and Rwanda (131–133); a note by the author explaining her connections to Ukraine and the Holodomor; a song and poem written by Mutala (144–145); and historical information about the recognition of the Holodomor by Ukraine, Western countries, the Government of Saskatchewan, three other Canadian provinces, and the Federal Government of Canada (142). By including so many paratexts, Mutala attempts to "authenticate" the story and show its historical correctness (cf. Kokkola 58). Yet children often do not read paratexts and sometimes such strong focus on didacticism can be counterproductive (cf. Kokkola 6–61; Pesonen 98).

In his review of the book included on the blurb on the cover, Bill Gulka from the University of Saskatchewan claims that *My Dearest Dido* describes the Great Famine "in a language and context that children can relate to," thus it can "serve to educate and sensitize the next generation to strive for peace and dignity among all people." However, it is difficult to agree with this openly positive statement. Mutala was, as she admits in the author's note, asked by Gulka to write a book whose form "came to [her], perhaps by the Holy Spirit" (5). *My Dearest Dido* is written in letters exchanged between the 17-year-old Hanka and her Ukrainian grandfather, Dido Bohdan, both living in different parts of Saskatchewan, Canada. The letters are intertwined with the girl's diary entries. While Dido came to Canada after the Holodomor, he lives where "[m]any Ukrainians settled [...] during the first wave of immigration in 1891," including his wife's family (97). In their letters both Hanka and Dido quote from numerous popular and scholarly sources. For example, talking about the devastation of his village, Dido paraphrases testimonies quoted in Applebaum's *Red Famine* and points to the Soviet ban on religion and traditional Ukrainian customs. The mention of Applebaum in Hanka's letter comes as the first suggestion that *My Dearest Dido* is indeed set in present-day Canada.[21]

Although the characters are fictional, their stories are based on various accounts of survivors of the Holodomor, mostly those mentioned by

Applebaum in *Red Famine*. Mutala includes the days and months of each letter/entry, but leaves out the year. This may be her attempt to make the book more universal and approachable to contemporary and future readers, hence more likely to provoke the transmission of next-generation memory. Still, considering that Hanka's grandfather was only eight during the Holodomor and he exchanges written letters with his teenage granddaughter, modern readers in technology-saturated times may find it challenging to identify with the narrative and the characters. This is especially important since research shows that "readers who become personally involved in the story also obtain a higher level of understanding than students who read efferently, or primarily to recall, paraphrase, or analyze" (Dressel 750). Identification with characters and their struggles is vital in the context of books for young readers, who are more likely than experienced readers to uncritically accept and assimilate the values conveyed to them in a text as long as the text fascinates them (cf. Richter 19). Becoming involved in *My Dearest Dido* may be difficult, thus the mnemonic potential of the novel is not as significant.

After learning about the Holodomor at school, Hanka decides to make it the topic of her history essay, a theme typical in Canadian children's and YA literature, including Langston's *Lesia's Dream* and Kirk's *A Drop of Rain*. Already in the first letter sent to her Dido, the girl quotes detailed historical information and mentions carrying out "research," despite hearing about the famine on the same day (7). Her words "[c]hildren died first, then the men, and then the women. That's crazy!" are supposed to instantly shock the young readers and highlight the atrocity of the famine (7). After being informed that her Dido is a survivor of the Holodomor, Hanka asks him to confirm the information she has already learned at school. In her question the girl seems to emphasize the importance of oral history and the intergenerational transfer of memory in understanding the past. After all, as Rothberg contends, cultural memory of such traumatic events "is primarily collective and historical, although it is never divorced from individuals and their biographies either" (14). By encouraging Dido to share his experiences with her, Hanka tries to make the difficult topic of the Holodomor more accessible to herself, hence also to contemporary Canadian readers.

Misinformation in children's historical fiction, as in *My Dearest Dido*, is dangerous because upon finding out about it, the readers may start questioning some historically accurate facts and dates found in the books (cf. Kokkola; Bosmajian). Instead of initially sharing his personal story, in the first letter, Dido Bohdan replies with a detailed historical statement, which reads like a passage from a textbook: "It is believed more people died in this Ukrainian genocide than any other genocide in world history" and "it is believed about 10,000,000 people died, 3,000,000 were children" (9). Here Mutala seems to deliberately quote exaggerated data while using "may," a modal verb expressing possibility, which comes as a surprise considering the historical sources listed at the end of the book.[22]

However, Mutala may be purposedly trying to shock the readers by showing them the scale of the Holodomor. She further does it by comparing the Holodomor to the Holocaust. When Hanka says that "Stalin was pure evil," she adds that "he killed off more people than Hitler did in the Holocaust!" (17). While this can be a reference to the total toll of the victims of Stalinism, an uninformed reader can mistake it for the toll of the Holodomor. Hanka also quotes her teacher's words, which echo the Holocaust remembrance discourse: "we must speak about this *Holodomor*, so people know the horrors that happened" (11; emphasis in original). Mutala uses a cliché usually associated with the Holocaust when Hanka writes: "[w]e need to [talk about it] so that history doesn't repeat itself" (11). Already in the second letter the teen protagonist mentions the past and present denial of the Holodomor by reporters and politicians, both in the West and in Soviet Russia; she includes direct references to Walter Duranty's infamous *New York Times* article "Russians Hungry, but not Starving" (11–12) where, in response to Gareth Jones' "Famine grips Russia," published a day before, Duranty claimed that "[t]here is no starvation or deaths from starvation but there is widespread mortality from disease due to malnutrition" (qtd. in Applebaum 302; cf. Shkandrij 49–50).

In *My Dearest Dido*, Mutala echoes the general attitudes of the diaspora and the problematic attempts at equaling the Holocaust with the Holodomor. After his spiritual awakening, Dido underlines the famine's status as a genocide saying: "[t]his tragedy, the *Holodomor*, occurred simply because [they] were Ukrainians" (92). Moreover, he voices the novel's most challenging words: "Let the Holodomor be remembered forever. Speak, remember. Like *other holocausts, genocides* and wars that occurred and are still happening. We need to speak against all injustices against so many people in the world" (91; emphasis mine). As Rothberg notes, "debates about collective memory and group identity are primarily struggles over injustices of recognition, over whose history and culture will be recognized" (20). Yet Ball and Rudling argue that instead of being productive, such comparisons between the Holocaust and the Holodomor are used to deploy the Great Famine "for the purpose of competitive victimology in the effort to appropriate the Holocaust's moral capital" (90). This seems to be the case in *My Dearest Dido*. After decades of repressing the traumatic memories, Dido suddenly becomes "on a mission" to share them as he wants all Canadians to know that: "Ukrainian people's story of genocide, the *Holodomor*, did truly occur [and he is] a survivor of this genocide" (87, 91). His words seem to echo typical Holocaust-remembrance narratives, especially when he says: "It is essential I speak up now, even if it leads to my death. Ukrainians cannot be silent anymore" (85).

On the one hand, Hanka's questions and initial lack of knowledge reflect the fact that for many years talking about the Great Famine was not allowed. However, they come as a surprise considering the role of the Holodomor in Ukrainian Canadian cultural memory and diasporic education (cf. Ulanowicz "We *Are* the People"; Kuryliw). In her letters Hanka asks Dido, who for years repressed his memories, immature and overwhelming questions: "[d]id your family talk about hushing [up] the situation? Did you hear talk like this from the Communist Party?" (13); "[w]ere you shocked when Stalin implemented this law of 'Five Stalks of Grain'?" (32). Hanka is persistent and becomes obsessed with the topic of the Holodomor when she recognizes its remembrance as an important element of her Ukrainian Canadian identity. Yet she seems to be incapable of grasping the history of the Great Famine without hearing her grandfather's own testimony. Therefore, Mutala emphasizes the role of storytelling and oral history in cultivating cultural memory. That is why Hanka constantly wants to validate the words of her teacher using her grandfather's testimony.

What seems to be another problematic aspect of *My Dearest Dido* is that although Dido initially does not want to talk about the past, his granddaughter continues asking questions, at times forcing the man to write about repressed memories. Dido's early hesitation to talk about his traumatic past reflects the experience of many survivors. As Applebaum notes, some "sought to describe these terrible months, in written accounts and thousands of interviews," yet "[f]or others who managed to live through this period, the experience was so awful that they were later unable to recall anything about it at all" (246–247). Dido represents the latter category, echoing Danylo, the grandfather in Skrypych's *Hope's War*, examined in Chapter 5. Hanka's determination has different consequences on her Dido, who, on the one hand, answers her letters, but on the other hand, at first avoids some questions and eventually falls ill. No sooner does he recover than he decides to share the entire story with Hanka.

Considering the novel's historical inaccuracies and Mutala's questionable narrative choices, it is improbable that *My Dearest Dido* has the potential to become the source of next-generation memory for the young readers, both mainstream and diasporic ones. Unlike in *Nettie's Journey*, *Lesia's Dream*, or *Andrei and the Snow Walker*, it is not as obvious who the giver and the receiver of memory is in *My Dearest Dido*.[23] After all, the teacher initiates the exchange between the two protagonists and it is Hanka who wants to "educate" her Dido by asking questions and quoting long passages from history books. Yet it is her persistence which makes him open up and try to work through the Holodomor trauma. Here I want to concur with Mingshui Cai that "[m]ediocre literature cannot give children an engaging aesthetic experience; neither can it move their hearts or enlighten their heads. A mediocre work, even if it is culturally correct, may not be very useful" (91). Thus, despite Mutala's praiseworthy attempts at popularizing the theme of the Holodomor, the novel is not believable and with the factual errors at times even disrespectful towards the young readers.

The Holodomor in Ukrainian Canadian Historical Fiction after 2019: Gal

Despite being based on true stories, most of the books examined in this chapter are fictionalized and to some extent tend to "spare the child," understood as concealing "atrocious history with reader-protective strategies" (cf. Bosmajian xv). Valentina Gal in *Philipovna: Daughter of Sorrow*, inspired by the story of her mother's childhood, also limits the descriptions of atrocities, but the novel is the most historically accurate and detailed book about the Great Famine. Because it is written in the form of a retrospective narrative, the mentions of the eventual migration to Canada and the hints at the survival of the young protagonist and her aunt make the story more hopeful, even with the depictions of starvation, death, and other brutalities. Such a narrative technique, as Lydia Kokkola argues, "reassure the reader that the outrageous protagonist does survive" (63).

Similar to Goldstone in *The Kulak's Daughter/Red Stone*, in the first part of the novel Gal focuses on the deterioration of the Ukrainian countryside during Stalin's collectivization. Vera Philipovna is introduced as a six-year-old orphan whose Aunt Xena promises to do everything to keep her safe. Against all odds, Xena keeps the promise; she loses almost her entire family to the famine, but Vera Philipovna survives. The second part of the novel centers around the worst months of the Holodomor in the winter of 1932–1933 and the protagonist's fight for survival. Like in *Enough* by Skrypuch and Martchenko, also here people try to hide their wheat in the ground. Yet unlike in the 2000 picturebook, in Gal's novel the attempts are unsuccessful as their food is found by the requisitioners who are searching for everything edible using metal rods, also at the cemeteries.[24]

With its depiction of a child survivor of the Holodomor, *Philipovna* challenges the "assumptions of and desire for a pastoral, innocent and joyous childhood" (Bosmajian xi). Initially Philipovna acts like a typical child: she plays in the forest with Mitya, a lonely boy she befriends, plays checkers with her family, believes in old wives' tales, and desperately wants to start school like her older cousins. However, throughout the novel, she quickly matures and at 9 acts like a much older person. Similar to Olga/Katya in Goldstone's series, Philipovna gradually becomes disenchanted with reality; yet she also never loses faith and hope. Philipovna is a very good student who quickly learns Russian, the new language of instruction.[25] Despite her young age, she starts questioning the teacher's words and seems more immune to the power of Soviet propaganda. Dissimilar to the previous Ukrainian teacher who was imprisoned by the regime,[26] the new Russian one is not sympathetic and treats the starving children with hostility when they lose their family members to the famine. Even during the worst period of the Holodomor the children have to attend school as "[t]here's no place for lazy brats in the new order" (157). While initially the children, including Philipovna, try to enjoy spending time together at school, they gradually become too tired and hungry to play.

The image of the starving and shamed Ukrainian children is juxtaposed with the well-fed young pioneers brought to the village as symbols of the success of Stalin's collectivization. The pioneers see the starved children as "filthy peasants" who can give them "pestilences" (159). Barely standing, with their stomachs swollen from malnutrition, the peasant children have to sing "songs about ripening fields and golden harvests and the glory of our motherland – Mother Russia" (163). Told not to interact with the "filthy peasants," the pioneers try not to look at them. When they do, it is always with disdain. The scenes contrasting two types of children reflect the power of the anti-Ukrainian and anti-peasant propaganda present in the cities, which was used to convince Soviet citizens that the starving farmers were "second-class citizens" and carriers of diseases (cf. Applebaum 236).

Moreover, Gal shows that the destruction of the social norms in the Ukrainian countryside affected the traditional relations between children and adults. After losing her young cousin Victor to starvation, Philipovna cannot mourn as she has to go to school. Yet she finds no compassion on behalf of the teacher. On the contrary, he openly ridicules her and victim-blames her family and other peasants. Despite her young age, in one of the novel's most touching scenes, Philipovna confronts the teacher. She screams that Victor died because of Stalin, his army, the Ukrainian requisitioners recruited by the Soviets, and school violence and propaganda, which were "the worst of all" (184). Philipovna blames the teacher who "beat [Victor] every day till he didn't want to live any more – till he hadn't enough strength to get water or play with [her] or go to the river to catch crayfish with [her] or pick flowers" (184). What makes the protagonist's angry words even more shocking to the teacher is that she openly mentions religion, saying that Victor is "in Heaven, with Mama and *Tahto* and Jesus where [the teacher] or Uncle Ivan or Father Stalin will never hurt him – ever again" (184). The teacher beats Philipovna, whose aunt faints when she sees her niece. The girl's open expression of faith is ridiculed as the communist state is supposed to become "her new Heaven and Father Stalin her ruler" (186). While Philipovna is only eight at the time of the confrontation with the teacher, she is immediately labeled as an "enemy of the people" and is to be imprisoned and deported to Siberia (186).

Gal's novel is the only Holodomor-themed text that explicitly addresses the issue of the Ukrainian collaborators. As Malko notes, during the Holodomor Ukrainians faced "existential threats" and had to make "ideological choices" (xv). While some of the collaborators were criminals who wanted to take advantage of their neighbor's hardships, others who joined the collective were afraid of losing their land or being exiled, as described in the novels by Goldstone and Gal (cf. Applebaum

122). As Applebaum notes, the recruiters and their policy were met with hostility, and "the peasants' stubborn opposition made the activists angrier, more prone to violence, and more convinced of the rightness of the cause" (120). This is reflected in *Philipovna* where some members of the protagonist's community collaborate with the Soviets. Gal shows two types of collaborators represented by Ivan and Paulo. Ivan is openly abusive and seems to enjoy tormenting his neighbors, including children. Paulo at first believes in collectivization but later realizes that the authorities are trying to starve his village; hence, he emerges as an implicated subject (cf. Chapter 5). This reflects Applebaum's arguments that "many local activists refused to carry out orders that they knew would kill their neighbours" (238; cf. Malko). Notably, Paulo is the one who advises Xena to take Philipovna away from the village and hints that Ivan plans to rape the girl. Remarkably, Paulo sees the survival of Vera Philipovna necessary for the survival of Ukraine: "If you young ones don't make it, our lives are worth nothing," he admits, adding "[o]ur history, our culture, it'll all surely die. I won't make it, but you must!" (189). Philipovna does make it, as Aunt Xena takes her to the orphanage in the city. This theme is historically accurate as some children survived the Holodomor only because their parents left them at orphanages (cf. Applebaum 204, 275–278).

Philipovna survives, but the journey to the city orphanage is dangerous. The borders between the cities and villages are closed and the police remove begging people from the cities. Instead of finding sympathy, in the city the girl is called "filthy little *Zaraza*" and ridiculed for her thinness and dirtiness (198). Hostility towards the victims of the Holodomor portrayed by Gal is not that surprising considering that the authorities "loudly and angrily blamed the Ukrainian peasants for their fate" (Applebaum 251). People in urban areas were especially unsympathetic towards those peasants who succeeded in getting through the police barricades and came to cities to beg because they saw them as potential carriers of disease. Gal portrays this type of hostility when an urban girl sees Philipovna and asks her mother: "[w]here do girls like that come from, Mama? And why is she so filthy?" (198). She is told: "[m]ake sure that you never become one of them" (198). This reaction echoes Sontag's words quoted at the beginning of this chapter, but it also reflects the fact that "the witnesses of intense suffering did not always feel – perhaps could not feel – pity. Instead, they turned their anger on the sufferer," in this case a helpless child (Applebaum 251). However, Gal also shows acts of kindness as Philipovna and Xena encounter a man who gives them bread and says, "God be with you. You look like you could use tens of those" (199). Such acts, however, were rare.

The experience of the orphanage is so traumatic that in the future Philipovna represses her memory, which may be Gal's way of suggesting that she does, to some extent, want to spare the readers.[27] The caregivers are a Russian female doctor called Ivanovna and a nurse who spend most of their time taking care of the infirmary, where very sick children go but never recover. Philipovna is also reluctant to befriend other children, being afraid of the potential young collaborators. It is at the orphanage where she learns to repress her feelings: "I learned to look through people and to turn off any feelings I had left inside," she admits (208). Staying at the orphanage is not pleasant because most of the children smell "of human filth and vomit," but at least being there, Philipovna is fed "enough to survive, but never enough to feel satisfied" (204, 207).

While Philipovna eventually forgets her own first name, Vera, which means faith in Ukrainian, she never loses faith and keeps secretly praying. By the time she is to celebrate her ninth birthday, the girl encounters death and the spread of contagious diseases. Remembering her aunt's treatment of her sick cousins, when there is no more medicine the girl encourages doctor Ivanovna to use folk remedies, including urine and poppy tea. "If anyone survives this misery, it will surely be you," the woman tells her as it turns out that Xena's healing methods work (245). Diseases spread quickly because Ivanovna uses the same spoon while giving medicine to the children. As Philipovna retrospectively explains: "[t]hose were the days before we knew about sharing spoons and gladded with others when they had contagious diseases" (216). Moreover, she informs the readers that "[t]here was no penicillin or any of the drugs we are used to today" (235). With no access to medicine and even basic products, Ivanovna is soon forced to "play the part of God as she decided who would live and who wouldn't" (233). The woman's negative attitude towards the famine and Ukrainians slowly changes when she realizes there is not enough food and medicine even in the city, and Stalin's propaganda is pure fiction.

The protagonist does not usually act her age, but the novel is retrospective, and at times it seems that the young Philipovna is intertwined with her older self.[28] Nevertheless, her maturity is not surprising as often children in books about genocides "are survivors and have strength beyond their age," a theme I further address in Chapter 5 (Fry 6). However, at times Philipovna seems quite naïve. Kokkola notes that "[t]o understand a character, even in a work of literature, we do not need to find him or her consistent, only believable" (140). Philipovna is overly mature for her age but sometimes acts gullibly and childishly, yet she emerges as a believable character trying to stay alive. Gal shows that hope and faith make it possible for Philipovna to survive. Such emphasis on the power of hope and faith is a common trope in many Holocaust books (cf. Kertzer 54). Nevertheless, Gal demonstrates that not everyone's spirit is as unbreakable as Philipovna's.[29]

Gal's portrayal of the destruction of the Ukrainian countryside with its traditional morality during the Holodomor is the most graphic and historically accurate. Afraid of the Soviet officials and local collaborators, the starving villagers mostly stay at home. People eat grass, bark, stray cats, dogs,[30] and nightingale eggs, with the latter symbolizing the destruction of "the soul of the Ukrainian countryside" (170). While Ukrainians are forced to eat the nightingale eggs, the Soviets kill the birds only for fun. As Philipovna retrospectively adds: "[i]t would be a good three years before the nightingales returned to their normal ways" (170). However, even long after the Holodomor Philipovna's countryside never fully returns to the pre-Soviet warm hospitality. Feeling defeated, most of the survivors join the *kolkhoz*. Talking about the Holodomor in public becomes forbidden: "as if the famine had never happened" (266). The destruction of the Ukrainian countryside further suppresses mnemonic practices, yet the memory of the famine survives in oral history.[31]

The Holodomor also changes Philipovna and her family. Being an orphan, Philipovna becomes "stigmatized, [and] untouchable," especially after "Father Stalin's decree that all of the orphans were his children" (267). At school children call her "Stalin's bastard" (271). Aunt Xena, after the loss of her husband and all children, except for her older daughter, is "a shell" of her old self (265). Philipovna's description of her post-Holodomor community as one of "suspicion and silence" (172) seems to reflect what Brent Bezo and Stefani Maggi demonstrate in their article on intergenerational transmission of Holodomor trauma (90). The children and grandchildren of the survivors, as they argue, "reported that family oral histories of Holodomor-related atrocities, coupled with the knowledge that Ukrainians were targeted, contributed to a general fear and mistrust of others" (90). Yet Stalin does not manage to break the spirit of Philipovna, her aunt, and cousin. The three of them survive and symbolically keep the Ukrainian cultural memory alive by embroidering using traditional Ukrainian colors: "the red is for love and the black is for sorrow" (267). As Aunt Xena says, "[they]'re all Ukrainians" whose "families have lived here together for over a thousand years" (271). They survive, but with the Soviet regime and the destruction of the countryside, the only place Ukrainians can cultivate their customs, keep the memory of the Holodomor alive for the next generations, and build a simulacrum of "the normal ways" is Canada. Only there Philipovna can "live in peace" because she "couldn't really live unless [she] was free" (274). There is no place for freedom in Soviet Ukraine.

Conclusion

Since the 1940s the Holodomor has been an important part of Ukrainian Canadian cultural memory, yet until the late 2010s it was of minor relevance in children's historical fiction. Although the events preceding the Great Famine have been present in Canadian literature since the 1970s, books like Smucker's popular *Days of Terror* do not explicitly focus on the experiences of ethnic Ukrainians and show them rather negatively. However, the chronotopes of the novels by Smucker, Dueck, and Goldstone depict the ethnoreligious diversity of the Ukrainian countryside before the Red Terror and Stalin's collectivization. This diversity, as

I have argued in Chapter 1, is also present is Ukrainian Canadian prairie narratives.

The visibility of the Holodomor in Anglophone historical fiction has significantly increased in the last few years. New books of different formats keep on appearing on the Canadian book market, including ones issued by major publishers, such as *Five Stalks of Grain* (2022), a graphic novel by Adrian Lysenko and Ivanka Theodosia Galadza, and *Winterkill* (2022) by Skrypuch, whose bestselling Second World War novels examined in Chapter 5 challenge the negative stereotypes associated with Ukrainians in North America. Another Holodomor-themed children's book, Katherine Marsh's *The Lost Year*, is set for an early 2023 publication.[32] The recently growing mainstream popularity of such books is significant considering that for decades the memory of the Great Famine in Canada was repressed and reduced to diasporic forms of commemoration.[33] This explains why most of the narratives discussed in this chapter were published by small, independent publishers or were self-published. Unfortunately, books with limited promotion, hence readership, are less likely to provoke the transmission of next-generation memory. Moreover, not all of them meet the criteria of *good* historical fiction, primary because of inaccuracies and counterproductive comparisons of the Holodomor to the Holocaust (cf. Chapter 5). The majority was written by second-, third-, or fourth-generation descendants of immigrants from present-day Ukraine who heard about the stories of the Red Terror, Stalin's collectivization, and the Holodomor from their family members. After all, the memory of such traumatic memories "affects not only the individual, but also the family and community-society, and retains a historical perspective" (Bezo and Maggi 93). By sharing these stories with young Canadian readers, the authors can contribute to the transfer of next-generation memory to the young readers whom they anticipate not to have tangible links to the history portrayed in these narratives. However, in order for this to happen, their books have to be widely available and read.

Notes

1 While the protagonist's name is Vera, Ukrainian for Faith, she is usually called by her patronym Philipovna because "[b]ack home the father's name was our legacy. It really mattered something, not like here in Canada" (Gal 4).
2 The first Holodomor-themed novel, Ulas Samchuk's *Maria*, appeared in 1934. The book was translated into English by Roma Franko as *Maria: A Chronicle of a Life* (2011).
3 It was also used by other writers, including émigré authors Ulas Samchuk or Vasyl Barka.
4 Some Ukrainian scholars argue that the 3.9 million figure is understated and the actual number of Holodomor victims was much higher (cf. Malko 196).
5 Writing about the memory wars between Ukrainian Canadians and Jewish Canadians, Karyn Ball and Per Anders Rudling argue that some

ultranationalist [...] lobby groups have often resorted to a competitive victimology as they exaggerate the death count associated with the Ukrainian famine of 1932–1933, sometimes referred to as the *Holodomor*, in order to appropriate and supersede the Jewish genocide's perceived moral capital.

(38)

However, it is worth noting that the expression "the Ukrainian holocaust" was first used by Wasyl Hryshko in 1978 when "holocaust" was defined as "a mass slaughter of people" (cf. Malko). I agree with Victoria A. Malko, who refers to the application of the term "holocaust" in the context of the Holodomor as "emphatic, yet misleading" (Malko xvii).

6 However, as I demonstrate in Chapter 1, the diaspora embraced Eastern Ukrainian myths and traditions.
7 Smucker briefly writes about the persecution of Mennonites in Southern Ukraine in the 1940s in *Henry's Red Sea*, a short novel set in post–Second World War Berlin, published in 1955. Although Canada is mentioned as the promised land where Henry's sister wants to move, the protagonist's family eventually moves to South America. This is caused by the fact that Rudy, a young orphaned boy Henry befriends in the DP camp, is disabled, and at that time, immigrants to Canada were expected to be healthy. Deciding not to leave Rudy and following the teachings of the Bible, Henry's family sacrifices their only opportunity to go to Canada.
8 *Days of Terror* won Canada Council Children's Literature Prize and Ruth Schwartz Children's Book Award. It is listed as one of three key books for children 10+ in Ron Jobe and Paula Hart's teacher guide *Canadian Connections: Experiencing Literature with Children* (47–48). Writing about the book Jobe and Hart do not use the word Ukraine and refer to Ukrainians as "Russian peasants" (48).
9 Most Mennonite families experienced starvation, rape, and diseases such as typhus (cf. Epp 416).
10 Jews from the Russian empire were emigrating to escape religious persecution already during the "as government-condoned pogroms and restrictions [which] escalated after the assassination of Tsar Alexander I in 1881" (Swyripa "Storied" 17).
11 On the other hand, Applebaum points to "[a]necdotal evidence" according to which some ethnic Germans during the Holodomor "did get food aid and other forms of help from German sources" (Applebaum 286). Yet Germans, similarly to Poles and Jews, "would become targets later on," mostly during the Great Terror and the Second World War (Applebaum 286).
12 The name Katya may be a tribute to Catherine the Great, who ruled Russia from 1762 to 1796. Born Sophia of Anhalt Zerbst, in 1744 she married the heir to the Russian throne. Catherine II is mentioned as an example of a powerful German Russian woman with whom Katya identifies with in *Tainted Amber* (cf. 218–219). Goldstone does not mention the complex legacy of Catherine II and the role her rule played in the Russification of Ukraine, the destruction of the Zaporozhian Sich, and the annihilation of the Ukrainian Catholic church.
13 Despite publishing award-winning children's books and being a member of Manitoba Writers' Guild, The Writers' Union of Canada, and Canadian Society of Children's Authors, Illustrators, and Performers no mention of

Goldstone appears in the 372 volumes of the *Something About the Author* series issued by Gale. The volumes include multiple entries on fellow Canadian authors of historical fiction, including Skrypuch, Langston, Dueck, and Kathy Kacer.

14 While Olga's family is not wealthy, they are landowners who "hire outside help," which is enough to be labeled "kulaks [...] rich peasants," as Franz is told (23). Because in the early 1930s *kulaks* became the enemies of the state and were persecuted, children at school in Goldstone's *Red Stone* hear that "[a]ll private landowners are bloodsuckers" (42). In this revised version of *The Kulak's Daughter*, pupils are taught that "[t]here is no such thing as a good kulak [...] All are exploiters. All are class enemies" (42). Olga's/Katya's father's resistance to join the collective, which leads to his family's exile to Siberia, echoes the reality as most farmers in Ukraine were hesitant to join the *kolkhoz*. When Gerda, the Halters' housekeeper is arrested and says: "I'm not a kulak. You can't just send me away. What's my crime?," the Soviet official replies "[w]e'll give you one. Article 58. Treason. Ten years of hard labour" ("Red Stone" 66), highlighting that even working with the *kulaks* was seen as treasonous.

15 Black Raven was a colloquial expression used to call the cars driven by Stalin's secret police, most notably during the Great Terror. Like real ravens, the cars, whose drivers arrested "enemies of the state" who often never returned home, symbolized death (cf. Kamińska-Maciąg; Oziewicz; Krahn).

16 Leo is also the one who brings to Katya's school a propaganda poster which "shows a giant tractor running over animals and farmers. The words, 'destroy the kulaks as a class,' are sprawled across it in big letters" ("Red Stone" 42).

17 Given the importance of the Holodomor in the collective memory of the Ukrainian diaspora in Canada, as well as the presence of collectivization in children's literature, it may come as a surprise that the Great Famine first appeared not in Canada but in France. In *Famine: L'arme des tyrans*, published in 1994, Muriel Pernin, an author also known for the first children's book about Babyn Yar, introduces the French readers to the Great Famine, which, as she writes, was strange, unnatural, as it acted as a weapon in the act of ethnic cleansing. The book is based on the memories of witnesses and survivors with whom the author met in Kyiv in the early 1990s. It is worth noting that *Famine: L'arme des tyrans* is not only a book about the Holodomor. Pernin juxtaposes it with the famine in Kosovo in 1993 and relates it to other genocides.

18 In *Crow Stone*, set at the end and right after the Second World War, it turns out that the man survived the Holodomor but was killed by the Soviets in 1937.

19 The first Ukrainian children's book about the Holodomor, Kateryna Ehorushkina's *A Chest*, illustrated by Iryna Rud-Volga (2020), is also a picturebook.

20 The educational value of "The Rings" is explored by Valentina Kuryliw in *Holodomor in Ukraine, The Genocidal Famine 1932–1933: Learning Materials for Teachers and Students* (98–99).

21 Similar to all other books examined in this chapter, also here Canada is depicted as the promised land, which is best shown in Dido's words: "I am so glad I came to Canada and you did not have to experience what happened to me" (46). Dido's sophisticated statements, such as "[t]he Holodomor was

an act of genocide against the Ukrainian people committed by the Soviet Communist regime" (49), may come as abrupt, but provoke the protagonist to question why she has never heard about the famine at school. Hanka realizes that "there are people in the world, in Canada, that survived and are living today to share their stories," once again emphasizing the importance of testimonies and oral history (55). Interestingly, as is the case in many Holocaust novels, the descriptions of atrocities in *My Dearest Dido* underline the status of Canada as the promised land and a safe place. As Hanka herself writes: "[s]tudying this has made me aware of how grateful I am to live in Canada, a free country" (61). Dido finally answers Hanka's last question: "[h]ow did you come to Canada?" (65). He talks about being an orphan and surviving with the help of a friend called Taras, named after Shevchenko. The novel ends with Dido giving Hanka, who barely speaks Ukrainian, tickets to Ukraine as a birthday gift. Symbolically newly reborn, he wants her not only to remember traditions but also to value her "ancestors and [her] culture, as it is [her] backbone and makes [her] who [she is] today" (101). When Hanka and Dido travel to Ukraine, the readers are informed that *My Dearest Dido* is indeed a contemporary narrative, as Dido mentions Ukraine's recognition of the Holodomor as an act of genocide and Hanka references "war in the east with Russia's invasion," "the 'Heaven's Hundred,'" and the 2013-2014 Revolution of Dignity (110, 120, 125).

22 While in "The Rings" Skrypuch also uses 10 million as the number of Holodomor deaths, the story was written 20 years before *My Dearest Dido* and published in 2006 when the historical knowledge about the Great Famine was not as extensive as it is now (48). This number was also quoted by Prime Minister Harper during his 2010 trip to Ukraine (cf. Ball and Per Anders Rudling 50–51). The author's note in *Bottle of Grain: A Holodomor Story*, a picturebook by Rhea Good and Natalie Warner (2021), based on a true story of a Holodomor survivor, also includes the number 6–12 million. Since *Bottle of Grain* was self-published, the use of this number – absent from recent books issued by major publishers – must have been the author's conscious decision.

23 The theme of intergenerational exchange of memory appears in another Anglophone children's book published in North America, yet one not authored by a Canadian. Carola Schmidt is a Ukrainian Brazilian pediatric oncology pharmacist and writer whose picturebooks *Tell Me a Story, Babushka* (2019) and *Babushka is Homesick* (2020), both illustrated by Vinicius Melo, are devoted to the Holodomor and the post–Second World War migration. In late 2022 *Tell Me a Story, Babushka* will be reissued in North America by Reycraft Books with new illustrations by Anita Barghigiani.

24 When a 15-year-old boy named Stepan Tymashenko tries to steal some wheat from the field, he is told: "[t]his is how you treat Father Stalin? [...] He gives you an opportunity to be part of his glorious plan and you steal the wheat from his field?" (Gal 174). After all, "the grain belonged to the state and Father Stalin," not to the people (Gal 175). As the local villagers are too weak to work on the harvests, city workers come to help. Yet they take away the grain and let it rot instead of feeding the starving. Both scenes emphasize the cruelty of the officials.

25 When Philipovna goes to school for the first time, the place is already a propagandist machine of the Soviet regime like in *The Kulak's Daughter/*

Red Stone. In Goldstone's novel children "have special meetings with guest speakers from the government" and are taught that "[t]he Soviet Union cannot become strong unless all its enemies are found"; that is why children have to spy on adults, including their parents ("Kulak's Daughter" 59–60; "Red Stone" 23). As Malko argues, although teachers were supposed "to enlighten the masses and lead them in the struggle for national liberation," some of them actively spread propaganda and participated "in collectivization, and even grain-requisition campaigns" (Malko xxiii; cf. Pauly). This seems to be the case in the novels by Goldstone and Gal. At school Olga/Katya learns in Russian about Stalin, whose picture hangs on the wall next to that of Lenin, "the father of communism," which "is going to make the whole world a better place" ("Kulak's Daughter" 32). It is at school where Olga/Katya hears that "Stalin is watching [...] sitting in his office in Moscow, quietly listening to all the people in the Soviet Union" (60). The Comrade teacher talks about "the big farms that Stalin wants to make" and his Five Years Plan (60). Children sing "The Internationale" "loudly and at rigid attention" ("Red Stone" 23). After all, the new communist country "must educate its young to be productive citizens of its future"; that is why propaganda promotes the image of "workers' paradise here on earth," an image radically different from the reality the children know ("Red Stone" 24). Also Philipovna is taught in Russian about "father Stalin" instead of learning about Ukrainian culture and the work of Taras Shevchenko, which all of her older cousins learned about in the past. As the new teacher says, "it is the Party and Mother Russia that dictate what you do" because "[t]hose who don't do what we tell you will pay dearly" (Gal 115). The children soon realize the seriousness of these words.

26 As is the case in *The Kulak's Daughter/Red Stone* and *Philipovna*, the authorities arrested prominent citizens, like teachers and priests, first, and took over their houses (cf. Applebaum 123; Malko xxiii). After all, the extermination of Ukrainians started with intellectuals and spiritual leaders (Applebaum 124; Malko xvii). Although, as the eponymous grandfather in Mutala's *My Dearest Dido* notes, most people from all social groups resisted collectivization, "weapons spoke louder than [their] words" (Mutala 33).

27 For many survivors of the Holodomor, "the experience was so awful that they were later unable to recall anything about it all" (Applebaum 246–247). This theme is also present in Mutala's *My Dearest Dido*.

28 While children keep on dying, new ones are brought to the orphanage. When an infant is left in a red shawl, surprisingly with "no insects in it," Philipovna chooses to take care of the baby and calls her Malenka (Eng. the little one). She also decides to become her godmother as "she had no one else to take care of her" (Gal 223). The child's clothes have no lice, and Philipovna discovers a gold cross hidden beneath them. With the spread of disease, quickly also Malenka gets sick. As there is still no medicine, Philipovna encourages Ivanovna to take the cross, go undercover, and buy medication for the children from a local doctor, who later turns out to be the same one who previously helped Aunt Xena. After Philipovna catches pneumonia, doctor Bednarenko treats her and eventually helps her get reunited with Aunt Xena.

29 Before going to the orphanage, Aunt Xena asks Philipovna to be faithful and pray that God lets her survive. The girl does, however, at times question

God's intentions. While Philipovna often thinks about her parents in heaven, she never loses faith. Moreover, praying helps her survive the abuse in the orphanage. On the one hand, she asks complex questions like: "[i]f I was a Child of God, why did I have to be here?"; but on the other hand, she quite naively believes that "[i]f [she] didn't pray, maybe they wouldn't let [her] into Heaven when it was [her] turn to go" (205). Her gullibility is emphasized when she wonders if she can be let into heaven as she is "too filthy" (214). In the orphanage, the children celebrate a secular version of the banned Christmas and have to say thank you for "being taken care of by Father Stalin" (210). They are given oranges by their Russian teachers who mock the old beliefs, traditions, and customs. Larysa, a girl who does not like Philipovna for no apparent reason, tells on the protagonist, who prays every day (211). After a "mock trial," the children are asked to denounce Philipovna and later mock her. While it is believed that "Father Stalin will break them no matter what they do," he never manages to break Philipovna (215).

30 During the Holodomor people did many things to survive, sometimes having to sacrifice their pets (Applebaum 267–268). Knowing that people eat dogs, Mitya, the best friend of Philipovna, protects his beloved dog Sharik, his closest companion. Milena Šubrtová observes that in most war novels "[t]he care of a pet was an attempt to create one's own micro-world in which solidarity, love and respect for the life of every creature holds true" (7). The world of Mitya, who is also an orphan, is shattered when his dog is shot by the Soviet officials (Gal 169). Some survivors quoted in Applebaum's *Red Famine* mention that the Soviets hunted for dogs, which "almost took on the aspect of a sport" (228). As Philipovna sarcastically notes: "Father Stalin had need of their furs for the good of the new order" (Gal 169). Notably, cannibalism was common during the Holodomor. While its occurrence was well-known in Moscow and Kyiv already in 1932, for years it remained a taboo topic. Still, it is graphically depicted in many contemporary famine-themed narratives, including Holland's *Mr. Jones*. Remarkably, the only person who is accused of committing it in *Philipovna* is Uncle Ivan, a local requisitioner and one of the novel's main antagonists.

31 Gal highlights the importance of cultivating traditional customs even in the most difficult times. Aunt Xena goes to the city dressed as an old woman to sell a silver spoon Philipovna found in the river. At that time it was typical for the peasants to exchange precious items for bread, which was beneficial for the Soviet regime, aware that "the famine would bring gold into the state coffers" (Applebaum 279). On her way to the city she encounters corpses, "piles of the bones of dead people who were frozen or starved to death [...] lying by the road" (Gal 145). She does not, however, share this image with Philipovna until years later, as she attempts to spare her.

32 Marsh is an award-winning American author. Her book will be issued in early 2023 by Roaring Brook Press, an imprint of Macmillan Publishers.

33 A few months after its publication, *The Memory Keeper of Kyiv* (2022), a novel for adults by American author Erin Litteken, became a bestseller and has already been translated into several languages. Although the novel has not been marketed as suitable for younger readers, it has a crossover potential.

Works Cited

"About Me," *gabriele goldstone ... writer ... reader ... meanderer*, www.gabrielegoldstone.com/p/about-me.html. Accessed 10 March 2021.

Altman, Illya (ed.). *Holokost na territorii SSSR: Jenciklopedija*. Moscow: Rossijskaja politicheskaja jenciklopedija, Nauchno-prosvetitel'skij centr "Holokost," 2009.

Applebaum, Anne. *Red Famine: Stalin's War on Ukraine*. Penguin Books, 2017.

Atwood, Margaret. *Survival*. Anansi Toronto, 1972.

Ball, Karyn and Per Anders Rudling. "The Underbelly of Canadian Multiculturalism: Holocaust Obfuscation and Envy in the Debate about the Canadian Museum for Human Rights." *Holocaust Studies: A Journal of Culture and History*, vol. 20, no. 3, Winter 2014, pp. 33–80.

Bertelsen, Olga. *In the Labyrinth of the KGB: Ukraine's Intelligentsia in the 1960s–1970s*. Lexington Books, 2022.

Bosmajian, Hamida. *Sparing the Child: Grief and the Unspeakable in Youth Literature about Nazism and the Holocaust*, Routledge, 2002.

Bougai, Nikolai. *The Deportation of Peoples in the Soviet Union*. New York: Nova Science Publishing, Inc., 1996.

Bezo, Brent, Stefania Maggi. "Living in 'Survival Mode:' Intergenerational Transmission of Trauma from the Holodomor Genocide of 1932–1933 in Ukraine." *Social Science & Medicine*, vol. 134, 2015, pp. 87–94.

"Brotlose Kunst," *gabriele goldstone ... writer ... reader ... meanderer*, 17 February 2021, www.gabrielegoldstone.com/2021/02/brotlose-kunst.html. Accessed 10 March 2021.

Cai, Mingshui. *Multicultural Literature for Children and Young Adults: Reflections on Critical Issues*. Greenwood Press, 2002.

Cipko, Serge. *Starving Ukraine. The Holodomor and Canada's Response*. University of Regina Press, 2018.

Dressel, Janice Hartwick. "Personal Response and Social Responsibility: Responses of Middle School Students to Multicultural Literature." *The Reading Teacher*, vol. 58, 2005, pp. 750–764. https://doi.org/10.1598/RT.58.8.5

Dueck, Adele. *Nettie's Journey*. Coteau Books, 2005.

Epp, Marlene. "The Semiotics of Zwieback: Ffeast and Famine in the Narratives of Mennonite Refugee Women." *Sisters or Strangers? Immigrant, Ethnic, and Racialized Women in Canadian History*, edited by Marlene Epp and Franca Iacovetta,. 2nd ed., University of Toronto Press, 2016, pp. 413–431.

Fry, Leanna. "'Never Again' International Children's Genocide Literature." *Bookbird*, vol. 47, no. 1, 2009, pp. 6–9.

Gal, Valentina. *Philipovna: Daughter of Sorrow*. MiroLand, 2019.

Gangi, Jane M. *Genocide in Contemporary Children's and Young Adult Literature: Cambodia to Darfur*. Routledge, 2017.

Goldstone, Gabriele. *Broken Stone*. Rebelight, 2015.

Goldstone, Gabriele. *Red Stone*. Rebelight, 2014.

Goldstone, Gabriele. *Tainted Amber*. Ronsdale Press, 2021.

Goldstone, Gabriele. *The Kulak's Daughter*. Austin, Tire Swing Books, 2010.

Good, Rhea. *Bottle of Grain: A Holodomor Story*. Illustrated by Natalie Warner. Columbia, SC 2021.

Grekul, Lisa. *Leaving Shadows: Literature in English by Canada's Ukrainians*. University of Alberta Press, 2005.

Jobe, Ron, Paula Hart. *Canadian Connections: Experiencing Literature with Children*, Markham, Ontario, Pembroke Publishers Limited, 1991.
Kamińska-Maciąg, Sylwia. "Pamięć o Wielkim Terrorze we współczesnej literaturze dziecięcej (na przykładzie *Breaking Stalin's Nose* Eugena Yelchina)." *Przegląd Rusycystyczny*, vol. 3, no. 171, 2020, pp. 90–104.
Kertzer, Adrianne. *My Mother's Voice. Children, Literature, and the Holocaust*. Broadview Press, 2002.
Kokkola, Lydia. *Representing the Holocaust in Children's Literature*. Routledge, 2003.
Krahn, Elizabeth. "Transcending the 'Black Raven': An Autoethnographic and Intergenerational Exploration of Stalinist Oppression." *Qualitative Sociology Review*, vol. 9, no. 3, 2013, pp. 46–73.
Kuryliw, Valentina. *Holodomor in Ukraine, The Genocidal Famine 1932-1933: Learning Materials for Teachers and Students*. Toronto: CIUS Press, 2018.
Louie, Belinda. "Development of Empathetic Responses with Multicultural Literature." *Journal of Adolescent & Adult Literacy*, vol. 48, no. 7, 2005, pp. 566–578.
Malko, Victoria A. *The Ukrainian Intelligentsia and Genocide: The Struggle for History, Language, and Culture in the 1920s and 1930s*. Lexington Books, 2021.
Marples, David R. *Heroes and Villains: Creating National History in Contemporary Ukraine*. Budapest-New York: CEU Press, 2007.
Montgomery, Lucy Maud. *Emily of New Moon*. [1923]. Mint Editions, 2021.
Mutala, Marion. *Kokhum's Babushka: A Magical Métis/Ukrainian Tale*. Illustrated by Donna Lee Dumont. Saskatoon: Gabriel Dumont Institute Press, 2017.
Mutala, Marion. *My Dearest Dido: The Holodomor Story*. Wood Dragon Books, 2019.
Oziewicz, Marek. "Bloodlands Fiction: Cultural Trauma Politics and the Memory of Soviet Atrocities in *Breaking Stalin's Nose, A Winter's Day in 1939* and *Between Shades of Gray*." *International Research in Children's Literature*, vol. 9, no. 2, 2016, pp. 146–161.
"Pandemic." *Britannica*. www.britannica.com/science/pandemic
Pauly, Matthew. *Breaking the Tongue: Language, Education, and Power in Soviet Ukraine, 1923–1934*. University of Toronto Press, 2014.
Pernin, Muriel. *Famine: L'arme des tyrans*. Syros, 1994.
Pesonen, Jaana. *Multiculturalism as a Challenge in Contemporary Finnish Picturebooks:. Reimagining Sociocultural Categories*. Tampere, 2015.
Petryshyn, Jaroslav. "The 'Ethnic Question' Personified: Ukrainian Canadians and Canadian-Soviet Relations 1917–1991." *Re-imagining Ukrainian Canadians: History, Politics, and Identity*, edited by Rhonda L. Hinther and Jim Mochoruk. University of Torotno Press, 2011, pp. 223–256.
"Reviews," *gabriele goldstone ... writer ... reader ... meanderer*, www.gabrielegoldstone.com/p/thank-you-to-dora-dueck-for-her-review.html. Accessed 10 March 2021.
Rothberg, Michael. *Multidirectional Memory Remembering the Holocaust in the Age of Decolonization*. Stanford University Press, 2009.
Satzewich, Vic. *The Ukrainian Diaspora*, Routledge, 2002.
Schmidt, Carola. *Babushka Is Homesick*. Illustrated by Vinicius Melo. Carolina Witchmichen Penteado Schmidt, 2020.

Schmidt, Carola. *Tell Me a Story, Babushka*. Illustrated by Vinicius Melo. Carolina Witchmichen Penteado Schmidt, 2019.

Shkandrij, Myroslav. "Ukrainization, Terror, and Famine: Coverage in Lviv's Dilo and the Nationalist Press of the 1930s." *Revolutionary Ukraine, 1917–2017: History's Flashpoints and Today's Memory Wars*. Routledge, 2019, pp. 42–67.

Skrypuch, Marsha Forchuk. *Enough*. Illustrated by Michael Martchenko. Fitzhenry & Whiteside, 2000.

Skrypuch, Marsha Forchuk. "The Rings." *Kobzar's Children: A Century of Untold Ukrainian Stories*, edited by Marsha Forchuk Skrypuch, Fitzhenry, & Whiteside, 2006, pp. 49–66.

Smucker, Barbara. *Days of Terror*. Clarke Irwin & Company, 1979.

Smucker, Barbara. *Henry's Red Sea*. Herald Press, 1955.

Sontag, Susan. *Illness as Metaphor and AIDS and Its Metaphors*. New York: Doubleday, 1989.

Šubrtová, Milena. "When Children Die in War: Death in War Literature for Children and Youth." *Bookbird*, vol. 47, no. 4, 2009, pp. 1–8.

Swyripa, Frances. *Storied Landscapes: Ethno-Religious Identity and the Canadian Prairies*. University of Manitoba Press, 2010.

Ulanowicz, Anastasia. "'We Are the People': The Holodomor and North American-Ukrainian Diasporic Memory in Marsha Forchuk Skrypuch's *Enough*." *Miscellanea Posttotalitariana Wratislaviensia*, vol. 2, no. 7, 2017, pp. 49–71.

Warner, Marina. *No Go the Bogeyman: Scaring, Lulling & Making Mock*. New York: Farrar, Straus and Goriux, 1998.

Warwaruk, Larry. *Andrei and the Snow Walker*. Regina, Saskatchewan: Coteau Books, 2002.

Yefimenko, Hennadiy. "More Iis Not Better. The Deleterious Effects of Artificially Inflated Holodomor Death Tolls," translated by Christine Chraibi. *Euromaidan Press*, http://euromaidanpress.com/2021/11/05/more-is-not-better-the-deleterious-effects-of-artificially-inflated-holodomor-death-tolls/?fbclid=IwAR2FrsXvjORY-4zLoG6jtupcXm_dUgONgPvP8R2eWdnvSelT5YPuXxMje0g Accessed 08 November 2021.

Yekelchyk, Serhy. "Stalinism: Famine and Terror." *Ukraine: Birth of a Modern Nation*. Oxford University Press, 2007, pp. 103–120.

Zacharias, Robert. "Learning Sauerkraut: Ethnic Food, Cultural Memory, and Traces of Mennonite Identity in Alayna Munce's *When I Was Young and In My Prime*." In *Canadian Literature and Cultural Memory*, edited by Cynthia Sugars and Eleanor Ty. Oxford University Press, 2014, pp. 103–117.

Zacharias, Robert. *Rewriting the Break Event: Mennonites and Migration in Canadian Literature*. University of Manitoba Press, 2013.

Zhuk, Sergei I. *KGB Operations Against the USA and Canada in Soviet Ukraine, 1953–1991*. Routledge, 2022.

5 Survivors, Oppressors, Implicated Subjects, and Entangled Bystanders
The Second World War and the Holocaust

> *Long life was before all the others who trysted that night in the old homestead orchard; but Cecily's maiden feet were never to leave the golden road.*
>
> (L.M. Montgomery, *The Golden Road*)

Before the February 24, 2022 attack on Ukraine, which echoed Hitler's 1939 takeover of Poland, Vladimir Putin, the president of the Russian Federation, outrageously argued that he wants to "de-Nazify" the country (cf. Snyder "The War in Ukraine"). Putin notoriously refused to acknowledge the separate culture and statehood of Ukraine, repeating the views of Joseph Stalin who, as Serhii Plokhy notes, believed that "Russians and Ukrainians were one and the same people" ("The Gates" 233). The consequences of Stalin's beliefs resulted in the genocide examined in Chapter 4 and other atrocities. While Putin's sentiment may seem surprising considering that Volodymyr Zelenskyy, Ukraine's president, is of Jewish background,[1] it also reverberates the long history of Soviet and Russian equating of any forms of Ukrainian cultural and national distinctiveness with fascism and/or bourgeois nationalism. Not accidentally, between 1953 and 1991 Ukrainian nationalism was the key target of the KGB (Zhuk loc. 481). The discourse used by Putin and his propaganda is reflected in the words of the protagonist of Marsha Forchuk Skrypuch's *Traitors Among Us* (2021), a novel set right after the end of the Second World War:

> they [the Soviets] didn't believe that Ukraine had a unique culture or country but that it was just part of Russia, so to say you were Ukrainian meant you were a traitor. They also thought anyone who didn't believe in Communism was a Nazi.
>
> (79)

Next-generation memory is always formed in social and cultural frameworks.[2] Despite the regular appearance of Holocaust-themed books and films directed at young audiences, a study by the Azrieli

DOI: 10.4324/9781003367918-6

Foundation shows that the majority of Canadians aged 18–34 do not know how many Jews fell victim to Nazism and 22% are not sure if they have heard about the Holocaust ("New Survey"). The results may be contributed to the fact that 69% of young Canadians do not personally know any Holocaust survivors or people who witnessed the Nazi atrocities and 89% have never visited a Holocaust museum; hence, they have not included the Shoah in their mnemonic repertoires. Moreover, 32% of young Canadians believe that the country had an open immigration policy during and after the war, and 37% are not sure what the policy was like. Interestingly – and surprisingly considering the other results – 82% of the respondents of the Azrieli study recognized the name Anne Frank, whose *The Diary of a Young Girl* (1947) is read in many North American schools. The recognition of Anne Frank points to the role literature can play in teaching history but also demonstrates that familiarizing young people with a single text is not enough to make them grasp its complexity. After all, reading a single book about the Shoah is not "sufficient in knowledge or understanding of Nazism and the Holocaust" (Bosmajian xx). It also does not explain the entangled and multilayered memory of the Second World War in Eastern Europe and the consequences it has had on global politics. Especially since many children's narratives about the Holocaust and the Second World War rely on the simple victim-oppressor binary, potentially leading to a one-dimensional and oversimplified reading of complex history (cf. Goldberg 649).

Agreeing with Hamida Bosmajian, who has argued that children's literature always reflects "the prevailing social climate" (xiv), in this chapter I investigate the multifaceted representations of the Shoah and the Second World War with its Ukrainian and Jewish actors in the novels written by Marsha Forchuk Skrypuch and Kathy Kacer. In my cross-sectional analysis of eight books, I maintain that contemporary historical fiction enables the transfer of next-generation memory, which challenges the victim-oppressor binary by showing the implicated position(s) of Eastern Europeans during the Second World War. While Bosmajian argues that after the war "memory became a primary problem for both perpetrators and victims," in the recent decades, the mnemonic discourse has been enriched by perspectives which exceed this binary (xiii). As I have so far demonstrated in *Next-Generation Memory*, the history of Ukraine – and Ukrainian Canadians – is complicated and cannot be explained using simple binaries. The complexity of the position(s) of Ukrainian subjects during the Second World War is reflected in the polyphonic mnemonic discourses produced in Canada, including historical fiction investigated in this chapter. In my considerations I apply a transcultural[3] perspective and agree with Michael Rothberg that "separating [the Holocaust] off from other histories of collective violence […] is intellectually and politically dangerous" because "it potentially creates a hierarchy of suffering (which is morally offensive) and removes that suffering from the field of historical agency (which is both morally and intellectually suspect)" ("Multidirectional" 9).

In my reading of the books by Kacer and Skrypuch, I argue that many of their characters can be described as "implicated subjects" or "entangled bystanders," categories introduced by Rothberg and Anna Wylęgała. Considering the importance of historical background, in the first part of this chapter, I use various historical perspectives to explain Ukraine's situation during the Second World War and demonstrate the role of the Holocaust in the Ukrainian Canadian mnemonic discourse since the mid-twentieth century. The following two sections show how Skrypuch's books address the stereotypical depiction of Ukrainian displaced persons (DPs) as alleged war criminals and portray the controversial Ukrainian Insurgent Army (UPA). Then I move to the portrayal of the complex Jewish–Ukrainian relations, concentrating my attention on the different approaches of Skrypuch and Kacer towards Ukrainian Righteous Among Nations. Reading Skrypuch's trilogies, I point to the entanglements of the rescuing of Jews and the underground operations of UPA, an organization accused of participating in pogroms. Finally, I study the framing role of Canada, the symbol of hope and a place where the Ukrainian memory of the Second World War can survive.

Ukraine during the Second World War

Discussing the history of Ukraine is crucial in understanding the socio-political situation of the country in the twentieth century and its relationships with other parts of Europe, Soviet Russia, and North America. Moreover, illustrating Ukraine's entanglements during the Second World War helps to show the limitations connected to the use of the simple victim-oppressor binary popularized by Western historiography and mass media after the war. Notably, such simplified images were also reproduced in Anglophone children's and YA literature, for example, Louis Begley's *Wartime Lies* (1991) or Philip Kerr's *Winter Horses* (2014). Introducing various historical perspectives on the complex war chronotope[4] of Eastern Europe may also explain the origins of Putin's outrageous claims that the 2022 invasion was motivated by Russia's attempt to fight Nazism in Ukraine, a country whose Jewish president won the 2019 presidential election with more that 73% of the vote and none of the right-wing parties secured enough votes to make it to the parliament.

When Hitler invaded present-day Ukraine in 1941, initially Ukrainians welcomed the Nazi troops as rescuers from the years of Soviet occupation (cf. Applebaum "Red Famine" 328). In his *Black Earth: The Holocaust as History and Warning* (2015), Timothy Snyder notes that the attitudes towards the 1941 German invasion were directly connected to the people's experiences of the Soviet rule: years of mass killing operations, including the Holodomor, deportations, the extermination of intelligentsia in the case of Soviet Ukraine; and mass arrests, killings, and deportations in Western Ukraine. Moreover, before the Soviet rule, Ukrainians in Austria-Hungary and Russia had also suffered from mass political violence. Hence it is not surprising that after decades of recurrent systemic violence, Ukraine became a "fertile ground for ideologies that rejected liberal and democratic values, and which turned instead to xenophobia and extremism" (Shkandrij "Jews" 168). Some nationalists in Galicia "could believe that a German invasion would advance their political interests" and they "told fellow Ukrainians that they could purge themselves of the stain of collaboration with the Soviets by killing one Jew" (Snyder "Black Earth" 155). The occurrence of well-documented pogroms in territories occupied first by the Soviets and then by the Nazis is a controversial aspect of the mnemonic discourse (cf. Wylęgała "Co jest nie tak?"). Anti-Semitism, however, was not more widespread among Ukrainians than other Slavic and Baltic nations which also experienced Stalin's regime. At first, many of them saw the Nazis as liberators, unaware that Hitler "did not see Ukrainians or Soviet citizens as subjects of politics, or even as full human beings" (Snyder "Black Earth" 55). As Anne Applebaum definitively states, "anyone who hoped for a better life under German occupation had their expectations swiftly dashed" ("Red Famine" 328).

Altogether 6.8 million people were killed during the Second World War in what is now Ukraine. As Snyder maintains, when Hitler called Slavs "a slavish mass crying out for their master" he primary had in mind Ukrainians, the inhabitants of bountiful lands (qtd. in Snyder 18). The Nazis used anti-Slavic propaganda positioning Slavs as "born slaves" in order to gain "living space" in the East (Janion 19). Ukraine, Europe's "breadbasket," was central not only in Stalin's Five-Year Plan, as discussed in Chapter 4, but also in Hitler's *Lebensraum* project, which was his plan "to wipe out the existing population all the way to the Volga" (Plokhy "The Gates" 259). Divided and conquered by both Hitler and Stalin, Ukraine experienced greater devastation than other Nazi-occupied countries (Lower 2).

Historian Grzegorz Rossoliński-Liebe claims that the mnemonic discourse of the North American diaspora was based on the narratives of "heroization and victimization" ("Holocaust Amnesia" 127). According to this belief, the diaspora commemorated Ukrainians during the Second World War either as "heroes (of the struggle for national independence) or victims (of other regimes or ideologies)" (127; cf. Marples "Heroes and Villains"). Because these two categories were appreciated by the diaspora, any mention of Ukrainian involvement in the Holocaust was disdained "as provocation or [Soviet] propaganda" (127–129).[5] Hence Rossoliński-Liebe argues that the diasporic mnemonic discourse has been "strongly anchored in the propaganda and self-understanding of the OUN [Organization of Ukrainian Nationalists] and UPA [Ukrainian Insurgent Army]," because it was formed by individuals who had been leading representatives of Ukrainian Nationalism, people who were aware of the Holocaust and the ethnic cleansing of Poles (141). Hereafter "the narrative that they propagated seems to have served as a protective shield in the ongoing struggle against the Soviet Union and for political status in their new places of residence" (141). John-Paul Himka, who has been openly critical of UPA-OUN, has argued that "the Holocaust hardly figured" in the collective memory of the diaspora and after "outsiders accused them of having collaborated with the Germans [...] they engaged, defensively" with the Shoah, and consequently, "they represented themselves, externally as well as internally, as freedom fighters against both the Nazis and the Soviets," promoting the OUN and UPA as their heroes ("The Reception" 648).

In order to grasp the complexity of the Ukrainian Canadian mnemonic discourse, it is necessary to explain the legacy of the Organization of Ukrainian Nationalists (OUN), which has been one of the most controversial aspects of Ukrainian cultural memory both in Ukraine and abroad. The OUN emerged in 1929 in Galicia in the place of the Ukrainian Military Organization led by Yevhen Konovalets (Plokhy "The Gates" 237). During the 1930s, the organization, inspired by the ideology of Dmytro Dontsov, gained a significant following in Western Ukraine, especially among the youth seeking "a radical solution to the Ukrainian problem," that is its statelessness (Hunczak 98; cf. Erlacher).[6] Initially of marginal status, the OUN quickly became an influential actor on the Ukrainian political scene.

In the early 1930s the OUN gained notoriety for the killings of two politicians: Bronisław Pieracki, accused of the repression of Ukrainian activists, and a Soviet diplomat, who was allegedly murdered in revenge for the Holodomor. Both assassinations were organized by the 25-year-old Stepan Bandera[7] (Plokhy "The Gates" 238). As Shkandrij observes, under the leadership of the OUN, who "saw the use of violence as inevitable in the struggle for independence," students and workers "were able [...] to organize an effective response to aggression," in this case when Ukrainians in Lviv were banned from attending the Polish university (Shkandrij "Jews" 151; Shkandrij "Ukrainian Nationalism" 52). In 1941 the organization split into two fractions: OUN-M led by Andrii Melnyk and OUN-B led by Bandera, with the latter supported mostly by younger people (Shkandrij "Ukrainian Nationalism" 59). The next year UPA (Ukrainian Insurgent Army), the OUN-B's paramilitary, and later partisan, formation started operating. As some scholars argue, "the OUN-B and UPA should be considered separate entities" as many young people joined the organization toward the end of the war and represented various political views (Shkandrij "Ukrainian Nationalism" 75).

Although "the Nationalist attitude toward Germany remained ambiguous," the OUN believed that Germany would help them gain independence (Shkandrij "Ukrainian Nationalism" 58). Instead of helping Ukrainians form a government, Hitler divided the country into the General Government and the Reich Commissariat Ukraine and prohibited Ukrainians to bear arms. The association of the OUN with the Nazis caused them damage in Eastern Ukraine, and in late 1941 "the organization began to shift to an anti-Nazi" line (59–61). The following year underground publications were referring to both Nazis and Soviets as Ukraine's enemies, and in 1943 the OUN-B formally "rejected both communism and fascism" (64–65). As Plokhy notes, "[t]he Bandera faction of the OUN went overnight from the Germans' loyal ally to their enemy" and the Nazis shot hundreds of members of the OUN ("The Gates" 266).

The complex relations between the OUN-UPA and Jews, Poles, and Germans remain the most challenging part of the legacy of Ukrainian nationalists next to their association with fascism (cf. Yurchuk 41). The attitudes towards the heritage of Ukrainian Nationalists and UPA still differ and remain a problematic aspect in the mnemonic debates. Ukrainian complicity in Jewish pogroms and the ethnic cleansing of Poles have become the key focus of recent studies by non-Ukrainian scholars; yet some Ukrainian historians either deny any wrongdoing committed by OUN-UPA or rationalize them (cf. Wylęgała "The Absent 'Others' "; Wylęgała "Co jest nie tak?"; Wylęgała "Bohaterowie"). Western historians, like Rossoliński-Liebe and Per Anders Rudling, believe that OUN was an unequivocally fascist organization and "the UPA was fighting for an independent Ukraine that was to take the form of an ethnically homogenous and authoritarian nation state" ("Holocaust Amnesia" 115). Others, like John Armstrong and Alexander J. Motyl, argue that OUN was only influenced by European fascists but was not fascist *de facto*. Ukrainian scholars like Petro Mirchuk, Volodymyr Kosyk, or Volodymyr Viatrovych deny any traces of fascist ideology of the OUN, believing "that nationalism is connected to national liberation, while fascism is a form of rule where there is already a nation with an established state;" hence in the case of Ukraine, it is difficult to talk about fascism (Yurchuk 46). However, long after the Second World War the Soviets "would link Ukrainian Nationalism with German fascism by constantly referring to the Ukrainian insurgents as 'German-Ukrainian nationalists' " (Plokhy "The Gates" 286).

After the collapse of the Soviet Union, the OUN and UPA – organizations based in Western Ukraine – became crucial topics in the national memory debates, often leading to regional and international tensions. Under the presidency of Viktor Yushchenko, who was elected after the 2004 Orange Revolution, leaders of the OUN and UPA began to be commemorated as national heroes, with the rehabilitation of Stepan Bandera receiving a widespread condemnation in Ukraine and abroad, especially Poland (cf. Motyka 650–670; Isakowicz-Zaleski 78; Wylęgała "Co jest nie tak?"; Wylęgała "Bohaterowie" 134–135; Plokhy "The Frontline" loc. 106). The 2013–2014 Revolution of Dignity and the Russian annexation of Crimea "became a catalyst for a governmental institutionalization and social mainstreaming of [...] the OUN and its leaders," because they openly fought against the Soviets (Umland and Yurchuk 186). One of the Ukrainian decommunization laws passed during the presidency of Petro Poroshenko "officially protects the two organizations [OUN-UPA] from derogation and condemnation in the public sphere" (Umland and Yurchuk 186; cf. Wylęgała "Co jest nie tak?"). The so-called "anti-communist law" proved to be divisive and in an open letter was unequivocally condemned by both Ukrainian, Ukrainian Canadian, and non-Ukrainian scholars (Marples "Open Letter").

A brief look at Ukrainian Second World War history demonstrates that in the context of Eastern Europe, the strict categories of victims, oppressors, and selfless saviors are inadequate because "all major ethnic groups residing in the area were subjected to mass violence: both by the occupier and their own neighbors" (Wylęgała "Entangled" 121; Himka "The Reception" 629). Thus, while writing about the war in Eastern Europe and its literary representations it is more suitable to use the categories of "implicated subjects" or "entangled bystanders." The "complexly implicated subject," a category introduced by Michael Rothberg, seems particularly appropriate in the context of the entanglements of many Ukrainians during the Second World War and Ukrainian Canadian DPs. Rothberg maintains that this notion can be used to describe "*beneficiaries* and *descendants, accomplices* and *perpetuators*, and it can even attach to people who have had shattering experiences of *trauma of victimization* and are thus situated within 'complex implication'" ("Implicated" 200; emphasis in original). Referring to Rothberg's observations, Polish scholar Anna Wylęgała has argued that Eastern Europeans were "entangled" in the complex and frequently changing situation, and sometimes victims would become victimizers, and *vice versa* ("Entangled" 121). Wylęgała observes that people who witnessed the Holocaust "might have benefited from the reality of the ethnic cleansing or not, but in fact were not given the choice of standing aside: they were thrown inside by the very fact of being born where they were" ("Entangled" 121). Notably, as Rothberg notes, "[a] discourse based on clear-cut visions of victims and perpetrators of innocence and guilt evacuates the political sphere of complexity and reduces it to a morality tale" ("Implicated" 139). As the distorted historical discourse used by Putin before and during the recent Russian invasion of Ukraine has demonstrated, simple binaries can be misused to ignite new conflicts.

Ukrainian Canadians and the Memory of the Second World War and the Holocaust

While the Second World War exceeds geographical and cultural borders, the national mnemonic discourses sometimes clash and lead to disagreements. The aforementioned entanglements of Ukraine's position during the Second World War have further complicated the evaluation of the country's history and provoked mnemonic divergences: for example, when North American Ukrainians, including UPA veterans, were accused of Nazi collaboration in the 1980s. The Ukrainian memory of the fight for independence, which challenges the Soviet Victory myth, was also repressed in Soviet Ukraine and later denied in post-Soviet Russia. Until recently, it was either not acknowledged or misunderstood in the West and associated with Nazism in Putin's propaganda.[8] However, UPA and the Ukrainian fight against the Soviets and the Nazis have remained an important element of Ukrainian Canadian cultural memory.

Unlike in Soviet Ukraine, where the memory of the Second World War was reduced to commemorating the so-called Great Patriotic War, in North America the OUN-B and UPA appeared in the diasporic mnemonic discourse already in the early 1950s. This was the consequence of the arrival of Ukrainian DPs, who were often sponsored by their relatives who had immigrated to Canada during the first two waves of immigration from Galicia and Bukovyna (Satzewich 101).[9] Although only 30,000 Ukrainians came to Canada during this period, they soon became the key actors in the diasporic sociopolitical and cultural life (Yekelchyk 22; cf. Grabowicz "A Great Literature"). However, already in the camps Ukrainians from the West and East "became painfully aware of the considerable social, cultural, and psychological differences between them" (Subtelny 557). The Banderites, as the supporters of Bandera became known, gained a following among most of the workers and peasants, but not the intellectuals (Subtelny 557). Despite the ideological dissimilarities between them, Ukrainian DPs managed to create a lively intellectual, cultural, and political life (Satzewich 97).

The "high degree of politicization, particularly the Melnykite/Banderite feud," caused the political fragmentation of the Ukrainian diaspora in North America, which at that time had already been well established (Subtelny 560; cf. Chapter 1). As Vic Satzewich notes, diasporic leftists "despised the DPs and were severely critical of them, and of the nationalists who worked to bring them to North America" (Satzewich 102). Unaware or dismissive of the DPs' experiences during the war (*Ostarbeiters*, *Lebensborn*), they believed that their reluctance to return to Soviet Ukraine "was a sign of their political conservatism and their guilt for atrocities that had been committed against Jews in Ukraine" (102). Interestingly, the Association of United Ukrainian Canadians tried "to convince the Canadian government and the wider population that the Ukrainian DPs were pro-Nazi and that the nationalists in the diaspora were knowingly trying to bring war criminals into the country" (103). Years later this contributed to the one-dimensional and negative perception of Ukrainian DPs as Nazi collaborators.

The new émigrés were generally better educated and politically more active; hence, they sometimes assumed central roles in diasporic organizations. They were, however, "relatively silent on the Jewish question," that is the Holocaust (Shkandrij "Jews" 200). On the one hand, this silence can be attributed to trauma of those who witnessed

Nazi atrocities. On the other hand, as some historians argue, not talking about the Holocaust became "a central element in the Ukrainian diaspora's early memory discourses" because the new immigrants wanted to show UPA and the OUN-B as heroes struggling against the regimes of the Nazis and the Soviets, at the same time, ignoring their participation in pogroms (Rossoliński-Liebe "Holocaust Amnesia" 120). Instead of addressing anti-Semitism, some DPs argued that UPA collaborated with Ukraine's Jews.[10]

Mnemonic discourses are "highly mediated," says Rothberg, yet while "individuals and groups play an active role on rearticulating memory," they usually do not have "complete consciousness or unimpeded agency" ("Multidirectional" 16). The allegations that Ukrainian DPs were anti-Semites and war criminals reemerged in North America in late twentieth century. First, the influential (and controversial) *Holocaust* miniseries (1978) positioned Ukrainians as Nazi collaborators. Second, the work of the Commission of Inquiry into Alleged War Criminals in Canada, also known as the Deschênes Commission, and the notorious case of John Demjanjuk in the USA,[11] further contributed to a one-dimensional and negative perception of the role Ukrainians played in the Second World War (Satzewich 103, 169).[12] Notably, as historians Sergei I. Zhuk and Olga Bertelsen demonstrate, the KGB used "active measures" in North America, most importantly disinformation, forgeries, and anti-Ukrainian propaganda to position Ukrainians as war criminals (Zhuk loc.171; Bertelsen "Introduction" 2).

Although the position of most Eastern Europeans during the Second World War can be described as that of implicated subjects or entangled bystanders, the Nazi-collaboration accusations provoked North American Ukrainians to feel victimized because they were "collectively, and unjustly, portrayed as inveterate racists, anti-Semites and war criminals" in the Western mass media (Satzewich 168). These allegations were especially unjust to the families of the 35,000–40,000 Ukrainian Canadians – 15% of their entire population – who enlisted for the Canadian armed forces during the Second World War and fought with the Allies (Subtelny 565).[13] They also challenged the image of Ukrainian struggle for independence based on fighting both Nazis and Soviets, at that time already well-established in the diaspora's collective memory.

Ukrainians and the Nazi Collaborator Stereotype in Canadian Children's Literature

Most of the authors whose books I have investigated in the previous chapters point to the role of Canada as the place where their characters finally find freedom and peace. For example, in the afterword to her 2021 novel *Tainted Amber*, Gabriele Goldstone writes: "here in Canada, we can flourish in an imperfect society. Let's never take it for granted" (254). However, in *Hope's War* (2001), her early novel set at the turn of the twenty-first century, Marsha Forchuk Skrypuch demonstrates that even long after finding shelter in Canada, Ukrainian DPs still could have been accused of Nazi collaboration. Kat Baliuk, the teenage protagonist of *Hope's War*, finds out that her grandfather Danylo Feschuk, who immigrated to Canada right after the Second World War, is accused of being a war criminal who lied to obtain Canadian citizenship.[14] Danylo is not guilty of the crimes, but the flashbacks position him as an implicated subject who had to make difficult choices while fighting against two totalitarian regimes, such as joining the auxiliary police and lying about his identity and war experiences at the DP camp. Skrypuch returned to the theme of the Nazi allegations against Ukrainians in two successful trilogies published by Scholastic between 2010 and 2021. However, in later novels like *Stolen Child* and *Traitors Among Us*, the accusations are addressed in a more subtle way than in *Hope's War*, which was written in the aftermath of the war-criminality accusations in North America.[15] The entanglements of Skrypuch's characters challenge the victim-oppressor binary; her child protagonists are forced to lie in order to get to Canada and escape from Soviet repressions. As I demonstrate at the end of this chapter, in the novels' chronotopes there is no place for Ukrainians in postwar Soviet Ukraine.

Hope's War is set predominately in Canada, yet its significant parts come in flashbacks depicting Danylo's war experiences in Ukraine. The third-person narrator provides the readers with an objective point of view, but Skrypuch at times gives voice to Danylo and his granddaughter Kat, a teenage foil character who positions Danylo as a sympathetic character. This type of focalization recalls the one frequently found in Holocaust narratives, which, as Sue Vice notes: "are structured in what is apparently the same temporally split manner," that is

> [s]elections about the traumatic past alternate with sections describing the present: either that of the post-war era, or the time of writing [...] Such texts are also divided between a child's and an adult's perspective; the past of the Holocaust is the time of childhood, its effects that of adulthood.
>
> (12)

Because Danylo has never talked about his pre-Canadian experiences with his family – it is his late wife, Nadiya, who was the giver of the seeds of memory – the accusations provoke him to symbolically go back to his teenage years in the form of flashbacks. The fact that in *Hope's War* and *Underground Soldier/The War Below*, a later novel whose protagonist resembles young Danylo, Skrypuch portrays teenage soldiers is particularly important considering Bosmajian's observation that "[t]he child with a gun startles and shocks, perhaps even more than the child as victim of starvation, rape mutilation, or murder" (xi).

First-person flashbacks and direct questions[16] used by Skrypuch position Danylo as a more relatable character and may provoke the readers to question the typical victim-oppressor binary found in most Second World War novels. Roger Luckhurst argues that

> [t]he flashback [...] can only ever be explained belatedly, leaving the spectator [or reader] in varying degrees of disorientation or suspense [...] It flashes back insistently in the present because this image cannot yet or perhaps ever be narrativized as past.
>
> (180)

Despite the allegations against him, from the flashbacks the readers learn that Danylo did not kill or torture Jews and never supported the Nazis. On the contrary, the trial makes Danylo finally return to the repressed traumatic moments when he had to fight both the Nazis and the Soviets in order to survive.

The flashbacks point to the complexity of Danylo's situation and position him as an implicated subject. When he finally shares his individual memory of the Second World War with his family and community, the testimony prompts a subjective transformation and becomes a polyvalent instrument of self-acceptance as well as a mechanism of potential political indignation for his close ones and, potentially, also for the readers. After seeing his parents killed, teenage Danylo was encouraged by his sister Kataryna to join UPA (Ukrainian Insurgent Army) and become an auxiliary Nazi police officer to gain information. Although at first he disagreed to cooperate with the Nazis, Kataryna threatened him with a pistol, saying: "[y]ou'll do what I say, brother, or I will shoot you myself" (88). Teenage Danylo had no choice and "knew better than to argue" (88). Unlike in her more recent novels, in *Hope's War* Skrypuch shows that not all Ukrainians joined UPA voluntarily. Whereas Danylo's reluctance to talk about his Second World War experience appears to be the consequence of postwar trauma, it may also be related to his awareness of the ambiguous legacy of UPA, an organization he initially did not want to join, and the unwillingness to be associated with atrocities he had not committed. In this context it is worth recalling Rothberg's observations that "discussions of memory and historical justice have almost always involved either around victims – mourning their deaths, working towards material and symbolic restitution – or around perpetrators whom one hopes to bring to justice in one way or another" ("Implicated" 57). Danylo's position goes beyond these binaries.

Instead of leaving any ambiguities unanswered, children's and young adult historical fiction has the tendency to oversimplify complex historical narratives and reduce ethical dilemmas to simple acts of forgiveness. As Bosmajian notes, authors or children's and YA historical books about the Holocaust "may conceal or limit the site of atrocious history with reader-protective strategies that intend to spare the child but also enable the author to censor, sublime, deny or release personally experienced traumatic events" (xv). Skrypuch's portrayal of the controversial UPA in *Hope's War* is irrefutably positive. She fails to mention not only their complicity in pogroms but also the problematic relationship between Ukraine and Poland during the Second World War. This comes as a surprise considering that the OUN-B's ethnic cleansing campaign against Poles living in Volhynia[17] has been the matter of a heated debate among historians (Shkandrij "Ukrainian Nationalism" 68–69; cf. Plokhy "The Gates" 239).[18] As Shkandrij writes, all available sources suggest that the anti-Polish action was seen "as a failure, a debilitating war between two populations that should have been allied in the struggle against Germany and the Soviets both" ("Ukrainian Nationalism" 70). However, this lack can also be contributed to the age of the implied readers and Skrypuch's focus on addressing the allegations of Nazi-collaboration directed at Ukrainian Canadians. Although Skrypuch seems to spare the child, *Hope's War* is not completely biased, because during the trial Danylo and scholars interviewed by the prosecutor admit that there were instances of collaboration between Ukrainians and the Nazis, showing young readers that applying such narrow categories of the victim, the oppressor, and the savior is problematic in the context of war atrocities.

While Danylo's adolescent experience is introduced in the form of flashbacks, at the trial, his version of the Second World War reality is challenged by the one described by historians and other witnesses. Danylo's defender, Mr. Vincent, keeps on rejecting the accusations, as the charges against Danylo are built on allegations and testimonies of only two witnesses. Moreover, they can be rebutted by 11 witnesses willing to testify on Danylo's behalf. As there is no factual evidence of his cooperation with the Nazis, the testimony of Mr. Abramovich makes Danylo appear as the perpetrator who tortured people in the village of Orelets. The use of flashbacks, however, allows us to see a different version of the same memory shared by Mr. Abramovich. Danylo was indeed supposed to kill a number of villagers but instead disobeyed the order, pointed the pistol, and made people do push-ups; thus, he saved them and put himself in danger. This scene echoes other Holocaust narratives where "the extremes of atrocious history" are understated and "acts of ingenuity and kindness" are highlighted "to inspire the young readers" (Bosmajian xvi). While the story of Danylo serves to familiarize young readers with the multifaceted political predicaments of Ukraine during the Second World War, one could argue that a singular act of saving a group of villagers from execution cannot eliminate the fact of systemic participation of organized groups of Ukrainians in atrocities mentioned by the prosecutor.

Rothberg maintains that "acknowledging implication – as opposed to identifying with either victims or perpetrators – can put the conflict on another footing more amenable and transformative" ("Implicated" 139). However, *Hope's War* imposes a didactic closure of "forgiveness" by the survivor. Though there is no clear happy ending to Danylo's story, as he is sentenced and his future is not clear, the young readers see that his case was built on allegations only. After the trial, a woman who protested in front of the house of the Baliuks approaches Danylo and says: "I survived the Holocaust [...] I remember [...] being led away at gun point by the Nazis, while the Ukrainians looked on. [...] What I realize now is that the Ukrainians were as hopeless as the Jews" (239). By holding out her hand to Danylo and introducing her own granddaughter to Kat, the Jewish woman symbolically shows her forgiveness. Notably, this act or reconciliation is significant as the allegations of war crimes deteriorated the "relations between the Ukrainian and Jewish diasporas" (Himka "Reception 649").

Skrypuch portrays two contradictory positions towards the accusations against Danylo in the Baliuk family. The reaction of Genya, Kat's assimilated sister, whom friends call Jenny, is nothing like the protagonist's. Kat's perfect, "beautiful in a blonde and blue-eyed way" (13) sister Danylo's "malenka ptashka" (little bird), who performs the role of *Nasha Meri* (cf. Chapter 3), instantly believes in the allegations against her grandfather as she is worried about their influence on her own well-being:

> If Dido truly cared about us, he would pack his bags and move back to Ukraine [...] He's obviously done something, and now we're all paying for his past. [...] We could lose our home because of him. And I probably won't be able to go to medical school.
>
> (69)

While initially Genya seems conformist and appears as Kat's contradiction, she gradually becomes more involved in the trial and eventually believes in her grandfather's innocence. For such a change to happen, Danylo has to testify and share his memory with the family. By doing so, his testimony and the three family photographs may become the basis of Kat's and Genya's intergeneration memory of Second World War. Skrypuch's narrative illustrates Anastasia Ulanowicz's point that such transfer of memory can occur only when an individual deliberately acknowledges "the ways in which her present circumstances have been mediated and shaped by past events that she herself did not directly experience" (4). The trial against Danylo seems to help Genya – who, unlike Kat, allows everyone to call her by an Anglophile name and feels little allegiance to her Ukrainianness – embrace her heritage and see how remembering and forgetting can influence her present and future.

In her Second World War novels, Skrypuch creates sympathetic characters and uses literature as not only a potential medium of the transfer of next-generation memory but also a means of challenging the stereotype of Ukrainians as anti-Semites and Nazi collaborators. Luka, the young protagonist of *Underground Soldier/The War Below* who, similar to Danylo, cooperates with UPA and also eventually settles in Canada, is told: "[y]ou need ... to live. To tell our story" (185) and "[y]ou will bear witness for us, Luka. For all those who have been silenced by death" (187). In keeping this memory, however, both Luka and Danylo seem not to recognize their own implication. After all, "most people refuse to see how they are implicated in – have inherited and benefited from – historical injustices: synchronic and diachronic injustices are intertwined" (Rothberg "Implicated" 20). Danylo in *Hope's War* demonstrates that bearing witness and keeping the memory can be a challenge, especially when it exceeds the victim-oppressor binary. For 50 years Danylo remains silent, which only further implicates him. However, he finally has to come clean, testify and bear witness not only for himself, but also "for those who have been silenced by death." He does, however, also need to accept his own entangled position.

Almost a decade after the publication of *Hope's War*, Skrypuch returned to the topic of the allegations against Ukrainian Canadians as Nazi collaborators in her two commercially and critically successful Second World War trilogies. However, she has approached this issue in a more nuanced way while problematizing the predicament of displaced persons coming from Western and Eastern Ukraine. Nadia, the 12-year-old protagonist of *Stolen Child*, moves from a DP camp to Brantford, Canada. She suffers from a memory loss caused by war trauma, but the moment she arrives to North America, she begins getting flashbacks of her life in Germany, including meeting Hitler and visiting a Jewish ghetto. "If I'd met Hitler – Hitler himself – then I must be a Nazi," she believes (45). In the DP camp she repressed her memories, but "the nightmares started up and the memories came back" the moment she arrived in Canada (71). Despite her adoptive parents' assurance that Nadia is not German, the fragmented recollections, combined with the girl's Aryan looks, convince her that she must have been a Nazi. Feeling ashamed, Nadia attempts to repress her memories, but the flashbacks come at various moments and are provoked by the encounters with smells, tastes, sounds, images, and objects.

Throughout the novel Nadia struggles with shame. Eventually, she partially reconstructs her memory and realizes that she is a Ukrainian girl named Larissa who, due to her Aryan looks, fell victim to the *Lebensborn* program at the age of five. Nadia was stolen from her grandmother and sister and lived with a Nazi family as Gretchen Himmel. Nadia/Larissa remembers the Nazi propaganda used to erase the memories of Slavic children: "*You are Aryans [...] The people you think were your parents are thieves. They stole you from your Aryan parents and now we will give you back*" (138; emphasis in original). Marusia, the Himmels' slave worker, realizes that Gretchen, who sings Ukrainian songs while playing and speaks German with an accent, is a stolen child. It is Marusia who helps the girl escape to a DP camp at the end of the war. Because Gretchen does not know her real name, Marusia decides to call the girl Nadia and registers her as her own daughter. After some time they immigrate to

Canada. Just like her adoptive parents, who were *Ostarbeiters*, Nadia could not return to Soviet Ukraine, where they would all be *"punished for letting [them]selves be stolen by the Germans"* (146; emphasis in original). Although Nadia is not a Nazi, she arrives in Canada pretending to be someone else, knowing that she cannot tell anyone that Marusia is not her biological mother, because "the Soviets would take [her] and [she] would be sent to Siberia" (67). Here Skrypuch refers to the fact that some DPs had to change their identity, which years later further provoked the accusations of Nazi collaboration, as is the case in *Hope's War*. The need to conceal one's identity is present in all of Skrypuch's Second World War novels, including *Making Bombs for Hitler* and *Underground Soldier/ The War Below*, where the child protagonists have to lie about being from Western Ukraine[19] in order to escape Soviet oppression and join Nadia/Larissa in Canada.

While in *Prisoners in the Promised Land: The Ukrainian Internment Diary of Anya Soloniuk* set in the 1910s, the Anglo-Canadian teachers deliberately ignore the bullying of "enemy aliens," in *Stolen Child* Skrypuch shows that after the Second World War this type of behavior is no longer accepted (cf. Chapter 2). Gradually reconstructing her memories, Nadia/Larissa also learns English and becomes "a Canadian girl" (33). The thought of being Canadian helps her overcome anxiety and trauma because "Canadian girls walk down the street by themselves without fear" (33). However, at school Nadia/Larissa is bullied by two boys, who call her "Nazi Nadia" or "Hitler girl," and say that "she looks like a Nazi" (63). Despite her own uncertainty about the past, Nadia does not understand why privileged Anglo-Canadian children, who never witnessed the war, judge her. She thinks: "Had he ever had his hair hacked off for lice? Could he even imagine such a thing?" (71). In addition to hatred, however, the girl also encounters kindness and befriends a girl named Linda. Remarkably, every time the teacher hears the bullying, she reacts. Miss Ferris sends the boys "to the principal's office," but David and Eric later continue calling Nadia/Larissa a Nazi (63). When David gives Nadia a note saying: *"Nazi Nadia, go back to Hitler-land"* (99; emphasis in original), Miss Ferris "grabbed David by the ear and marched him out of the room" (101). Notably, when Miss Ferris initially calls her Natalie, Nadia/Larissa corrects her. Although she wants to become Canadian and throughout the novel learns English by reading books like *Freddy Goes to Florida*[20] and attending extra classes with Miss McIntosh, she does not want to once again repress her Ukrainianness, which she was forced to do while being Gretchen Himmel.

Although in *Hope's War* and *Stolen Child* Skrypuch focuses on unfounded Nazi allegations against Ukrainians, in her other novels she shows that some of the DPs were indeed war criminals using forged documents. This is further explored in *Traitors Among Us*, where Maria, one of the two protagonists, admits: "There were well-fed people hiding among the refugees [in a DP camp]. Those who had profited from Hitler's rule" (10). Among them is Sophie, a Nazi girl and the daughter of the kind Austrian family for whom Maria is a slave worker in *Trapped in Hitler's Web*. In *Traitors Among Us* Sophie is a Nazi *Werwolf* (werewolf) pretending to be a Polish girl named Bianka. She is the one who tells the Soviet soldiers that Maria and her sister Krystia are "Nazi collaborators" ("Traitors Among Us" 12). Consequently, the three girls are taken to the Soviet zone where they are questioned and tortured by the Soviet secret police, who know that Maria and Krystia worked with UPA and that Sophie is using forged documents.

In all of Skrypuch's Second World War novels the complexly implicated position of the Ukrainian characters results both from their association with UPA and the Soviet and Western lack of recognition of Ukraine's separate political agency and cultural identity. When the protagonists of *Traitors Among Us* are captured by the Soviet secret police, "the Soviet equivalent of the Nazi Gestapo: the killers, the interrogators" (78), Krystia tells her sister: "No matter what, we can't say anything about the Ukrainian Insurgent Army" (44). Maria shares her sentiment and replies: "Death would be preferable to betraying our friends" (44). While the protagonists refuse to talk about UPA with the Soviet soldiers, Sophie admits to being a Nazi. Unlike her, the sisters manage to escape to the American zone and eventually settle in Canada. The following question asked by one of the sisters echoes the accusations of Nazi collaborators which Ukrainians faced in the Soviet Union and later in North America: "What would the Soviets do to us if they found out about our work helping to rescue Jews from the Nazis and working with the Ukrainian Underground to defeat both dictatorships?" (44). Krystia and Maria know that they should not be talking about UPA, suspecting that "the Ukrainian Insurgent Army [will be] seen as a future threat" (80). However, at the same time they wonder: "how could [they] not talk about the Underground? Fighting for equality was so much a part of everything [they] did" (81). These words highlight the protagonists' overly positive depiction of UPA, whom they only know for the courageous actions.[21]

UPA as Underground Soldiers

Historical fiction encourages young readers to identify with characters and their close ones. As Sara L. Schwebel argues, "[t]his enables an intimate, visceral connection with the past, but it is also limiting" (3–4). Because all of the novels investigated in this chapter are focalized by child protagonists who survived the Soviet and Nazi occupation, they never move beyond their world. This allows Skrypuch to focus on certain perspectives and overlook others, most importantly when it comes to the complex legacy of UPA. Mentions of UPA appear in all of Skrypuch's Second World War novels, where its members usually belong to the protagonists' family. Writing about the Holocaust Kokkola observes that "positioning the threat outside the family enables a celebration of family life to take place within the context of the fear" (Kokkola 135). In Skrypuch's fiction the celebration of family ties also allows for an irrefutably positive depiction of UPA.

In the afterword to *Underground Soldier/The War Below* (2014), a novel published more than a decade after *Hope's War*, Skrypuch explains:

> I first heard about the Ukrainian Insurgent Army (UPA) almost two decades ago. Could it really be true that there was an underground army that fought the two most bloodthirsty dictatorships of the twentieth century? People who wouldn't take the tyranny anymore, so they went into the woods and the mountains, built hiding places and underground hospitals, and fought back for freedom, even though they'd likely die in the process?
>
> (241)

Such unequivocally positive attitude towards UPA may be attributed to the mnemonic discourse promoted by the diaspora since the 1950s. However, as Rothberg observes, "[t]he dynamics of memory [...] do not obey a zero-sum logic, but are instead generative: the conflict of memories produces more, not less memory" ("Implicated" 122). Many Ukrainians were victims of both regimes, and millions of them were killed by the Soviets and the Nazis. Nevertheless, the questionable actions committed by the OUN-B and UPA have led to the appearance of clashing mnemonic discourses.

Hitler's rise to power in 1933, and the subsequent spread of anti-Semitism in Germany, led to the growth of anti-Jewish sentiments in other countries, including Ukraine (Shkandrij "Jews" 151). As Snyder notes, "Ukrainian nationalists helped organize pogroms in reinvaded southeastern Poland in summer 1941" and assisted "the Germans to translate the experience of Soviet rule into a fantasy of Ukrainian innocence and Jewish guilt" ("Black Earth" 155). Skrypuch does not focus on the instances of anti-Semitism among UPA, which scholars like Himka and Karel Berkhoff believe to have been a key element of the OUN ideology (Himka "War Criminality"; Berkhoff 83; Yurchuk 49). This can be explained by the fact that "the collaboration of the OUN, UPA and the local population in the killing of Jews is taboo in the Ukrainian society [and the diaspora – M.Ś] where the traces of Jewish life and wartime atrocities are almost totally erased" and remains a source of disagreements within the diaspora (Yurchuk 50). Rossoliński-Liebe argues that in Ukrainian diasporic memory the theme of Jews rescued by UPA became a significant part of the mnemonic discourse. However, as he notes, some Jews survived with the help of the Ukrainian resistance, but they "usually remained with the UPA against their will, and were forced to treat UPA partisans" (140). Yurchuk observes that "individual instances of kind treatment of Jews by the OUN were the exception rather than the rule," however, the "story about Jewish doctors who helped the UPA was used after the war in order to whitewash the dark side of the history of the UPA" (Yurchuk 50–51).

Skrypuch's novels reflect the fact that most Ukrainians sympathetic towards the idea of German-Ukrainian cooperation initially did not know that Germany saw Ukraine "in terms of a master-slave relationship" (Hunczak 98). As Shkandrij notes, they "believed that any change in Eastern Europe had to be for the better," even if it included working with Hitler ("Ukrainian Nationalism" 57). In her Second World War books Skrypuch does not ignore the existence of collaborators: for example, the father of Luka in *Underground Soldier/The War Below* is arrested not by Germans, but by the Ukrainian Soviet police, who later started collaborating with the Nazis. This seems to echo the words of Snyder who, using the example of Dubno, observes that:

> Ukrainians who spent the first two years of the war helping the local NKVD commander (who was Jewish) deport Poles, Jews, and Ukrainians shifted to helping the SS kill Jews, Ukrainians and Poles whom they – actual Soviet collaborators – denounced as Soviet collaborators.
>
> ("Black Earth" 155)

Skrypuch also mentions instances of denunciation which were frequent in double occupied territories and further problematize the Eastern European mnemonic discourse. However, the image of UPA she wants her readers to include in their mnemonic repertoire is undeniably positive and built on the instances of collaboration between Ukrainians of different religions and backgrounds.

Many Ukrainians during the Second World War were implicated subjects entangled in morally and emotionally complex situations. In Skrypuch's second war trilogy consisting of *Don't Tell the Enemy*, *Trapped in Hitler's Web*, and *Traitors Among Us*, UPA are close members of the protagonists' family who help them and their Jewish neighbors and are "fighting for freedom" ("Traitors Among Us" 193). Unlike most adults who believe in the possible German-Ukrainian collaboration, in *Don't Tell the Enemy* Krystia quickly starts doubting the good intentions of the Nazis who, as she believes, "had not come to liberate Ukraine, but to take [it] over" (41). She is right, as soon Ukrainian leaders in Lviv are arrested and, as her Uncle Ivan says, Ukrainian "independence is dead" (66).

Although UPA was established in 1942, in *Don't Tell the Enemy* Skrypuch demonstrates earlier actions of the partisans, probably members of the OUN. Krystia and Maria are introduced to the Ukrainian underground by their cousin Borys, who believes that Ukraine "doesn't belong to Stalin, and it doesn't belong to Hitler" (66). He informs the sisters of the secret actions of the local insurgents who have been gathering stolen weapons, and the existence of a network of "similar encampments all over Ukraine" (87).[22] While Borys' brother Josip is killed by the Soviets, he is captured by the Nazis and executed. Eventually Krystia realizes that the Nazis do not only kill Jews as "[a]ll of the people in today's mass grave were Ukrainian" (95). At the end of the novel, when Krystia's mother is murdered for hiding Jews, the protagonist goes to the underground encampment where she uses the secret code Borys taught her. There Aunt Iryna, Borys' mother who lost her husband and sons, nurses the protagonist back to health.

In *Traitors Among Us* Krystia openly mentions UPA, saying that she lived "in the woods at the encampment for the Ukrainian Insurgent Army" (120). While at first OUN collaborated with the Nazis, in *Don't Tell the Enemy*, Skrypuch points to the numerous instances of collaboration between Jews and the UPA.[23] Krystia admits that she "acted as a courier between prisoners in the ghetto and insurgents in the woods," further highlighting the collaboration between UPA and the local Jews and her own implication ("Traitors Among Us" 66).[24] Some Jews manage to escape with the false documents made by Mr. Segal, the father of Maria's friend Nathan, and Krystia's Uncle Ivan. Krystia continues smuggling pictures from Mr. Segal but only realizes what he and the insurgents are doing when she sees: "Nathan Segal's picture staring up [...] In the spot where it should have said his name, it read Bohdan Sawchuk, one of the Ukrainians who had been tortured to death by the Soviets" ("Don't Tell" 90). At first Krystia struggles to understand what is happening, but Mr. Segal explains that he is helping to "get people out of here," because he "want[s] [his] son to *live*" ("Don't Tell" 91; emphasis in original). As it turns out in *Trapped in Hitler's Web*, because of the forged documents, and Maria's support, Nathan survives.

UPA, usually referred to only as the Underground, is also present in other books by Skrypuch. In *Stolen Child* it is briefly mentioned when Ivan, Nadia's adoptive father, tells her that he fought against the Nazis and the Soviets. However, the only novel where UPA is not framed within the protagonist's family is *Underground Soldier/The War Below*, which was shortlisted for the 2016 KOBZAR Award and the Geoffrey Bilson Award. It is also the only novel where the readers can learn more about the work of UPA, here depicted at the end of the war as a partisan organization fighting against the Nazis and the Soviets. References to UPA can be found already in the novel's title, both the Canadian (*Underground Soldier*) and American ones (*The War Below*). The novel begins in 1943 when Luka, a 12-year-old boy from Kyiv, manages to escape from the Nazi labor camp where he and other prisoners, including Lida, made bombs. He gets out of captivity by pretending to be dead, lying on a truck filled with corpses.

Although *Underground Soldier/The War Below* focuses on Luka's escape from the camp and struggles to stay alive, Skrypuch also uses flashbacks to familiarize the readers with the boy's life in Kyiv and explain his hatred towards the Soviets, which later convinces him to join UPA. Moreover, this technique allows Skrypuch to provide a historical background for many important events and later explain the position of Luka, who comes from Soviet Ukraine and has to lie about his identity before he can leave for Canada. In the flashbacks Luka talks about his father, a pharmacist who taught him folk remedies. This knowledge saves the boy's life after he is wounded and has no medicine. The fact that Luka respects the legacy shared by his ancestors and does not abandon his Ukrainianness in difficult situations saves the lives of both him and others who need his help.[25] Although it allows him to work as a medic in the local UPA unit, as a member of the insurgence Luka also has to know how to shoot.

Luka gets his chance to symbolically avenge his parents, who were killed by the Soviets and the Nazis, when he comes across UPA.[26] His first encounter with the organization occurs when together with Martina, a Czech girl he befriends running away from the Nazis, they meet soldiers who surprise the children with their kindness. The men tie Luka's and Martina's eyes with a band and carry them to an underground base. Tired and hungry, the children lose consciousness. Luka wakes up, but he is confused, especially after seeing a wounded Wehrmacht soldier lying on a berth nearby. The protagonist realizes he is safe only when the German man recovers and the underground soldiers let him out saying: "You can tell your superiors that your life was saved by the Ukrainian Insurgent Army" (137–138). Unlike in *Hope's War*, here the readers can learn more about the way UPA worked. When Luka realizes that he cannot help his family, but finally has the opportunity to "fight for freedom," he decides to join the ranks of the underground army (137–138). In the booklet he gets from one of the soldiers, Luka reads that "The Ukrainian Insurgent Army – also called the UPA – is fighting against the Nazis and the Soviets" (137–138). Such a positive picture of the organization persists throughout the book; here UPA consists of brave civilians and soldiers, with the underground hospital healing wounded soldiers from both sides and sending them back to freedom with a warning.

Although the insurgents in *Underground Soldier/The War Below* are not members of Luka's family, they emerge as one-dimensional, supporting characters without flaws, full of courage and selfless dedication. Younger members of UPA also give the impression of being fearless and experienced beyond their age, simply by belonging to this organization. The death of Martina, which occurs as a result of the injuries suffered during the evacuation of the camp in fear of being found by the Soviets, is never blamed on any adults who allowed the children to take part in the dangerous operations. Vera, a medical officer, even lets Luka assist in an attempt to rescue Martina on the operating table. The subject of responsibility for the lives of underage subordinates is omitted from the book, and any remorse that adults would have to face is ignored.

Skrypuch, like other authors of children's literature who "depict war and death (especially the death of minors) as absurd and useless," highlights the absurdity of killing (Šubrtová 3). Although Luka quickly establishes himself amongst the troops and goes through training, collaborating with UPA leaves an important scar on his psyche. When Luka is on a mission, he has to kill a Gestapo man to save himself and innocent people: "I raised my rifle and shot. His chest exploded and he slumped down" ("The War" 167). Then he "bent over, and threw up on the floor," showing the impact this act has on him (168). "I reasoned that his death meant that many innocent people would live, but my conscience didn't buy that," he thinks, but asks his superiors not to tell anyone about it (168). Killing, even in this situation, is something of which Luka is ashamed.[27] Moreover, it further positions him as an implicated subject.

Righteous Among Nations – Ukrainians as Rescuers of Jews

The historical discourses on the Ukrainian position(s) during the Second World War have been changing over the last decades and still vary depending on the context of the historian. Historical fiction reflects this discursive diversity and, as Schwebel notes, the chronotopes created by the authors of such novels demonstrate their "knowledge, politics, and worldview [...] at a particular moment in time" (Schwebel 3). As the previous chapters of *Next-Generation Memory* have demonstrated, historical narratives are often children's first encounters with culturally, temporally, and geographically distant events. Hence the authors' beliefs and attitudes reflected in the text shape the readers' next-generation memory of such history. After all, as Rothberg notes, "memory is closely aligned with identity" ("Multidirectional" 4). Despite writing about similar time and space, Skrypuch and Kacer represent different approaches to the position of Ukraine and Ukrainians – Christian and Jewish – during the Second World War. However, the young characters in their novels emerge as active agents[28] and survivors who never lose faith and hope, in Skrypuch's books symbolized by Canada.

Although "memory is not a zero-sum game," the position of the author of historical fiction has a direct influence on the form of next-generation memory (Rothberg "Multidirectional" 11). Writing about Holocaust narratives, Bosmajian notes that children can "appropriate a memory" when they read "consciously, critically, and empathically," yet they usually learn little about history (xvi–xvii). However, Bosmajian's *Sparing the Child: Grief and the Unspeakable in Youth Literature about Nazism and the Holocaust* was published two decades ago and the books discussed in it were aimed at different implied readers. The novels by Skrypuch and Kacer challenge the belief that historical fiction about the Holocaust is mostly centered around the author's grief, because they point to the complexity of the Ukrainian position during the Second World War and the complicated Jewish-Christian dynamics without focusing on the simple victim-oppressor binary. However, after providing a brief historical background on the complex Ukrainian-Jewish relations, in this section I demonstrate that Skrypuch and Kacer approach this complexity in different ways.

Living among hostile and antagonistic national groups forced Eastern European Jews to "identify the stronger without fail"; the fact that Ukrainians usually happened to be the weaker side contributed to the spread of the belief that Jews were not sympathetic towards the Ukrainian national cause (Matusiak 7).[29] In his *Jews in Ukrainian Literature: Representation and Identity* (2009), Shkandrij demonstrates the multi-layered and complex position of Jews in Ukrainian history, including the mutual resentments, especially due to the pogroms (1648–1657, 1759, 1919), the Jewish participation in the Cheka, and their cooperation with the Soviets. Notably, in *Ukrainian Nationalism: Politics, Ideology, and Literature, 1929–1956* (2015), Shkandrij argues that "racial prejudice was present," yet Ukrainian anti-Semitism differed from that of the Nazis because it "was based not on racial beliefs but on the perception of political and economic antagonisms" ("Ukrainian Nationalism" 55). Himka contends that the Nazis used some Ukrainian intellectuals who believed in the possibility of Ukrainian-German collaboration; they were encouraged "to depict Jews as responsible for Bolshevik crimes, as exploiters of the Ukrainian people, as corrupters of morals and conspirators, as a vicious enemy that had to be destroyed" ("The Reception" 622). Hence during the Second World War anti-Semitism was boosted by the Nazi propaganda which associated Jews with bolshevism ("Ukrainian Nationalism" 55).

In 1941 the territory of present-day Ukraine was inhabited by people representing various ethnicities and religions, including approximately 2.7 million Jews: that is "one-third of all world Jewry" (Shkandrij "Jews" 9). About 100,000 of them survived the war in hiding, while about 900,000 of those living in Eastern Ukraine escaped to the Soviet Union with the Red Army. Most of Ukraine's Jews, however, lived in Western Ukrainian provinces of Galicia and Volhynia; therefore, after 1939 they had little chance of fleeing the Nazi-occupied region. Before the Soviet Union's invasion, about 570,000 Jews lived in Galicia, yet most of them were killed in the Belzec extermination camp, shot in the local forests or in the ghettos, and others died in work camps. Hence only 15,000 Jews survived the Holocaust in Western Ukraine. While some were helped by the local population – 2,673 Ukrainians were given the *Righteous Among the Nations* title by Yad Vashem – others were killed by the Nazis and Nazi collaborators.

"Ukrainians hiding Jews. That was like the doomed hiding the more doomed," says Maria, the protagonist of Skrypuch's *Trapped in Hitler's Web*, when she hears that her mother and sister hid their Jewish friends (209). This quote echoes the solidarity and collaboration between Ukrainians and Jews present in all of Skrypuch's Second World War books. Krystia, Maria's sister, is the central character in *Don't Tell the*

Enemy, published in the USA as *Don't Tell the Nazis*. Skrypuch's inspiration for the novel's plot was the true story of Kateryna Sikorska and her daughter Krystia, who risked their lives during the Holocaust by hiding three Jewish friends under their kitchen floor in the town of Pidhaitsi and were acknowledged as *Righteous Among the Nations* by Yad Vashem.[30] Although at first Skrypuch planned to write a nonfiction book, she became aware of the limitations connected to this genre. Realizing that "the story extended far beyond Krystia and her family," she eventually settled for historical fiction,[31] which allowed her to publish two companion novels and focus on showing Ukrainians, civilians and partisans, in a more nuanced way ("Don't Tell" 180).[32]

Don't Tell the Enemy begins on June 28, 1941 in Viteretz, a small town in Western Ukraine, based on Pidhaitsi (pl. Podhajce), at that time part of Poland that faced both Soviet and Nazi occupation. When the readers are introduced to Krystia, the protagonist and first-person narrator, she has experienced two years of constant fear under the Soviet occupation, which included the arrest and murder of many members of her community, including Ukrainian intelligentsia. Krystia's father died of cancer before the occupation, and her mother Kateryna works for the Kitais, a wealthy Jewish family. Although they "could have been deported to Siberia as 'bourgeois,'" Doctor Mina Kitai gets away with having a servant because she treats Soviet officers (8). With the inevitable arrival of German soldiers, the local community seems hopeful and believes that they "would banish the Soviets once and for all" (8).[33] After the Nazi invasion and the spread of anti-Semitism, Krystia's mother is forced to start working for the Commandant and his wife. The Nazis move to the Tarnawsky residence where Kataryna had worked before the Soviets took it away from a wealthy Polish family. Krystia and her sister Maria help their mother, which gives the protagonist an opportunity to eavesdrop and get to know more about the atrocities committed by the Nazis and share them with her Jewish and UPA friends.

With a predominantly Jewish and Polish population and a Ukrainian minority, at the beginning of the Second World War the real Pidhaitsi welcomed a number of Jewish refugees from the West. After the Nazi occupation a Jewish ghetto was built in the town and the head of the local *Judenrat* was Leibish Lilienfeld. Importantly, in the novel Skrypuch refers to real Nazi *Aktions* taking place in the town. A few months after the arrival of the Nazis many local Jews died in the winter of 1941–1942 of hunger and typhus. The next year, on September 21, 1942, the day of Yom Kippur, more than 1,000 Jews from the local ghetto were sent to the nearby Belzec extermination camp. A month later, on October 30, 1,500 Jews were deported to Belzec. Many others were murdered in the area by Nazi and Ukrainian police, but some were rescued by Ukrainian and Polish families (Gołębiowski 45–54). As of 2022 there are no Jewish inhabitants in Pidhaitsi. While the local synagogue survived, it is ruined and closed, because communists turned it into a market after 1945.

Writing about the experiences of Krystia, Skrypuch also attempts to save the story of the Jews of Pidhaitsi – and their few rescuers – from oblivion.

The choice of historical fiction allowed Skrypuch to highlight the entanglements of various communities in multiethnic Ukraine *and* Canada. When Krystia shows her Jewish friend Dolik an old picture depicting the protagonist's mother with her siblings, Aunt Stefa from Toronto and Uncle Ivan, the boy says: "You'd never know it by looking at them as children that they'd all grow up to be so brave" ("Don't Tell" 154). With Dolik's words, Skrypuch seems to equalize the experiences of Krystia's mother, who hid Jews during the war, her sister, who emigrated to Canada, and their brother, who collaborated with UPA. Introducing modifications impossible in nonfiction narratives, for instance simplifying the complex Ukrainian-Polish relations and making Krystia and Maria, who were only eight and seven in 1941, 12 and 11, Skrypuch wanted to make it easier for young readers to identify with the protagonists whose "courageous actions," as she believes, "were that of a mature individual" (182).

Although Skrypuch kept the timeline of *Don't Tell the Enemy* historically accurate, she changed the town's name to Viteretz and made its population significantly smaller. Like in the real Pidhaitsi in 1941, Ukrainians are a minority in Viteretz: "only eight hundred were Ukrainians, with about sixteen hundred Poles and the same number of Jews" (9). However, Skrypuch mentions that the surrounding villages are predominantly Ukrainian. What is quite puzzling, though, is the absence of Polish characters in a city with a Polish majority. While only four Ukrainian families live on Krystia's street, including "Mr. Zhuk, a bookkeeper, [who] had been deported to a Siberian slave camp," the protagonist notes that "the surrounding farmlands were the opposite – mostly poor Ukrainian farmers with just a few Polish and Jewish families mixed in" (8–9). This information is accurate and makes it easier for the readers to better understand Ukrainian nationalist hopes and the joy with which many Ukrainians welcomed the Nazis after years of Soviet occupation, at first seeing them as saviors who would help them gain independence.

Don't Tell the Enemy portrays the initial optimism caused by the arrival of Germans and then the disenchantment after the expected liberation turns out to be another occupation. When the Soviets leave Viteretz, Krystia's neighbor informs her that "Ukraine is free!" after seeing "a proclamation of statehood for Ukraine, independent of Germany and the Soviet Union" nailed on the church door (16). Here Skrypuch refers to when on June 30, 1941, Iaroslav Stets'ko, "one of the leading members of the OUN-B [...] proclaimed the Ukrainian state in the capital of western Ukraine, the city of Lviv" (Rossoliński-Liebe 112). Krystia questions the validity of the poster and the independence claims by asking: "[b]ut are we truly independent? (20). Uncle Ivan, who is a member of UPA, evasively explains that "the Ukrainians got to Lviv right after the Soviets fled and before the Germans arrived" and "seized the radio station and posted signs all over, declaring Ukrainian independence" (20). The man is right when he says that independence is "a ploy" as "[t]he proclamation was a complete surprise to the Germans" (20). However, he seems hopeful and says that "right now the crowds see the Germans as liberators," which may provoke the Nazis to "realize it's on their interest to support Ukrainian independence" (20). As it soon turns out, he is wrong. The initial joy is short lived as the poster quickly disappears and "huge German tanks rumbled in from the west" (17).

Ukrainian statehood in the novels is seen as the cause of all Ukrainians, including the local Jews; hence, they also seem optimistic about the Nazis. For example, Mr. Kitai says: "[g]ood things come from the West, bad things come from the East" ("Don't Tell" 20). It is Ukraine's Jews, the Segals, who document the arrival of the Nazis[34] and life under their occupation in *Don't Tell the Enemy*, including the initial belief they all share – that the Nazis would be better than the Soviets. Skrypuch shows the positive reactions of the locals to the arrival of the Nazis but explains them as the consequence of the years of occupation and Soviet propaganda, which did not inform the citizens about all of the Nazi atrocities and the level of anti-Semitism. Remembering the Soviet atrocities, Krystia wonders "how could the Germans possibly be worse" (20). The girl believes that "[t]he slave camps, executions, hunger – these were over now" and even says that she feels free and "[is] so excited that [she] thr[ows] flowers in the streets" (17). The protagonist notices significant differences between the "ragtag" Soviets and the Nazis, who "seemed so scrubbed and orderly" and give the poor "coffee and chocolate (17). Also in *Underground Soldier/The War Below* the Nazi takeover of the city looks like a parade, with people smiling and waving to the soldiers in fresh uniforms and trucks. The inhabitants of Kyiv, who remember the Soviets' warnings about the "bloodthirsty" Nazis, seem to be surprised by the manifestation of friendship on the part of the soldiers: "At first they seem friendly. It looks like they are trying to create an order" ("The War" 78). But soon it turns out that the initial uncertainty was justified.

Don't Tell the Enemy illustrates the way Nazi propaganda presented the executioners of Ukrainians whose corpses were found in NKVD prisons as Jews (cf. Snyder "Black Earth" 155). Dolik Kitai informs Krystia that the Nazis have discovered rotten corpses in a local Soviet prison in Velicky Selo. Krystia's family is asked to identify the bodies and goes there with a Nazi officer. They find the corpse of her cousin Josip, which "[is] so mutilated that the face was unrecognizable" ("Don't Tell" 32). Although at first the Nazis openly say that the corpses were left by the Soviets, the murders are eventually blamed on 100 local Jews. While Krystia knows this is a lie, the men are sentenced to death. Initially the local Jews believe this accusation to be a misunderstanding. Mr. Kitai approaches the Commandant and says: "those murders were an affront to us all, and we all thank you for trying to punish the culprits [...] But *these* men did not do it" (49). Then he explains that "[i]t was the Soviet secret police – the NKVD – who killed and tortured those young men, but the murderers left *before* you got here" (49; emphasis in original). Instead of answering, the Commandant asks if he is Jewish and tells him to join "these murderers," threatening others by saying "[w]e have plenty of room for new graves" (50). Eventually all of the Jewish men whom the Nazis accuse of murdering Ukrainians are killed.

Skrypuch indicates that the Ukrainian reactions to the anti-Semitic allegations differed. While a man shouts "Kill them!" and a woman adds "[t]he Jews deserve to die. Let's get them all," Petro Zhuk yells to them "[s]hut your drunken mouth!" ("Don't Tell" 48). Interestingly, later Zhuk, whose father was exiled to Siberia by the Soviets, emerges as an implicated subject when he becomes an auxiliary police officer guarding the entrance to the ghetto. He confronts Krystia, who smuggles food for her friends, by saying: "please realize that if the Nazis knew what you were doing, you would be shot. And if they thought that I was bending rules for you, *I* would be shot" (129). This scene illustrates Zhuk's implication, as well as the predicament of many Ukrainians at that time. As Snyder notes, "the Germans gave Ukrainians who had collaborated with the Soviets a chance, which they quickly took," that is "Ukrainians identified Jews as communists and Soviet collaborators, thereby sheltering themselves and their families" ("Black Earth" 156). By saving themselves, they had to sacrifice the lives of others.

A similar scene showing the use of anti-Semitic propaganda appears in a flashback in *Underground Soldier/The War Below*. Here Luka remembers that when the Nazis entered Kyiv, the slogan "Kyiv was, is, and will be Soviet" was immediately replaced by a new one: "Kyiv is now in German hands. You have been liberated from the Soviets" (38). After the capitulation of the Soviet army, the Nazis learn about the mass grave that was found in the forest on the outskirts of Kyiv. Destroying the evidence of their crimes, the Soviets wanted to get rid of the traces of the past. When the city residents are called in to identify the bodies, Luka hears two German officers saying: "top layer of bodies had been very fresh – executed over the summer – but the pit seems limitless ... the pit has been used for years" (84). The Nazis blame the murders on the local Jews. In both *Don't Tell the Enemy* and *Underground Soldier/The War Below* Skrypuch shows that the retreat of the Soviets was connected with the mass executions of political prisoners, including Ukrainian nationalists, which was blamed on Jews. Hence she further points to the complex situation of Ukrainians after the Soviet occupation and the hope that the Nazi "liberation" provoked.

Despite their initial doubts, many people start believing in the Nazi propaganda. Eventually, the Nazis order all Jews to pack and gather next to the graveyard to be transferred to a camp. Luka remembers seeing his Jewish best friend David for the last time: "Two days later, we found out that there had been no train. The Nazis murdered the Jews of Kyiv. Their bullet-riddled bodies now filled the ravine of Babyn Yar" ("The War

92). Here Skrypuch refers to one of the largest massacres in the history of the Holocaust which took place on September 29–30, 1941. The Nazis killed approximately 33,771 Jews. During German occupation of Kyiv about 100,000 and 150,000 people were killed at Babyn Yar (Babi Yar), including Ukrainian nationalists. As Shkandrij notes, "[p]ractically all the Jews who had not escaped or left Kyiv were killed in the last days of September 1941 in Babyn Yar" ("Jews" 167). Although after the Second World War the Soviets "avoided discussing the mass killings of Jews by the Nazis or their own discriminatory practices," in the last few decades the ravine has become the center of Ukrainian Holocaust commemoration (Shkandrij "Jews" 168, cf. Matusiak 17).[35]

As I have already demonstrated in the earlier part of this chapter, there are few references to Ukrainian-Nazi collaboration in *Don't Tell the Enemy*, but Skrypuch does not portray all Ukrainians as unequivocally blameless. However, she does not mention the pogroms which the Nazis organized with the assistance of Ukrainian nationalists, for example the one which took place in Lviv on June 25, 1941 (cf. Snyder "Black Earth" 155). This may be explained by the complexity of the issue and the fact that Skrypuch wants to focus on the rescuers of Jews and the instances of collaboration between Jews and the insurgents. However, it must be noted that, as Snyder argues, Ukrainian participation in pogroms should be linked not only to the effectiveness of the anti-Semitic propaganda and the Judeobolshevik myth, but also to the fact that "it provided useful political cover for the large number of Ukrainians who ha[d] been communists or Soviet collaborators or both" ("Black Earth" 155).

Similar to Skrypuch's *Don't Tell the Enemy*, Kacer's *Louder Than Words* is loosely based on the true story of a Ukrainian Righteous Among Nations. The novel's central adult character is based on Ludviga (Nina) Pukas, a Christian woman who saved Jewish children in Proskuriv[36] (now Khmelnytskyi, Ukraine). Notably, *Louder Than Words* is the third book in Kacer's *Heroes Quartet Series* devoted to rescuers of Jews during the Holocaust (cf. Świetlicki "It Felt Better"). Unlike in the novels by Skrypuch, focalized by gentile rescuers, the central characters in *Louder Than Words* are Jewish sisters named Eldina (Dina) – the focalizer –, Gennadiy (Nadia), and Galya Sternik. After a gradual spread of anti-Semitism before and after the Nazi invasion of Ukraine, a fire destroys the Sterniks' apartment. In order to save the family, Nina, their Christian nanny, registers the girls as her own children. Nina is given a new apartment in a different part of town, because the officials believe that the Aryan-looking children are hers and that Mrs. Frima Sternik is the babysitter. Unlike her children, Dina's mother's hair is dark and she looks Jewish. When the girls' mother goes shopping, a local vendor, Mrs. Timko, recognizes her and denounces to the police. Consequently, despite having new documents, Frima is taken to the ghetto. Although in

Kacer's novel she dies there, according to the website of Yad Vashem, "Pukas sent Sternik to her brother's home in a nearby village but, on her way there, Sternik was caught and killed" ("Ludviga Pukas").

While Kacer shows the steady growth of anti-Semitic sentiments in Ukraine, this is achieved through some questionable narrative choices, such as the use of a significantly altered timeline and inaccuracies not addressed in the author's note. The fate of Frima Sternik is not the only factual error in *Louder Than Words*. Although the real Nina Pukas started working for the Sterniks in 1937, in Kacer's novel, she does so in 1941 and, after only a few months with the children, starts calling them family. Moreover, Galya was Pukas' biological daughter. The novel begins in September 1941, but most of the action takes place six months earlier. As Kacer explains in the author's note, "[f]or the *dramatic purpose* of this story, and to show how the lives of Ukrainian Jews were affected by the Nazi occupation," she decided to change "the timeline of events so that the restrictive laws came into effect first, leading up to the invasion" (229; emphasis mine). Kacer briefly addresses the historical inaccuracies in the author's note, but children do not always read paratexts. I concur with Kokkola that the text itself should contain the truth and explain "a dialogic relationship between fictionality and factuality" (61). Kacer seems to have sacrificed it for the sake of the dramatic purpose, yet it allowed her to depict the gradual spread of anti-Semitism in Poskurov, a city in Western Ukraine, about which Dina's father "had always said that it was amazing how many armies had fought over this small piece of land – *hardly worth all the fuss*" (15; emphasis in original). The real Nazi occupation of Proskurov happened between July 8, 1941 and March 25, 1944. In early November 1941, 5,300 Jews living in the town and the nearby villages were shot by *Einsatzgruppe*. The following month a ghetto was established. In late 1941 or early 1942 all of its surviving inhabitants were murdered (Arad 271). While in Kacer's novel the timeline is altered, the Nazi *Aktions* she refers to are accurate.

Like Skrypuch's protagonists, Dina in Kacer's *Louder Than Words* knows that Ukraine is trapped between two regimes, the Nazis and the Soviets: "*my country* was a pawn, caught in the middle of a war over land and power, and it was being destroyed. And neither the Germans nor the Russians wanted the Jews" (207; emphasis mine). Notably, throughout the novel, Dina refers to Ukraine as her country and identifies as both Ukrainian and Jewish. However, unlike Skrypuch's gentile characters, Kacer's Dina knows that "there was a long history in [her] country of Jewish people being mistreated and persecuted (15). Most notably, she mentions the pogrom of 1919, which happened

> in the center of the city by Kamenetsky Street [...] thousands of Jewish people had been killed by groups of soldiers from the Ukrainian army. It happened before anyone knew what was going on – like

thunder on a clear day, Papa had said. These days, Mama shopped here for groceries every week.

(24–25; emphasis in original)

In reality, the Proskurov pogrom was carried out by Ivan Samosenko's soldiers on February 15, 1919, and in a few hours more than 1,500 Jews were killed using lances and bayonets, with 1,000 left wounded (Vital 716–717).[37] Kacer mentions the 1919 pogrom but does not dwell on the traumatic pre–Second World War history. Although she is trying not to misinform the readers, she also spares them from a more detailed – and graphic – descriptions which may be beyond their comprehension.

Both Skrypuch and Kacer depict the gradual spread of Nazi propaganda and the consequences it had on the lives of Jewish and Christian Ukrainians. In Skrypuch's novels, the only beneficiaries of the invasion are the Nazis and *Volksdeutsche* Germans. In the fall of 1941 Viteretz, where Skrypuch's *Don't Tell the Enemy* is set, officially becomes German; its name is changed to Lebhaft and the names of all streets and places are Germanized. In late August, Jews are ordered to wear armbands with a Star of David,[38] and those who refuse are killed or "forced into labour" ("Don't Tell" 74). The Nazis humiliate Krystia's neighbors, wealthy and educated Jews; for example, the Segals are "made to collect up the horse dung from the streets with their bare hands and dispose of it in the Jewish cemetery" (75). The emergence of *Judenrat* managing work groups is seen by the Jews as an improvement of their situation. Although many Jews, for instance Dolik, believe that being "useful" was synonymous with being "safer," it quickly turns out that no one is safe in the Nazi-occupied territory, including Ukrainians (75).

The hopelessness of the situation of the local Jews becomes obvious when the Nazis begin killing them *en masse*. The Commandant gives the Jews some time off for Yom Kippur, arguably the most important celebration in the Jewish calendar. The next day: "*All Jewish males are ordered to report to the town square at noon*" ("Don't Tell" 100; emphasis in original). While the previous gathering of Jews, which led to the murder of Jewish men, was met with the interest of the local people, this time gentile inhabitants of Viteretz "stayed away from the square at noon, for fear of being targeted by mistake" (100). Among the only witnesses are Krystia and her family, who want to support their friends, the Kitais and the Segals. The Commandant accuses the Jews of "hoarding gold" and demands "one kilogram of gold to be collected from them" (101). He also asks the head of the *Judenrat* to choose 40 of the finest Jewish men; instead, the man chooses the elderly or those of poor health. The reaction of the Commandant surprises everyone, as he says: "Why, you didn't even call up Mr. Baruch, who is on the *Judenrat* with you" (101; emphasis in original). It becomes clear that even the *Judenrat* can be killed by the Nazis. The men are held hostage and the people somehow collect a kilogram of gold. But as the holiest day begins, they are all shot.

Skrypuch challenges the traditional depiction of the oppressors in Holocaust narratives "as completely dehumanized monsters" (Kokkola 134). Kokkola notices that usually "there is little humanity associated with Nazi characters in most children's novels, and almost no attempt to encourage child readers to understand the position of the perpetrators" (Kokkola 134). Although Skrypuch portrays dehumanized Nazis, most notably in *Don't Tell the Enemy* and *Making Bombs for Hitler*, in all of her novels she also points to the numerous examples of humane behaviors and actions of Germans. In *Trapped in Hitler's Web* it is a Nazi who suggests Maria that Nathan should flee to Switzerland, and in *Underground Soldier/The War Below* German farmers, the parents of a Nazi officer, look after Luka when he escapes from the slave camp. As Rothberg argues, "[i]mplication is [...] multidirectional," meaning that "it does not remain limited to one set of entanglements but encompasses a range of powers and interests that frame our actions" ("Implicated" 145). The various intersections of power and interests appear in all of Skrypuch's novels. She points to the entanglements of the characters' situation, provoking the readers to question some of the actions committed by individuals who cannot be categorized using the victim-oppressor category. However, despite individual acts of kindness, they emerge as implicated subjects benefiting from the Holocaust and the Nazi occupation.

The altered timeline in *Louder Than Words* allows Kacer to show the gradual appearance of restrictions and anti-Semitic laws before the Nazi invasion and position Ukrainians as their beneficiaries. Progressively, Jews are not allowed to go to movie theaters, stores, libraries, or even walk on the sidewalks. Eventually, Dina's mother loses her job as a teacher. The Nazis in Kacer's novel are dehumanized, but they are only briefly mentioned. Instead, *Louder Than Words* focuses on showing the various instances of anti-Semitic acts before and after the Nazi occupation. Dina believes that both Stalin and Hitler hate the Jews. Still, it is only when the Nazis come into Ukraine and take over the city that more serious acts of physical and symbolic violence committed by Ukrainians start occurring. Right before the occupation, Dina encounters acts of anti-Semitism at school. For example, her friend Esther is told by a boy named Ivan that "Jews have no brains" (15–16). Kacer shows that by bullying Jews, mostly the weaker ones, including Avrum, "the smallest person in class," the poor Ukrainian child is trying to gain popularity at school (31). Although Kacer points to *"kind families"* hiding Jews, most secondary Ukrainian characters in *Louder Than Words* emerge as implicated subjects, who believe in the anti-Semitic propaganda and see the Nazis as liberators, or entangled bystanders, who are too afraid to help Jews (207; emphasis mine).[39]

The Ukrainian woman named Mrs. Timko epitomizes the sudden and shocking growth of anti-Semitism among Christian Ukrainians. Dina first introduces her as a cheerful and smiling person, who "always had candies to pass out to any child who walked by" (26). Furthermore, the kind woman shows her sympathy when she tells Dina: "Your mother has to deal with so much. But the Lord never gives us more than we can handle" (27). The mention of "the Lord" is of great significance as throughout the novel Kacer highlights Mrs. Timko's religiosity: she "was always talking about what the Lord did and didn't do" (27). While in Skrypuch's books Christians are presented in a positive way, often risking their lives to save Jews, here the kind churchgoing woman suddenly becomes anti-Semitic. When Mrs. Timko sees Dina right after the Nazi invasion, she refuses to give "candy for the JEWISH girl" (89). Dina recalls that the woman's unexpected words sounded as if "she had put [Dina's] religion in capital letters and shouted it loudly so that everyone around her could hear" (89). The attitude and words of Mrs. Timko resonate the anti-Semitic Nazi propaganda, especially when she says: "The Jews will take over our business and schools if we let them" (90). Although Mrs. Timko's behavior demonstrates the power of propaganda, her complete transformation is rapid and may puzzle the reader.[40]

Notably, Mrs. Timko is not the only Christian depicted as anti-Semitic in *Louder than Words*. As Nina says, the "church teaches us that Jewish people tortured Christian children – even sacrificed a child once during the Easter celebration" (58). She also wonders "[w]hy would my church teach such a horrible thing?" (58). Such a one-dimensional portrayal of "the church" dismisses the complex religious situation in Ukraine and the differences between Orthodoxy and Catholicism. It is also significantly different from the positive representation of Christians in Skrypuch's novels. Moreover, Kacer's depiction of the church seems problematic because some Catholic churches helped to hide Jews, a fact she acknowledges in *Masters of Silence*, a novel set in France (cf. Świetlicki "It Felt Better").[41]

In *Louder Than Words* the sudden spread of anti-Semitic propaganda turns Mrs. Timko into a perpetrator. When Dina sees her mother for the last time near the ghetto fence, Frima tells her daughter that it was Mrs. Timko who denounced her to the Nazis. Although according to Yad Vashem this is not historically accurate, making Mrs. Timko the one responsible for the death of the protagonist's mother allows Kacer to create a foil character representing all gentile collaborators. The fact that it is "[t]he candy lady [...] with the forever smile and sweets for everyone," who betrays Dina's mother, makes the treachery even more upsetting (202). However, it suggests that one did not have to be a dehumanized monster to support the Nazis.

Mr. Petrenko, Dina's teacher, emerges as an entangled bystander, who unlike Mrs. Timko, undergoes a moral evolution throughout the novel. At first, the man is too afraid to act when he sees Ukrainian children bullying Jews. Seeing the abuse, he says: "You all need to work out your ... your disagreements on your own" (32). Dina notices "the look of embarrassment in his eyes" (33). The teacher seems ashamed when he later has to segregate the students, forcing the Jewish ones to sit in the back of the classroom. Notwithstanding his initial apathy, Mr. Petrenko acts differently when Dina meets him on her way to see her mother in the ghetto. The man instantly recognizes his former student, but instead of denouncing Dina, he helps the girl find out what has happened to her mother. This is possible because he knows someone "connected to the authorities," who despite collaborating with the Nazis, "[i]s a good man" (189). Although the teacher's initial passivity is caused by fear, and he tells Dina that he "wish[es] there was more [he] could do to help," his inability to stand up against anti-Semitism positions him as an entangled bystander (191).

Dina's uncle, who converted to Christianity, and his gentile wife, also emerge as implicated subjects who detach themselves from Jewishness. After the fire, together with Nina and their mother, the Sternik sisters are forced to pay the uncle a visit. While the aunt gives them some clothing, she is scared and reluctant to help, asking: "[w]hat is it that you want from us? [...] Jews are not wanted in any neighborhood" (133–134). Afraid of the Nazis, the couple need to make a difficult and morally ambiguous decision: to risk their own lives or sacrifice the ones of Dina and her sisters. Although they choose to save themselves, in the epilogue, taking place after the war, they want to reconcile and be reunited with the Sternik children. However, at this point, the girls prefer to stay with Nina, whom they call mother.

Writing about the collaboration between Jewish and Christian Ukrainians, in *Don't Tell the Enemy* Skrypuch informs her readers of the consequences of helping Jews. Unlike in Western Europe, for example the Netherlands, helping or hiding Jews was punishable by death: "the Commandant decreed that Jews found outside the ghetto without permission would be shot on sight. Slavs who gave Jews food would be shut" (115). To discourage Slavs from helping Jews, Nazi propaganda portrayed them as carriers of contagious diseases (cf. Chapter 4). Krystia and her family are immune to the propaganda. Despite the danger and the fact that the ghetto is barbed with wire, the protagonist decides to risk her life and help her friends by regularly sneaking in food, medical supplies, and small hacksaws that her father used to make; she believes that they may be useful when the Jews will be deported.

Both Skrypuch and Kacer depict the chronotope of the ghetto and the gradual killing of the Jews living there. In *Louder Than Words* the ghetto is located "near the market on Kamenetsky Street," close to the place where the 1919 pogrom took place (168). When Dina is looking for her mother there, she sees her close friends "all imprisoned behind wire bars, cages as if they were dangerous animals" (199). The Jews in the ghetto are surrounded by gentile Ukrainians who "walked past the ghetto, starring at the Jews inside as if they were exhibits in a zoo, pausing every now and then to point and whisper to one another" (199–200). Although these people do not directly contribute to the predicament of the imprisoned Jews, they are described as entangled bystanders observing a genocide. In

Louder Than Words, there are no gentile Ukrainians helping their former neighbors behind barbed wire. Notably, Kacer uses typical Holocaust imagery and points to Dina's survivor guilt. In the ghetto Dina spots her best friend, Esther, wearing a red coat, which she describes as a sign of "color in a sea of gray" (203). The color of Esther's coat is a clear reference to the girl in the red coat, a symbol of innocence in Steven Spielberg's *Schindler's List* (1993), one of the most popular Holocaust-themed films. Instead of talking to her friend, Dina decides to look away: "What would I have said? And how could I have explained my freedom when she was imprisoned like this?" (203). Although she is trying to survive, the girl feels guilty because she cannot help those behind the wire.

Before the establishment of the ghetto in *Don't Tell the Enemy*, some local Jews escape using forged documents. However, Doctor Mina Kitai and the Segals stay in Viteretz and together move to an overpriced single room. Because the Jews are allowed to bring just a single suitcase to the ghetto, Doctor Mina cannot take her medical supplies. However, instead of destroying them or leaving for the Nazis, she gives most of them to the local UPA unit. One box of essentials stays hidden in Krystia's loft. When the girl later sneaks into the ghetto, she sees countless people sleeping on the ground with their suitcases, too poor to afford a room. In a manner more detailed than Kacer, Skrypuch describes the various ways in which the Nazis tortured and killed the Jews living behind the barbed wire. Some are to be taken to a work camp, but this turns out to be a lie as "they are shot dead just a few kilometers out of town" (125). Among them is the 12-year-old Nathan Segal, who is buried alive, but manages to escape and share with Krystia's family what has happened. Notably, his words are reminiscent of the testimonies of Holocaust survivors:

> When the person beside me was shot and fell into the pit, I stumbled and fell in after him. I lay very still as the Volksdeutsche covered us with shovelfuls of dirt. After they left, I climbed out and ran. All I had on was my underwear.
>
> ("Don't Tell" 137; cf. Snyder)

Krystia's mother gives the boy some clothes left by Aunt Iryna. The next day it turns about that Nathan has escaped with Maria. Maria and Nathan go to Lviv where they enlist as Eastern workers and in *Trapped in Hitler's Web* travel to Austria. Hence, because of Maria and the documents forged by UPA and Mr. Segal, Nathan is one of the few Jews from Viterets who survive the Holocaust.

Maria, unlike Lida in *Making Bombs for Hitler* and Marusia in *Stolen Child*, volunteers to become an Eastern worker. However, she does it "not because [she] wanted to help the Nazis" but to save Nathan ("Traitors Among Us" 128). Maria knows that staying in Ukraine is not an option for the boy because of the Nazis and the fact that "everyone in Viteretz knew that the real Bohdan had been killed by the Soviets"

("Trapped in Hitler's Web" 1–2). Hence Maria seems to recognize the danger of not only the Nazis but also the possible denouncers. Notably, for some time, Maria and Nathan hide in the woods with the assistance of UPA. To make his passing as a Ukrainian more believable, before going to Austria, Maria teaches Nathan Catholic prayers and songs, as well as Taras Shevchenko's poetry. On their way to Salzburg, Maria and Nathan are separated by the Nazis, who force Nathan to work as a bridge constructor. Despite their separation, the protagonist is relieved that her best friend "was out of the war zone. Away from the units that hunted down Jews" (36).

Although in *Trapped in Hitler's Web* Skrypuch focuses on the struggles of Maria as a slave worker, throughout the novel the protagonist witnesses acts of anti-Semitism, which she openly condemns. When Sophie, the Hitler girl, shows her an ornament of "[a] hanged Jews swinging on a scaffold," and asks "Isn't that funny?," Maria replies: "No, it's not funny [...] It's celebrating murder and it's sick" (102). She also questions whether the only thing Sophie learns from the Hitler Youth is "[h]ow to hurt and to hate" (103). The ornament makes the protagonist think about Nathan: "Was that his fate if he stayed in the Reich? How could I stop that from happening?" ("Trapped in Hitler's Web" 104). Bosmajian argues that "the implied reader is to undergo both identification and rejection" when they are presented with a Hitler Youth character (xvi). The juxtaposition of a Christmas decoration and an anti-Semitic ornament positions Sophie as cruel and brainwashed by propaganda. While Maria is punished for her reaction, she knows that all instances of anti-Semitism are morally wrong. Hence she emerges as a sympathetic character, different from the dehumanized Nazi girl.

Unlike all other main characters who survive the Second World War in Skrypuch's books, Nathan does not immigrate to Canada, instead, he reconnects with "distant cousins" and "move[s] to Israel" ("Traitors Among Us" 263). With the help of the advice given by Sophie's older brother, a kind soldier, who does not believe in the inferiority of Slavs and Jews, Maria is briefly reunited with Nathan, and she encourages him to escape to Switzerland. Although Nathan is like a brother to Maria and wants her to join him, she decides to stay at the farm, hoping to find her sister after the war. Maria receives a letter from Nathan with the words "*Falcon is free,*" which recall the secret UPA code ("Trapped in Hitler's Web" 265; emphasis in original). Because of Maria's help, Nathan survives, but the Nazis kill his family and friends.[42]

The theme of Ukrainian rescuers of Jews is central to *Don't Tell the Enemy* and its two sequels. In late July the inhabitants of the ghetto in Viterets are to be taken to Belzec, a death camp, but Nathan's father escapes with the help of the hacksaw which he got from Krystia. Krystia's mother lets Mr. Segal hide in the kitchen, in a hole under the stove. Soon he is joined by Dolik and Leon, who also escape.[43] Krystia prays that other Poles and Ukrainians are also hiding Jews. As the protagonist recalls in *Traitors Among Us*, her mother "knew the risk" of hiding Jews, but "decided that [they] had to take the chance, even if we both died trying" (241). Notably, it is Uncle Ivan, a member of UPA, who helps dig the hole. In the third book it turns out that the Soviets know that nationalists helped Krystia and her mother who "were in constant contact with the underground group" ("Traitors Among Us" 123). Hence they use this information to allege that Krystia is a Nazi collaborator.

In *Don't Tell the Enemy* Skrypuch refers to the accusations that Slavs who risked their lives helping Jews did so only for financial profits, which were common in the Eastern Bloc after the war (cf. Świetlicki and Michułka; Snyder "Black Earth" 275). In the spring of 1943 the Commandant comes to Krystia's house and accuses her mother of hiding Mr. Segal. Although she denies the accusation, the Nazis find the hidden man and accuse Kateryna of helping Jews in exchange for gold: "Slavs are despicable people. You wouldn't hide Jews if not for the gold" (166). The Commandant finds no gold, and Krystia's mother is hanged. The man also tears the family portraits which Krystia and Dolik draw, which symbolizes the destruction of Viterets with its Christian and Jewish inhabitants (169–170). Notably, it is Aunt Iryna, who lives in the woods with UPA, who glues the portraits together and encourages Krystia to look for her sister, go to Canada, and keep the memory of Ukrainians *and* Ukrainian Jews alive: "Who will remember them if you give up?," she asks (177).

Nina Pukas, the Righteous Among Nations in Kacer's *Louder Than Words*, is portrayed as a simple, illiterate woman from Western Ukraine, who asks the children to call her by her name: "If we're to be friends, then we should know one another by our first names" (11). She does, however, call their mother Mrs. Sternik, a sign of respect and class division absent from Skrypuch's novels. Nina wears traditional, colorful scarves, and her depiction echoes the stereotypical *baba* (cf. Chapter 3). At first Dina's perception of the woman is irrefutably negative; she even compares Nina to "a troll" (9). According to Dina, Nina is a short woman who is

> as small as she was wide [...who] wore a simple long skirt and flowered cotton blouse, and a bright red scarf was wrapped tightly around her head and tied under her chin. Her skin was worn and lined, like old leather. She had a deep dimple only on one side of her face. It disappeared, like a crater, into the folds of her skin. I had no way of knowing how old she was. Twenty? Forty? A hundred?
>
> (9)

Despite this depiction, in the next few months Nina earns the children's sympathy and trust. To make Dina like her, Nina cooks traditional Ukrainian *varenyky* or pierogi, the girl's favorite dish. Most notably, however, Nina asks Dina to "tell [her] more about being Jewish" (43).

Her willingness to learn about the Sterniks' customs brings Nina closer to the protagonist.

Although in the prologue to *Louder Than Words* Dina says that Nina "never stopped helping [them], no matter how dangerous it was," Nina is reduced to a foil character, a typical brave rescuer in Holocaust fiction who risks her life to help the children she has recently met (227). Nina is illiterate and can only write down her name. It is Dina who starts teaching Nina in secret, which brings them even closer and makes the child protagonist feel in charge of the situation. Although Nina proposes to pretend to be the children's mother, she never emerges as a character with any agency. When she goes to the Nazi office to register the children as her own, Nina has to write down their names. This surprises Mrs. Sternik, because the woman does not know that Dina has been teaching Nina to read and write. While it is Nina who risks her life, it is possible only because of Dina's lessons.

The theme of rescuers of Jews is also present in Skrypuch's *Making Bombs for Hitler* and *Stolen Child*. A significant scene in *Making Bombs for Hitler* involves Lida, the protagonist, who turns nine but pretends to be 13, a common practice as many children who survived the Second World War were passing as adults (Kertzer 198).[44] Lida gives her precious necklace with a cross to Zenia, a Jewish girl she meets in the slave camp, believing that it may save her. Even though Lida does not know Zenia well, she does what her mother would have liked her to do. After all, the woman was killed by the Nazis for hiding Lida's friend Sarah and her family ("Making Bombs" 47). Seeing Zenia, Lida thinks that "[her] simple cross was not just jewelry and it was not only a symbol of [her] beliefs. It was all that [she] had left of [her] parents. But it also showed that [she] wasn't Jewish" (47–48). Thanks to Lida's support in the camp, Zenia manages to survive and, after the war, settles in Israel.

Although Skrypuch's protagonists are Slavic Christians, they are sympathetic towards Jews and recognize that as terrible as their own situation is, it is still better. Lida in *Making Bombs for Hitler* knows that the Slavs are "treated terribly, but one glance told [her] that these Jewish people had it even worse" and is "grateful that no one at the camp realized Zenia was Jewish" (122). When the readers are introduced to Lida's sister Nadia/Larissa in *Stolen Child*, the girl recalls the first propaganda lessons she had after being kidnapped by the Nazis: "*Ukrainians and Poles are sub-human. Those who are allowed to live will be slaves to the Aryans [...] Jews are rats [...] None deserve to live*" ("Stolen" 138; emphasis in original).[45] Among the memories which return to her in Canada is one of a "girl in the yellow dress with the yellow star, standing in a lineup just like this" (65). Living with the Himmels, Nadia/Larissa subconsciously thinks about the fate of Europe's Jews. She even refuses to eat the sophisticated dishes prepared by their cook: "*I think of the women and children with the yellow stars. How can I eat this when it seems they have nothing?*" (106; emphasis in original). Nadia/Larissa, who was herself kidnapped and lost her family, is haunted by the image of the girl with the yellow star. In the flashbacks, Nadia/Larissa remembers instances of her subliminal rejection of anti-Semitism. When she is given a propaganda book titled "Das [sic!] Giftpilz," Nadia/Larissa tries to like it, but it is not possible because "*[i]t talks about Jews and how they are poisonous toadstools but Germans are wholesome mushrooms*" (75). Despite the propaganda she is fed with, Nadia/Larissa knows that anti-Semitism "*is wrong*" (76; emphasis in original).

The Nazi occupation destroys Skrypuch's and Kacer's multiethnic Ukraine inhabited by people of various ethnoreligious backgrounds.[46] Although both authors approach the topic of the Righteous Among Nations differently, they highlight that their Jewish characters identify as Ukrainians. In *Louder Than Words* Dina says: "It didn't matter that we were all *young Ukrainian boys and girls – proud of our country*. The only thing that seemed to matter was our religion, and mine was the wrong one to have" (78; emphasis mine). Eventually all Jews in the novel become the targets of the Nazis, which makes Dina think that: "the Jews of *my country* might be in danger" (70; emphasis mine). In *Don't Tell the Enemy* the Segals and the Kitais are important members of the community who want Ukraine to become independent. They also actively collaborate with UPA, which allows Skrypuch to discreetly address the allegation that Ukrainian insurgents were anti-Semitic. After the war there is no place for Skrypuch's characters in Ukraine, with the surviving Jews settling in Israel and Ukrainians finding new home in Canada.

Home-Away-Canada

"We're together. We're safe. We'll be in Canada soon," says Krystia to her sister Maria when they are finally reunited in a DP camp ("Traitors Among Us" 6). Skrypuch frames her Second World War books with the mentions of Canada, which protects the readers and may encourage them to think that the novels' protagonists will not only survive but also emigrate and escape the Soviet occupation. Canada emerges as the only place where Skrypuch's protagonists can find peace, yet getting there is not simple. Although she does not directly mention the restrictive immigration laws in Canada during and right after the war, all of the children in Skrypuch's novels have to spend a few years in camps for displaced persons. In the spring of 1946 a bill was passed to let Canadian citizens sponsor close relatives and orphaned nieces and nephews who had not yet turned 16. Many DPs did not have any documents and/or family in Canada. In 1947 Canada started receiving non-sponsored DPs among those considered "acceptable."

Canada is the place which gives Skrypuch's protagonists hope for a better future during the war. This hope is exemplified by the numerous mentions of Aunt Stefa from Toronto, the sister of Krystia's and Maria's mother, in *Don't Tell the Enemy*, *Trapped in Hitler's Web*, and *Traitors*

Among Us. In the first novel Krystia finds a letter from Aunt Stefa, some pictures, and stockings. The woman looks like the girls' mother, "except happy and well fed" ("Don't Tell" 109). Seeing the photographs, Krystia wonders: "[w]hat would our life be like now if we lived in Canada instead of Viteretz? We'd have enough to eat, and there would be no war happening all around us [...] It sounded almost like heaven" ("Don't Tell" 110). Krystia wishes her family was safe in Toronto where there are no Nazis. Although her wish is fulfilled only in *Traitors Among Us*, the gifts sent by Aunt Stefa help the protagonist's family and neighbors survive hunger. Krystia suggests her mother to go to Lviv and sell the stockings on the black market. After three days the woman returns with buckwheat that the protagonist shares with her friends in the ghetto.

As Kokkola argues, "Holocaust literature destroys some of the most basic premises of children's literature," including "the basic home-away-home pattern of much children's literature" (154). While in Skrypuch's novels home is also lost, Canada brings closure and offers the protagonists the opportunity to build a simulacrum of their home in pre-War Ukraine. The vision of safety in Canada is a frame giving the characters, and the readers, hope, but it also shows that remaining in Ukraine is impossible. In *Underground Soldier/The War Below*, Luka wonders whether he will fit and "truly be at home" in Canada (240). The only thing he is sure of is that unlike in Soviet Ukraine, in Canada he can "be happy" (240). Krystia in *Don't Tell the Enemy* hears that she needs to do everything to go to Canada. When she wonders if her sister is alive, Dolik's brother Leon says: "you should find Maria, and the three of you should go to Canada and live with your Aunt Stefa" (155). After Krystia's mother's death, Aunt Iryna encourages the girl to find Maria and Nathan and go to Canada. She tells her niece that her mother always wanted to go to Canada, adding that she "would rest easy in her grave" knowing that the girls were reunited with Aunt Stefa ("Don't Tell" 178). After spending a few years in a DP camp, Krystia and Maria find safety in Toronto and can pray for the souls of the close ones – both Christian and Jewish – whom they lost to Nazism and Stalinism. Hence immigration to Canada is synonymous with a structural and psychological closure for Skrypuch's characters.[47]

Juxtaposing the war-struck Eastern Europe with the safe chronotope of Canada, where many Ukrainians live, allows Skrypuch to show how different the war experiences in North America and Eastern Europe were. When in *Trapped in Hitler's Web* Maria arrives in Salzburg, the "food and luxury items" she sees everywhere remind her of "how [she] imagined Auntie Stefa's Toronto" (143). Unlike later in Canada, in Salzburg the girl is met with Nazism, anti-Semitism, and hatred towards Slavs. Eventually, even Salzburg is bombed and destroyed. As Mychailo, a friend of Nadia/Larissa, says in *Stolen Child*, the best thing about Canada is the absence of bombing and the haunting smells of "[g]unpowder and rot and blood" (122). Instead, as Nadia/Larissa adds, in Brantford "everything smelled like it had just been washed" (122). Although at first seeing the cleanliness and wealth of Canada the girl believes that "it was not a world war after all," eventually Nadia/Larissa realizes that many Canadian soldiers died fighting in the war (30). By framing her novels with Canada, Skrypuch further highlights the transcultural and multidirectional character of the memory of the Second World War.

Conclusion

Writing about implicated subjects, Rothberg maintains that "radical discontinuities" caused by the destruction of a people "cannot simply or immediately be undone by the cessation of killing, formal independence, or emancipation from bondage" ("Implicated" 56). Hence, it comes as no surprise that the Shoah remains in the center of mnemonic debates in North America and Europe, often positioned next to other genocides and slavery. Next-generation memory of the Holocaust and the Second World War shaped by the books examined in this chapter appears as significantly different from the past narratives based on the simplified victim-oppressor binary.

Similar to multidirectional memory discussed by Rothberg, next-generation memory can lead to the formation of "new forms of solidarity and new visions of justice," which go beyond the victim-oppressor binary ("Multidirectional" 5). The texts I have discussed challenge the formulaic and one-dimensional depiction of the role Ukrainians played in the Holocaust. I agree with Kokkola that "[i]n silence we become complicit with the oppressor, we hush up the past" (15). Writing novels which explain the complexity of Ukrainian history, Skrypuch addresses some of the silenced experiences of Ukrainian rescuers of Jews but also points to the problematic instances of denunciation and collaboration. She also confronts the stereotypes concerning the Ukrainian participation in the Holocaust and the war-criminal allegations against North American DPs. Although Skrypuch's depiction of UPA and the Polish-Ukrainian relations is simplified, this can be attributed to the limitations caused by the novels' focalization.[48] However, none of the books contain any major and misleading inaccuracies and many of her characters emerge as implicated subjects or entangled bystanders.[49] Despite the instances of historical inaccuracies and generalizations in *Louder Than Words*, Kacer's novel also addresses the complexity of the Ukrainian situation and introduces sympathetic Ukrainian characters while stressing that many Ukrainian Jews identified as Ukrainian.

Historical novels may help young readers understand the complexity of Ukrainian past *and* present. This seems to be of particular importance considering that in his recent "de-Nazification" campaign, that is the genocide of Ukraine and its people, Putin has regularly pointed to the distorted memory of the Holocaust. Although after Russia's attack on

Ukraine in 2022, the question of Ukraine's complicity in the Holocaust has been used in Putin's propaganda, the war has led to instances of reconciliation between Ukrainians and Jews. For example, President Zelenskyy was awarded the Jan Karski Eagle Award (Nagroda Orła Jana Karskiego) for his "heroic defense of Ukraine and the moral values of Western civilization" ("Nagroda Orła"; cf. Motyl "Op-Ed"). Rabbi Abraham Skórka, a member of the Eagle Award committee, compared Putin's invasion to the Holocaust: "Let us take heed that the sin of omission toward Ukraine and the brave nation does not come to persecute us, like the sin of omission in the face of the Holocaust" (Motyl "Op-Ed"). This act was of great symbolic significance considering the complex history of Ukrainian-Jewish-Polish relations and the various ways they are remembered in cultural memory. On March 1, Putin's army bombed Babyn Yar in Kyiv, a place where the NKVD and Nazis murdered thousands of Jews. Putin's "de-Nazification" did not stop there. In March all monuments and Jewish sites of memory in Kharkiv were damaged or destroyed, including the Kharkiv choral synagogue and Drobytsky Yar where about 20,000 Jews were killed during the Holocaust.[50] Despite the memory wars connected to the polarizing assessment of the position of Ukrainian Nationalists during the Second World War, present-day Ukraine which Putin is attempting to "de-Nazify" "is expansive, diverse, tolerant and committed to freedom and democracy" (Motyl "Op-Ed"). However, as Serhii Plokhy notes in the preface to *The Frontline*, "history is central to Ukraine's current war with Russia and its relations with the West" (loc. 83). As I have shown in this and the previous chapters of *Next-Generation Memory*, history is also central to Ukrainian Canadian children's literature.

Notes

1 In 2022 Russian Foreign Minister Sergey Lavrov, who accused the USA and Canada of helping "neo-Nazis," openly compared Zelenskyy to Hitler who, as Lavrov believes, "also had Jewish blood" ("Lavrov Compares").
2 In the last few decades the history of the Second World War, especially the Holocaust, has become a significant part of literature, popular culture, and school curricula both in Europe and North America (cf. Marshman; Wójcik-Dudek; Świetlicki "It Felt Better"; Świetlicki and Michułka). Most of the books by best-selling authors of children's and YA literature – like Kathy Kacer, Edeet Ravel, and Jennifer Nielsen – concentrate on the atrocities committed by the Nazis against Europe's Jews and their noble rescuers. More recently, writers like Skrypuch or Amanda McCrina have focused on various complex issues, such as the *Lebensborn* project, *Ostarbeiters* (Eastern workers), Jewish-Christian collaboration, or the atrocities committed by Stalinists against the multiethnic populations of Eastern Europe.
3 Serhii Plokhy argues that applying a transcultural perspective in the reading and writing of Ukrainian history may be particularly beneficial due to its long-term statelessness ("The Frontline" loc. 348).
4 I refer here to the notion introduced by Bakhtin. See Chapter 1 endnote 3.

5 However, as Zhuk observes in *KGB Operations Against the USA and Canada in Soviet Ukraine, 1953–1991* (2022), Soviet intelligence *did* target diasporic organizations and attempted to undermine the Ukrainian-American collaboration by discrediting Ukrainian leaders (loc. 563).
6 For more about the genesis of Ukrainian Nationalism see Erlacher 2021 and Shkandrij 2015.
7 Examining the political myth of UPA and Bandera in Canada, Rossoliński-Liebe writes that this heroization is among "the most problematic components of Canadian's heterogeneous history" because it "stimulated parts of the Ukrainian diaspora in Canada and other countries to pay homage to a fascist, anti-Semitic and radical nationalist politician" (Rossoliński-Liebe "Celebrating" 1). Nevertheless, in the last two decades Bandera has been commemorated as a hero, which has been met with varied reactions (cf. Wylęgała "Bohaterowie").
8 It started to change with the publication of books by Anne Applebaum (2003), Timothy Snyder (2010), Norman Davies (2006), and other Western historians.
9 In the early 1930s some Ukrainian First World War veterans who found refuge in Canada openly displayed Nazi sympathies (cf. Martynowych).
10 The main proof of this cooperation, the 1957 memoir by a Jewish-Ukrainian woman named Stella Krentsbach, is widely believed to be fabricated by either diasporic intellectuals or Soviet propaganda (Himka "Falsifying"; Goble; McBride).
11 Demjanjuk was accused of being "Ivan the Terrible," the notorious Nazi camp guard at three extermination camps.
12 The Commission of Inquiry found some evidence against 20 individuals – out of the 774 accused. The initial high numbers of alleged war criminals may have been the consequence of the KGB propaganda against Ukrainians (Satzewich 173; cf. Zhuk). The Soviets may have been attempting to weaken the "cooperative relations" emerging between Jews and Ukrainians by providing North American governments with forged documents about the alleged cooperation of Ukrainian with the Nazis (Satzewich 173; cf. Zhuk).
13 Notably, the mere mention of young Ukrainian *Canadians* fighting for both of their homelands is the only reference to the Second World War in Gloria Kupchenko Frolick's *Anna Veryha*, examined in Chapter 3. Apart from Ukrainian Canadians, a few million Ukrainians were in the Red Army.
14 Skrypuch's *Hope's War* echoes the real-life trials of North American Ukrainians accused of collaborating with the Nazis. In the author's note she admits that all "[w]ar criminal must be brought to justice," however she stresses that "justice demands that they be presumed innocent until proven guilty" ("Hope's War" 243). Skrypuch refers here to the – at the time ongoing – trials of Wasyl Odynsky, Vladimir Katriuk, and Helmut Oberlander, men accused of collaborating with the Nazis and concealing their past. In 2001 they were set to be deported and stripped of their Canadian citizenship under subsection 10(1) of the Citizenship Act, R.S.C. 1985, c. C-29. Skrypuch also brings out the case of Serge Kisluk who died during proceedings in 2001. In 2007 the Federal Court found that Odynsky and Katriuk, who was accused of participating in the Khatyn massacre, had lied to obtain their citizenship, but there was no evidence of their personal involvement in war crimes. Both men died in Canada long after the publication of *Hope's War*, Odynsky in 2014 and Katriuk in 2015. In 2007 Oberlander was stripped of Canadian

citizenship and died in 2021 before his extraction. Katriuk and Oberlander were among the Most Wanted Nazi War Criminals according to the Simon Wiesenthal Center. The question of war criminals is also addressed in *To Look a Nazi in the Eye: A Teen's Account of a War Criminal Trial* (2017) by Kacer and Jordana Lebowitz, where they familiarize young readers with the trial of Oskar Groening, a German senior who was accused of being a Nazi. While Danylo's and Groening's cases differ significantly, they both involve sympathetic elderly citizens who claim to be innocent and represent contradictory approaches of teenagers towards the allegations. Unlike Kat in *Hope's War*, the Jewish protagonist of *To Look a Nazi in the Eye* has no personal relationship with the accused. Still, she has a cognitive dissonance when she listens to Groening's convincing testimony and then the testimonies of the Holocaust survivors.

15 The first one consisting of *Stolen Child/Stolen Girl* (2010/2019), *Making Bombs For Hitler* (2012), and *Underground Soldier/The War Below* (2014/2018), as well as the second one formed by *Don't Tell the Enemy/Don't Tell the Nazis* (2018), *Trapped in Hitler's Web* (2020), and *Traitors Among Us* (2021). The novels, however, can also be read separately.

16 During the trial described at the end of the novel, Danylo's defender asks the following questions: "Imagine yourself as a teenager in a Canada with no government, no army, no weapons [...] What would you do? Would you do what Danylo did when he was a teen? Would you fight for your country as he did?" (229). Answering them may provoke the readers to sympathize with Danylo and further position him as a complexly implicated subject.

17 For a more detailed discussion of the complex situation of the region before and during the Second World War, see Plokhy "The Gates" 239–241. As he notes, Volhynia "was a hotbed of Russian nationalism," which was later incorporated into Poland and Polonized; thus, it became "a sphere of competition between two Ukrainian nation-building projects" and then "a stronghold of Ukrainian nationalism with powerful anti-Polish overtones" ("The Gates" 239, 241).

18 The only other Ukrainian Canadian author who mentions the issue of Ukrainian collaboration with the Nazis is Lisa Grekul. Unlike Skrypuch, Grekul, whose coming-of-age novel *Kalyna's Song* (2003) is directed at adult and young adult readers, explores Poland and Ukraine's battle over the past, especially UPA's campaign of mass terror against the Polish minority in Volhynia in 1943 when "between 70,000 and 100,000 Polish civilians were murdered by the UPA" (Rossoliński-Liebe 115). She also mentions the history of Polish colonization of Ukraine. However, Collen, Grekul's protagonist, distances herself from these atrocities: "I might not speak Ukrainian, but I still feel Ukrainian. And I might feel Ukrainian, but that doesn't mean I'm guilty for every historical injustice perpetrated by other Ukrainians" ("Kalyna's Song" 414). This sentence, as well as the following quotation demonstrate the complex situation of Ukrainian Canadians when it comes to the Second World War memory: "It wasn't me [...] I wasn't there. My grandparents weren't there. They never lived in Kiev [sic!]. They were farmers. They moved to Canada before the war, years before. In 1899" ("Kalyna's Song" 322). However, as I show in this chapter, the postwar immigration and the accusations of Nazi collaboration influenced all Ukrainian Canadians, including those whose ancestors immigrated during the first two waves.

19   Moreover, just like Danylo, Luka decides not to tell the American soldiers about his collaboration with UPA.
20   Only in Canada does Nadia/Larissa get to read non-propaganda children's books, and reading becomes her greatest passion.
21   When Krystia is question by the NKVD, she is told "that the Ukrainian Insurgent Army is a pro-Nazi group," and "a group traitorous to the Soviet Union" ("Traitors Among Us" 122, 124). These words provoke her to say that UPA "is an anti-Nazi group" (122). While Krystia is forced to make a false confession against the local UPA, she does not break, preferring to die than betray her family and friends. Before the interrogation, the readers learn that the Ukrainian insurgence "fought the Nazis during the war" and "that Ukraine's biggest threat came from the Soviets," who "want to cut the freedom movement off at its knees" and kill all remaining members of UPA, including Krystia's uncle and aunt (104).
22   To get there, Borys has to make the call of the falcon and after five minutes is asked to say the code which is "Ukraine is not yet dead" ("Don't Tell" (86). Only later does Krystia realize that a falcon in flight looks like the Tryzub (trident), the national symbol of Ukraine. The code is the chorus of a song: "If we had our own country, that song could be its anthem," she thinks ("Don't Tell" 88). Here Skrupych refers to "Shche ne Vmerla Ukrayiny ni Slava, ni volya" ("Ще не вмерла України ні слава, ні воля"), the national anthem of Ukraine adopted in 1992, with the final version of the lyrics approved in 2003. The piece is based on Pavlo Chubynsky's 1862 poem with music composed in 1896 by Mykhailo Verbytsky and was used as the national anthem of the Ukrainian People's Republic, Carpatho-Ukraine, and West Ukrainian People's Republic.
23   In Skrypuch's second trilogy, Maria and Krystia are both said to have collaborated with the resistance, "which both the Nazis and the Soviets hated" ("Traitors Among Us" 44). Yet they do so to save their family and Jewish friends. Moreover, in the chronotope of the books, members of UPA help not only Ukrainians but also local Jews. Unsurprisingly, both Krystia and her sister Maria have close Jewish friends, such as the children of the Kitais (Dolik and Leon) and the Segals (Nathan). While Maria is close with Nathan Segal, whom she eventually helps escape to Austria, Krystia's relationship with Dolik Kitais is more complex. Krystia likes Dolik but is jealous, not of his family's money but of the fact that he has a father. Krystia does not share her thoughts with Dolik until the end of the novel when he is hiding with Leon and Mr. Segal under her kitchen floor.
24   At the beginning of *Trapped in Hitler's Web* Nicoletta, a woman collaborating with UPA, gives Maria and Nathan food when they are escaping to Austria.
25   The earliest chronological reminiscence appears in the first chapter when the boy leaves the labor camp. He goes back to 1941 when the inhabitants of Kyiv were forced to destroy all valuable objects before the city was besieged by the Nazis. Skrypuch refers here to a Soviet practice used in the retreat, called the "scorched earth" tactic – that is leaving nothing of value to the enemy (Hrycak 234). Instead of being protected by the Soviet army, Ukrainians were abandoned as "Stalin says that everything must burn in Kyiv" ("The War" 76). The flashbacks also explain what happened to Luka's father. Even when he did not have any medicine, he refused to leave the people without help and

used folk methods until he was hailed as a Nazi spy by one of his neighbors. The NKVD agents find a book of medical prescriptions "written by a German nun in the Middle Ages" and arrest Luka's father (10). The language in which it is written is sufficient for the suspect to become accused of treason.

26   Although Luka's father and grandfather are killed by the Soviets, his mother is taken by the Nazis to Germany as an *Ostarbeiter*. Hence it is not surprising that the boy wants to fight against both regimes.

27   While Luka is brave and reasonable, Skrypuch writes from the point of view of a 13-year-old. He is mature for his age, but his thoughts often betray his childish side. When in chapter 13 Martina saves his life, blurring the traces behind him so that he is not traced by soldiers combing the forest, his first instinct is shame. "How humiliating to owe my life to a girl – and one who was likely younger than me, about ten or so" ("The War" 103). Though they befriend, Luka is jealous of Martina's shooting skills. Despite his courage, Luka prefers healing, not killing. Still, he quickly deals with envy when instead of a shooter, he becomes Vera's assistant at the underground hospital. "I was frustrated by that at first, stung by the thought that Danylo didn't have a faith in my abilities as a soldier, but secretly I was relieved to be healing instead of shooting," he says (174). Luka is sometimes naïve, especially in chapter 26 when he voluntarily falls into the trap set by the NKVD after the end of the war, a theme Skrypuch also mentions in *Making Bombs for Hitler* and *Traitors Among Us*. Eventually, like Danylo in *Hope's War*, Luka finds shelter in Canada.

28   This seems to challenge the belief that "[c]hildren are used and abused in history; they have no power though they are the inheritors of the future" (Bosmajian xii).

29   For centuries Ukrainians and Jews were marginalized minorities trying to survive within the borders of countries ruled others, in the case of the latter, in their own homeland (cf. Matusiak 5–6; Shkandrij "Jews" 1). As Yurchuk notes, "the war unleashed interethnic conflicts which were fuelled during the decades of the interwar period"; hence, understanding the complexity of the Ukrainian-Jewish relations during the Holocaust is impossible without referring to the history of these interethnic conflicts (Yurchuk 49). The Ukrainian-Jewish relations are more complex than studies on their entanglements during the Second World War may suggest.

30   In the author's note Skrypuch informs her readers that "more than twenty-five hundred Ukrainians have been recognized as Righteous Among the Nations by Yad Vashem for their efforts in rescuing Jews during the Holocaust" ("Don't Tell" 183).

31   The protagonist of *Don't Tell the Enemy* "is true to the real Krystia" and so are many significant details, such as Maria being the name of her sister, her father's illness and profession, as well as the existence of Aunt Stefa who lived in North America (181). The main antagonist, the Nazi Commandant, is also inspired by a historical figure, "a Kriminalpolizei officer named Willi Hermann who was personally involved in the liquidation of the Jews in the area" (182).

32   The first, *Trapped in Hitler's Web*, depicts the experience of Maria saving a Jewish boy named Nathan and working as an *Ostarbeiter* in Austria. In the next, in *Traitors Among Us*, the girls are reunited in a DP camp, but have to confront the Soviet allegations of being Nazi collaborators.

33 The novel begins with the Soviets leaving the town "like angry bees, attacking [..] *civilians* and stealing all they could as they fled" (2; emphasis in original). Krystia describes the Soviets as cruel, crude savages and thieves, and seems relieved seeing them leave with two trucks: "[o]ne was piled high with stolen goods; the other carried half a dozen soldiers clutching rifles" (11). Thus, in the novel Skrypuch shows the crimes committed by the Soviet occupiers.

34 After the death of her mother and Jewish friends, Krystia goes back home and finds the photograph of her family which Mrs. Segal took "on the day the Nazis arrived in Viteretz" ("Don't Tell" 169). Looking at it she reflects: "[w]e had all been so hopeful then, thinking the war was over, thinking we would have our own country. How could we ever have guessed, back then, just how evil the Nazis truly were?" (169).

35 Babyn Yar has become a common reference in popular culture and Holocaust literature, most notably in poetry by Yevgeny Yevtushenko, Lyudmila Titova, Mykola Bazhan, and Muriel Pernin's children's book *Kiev 41: Babi Yar* (1995).

36 Here spelled using the Russian transliteration as Proskurov.

37 Unsurprisingly, Kacer refers to the anarchy in Ukraine in 1919, mentioned in Chapter 4, and pogroms, as its "worst aspects" (cf. Subtelny 363). As Subtelny notes, because of the Ukrainian-Russian conflict "old animosities towards the Jews were heightened by the widespread impression that Jews were pro-Bolshevik" (363). Although

> most Jews were apolitical and those who were Marxists usually favored the Mensheviks [...] Jews were also disproportionately prominent among the Bolsheviks, notably in their leadership, among their tax- and grain-gathering officials, and especially in the despised and feared Cheka.
>
> (Subtelny 363)

Hence they "became the targets of old resentments and new frustrations," resulting in the death of 35,000–50,000 Jews (Subtelny 363).

38 When all Jews are forced to wear the Star of David in *Louder Than Words*, Dina feels "nothing but shame," but Nina, who helps the family sew the stars on their clothes, tells the girl that they should never stop appreciating being Jewish (85).

39 Although Dina thinks that "no one was coming to help [them]" and "[they] were all alone," she is together with Nina (127). By hiding Jews, the woman risks her life (cf. Świetlicki and Michułka 2022).

40 Nina confronts Mrs. Timko saying that Dina is "only a child," but the woman replies saying: "[a] Jewish child" (90). Just like Skrypuch's protagonist, Nina, also a gentile woman, does not believe in the Nazi propaganda. Like Dina, she is disappointed with Mrs. Timko, whom she believed to be "a good person – a kind person" (98). Nina seems to be immune to the spreading anti-Jewish hatred, which causes her to "feel ashamed that Jewish people are being treated like this" (93). Hearing her words Dina, who is initially skeptical towards Nina, hugs her for the first time. Throughout the novel they grow closer, especially since Nina wants to learn more about Jewish culture.

41 In the context of Ukraine it is worth noting that Andrei Sheptyts'kyi, the metropolitan of Halych, archbishop of Lviv, and bishop of Kamianets-Podilskyi, "quickly came to believe that Nazi occupation was worse" that the

Soviet regime (Snyder 2015, 288). As Snyder notes, Sheptyts'kyi, who was known for his respect for Jews,

> protested to Himmler, protested to Hitler, and asked the pope to intervene to protect Jews [...] He issued pastoral letters reminding his flock of the divine commandment not to murder. He also classified murder as a reserved sin, which meant that Greek Catholics who killed human beings had to confess personally to him.
>
> ("Black Earth" 288)

After his death "[t]he Soviets forcibly subordinated the Greek Catholic Church to the Moscow Patriarchate of the Orthodox Church, which they had long before humiliated and tamed" ("Black Earth" 288).

42 The only close friend of Krystia taken to Belzec is Doctor Mina, who refuses to escape and leave her patients. Hence the woman may be interpreted as Skrypuch's take on "the Old doctor" archetype, usually associated with Janusz Korczak (cf. Żurek). All Jews from the ghetto are eventually killed in the last Nazi *Aktion*. As Krystia recalls, "[t]he *Judenrat* was not spared. Doctor Mina was not spared" ("Don't Tell" 161). On the day of her death, Krystia and Dolik silently draw pictures of the Kitai family and the house the boy once lived in.

43 At night the children recall their happy childhood as they "had a secret agreement to talk only of happier times" ("Don't Tell" 169). Not allowed to go to the outhouse, they use a chamber pot and spend their days in the darkness under her kitchen floor. They come out at nights to eat and play Remi. Sometimes they are joined by Uncle Ivan and Aunt Iryna.

44 Interestingly, while Lida changes her age to survive and acts like an older individual, in *Don't Tell the Enemy* Skrypuch altered the age of the real Krystia. Knowing that some "might have difficulty understanding that someone so young could accomplish all that Krystia did," Skrypuch decided that "making [Krystia] older would make her actions more relatable" to the young readers (182).

45 Nadia/Larissa remembers hearing Eva, her adoptive Nazi sister, asking their "mother" about *Ostarbeiters* using a reference to Jews: "[a]re they animals like the Jews, Mutti?" ("Stolen" 94). The woman replies: "Yes, dear, that's why they work in the munitions factory. You wouldn't want Germans to get bombed, would you?" (94).

46 Edeet Ravel's *A Boy Is Not a Bird* begins with a description of Zastavna in Ukraine's Bukovyna (currently in Chernivtsi Oblast) as a place where five different languages are spoken. When the Soviets occupy Zastavna, Natt, the book's young protagonist, believes that Russian will become the sixth language. However, the novel showcases the forced russification of the region. Although the book is set predominantly in Ukraine, Ravel does not use the name Ukraine to describe the region. While the Ukrainian language is mentioned eight times, the only character referred to as Ukrainian is a poor peasant woman who brings her own mattress on the train to Siberia and is accused by a Romanian man of infesting people with lice.

47 As Kokkola notes, the first one "brings the plot a satisfactory conclusion, whereas psychological closure brings the protagonist's personal conflicts into balance" (155).

48 Notably, *Traitor* (2020) and *The Silence Unseen* (2022), recent YA novels by American author Amanda McCrina, focus on the complexity of the Ukrainian-Polish relations and the legacy of UPA.

49 Skrypuch's novels contain minor factual errors, yet mostly connected to geography. For example, she locates Rivne and Tarnopol outside of Poland in *Trapped in Hitler's Web* and in *Underground Soldier* incorrectly states that Wrocław (Breslau) was a Polish city occupied by the Nazis.
50 Among the only known survivors are musicians Zhanna Arshanskaya Dawson and her sister Frina, whose story inspired *Alias Anna: A True Story of Outwitting the Nazis* (2022), a novel in verse by Susan Hood and Greg Dawson, which is a retelling of *Dawson's Hiding in the Spotlight: A Musical Prodigy's Story of Survival, 1941–1946* (2009).

Works Cited

Applebaum, Anne. *Gulag: A History*. Doubleday, 2003.
Applebaum, Anne. *Red Famine: Stalin's War on Ukraine*. Penguin Books, 2017.
Arad, Yitzhak. *The Holocaust in the Soviet Union*. University of Nebraska Press, 2009.
Berkhoff, Karel. *Harvest of Despair: Life and Death in Ukraine under Nazi Rule*. Cambridge: Belknap Press, 2008.
Bertelsen, Olga. "Introduction: A Blind Spot of Active Measure." *Russian Active Measures: Yesterday, Today, and Tomorrow*, edited by Olga Bertelsen. Ibidem Press and Columbia University Press, 2021, pp. 15–35.
Bosmajian, Hamida. *Sparing the Child: Grief and the Unspeakable in Youth Literature about Nazism and the Holocaust*, Routledge, 2002.
Erlacher, Trevor. *Ukrainian Nationalism in the Age of Extremes: An Intellectual Biography of Dmytro Dontsov*. Harvard Ukrainian Research Institute, 2021.
Goble, Paul A. "Russia Special Services Again Play the 'Jewish Card' against Ukraine." *Moldova.org*, July 9, 2009, www.moldova.org/en/russia-special-services-again-play-the-jewish-card-against-ukraine-202438-eng/. Accessed 12 May 2022.
Goldberg, Robert A. *The Bystander during the Holocaust*. UTAH Law Review, 2017.
Goldstone, Gabriele. *Tainted Amber*. Ronsdale Press, 2021.
Gołebiowski, Grzegorz. *Śladem przodków – Podhajce*. Warsaw: Difin, 2010.
Grabowicz, George G. "A Great Literature." *The Refugee Experience: Ukrainian Displaced Persons after World War II*, edited by Wsevolod W. Isajiw, Yury Boshyk, and Roman Senkus. Canadian Institute of Ukrainian Studies Press, University of Alberta, 1992, pp. 240–268.
Grekul, Lisa. *Kalyna's Song*. Coteau Books, 2003.
Grekul, Lisa. *Leaving Shadows: Literature in English by Canada's Ukrainians*. Edmonton: University of Alberta Press, 2005.
Himka, John-Paul. "A Central European Diaspora under the Shadow of World War II: The Galician Ukrainians in North America." *Austrian History Yearbook*, vol. 37, 2006, pp. 17–31.
Himka, John-Paul. "Falsifying World War II history in Ukraine." *Kyiv Post*, May 8, 2011. www.kyivpost.com/article/opinion/op-ed/falsifying-world-war-ii-history-in-ukraine-103895.html?cn-reloaded=1
Himka, John-Paul. "The Reception of the Holocaust in Postcommunist Ukraine." *Bringing the Dark Past to Light. The Reception of the Holocaust*

in *Postcommunist Europe*, edited by John-Paul Himka and Joanna Beata Michlic, Lincoln, 2013, pp. 626–653.

Himka, Johh-Paul. "Ukrainian Collaboration in the Extermination of the Jews during the Second World War: Sorting Out the Long-Term and Conjunctural Factors." *The Fate of the European Jews 1939–1945: Continuity or Contingency? Studies in Contemporary Jewry XIII*, edited by Jonathan Frankel. Oxford University Press, 1997, pp. 170–189.

Himka, John-Paul. "War Criminality: A Blank Spot in the Collective Memory of the. Ukrainian Diaspora." *Spaces of Identity*, vol. 5, no. 1, 2005, pp. 9–24.

Hirsch, Marianne. "The Generation of Postmemory." *Poetics Today*, vol. 2, no. 1, 2008.

Hrycak, Jarosław. *Ukraina. Przewodnik Krytyki Politycznej. Z Jarosławem Hrycakiem rozmawia Iza Chruślińska*. Warszawa–Gdańsk: Krytyka Polityczna, 2009.

Hunczak, Taras. "Between Two Leviathans: Ukraine during the Second World War." *Ukrainian Past, Ukrainian Present: Selected Papers from the Fourth World Congress for Soviet and East European Studies, Harrogate, 1990*, edited by Bohdan Krawchenko. St. Matin's Press, 1993, pp. 97–106.

Isakowicz-Zaleski, Tadeusz. *Przemilczane ludobójstwo na Kresach*. Kraków 2008.

Janion, Maria. *Niesamowita słowiańszczyzna. Fantazmaty literatury*. Wydawnictwo Literackie, 2006.

Kacer, Kathy. *Louder Than Words*. Annick Press, 2020.

Kacer, Kathy and Jordana Lebowitz. *To Look a Nazi in the Eye: A Teen's Account of a War Criminal Trial*. Second Story Press, 2017.

Kertzer, Adrianne. *My Mother's Voice. Children, Literature, and the Holocaust*. Broadview Press, 2002.

Kokkola, Lydia. *Representing the Holocaust in Children's Literature*. Routledge, 2003.

"Lavrov Compares Ukraine's Zelenskyy to Hitler, Who Also 'Had Jewish Blood'." Haaretz May 1, 2022. www.haaretz.com/world-news/europe/.premium-lavrov-compares-zelenskyy-to-hitler-who-also-had-jewish-blood-1.10774213

Lower, Wendy. *Nazi Empire-Building and the Holocaust in Ukraine*. University of North Carolina Press, 2005.

Luckhurst, Roger. "Beyond Trauma: Torturous Times." *European Journal of English Studies*, vol. 14, no. 1, 2010, pp. 11–21.

"Ludviga Pukas." Yad Vashem. www.yadvashem.org/yv/en/exhibitions/righteous-women/pukas.asp

Marples, David R. *Heroes and Villains. Creating National History in Contemporary Ukraine*. Budapest–New York: Central European Press, 2008.

Marples, David R. "Open Letter from Scholars and Experts on Ukraine Re. the So-Called 'Anti-Communist Law.' *Krytyka*, March 2015, https://m.krytyka.com/en/articles/open-letter-scholars-and-experts-ukraine-re-so-called-anti-communist-law Accessed 12 May 2022.

Marshman, Sophia. "From the Margins to the Mainstream? Representations of the Holocaust in Popular Culture." *eSharp*, vol. 6, no. 1, 2005, pp.1–20.

Martynowych, Orest T. "Sympathy for the Devil: The Attitude of Ukrainian War Veterans in Canada to Nazi Germany and the Jews, 1933–1939." *Reimagining Ukrainian Canadians: History, Politics, and Identity*, edited by Rhonda L. Hinther and Jim Mochoruk. University of Toronto Press, 2011, pp. 173–220.

Matusiak, Agnieszka. "Holokaust: rewitalizacja ukraińskiej pamięci? W osiemdziesiątą rocznicę wydarzeń w Babim Jarze." *Iudaica Russica*, vol. 2, no. 7, 2021, pp. 5–44.
McBride, Jared. "Ukraine's Invented a 'Jewish-Ukrainian Nationalist' to Whitewash Its Nazi-era Past." *Haaretz*, November 9, 2017. www.haaretz.com/opinion/ukraine-nationalists-are-using-a-jew-to-whitewash-their-nazi-era-past-1.5464194. Accessed 12 May 2022.
Montgomery, Lucy Maud. *The Golden Road*. L.C. Page & Co., 1913. www.gutenberg.org/cache/epub/316/pg316-images.html
Motyka, Grzegorz. *Ukraińska partyzantka 1942–1960*. Warszawa, 2006.
Motyl, Alexander J. "Op-Ed: Is Zelensky Ukraine's George Washington?" *Los Angeles Times*, February 26, 2022, www.latimes.com/opinion/story/2022-02-26/volodymyr-zelensky-ukraine-invasion-george-washington-vladimir-putin?fbclid=IwAR0QyAu8T0wU5vZu8ZCG_VXQwKEQN5PaRpvT0GNQUGjZNkgI8GbgyBhT6NY
Motyl, Alexander J. *The Turn to the Right: The Ideological Origins and Developments of Ukrainian Nationalism, 1919–1929*. Columbia University Press, 1980.
"Nagroda Orła Jana Karskiego dla prezydenta Ukrainy Wołodymyra Zełenskiego." *Dzieje.pl* Feb. 25, 2022, https://dzieje.pl/wiadomosci/nagroda-orla-jana-karskiego-dla-prezydenta-ukrainy-wolodymyra-zelenskiego. Accessed 12 May 2022.
"New Survey by the Azrieli Foundation and the Claims Conference Finds Critical Gaps in Holocaust Knowledge." *Claims Conference*, www.claimscon.org/study-canada/. Accessed 7 January 2020.
Plokhy, Serhii. *The Frontline – Essays on Ukraine's Past and Present*. Harvard University Press, 2021.
Plokhy, Serhii. *The Gates of Europe: A History of Ukraine*. Basic Books, 2015.
Ravel, Edeet. *A Boy Is Not a Bird*. Groundwood Books, 2019.
Rossoliński-Liebe, Grzegorz. "Celebrating Fascism and War Criminality in Edmonton. The Political Myth and Cult of Stepan Bandera in Multicultural Canada." *Kakanien Revisited*, vol. 12, 2010, pp. 1–16.
Rossoliński-Liebe. Grzegorz. "Holocaust Amnesia. The Ukrainian Diaspora and the Genocide of the Jews." *Holocaust and Memory in Europe*, edited by Thomas Schlemmer and Alan E. Steinweis. Berlin, Boston: De Gruyter Oldenbourg, 2016, pp. 107–143.
Rothberg, Michael. *Multidirectional Memory: Remembering the Holocaust in the Age of Decolonization*. Stanford University Press, 2009.
Rothberg, Michael. *The Implicated Subject: Beyond Victims and Perpetrators*. Stanford University Press, 2019.
Rudling, Per Anders. "Multiculturalism, Memory, and Ritualization: Ukrainian Nationalist Monuments in Edmonton, Alberta." *Nationalities Papers*, vol. 39, no. 5, 2011, pp. 733–768.
Rudling, Per Anders. "The OUN, the UPA and the Holocaust: A Study in the Manufacturing of Historical Myths." *The Carl Beck Papers in Russian & East European Studies*, vol. 2107, 2011.
Satzewich, Vic. *The Ukrainian Diaspora*. Routledge, 2002.
Schwebel, Sara L. *Child-Sized History: Fictions of the Past in U.S. Classrooms*. Nashville: Verderbilt University Press, 2011.

Shkandrij, Myroslav. *Jews in Ukrainian Literature: Representation and Identity.* Yale University Press, 2009.
Shkandrij, Myroslav. *Ukrainian Nationalism: Politics, Ideology, and Literature, 1929–1956.* Yale University Press, 2015.
Skrypuch, Marsha Forchuk. *Don't Tell the Enemy.* Scholastic Canada, 2017.
Skrypuch, Marsha Forchuk. *Don't Tell the Nazis.* Scholastic, 2019.
Skrypuch, Marsha Forchuk. *Hope's War.* Dundurn, 2001.
Skrypuch, Marsha Forchuk. *Making Bombs for Hitler.* Scholastic Canada, 2012.
Skrypuch, Marsha Forchuk. *Stolen Child.* Scholastic Canada, 2010.
Skrypuch, Marsha Forchuk. *Stolen Girl.* Scholastic, 2020.
Skrypuch, Marsha Forchuk. *The War Below.* Scholastic, 2018.
Skrypuch, Marsha Forchuk. *Traitors Among Us.* Scholastic Canada, 2021.
Skrypuch, Marsha Forchuk. *Trapped in Hitler's Web.* Scholastic Canada, 2020.
Skrypuch, Marsha Forchuk. *Underground Soldier.* Scholastic Canada, 2014.
Snyder, Timothy. *Black Earth: The Holocaust as History and Warning.* Tim Duggan Books, 2015.
Šubrtová, Milena. "When Children Die in War: Death in War Literature for Children and Youth." *Bookbird*, vol. 47, no. 4, 2009, pp. 1–8.
Subtelny, Orest. *Ukraine: A History*, 4th ed. University of Toronto Press, 2009.
Świetlicki, Mateusz. "'It Felt better to Stay Quiet' Miming as a Non-Verbal Way of Coping with Trauma in Kathy Kacer's *Masters of Silence* (2019)." *Silence and Silencing in Children's Literature*, edited by Elina Druker, Björn Sundmark, Åsa Warnqvist, and Mia Österlund. Makadam: Göteborg and Stockholm, 2021, pp. 340–352.
Świetlicki, Mateusz and Dorota Michułka. "Unburied Practices of Memory: The Holocaust and the Polish-Jewish Relations in Joanna Rudniańska's *Kotka Brygidy* (2007) and *XY* (2012)." *Children's Literature in Education*, 2022. https://doi.org/10.1007/s10583-021-09473-6
Ulanowicz, Anastasia. *Second-Generation Memory and Contemporary Children's Literature: Ghost Images.* Routledge 2013.
Umland, Andreas and Yuliya Yurchuk. "Introduction: The Organization of Ukrainian Nationalists and European Fascism During World War II." *Journal of Soviet and Post-Soviet Politics and Society*, vol. 6, no. 1, 2020, pp. 181–203.
Vice, Sue. *Children Writing the Holocaust.* Palgrave, 2004.
Vital, David. *A People Apart: The Jews in Europe, 1789–1939.* Oxford University Press, 1999.
Wójcik-Dudek, Małgorzata. *Reading (in) the Holocaust: Practices of Postmemory in Recent Polish Literature for Children and Young Adults*, translated by Patrycja Poniatowska. Peter Lang, 2020.
Wylęgała, Anna. "Bohaterowie czy kolaboranci? Pamięć o UPA na Ukrainie Zachodniej." *20 lat rzeczywistości poradzieckiej. Spojrzenie socjologiczne*, edited by Małgorzata Głowacka-Grajper and Robert Wyszyński. Warszawa: Wydawnictwo Uniwersytetu Warszawskiego, 2012, pp. 134–154.
Wylęgała, Anna. "Co jest nie tak? Raz jeszcze o polskoukraińsko-żydowskim trójkącie." *Kultura Liberalna*, August 2, 2018, https://kulturaliberalna.pl/2018/08/02/wylegala-polityka-historyczna-ukraina-pamiec-wolyn/. Accessed 12 May 2022.
Wylęgała, Anna. "Entangled Bystanders: Multidimensional Trauma of Ethnic Cleansing and Mass Violence in Eastern Galicia." *Trauma, Experience and*

Narrative in Europe after World War II, edited by Ville Kivimäki and Peter Leese. Palgrave, 2022, pp. 119–149.

Wylęgała, Anna. "The Absent 'Others': A Comparative Study of Memories of Displacement in Poland and Ukraine." *Memory Studies*, 2015, pp. 1–17.

Yekelchyk, Serhy. *Ukraine: What Everyone Needs to Know*, 2nd ed. Oxford University Press, 2020.

Yurchuk, Yuliya. *Reordering of Meaningful Worlds: Memory of the Organization of Ukrainian Nationalists and the Ukrainian Insurgent Army in Post-Soviet Ukraine.* Stockholm University, 2014.

Zhuk, Sergei I. *KGB Operations against the USA and Canada in Soviet Ukraine, 1953–1991.* Rutledge, 2022.

Żurek, Sławomir. "*Noc żywych Żydów* [Night of the Living Jews] by Igor Ostachowicz–Judaic and Shoah Topoi." *Filoteknos*, vol. 11, 2021, pp. 35–51.

Conclusion

> ... for years the memory had been dim, crowded into the background of consciousness by the more exciting events of her busy life. Now it came back with a rush.
>
> (L.M. Montgomery, "Little Joscelyn")

The books discussed in *Next-Generation Memory* are focalized by child or adolescent protagonists, who emerge not only as the bearers of Ukrainian Canadian cultural memory but also as universal symbols of humanity and hope in chronotopes[1] filled with hatred and injustice. Their authors portray Ukrainian and Ukrainian Canadian history in dialogue with cultural memories of other ethnic groups in Canada and with the present. I agree with Michael Rothberg that "such dialogue can create solidarity even as it reveals implication" ("Implicated" 20). Hence I have tried to argue that these books can become the seeds of next-generation memory for their young readers. Notably, all of the texts I examine were written and published *before* 2022. Since then, in addition to transmitting the memory of the distant past and educating Anglophone children about Ukraine and its complex history, popular and widely available historical fiction has been helping them understand the 2022 war and its main actors: Ukrainians.

The number of historical children's books about the twentieth century keeps increasing. At the same time, as the 2022 ban on Art Spiegelman's *Maus* in Tennessee demonstrates, the discussion of whether war and genocide are appropriate topics in children's literature is still ongoing in North America (cf. Mangan). Debating about the past can be uncomfortable, because, as Rothberg notes, "practices of memory – even multidirectional practices – intersect with power dynamics, forms of complicity and distancing, and risks of forgetting" ("Implicated" 26). Hence the matter of addressing the past emerges as one always connected to the mnemonic practices of the present. Adrianne Kertzer has argued that by being afraid to show children violence and inhumanity, "we tell stories whose delicate and sensitive language persuades us that, despite the Holocaust, human values remain the same" (54). We promote the idea that the Shoah "was an aberration" but "our humanistic values remain strong" (54). This becomes especially problematic when we are faced with other global conflicts and genocides, like the ones which have happened around the world after 1945, including the recent war in Ukraine.

When I started working on this book in 2018, Ukraine was not in the center of the world's media attention. Everything changed on February 24, 2022. As Masha Gessen argues in an essay published in *The New Yorker*: "Europe will no longer be defined by the history of the Second World War. The next era of European history, whenever it begins, will be the aftermath of the war in Ukraine" (35). It will be a new era of *world's* history, because similar to the memory of the twentieth-century atrocities discussed in this book, the legacy of the 2022 war in Ukraine has already traveled through continents. In a media-saturated world, this genocide – as Timothy Snyder, Joe Biden, and Canadian lawmakers have already billed the Russian war crimes – cannot be hidden like the Holodomor, the Holocaust, or the Internment (cf. Singh; Snyder; Tabarovsky and Finkiel; Motyl). Although usually "most people deny, look away from, or simply accept the benefits of evil in both its extreme and everyday forms," we cannot hide from the war in Ukraine and the impact it has on global politics (Rothberg "Implicated" 20).

"We need a record for humanity of what happened here [in Ukraine]: not just justice, but a record, because memories fade," argues international human rights lawyer Flynn Coleman while discussing the use of crowdsourced evidence during the 2022 war (qtd. in Bergenduen 17). Unlike most previous wars and conflicts connected to Ukraine, proof of atrocities committed by Russian soldiers is available instantly. The massacres in Bucha and Mariupol cannot be denied in the same way the Soviet authorities denied the occurrence of the Holodomor and pogroms, discussed in Chapters 4 and 5. However, some people chose to turn around, not recognizing their implicated position. Yet to once again quote Rothberg, "[a]s taxpayers, we are indeed all implicated in the actions of our government, whatever our ideological opposition to or affective disengagement from particular policies" ("Implicated" 19). Although recording atrocities is of great importance, even well-documented events can fall into oblivion when they are not discussed and commemorated.

As I have tried to argue in *Next-Generation Memory*, popular historical books have the potential to prevent memory – even complex memory – from fading. Chapter 1 showed that narratives set at the turn of the twentieth-century position Ukrainians as the "founding fathers" of the prairies but also as colonizers of lands traditionally inhabited by Indigenous Peoples. Chapter 2 further demonstrated the ambiguous status of Ukrainian Canadian "founding fathers," who were considered enemy aliens during the First World War, with many put under barbed wire in internment camps. For decades, the memory of these Great War operations remained on the margins of Canadian and Ukrainian Canadian cultural memory. However, since the mid-1990s, it has become an essential topic in children's literature, with new books of different formats appearing regularly. In Chapter 3, I showcased that in most historical texts set in Canada, it is girls who are portrayed as the keepers of Ukrainian memory and ethnoreligious identity. Unsurprisingly, predominantly female characters are the protagonists of most books analyzed in Chapters 4 and 5 of *Next-Generation Memory*. There I argued that the Holodomor has gradually become a popular topic with children's authors over the last three decades. However, until recently, most books devoted to the Great Famine were either self-published or issued by independent publishers, thus receiving less attention than texts printed by professional press. The ultimate chapter, focused on the mnemonic entanglements of the past/present and North America/Eastern Europe, illustrated that in the last decade, Second World War– and Holocaust-themed books for young readers have become more inclusive and less dependent on simple binaries and stereotypes. This change is fundamental as familiarizing young readers with past war experiences can help them identify the threats of the globally rising nationalism(s), the complex sociopolitical situations in North America and Europe, and the transnational consequences of war. Despite the richness of issues covered in the 41 books examined in this study, it is worth noting that there are still topics that have not been explored in children's historical fiction or have only been signaled; for example, the periods between the world wars and the cold war. Moreover, I hope that in the future, *Next-Generation Memory* will be followed by investigations of diasporic presses for children, texts published before 1991, and the ones released after I had completed this project.

In addition to the war in Ukraine, parts of this book were written during a global pandemic. For a few years the entire world was struggling with COVID-19, which resulted in the deaths of more than 6 million people, extended unemployment, collapsing hospitals, interruption of schooling, closed universities, invasive practices of state surveillance, and a severe economic crisis. In these challenging and uncertain times, when politicians in various countries used people's anxieties and resentments, often directing them at ethnic, religious, or sexual minorities, remembering about past periods of social and political upheavals and how they take place in collective memories was of particular importance. On March 16, 2020, encouraging young people to follow the rules of social distancing, Marsha Forchuk Skrypuch posted the following statement referring to the pandemic and the Second World War on her Facebook profile: "[y]our grandparents were called to war. You're being called to sit on the couch. You can do this!" Skrypuch was not the only one who compared these two very different events two years before the world changed due to the war in Ukraine. The students taking my undergraduate online course *Memory and Trauma in North American Children's Literature and Film* told me that historical fiction we discussed in class, including the texts I examine in *Next-Generation Memory*, helped them process the feelings of isolation and fear caused by the pandemic. They also argued that their own emotions and experiences related to the current situation allowed them to better understand distant war atrocities and the importance of keeping the memory of the Second World War in the mnemonic repertoires of the next generations. Little did we know that the war atrocities would become so close two years later. I believe that many historical books examined in this study, regardless of their format, display a capacity to develop empathy in young readers. Most importantly, however, they can help the seeds of next-generation memory to sprout.

Note

1 See Chapter 1, endnote 3.

Works Cited

Bergenduen, Vera. "How Ukraine is Crowdsourcing Digital Evidence of War Crimes." *Time*, May 9/16, 2022, pp. 16–17.

Gessen, Masha. "Letter from Kyiv. The Memorial: A Holocaust Atrocity Was about to Be Commemorated. Then Came Another War." *The New Yorker*, April 18, 2022, pp. 26–35.

Kertzer, Adrianne. *My Mother's Voice. Children, Literature, and the Holocaust.* Broadview Press, 2002.

Mangan, Dan. "Tennessee School Board Bans Holocaust Graphic Novel 'Maus' – Author Art Spiegelman Condemns the Move as 'Orwellian'." *CNBC*, January 26, 2022, www.cnbc.com/2022/01/26/tennessee-school-board-bans-holocaust-comic-maus-by-art-spiegelman.html Accessed 12 May 2022.

Montgomery, Lucy Maud. "Little Joscelyn." *Chronicles of Avonlea*, edited by L.M. Montgomery. McClelland & Stewart, 1912. www.gutenberg.org/files/1354/1354-h/1354-h.htm#link2H_4_0005

Motyl, Alexander J. "Is Putin Committing Genocide in Ukraine?" *Tablet*, May 23, 2022, www.tabletmag.com/sections/news/articles/is-putin-committing-genocide-in-ukraine?fbclid=IwAR169gwupKJ9epHa-742TzWJ8aHUx1Bc41pH0W7HmPq7mw0Qm_YI5QqfL3A Accessed 23 May 2022.

Rothberg, Michael. *The Implicated Subject: Beyond Victims and Perpetrators.* Stanford University Press, 2019.

Singh, Kanishka. "Canada Lawmakers Vote Unanimously to Label Russia's Acts in Ukraine as 'Genocide'." *Reuters*, April 27, 2022, www.reuters.com/world/canada-lawmakers-vote-unanimously-label-russias-acts-ukraine-genocide-2022-04-27/ Accessed 12 May 2022.

Snyder, Timothy. "Russia's Genocide Handbook. The Evidence of Atrocity and of Intent Mounts." *Thinking about: Snyder*, April 8, 2022, https://snyder.substack.com/p/russias-genocide-handbook?s=r Accessed 12 May 2022.

Tabarovsky, Izabella and Eugene Finkiel. "Statement on the War in Ukraine by Scholars of Genocide, Nazism and World War II." *Jewish Journal*, February 27, 2022, https://jewishjournal.com/news/worldwide/345515/statement-on-the-war-in-ukraine-by-scholars-of-genocide-nazism-and-world-war-ii/ Accessed 12 May 2022.

Appendix

Corpus of Ukrainian Canadian and Ukrainian-Themed Children's and Young Adult (YA) Books Distributed in Canada between 1991 and 2021

Ukrainian Canadian Books

Borsky, Mary. *Benny Bensky and the Giant Pumpkin Heist*. Illustrated by Linda Hendry. Tundra Books, 2002.
Borsky, Mary. *Benny Bensky and the Parrot-Napper*. Illustrated by Linda Hendry. Tundra Books, 2008.
Borsky, Mary. *Benny Bensky and the Perogy Palace*. Illustrated by Linda Hendry. Tundra Books, 2001.
Clark, Pam. *Kalyna*. Stonehouse Publishing, 2016. E-book.
Gal, Valentina. *Philipovna: Daughter of Sorrow*. MiroLand, 2019.
Good, Rhea. *Bottle of Grain: A Holodomor Story*. Illustrated by Natalie Warner. Columbia, 2021.
Grekul, Lisa. *Kalyna's Song*. Coteau Books, 2003.
Keefer, Janice Kulyk. *Anna's Goat*. Illustrated by Janet Wilson. Orca Book Publishers, 2001.
Kupchenko Frolick, Gloria. *Anna Veryha*. Maxwell Macmillan, 1992.
Langston, Laura. *Lesia's Dream*. HarperThrophy Canada, 2003.
Luciuk, Kassandra and natalie marie burton. *Enemy Alien: A Graphic History of Internment in Canada during the First World War*. Toronto: Between the Lines, 2020.
Mutala, Marion. *Baba's Babushka: A Magical Ukrainian Christmas*. Illustrated by Wendy Siemens. Regina: Your Nickel's Worth Publishing, 2010.
Mutala, Marion. *Baba's Babushka: A Magical Ukrainian Easter*. Illustrated by Wendy Siemens. Regina: Your Nickel's Worth Publishing, 2012.
Mutala, Marion. *Baba's Babushka: A Magical Ukrainian Wedding*. Illustrated by Amber Rees. Regina: Your Nickel's Worth Publishing, 2013.
Mutala, Marion. *Baba's Babushka: Magical Ukrainian Adventures*. Illustrated by Wendy Siemens, Amber Rees, and Olha Tkachenko. Regina: Your Nickel's Worth Publishing, 2020.
Mutala, Marion. *Grateful*. Illustrated by Elisha Revke. Regina: Your Nickel's Worth Publishing, 2014.
Mutala, Marion. *Kokhum's Babushka: A Magical Métis/Ukrainian Tale*. Illustrated by Donna Lee Dumont. Saskatoon: Gabriel Dumont Institute Press, 2017.

Mutala, Marion. *More Babas, Please!* Illustrated by Olha Tkachenko. Regina: Your Nickel's Worth Publishing, 2017.
Mutala, Marion. *My Buddy, Dido!* Illustrated by Olha Tkachenko. Regina: Your Nickel's Worth Publishing, 2018.
Mutala, Marion. *My Dearest Dido: The Holodomor Story.* Wood Dragon Books, 2019.
Skrypuch, Marsha Forchuk. "An Unexpected Visitor." *A Christmas to Remember: Tales of Comfort and Joy.* Scholastic Canada, 2009 – also available in French.
Skrypuch, Marsha Forchuk. *Dance of the Banished.* Pajama Press, 2014.
Skrypuch, Marsha Forchuk. *Don't Tell the Enemy.* Scholastic Canada, 2017 – also available in French.
Skrypuch, Marsha Forchuk. *Don't Tell the Nazis.* Scholastic, 2019 – also available in French.
Skrypuch, Marsha Forchuk. *Enough.* Illustrated by Michael Martchenko. Fitzhenry & Whiteside, 2000.
Skrypuch, Marsha Forchuk. *Hope's War.* Dundurn, 2001.
Skrypuch, Marsha Forchuk. *Making Bombs for Hitler.* Scholastic Canada, 2012 – also available in French.
Skrypuch, Marsha Forchuk. *Prisoners in the Promised Land. The Ukrainian Internment Diary of Anya Soloniuk.* Scholastic Canada, 2007 – also available in French.
Skrypuch, Marsha Forchuk. "Red Boots." *Kobzar's Children: A Century of Untold Ukrainian Stories*, edited by Marsha Forchuk Skrypuch. Fitzhenry & Whiteside, 2006, pp. 70–80.
Skrypuch, Marsha Forchuk. *Silver Threads.* Illustrated by Michael Martchenko. Toronto: Fitzhenry &Whiteside, 2004.
Skrypuch, Marsha Forchuk. *Silver Threads.* Illustrated by Michael Martchenko. Toronto: Viking (Penguin Books Canada), 1996.
Skrypuch, Marsha Forchuk. *Stolen Child.* Scholastic Canada, 2010 – also available in French.
Skrypuch, Marsha Forchuk. *Stolen Girl.* Scholastic, 2020 – also available in French.
Skrypuch, Marsha Forchuk. "The Rings." *Kobzar's Children: A Century of Untold Ukrainian Stories*, edited by Marsha Forchuk Skrypuch. Fitzhenry & Whiteside, 2006, pp. 49–66.
Skrypuch, Marsha Forchuk. *The War Below.* Scholastic, 2018.
Skrypuch, Marsha Forchuk. *Traitors Among Us.* Scholastic Canada, 2021.
Skrypuch, Marsha Forchuk. *Trapped in Hitler's Web.* Scholastic Canada, 2020.
Skrypuch, Marsha Forchuk. *Underground Soldier.* Scholastic Canada, 2014 – also available in French.
Warwaruk, Larry. *Andrei and the Snow Walker.* Regina: Coteau Books, 2002.
Warwaruk, Larry. *Brovko's Amazing Journey.* Regina: Coteau Books, 2013.

Ukrainian-Themed Canadian Books

Dueck, Adele. *Nettie's Journey.* Coteau Books, 2005.
Goldstone, Gabriele. *Broken Stone.* Rebelight, 2015.
Goldstone, Gabriele. *Red Stone.* Rebelight, 2014.
Goldstone, Gabriele. *Tainted Amber.* Ronsdale Press, 2021.

Goldstone, Gabriele. *The Kulak's Daughter*. Austin, Tire Swing Books, 2010.
Huser, Glen. *Firebird*. Ronsdale, 2020.
Kacer, Kathy. *Louder Than Words*. Annick Press, 2020.
Smucker, Barbara. *Days of Terror*. Puffin, 2008 [1979].[1]
Smucker, Barbara. *Henry's Red Sea*. Herald Press, 2012 [1955].
Ravel, Edeet. *A Boy Is Not a Bird*. Groundwood Books, 2019.
Ravel, Edeet. *A Boy Is Not a Ghost*. Groundwood Books, 2021.

Other Books Set in Ukraine by Non-Canadian Authors

Begley, Louis. *Wartime Lies*. New York: Ivy Books, 1991.
Gosline, Andrea Alban. *Anya's War*. Macmillan, 2011.
Kerr, Phillip. *The Winter Horses*. Knopf Books for Young Readers, 2014.
McCrina, Amanda. *Traitor*. New York: Farrar Straus Giroux, 2020.
Schmidt, Carola. *Babushka Is Homesick*. Illustrated by Vinicius Melo. Carolina Witchmichen Penteado Schmidt, 2020.
Schmidt, Carola. *Tell Me a Story, Babushka*. Illustrated by Vinicius Melo. Carolina Witchmichen Penteado Schmidt, 2019 (second edition: Schmidt, Carola. *Tell Me a Story, Babushka*. Illustrated by Anita Barghigiani, New York: Reycraft, 2022).
Spradlin, Michael P. *The Enemy Above: A Novel of World War II*. Scholastic, 2016.

Francophone Ukrainian-Themed Books

Brien, Sylvie. *Spirit Lake*. Paris: Gallimard Jeunesse, 2008.
Pernin, Muriel. *Famine: L'arme des tyrans*. Syros, 1994.
Pernin, Muriel. *Kiev: Babi Yar*. Syros, 1995.

Historical Books Studied in *Next-Generation Memory*

Clark, Pam. *Kalyna*. Stonehouse Publishing, 2016. E-book.
Dueck, Adele. *Nettie's Journey*. Coteau Books, 2005.
Gal, Valentina. *Philipovna: Daughter of Sorrow*. MiroLand, 2019.
Goldstone, Gabriele. *Broken Stone*. Rebelight, 2015.
Goldstone, Gabriele. *Red Stone*. Rebelight, 2014.
Goldstone, Gabriele. *Tainted Amber*. Ronsdale Press, 2021.
Goldstone, Gabriele. *The Kulak's Daughter*. Austin: Tire Swing Books, 2010.
Good, Rhea. *Bottle of Grain: A Holodomor Story*. Illustrated by Natalie Warner. Columbia, 2021.
Grekul, Lisa. *Kalyna's Song*. Coteau Books, 2003.
Huser, Glen. *Firebird*. Ronsdale, 2020.
Kacer, Kathy. *Louder Than Words*. Annick Press, 2020.
Kupchenko Frolick, Gloria. *Anna Veryha*. Maxwell Macmillan, 1992.
Langston, Laura. *Lesia's Dream*. HarperThrophy Canada, 2003.

---

1 Although Smucker's books were initially published before 1991, they are still in print and in circulation.

Luciuk, Kassandra and natalie marie burton. *Enemy Alien: A Graphic History of Internment in Canada during the First World War*. Toronto: Between the Lines, 2020.

Mutala, Marion. *Baba's Babushka: A Magical Ukrainian Christmas*. Illustrated by Wendy Siemens. Regina: Your Nickel's Worth Publishing, 2010.

Mutala, Marion. *Baba's Babushka: A Magical Ukrainian Easter*. Illustrated by Wendy Siemens. Regina: Your Nickel's Worth Publishing, 2012.

Mutala, Marion. *Baba's Babushka: A Magical Ukrainian Wedding*. Illustrated by Amber Rees. Regina: Your Nickel's Worth Publishing, 2013.

Mutala, Marion. *Kokhum's Babushka: A Magical Métis/Ukrainian Tale*. Illustrated by Donna Lee Dumont. Saskatoon: Gabriel Dumont Institute Press, 2017.

Mutala, Marion. *My Dearest Dido: The Holodomor Story*. Wood Dragon Books, 2019.

Ravel, Edeet. *A Boy Is Not a Bird*. Groundwood Books, 2019.

Skrypuch, Marsha Forchuk. "An Unexpected Visitor." *A Christmas to Remember: Tales of Comfort and Joy*. Scholastic Canada, 2009.

Skrypuch, Marsha Forchuk. *Dance of the Banished*. Pajama Press, 2014.

Skrypuch, Marsha Forchuk. *Don't Tell the Enemy*. Scholastic Canada, 2017.

Skrypuch, Marsha Forchuk. *Don't Tell the Nazis*. Scholastic, 2019.

Skrypuch, Marsha Forchuk. *Enough*. Illustrated by Michael Martchenko. Fitzhenry & Whiteside, 2000.

Skrypuch, Marsha Forchuk. *Hope's War*. Dundurn, 2001.

Skrypuch, Marsha Forchuk. *Making Bombs for Hitler*. Scholastic Canada, 2012.

Skrypuch, Marsha Forchuk. *Prisoners in the Promised Land. The Ukrainian Internment Diary of Anya Soloniuk*. Scholastic Canada, 2007.

Skrypuch, Marsha Forchuk. *Silver Threads*. Illustrated by Michael Martchenko. Toronto: Fitzhenry & Whiteside, 2004.

Skrypuch, Marsha Forchuk. *Silver Threads*. Illustrated by Michael Martchenko. Toronto: Viking (Penguin Books Canada), 1996.

Skrypuch, Marsha Forchuk. *Stolen Child*. Scholastic Canada, 2010.

Skrypuch, Marsha Forchuk. *Stolen Girl*. Scholastic, 2020.

Skrypuch, Marsha Forchuk. "The Rings." *Kobzar's Children: A Century of Untold Ukrainian Stories*, edited by Marsha Forchuk Skrypuch. Fitzhenry & Whiteside, 2006, pp. 49–66.

Skrypuch, Marsha Forchuk. *The War Below*. Scholastic, 2018.

Skrypuch, Marsha Forchuk. *Traitors Among Us*. Scholastic Canada, 2021.

Skrypuch, Marsha Forchuk. *Trapped in Hitler's Web*. Scholastic Canada, 2020.

Skrypuch, Marsha Forchuk. *Underground Soldier*. Scholastic Canada, 2014.

Smucker, Barbara. *Days of Terror*. Puffin, 2008 [1979].

Smucker, Barbara. *Henry's Red Sea*. Herald Press, 2012 [1955].

Warwaruk, Larry. *Andrei and the Snow Walker*. Regina: Coteau Books, 2002.

Warwaruk, Larry. *Brovko's Amazing Journey*. Regina: Coteau Books, 2013.

Index

Note: Endnotes are indicated by the page number followed by "n" and the note number e.g., 62n4 refers to note 4 on page 62.

Achilli, Alessandro 66
Act C-331 Internment of Persons of the Ukrainian Origin Recognition Act (Bill C-331) 19, 74–75, 82
active reading 21; *see also* Ingarden, Roman
Alcoff, Linda 44, 67
Alter, Grit 63, 67
Altman, Illya 142, 165
Anderson, Benedict 39, 85; *see also* imagined community
Ankersmit, Frank R. 9, 24
Anne of Green Gables xi, 84, 106, 110, 116–117, 120, 128; *see also* Montgomery, L.M.
Aponiuk, Natalia 17, 23, 24
Applebaum, Anne 40, 64, 67, 133–165, 170–171, 208, 214
Arad, Yitzhak 195, 214
Arizpe, Evelyn 76, 99, 101, 103
Armenian Genocide 98–99n7, 127n13
Arshanskaya Dawson, Zhanna 214
Asikinack, William 58, 67
assimilation 13, 18, 20, 73–76, 82–88, 110, 117–123, 125–126, 129
Assmann, Aleida 7, 24, 34, 43, 67, 73–74, 81, 89, 98, 101
Assmann, Jan 6, 24
Atwood, Margaret 18, 24, 58–59, 67, 75, 101, 137, 165

baba 13, 20, 31, 52, 54, 107–115, 124, 126–127, 202
Babyn Yar (Babi Yar) 161, 193–194, 207, 121
Bader, Barbara 99, 101
Bainbridge, Joyce 80, 102, 104

Bakhtin, Mikhail Mikhailovich 62n3, 67, 207n4; *see also* chronotope
Balan, Jars 16, 24, 125, 127, 130
Ball, Karyn 14, 24, 152, 159, 162, 165
Bandera, Stepan 172–175, 208, 216
Barghigiani, Anita 162, 225
Barka, Vasyl 159n3
Barrett Browning, Elizabeth 87
Barrie, J.M. (James Matthew) 91
Battle of Batoche 46, 57, 65n17
Baudrillard, Jean 31, 62n4, 67; *see also* simulacrum
Baum Singer, Melina 27–28
Bazhan, Mykola 212n35
Begley, Louis 22, 24, 170, 225
Bell, Katherine 83, 101
Bellah, Robert N. 9, 24
Bergenduen, Vera 220, 222
Berkhoff, Karel 184, 214
Bernsztajnowa, R. 128n19; *see also Anne of Green Gables*
Bertelsen, Olga 135, 165, 176, 214
Bezo, Brent 148, 158, 159, 165
Bible 19, 40, 43–44, 47, 56, 160
Biden, Joe 220
Bloodlands 15; *see also* Snyder, Timothy
Boccaccio, Giovanni xi
Bociurkiw, Bohdan 12, 24
Bociurkiw, Marusya 115
Boraks-Nemetz, Lillian 128n19
Borsky, Mary 223
Bosmajian, Hamida 8, 24, 151, 154, 165, 169, 177–179, 188, 201, 211, 214
Bougai, Nikolai 144, 165
Bourdieu, Pierre 33, 67; *see also* capital of consecration

228 Index

Bowlby, Ewan 128, 130
Bradford, Clare 5, 24, 33, 45, 65, 67
Branach-Kallas, Anna 73, 97, 101
Brien, Sylvie 99–100n17, 101, 225
Buchholtz, Mirosława 12, 24, 69
Budka, Nicetas 100n18
Bukovyna 10, 77, 85, 175, 213
Burke, Marguerite V. 12–13, 24
burton, nicole marie 20, 82, 94, 103, 223, 226
Bush, Kate 66n24
Butler, Judith 129n22, 130

Cai, Mingshui 153, 165
Cairns, Alan C. 62, 67
Calver, Cheryl 67, 130
Canadian mosaic 5, 14, 101
The Canadian Multiculturalism Act (CMA) 12–13, 18
Carpenter, Carole Henderson 11, 25
Catherine the Great 140, 160n12
Chaikovsky, Andriy 63n11, 71
Chaplin, Charlie 86, 90
Chernetsky, Vitaly 39, 67, 126n7, 130
chronotope 62n3; *see also* Bakhtin, Mikhail Mikhailovich
Chruślińska, Iza 68, 215
Chubynsky, Pavlo 210
Cipko, Serge 134, 165
Clark, Pam 63, 94, 101, 104, 130, 223, 225
Clifford, James 10
Coleman, Flynn 220
collective memory 6, 9, 14, 20, 54, 74–75, 79, 81, 97, 134–138, 149–152, 161, 172, 176
collectivization 142–148, 154–155, 159, 161–163
Colomer, Teresa 76, 101
Connell, R.W. (Raewyn) 127, 130
Connerton, Paul 54, 67
Conquest, Robert 40, 67, 136
Conrad, Margaret 65, 67, 98n4, 101
Cook, Lyn 17, 99n9
Corse, Sarah M. 9, 25
Cossack 11, 13, 19, 30, 32–33, 36–50, 55–61, 63–65
Coulthard, Kathy 76, 101
COVID-19 221
Cree 30, 32–33, 42–43, 48–50, 57–58, 65–66, 96
Creet, Julia 23n14, 25
cultural memory 3–6, 10, 13–17, 19, 20–21, 36–37, 43, 61, 81–82, 89–91, 96–98, 106–107, 110–111,
122–124, 133–134, 149–151, 153, 158, 172, 175, 207, 219–220

Davey, Frank 54, 130
Davies, Norman 208
Davis, Marie 17, 25
Dawson, Greg 22n11, 214n50
Dean-Ruzicka, Rachel 7–8, 15, 25
Dear Canada 92, 95, 112
dekulakization 142–148, 161–163; *see also* collectivization
Demjanjuk, Ivan 176, 208n11
Deszcz-Tryhubczak, Justyna 63n10, 67
Devereux, Cecily 116, 126, 130
Diakiw, Jerry 6, 25
diaspora 1–23, 32, 37, 39, 61, 65, 80–81, 85, 106–107, 111–113, 122–124, 134–138, 152, 160–161, 171–176, 180, 184, 186, 208
Dickens, Charles 97, 89, 95
Dontsov, Dmytro 172, 214; *see also* Organization of Ukrainian Nationalists
Douglas, Mary 35, 67
Drach, Ivan 135
Dressel, Janice Hartwick 136, 151, 165
Drewniak, Dagmara 12, 17, 21, 25
Druker, Elina 217
Dueck, Adele 20, 140–141, 147, 158, 161, 165, 224–225; *see also* Mennonites
Dumont, Donna Lee 19, 31, 51, 54, 69, 166, 223, 226; *see also* Mutala, Marion
Dumont, Gabriel 46
dumy 40, 64n14
Duranty, Walter 152
Durbin, Deanne 106, 117–118, 129
Dzubak, Luba 34, 70, 101

Eaton catalog 128–129n21
Edwards, Gail 13, 25, 76, 101
Egoff, Sheila 7, 25
Ehorushkina, Kateryna 16n19
Eleniak, Vasyl 10
enemy aliens 10, 14, 19, 60, 74, 90–92, 95–97, 98, 100, 126, 182, 220; *see also* internment of Ukrainians in Canada
Engelhart, Margaret S. 114, 131
entangled bystander 21, 170, 174, 176, 198–199, 206; *see also* Wylęgała, Anna
Epp, Marlene 35, 124, 130, 140–141, 160, 165

Erlacher, Trevor 172, 208, 214; *see also* Dontsov, Dmytro
Erll, Astrid 3–4, 7, 25, 27, 67, 101–102, 138; *see also* travelling memory
Evans, Janet 76, 102
Ewers, Hans Heino 7, 25
exiles to Siberia 11, 144, 146, 155, 161, 182, 190, 191, 193, 213; *see also* collectivization

Federici, Silvia 107, 130
Fee, Margery 67, 101, 113, 130
Finkiel, Eugene 220, 222
First World War 7, 9–10, 19, 72–78, 82, 84, 87, 90, 94, 96–97, 112, 146, 208, 220; *see also* internment of Ukrainians in Canada
Fondrie, Suzanne 54, 68
frameworks of memory 6; *see also* Halbwachs, Maurice
Frank, Anne 84, 169
Frankenberg, Ruth 117, 131
Franko, Ivan 65n16
Freeman, Mark xi
Fry, Leanna 157, 165

Gal, Valentina 20, 134, 143, 154–159, 162–165, 223, 225
Galadza, Ivanka Theodosia 159
Galicia 10, 17, 33–36, 47, 83–88, 90, 100, 171–172, 175, 189
Galway, Elizabeth A. 17, 25, 36, 47, 50, 59–60, 66, 68, 72, 102, 116, 131
Gammel, Irene 132
Gandhi, Mahatma 118
Gangi, Jane M. 8, 25, 135, 165
Garland, Judy 117
gender 129n22; *see also* Butler, Judith
gender roles 106, 110, 113–120, 126; *see also* patriarchy
genocide 135–136, 151–152, 162, 206, 219–220
George V 77, 91, 97, 99
Germans in Ukraine 138, 142–149, 160
Gertridge, Alison 99, 101
Gessen, Masha 220, 222
ghetto 181, 199–200, 213; *see also* Holocaust
ghost images 3
Głowacka-Grajper, Małgorzata 217
Goble, Paul A. 208, 214
Gogol, Nikolai 38, 59, 68

Goldberg, Robert A. 169, 214
Goldie, Terry 5, 25, 31, 48, 68
Gołebiowski, Grzegorz 190, 214
Goldstone, Gabriele 20, 134, 224–225; *Broken Stone* 144–148; *Crow Stone* 145; *The Kulak's Daughter/Red Stone* 143–149, 155, 158, 160–163, 165; *Tainted Amber* 146, 148–149, 160, 165, 176, 214
Gonzalez, Ismel 52, 68
Good, Rhea 162, 165, 223, 225
Gosline, Andrea Alban 225
Grabowicz, George G. 38–40, 68, 175, 214
graphic novel 20, 93–94, 159
Gray, Paige 116, 131, 166
Grekul, Lisa 12–19, 23n17, 25–28, 104, 105, 125n1, 131, 141, 143, 165, 209n18, 214, 223, 225
Gubar, Marah 100, 131
Guillet, Jojo 52, 68
Gunew, Sneja 23n19, 26
Gunkel, Ann Hetzel 88, 102

Hałas, Elżbieta 15, 26
Halbwachs, Maurice 6; *see also* frameworks of memory
Harde, Roxanne 51–52, 68, 132
Hart, Paula 160, 166
Haskett, Mary Manko 92, 96; *see also* internment of Ukrainians in Canada
Hazzard, Claire 82, 102
hegemonic masculinity 127n15; *see also* gender
Henderson, Jennifer 23n17, 26–27, 51, 83, 92, 102–103
Herodotus 42, 68
Hesse, M.G. 23, 26
Himka, Johh-Paul 10, 26, 172, 174, 180, 184, 189, 208, 214–215
Hinther, Rhonda L. 27, 68, 166, 215
Hirsch, Marianne 2–3, 26, 215
Hnatiw, Chrystia 125–126, 131
Holland, Agnieszka 150, 164; *see also* Jones, Gareth
Hollindale, Peter 22n7, 26
Holocaust 2, 4, 8, 14–15, 20–21, 75, 92, 135–137, 152, 157–160, 162, 168–214, 219–220
Holodomor (Great Famine of 1932-1933) 57, 112, 124, 133–138, 140, 143–144, 148–154, 156–164
Howard, Vivian 5, 26, 76, 102
Hrushevsky, Mykhailo 40–41, 64n12, 70

Hrycak, Jarosław 38, 41, 68, 211, 215
Hryniuk, Stella 12, 26, 132
Hryshko, Wasyl 160
Hughes, Monica 18, 99n9
Hulan, Renée 5, 61
Hunczak, Taras 172, 185, 215
Hunt, Peter 7, 26, 51, 68, 103
Huser, Glen 74, 225; *Firebird* 82, 85–87, 89–94, 96, 99, 102, 110
Hutcheon, Linda 5, 26

Iacovetta, Franca 124, 130, 165
imagined community 39, 85; see also Anderson, Benedict
implicated subject 21, 31, 46, 156, 168, 170, 174–178, 185–188, 193, 197–199, 206, 209, 220; see also Rothberg, Michael
The Indian Act 30
Ingarden, Roman 21n3, 26; see also active reading
Innocenti, Roberto 8, 26
internment of Ukrainians in Canada 1, 4, 7, 19–20, 31, 44, 50, 65, 73–76, 78–84, 91–99, 101, 108, 113, 115, 120, 126, 128, 182, 220; see also enemy aliens
Isajiw, Wsevolod W. 215
Isakowicz-Zaleski, Tadeusz 173, 215

Janes, Daniela 72, 102
Janion, Maria 171, 215
Jaques, Zoe 63n10, 67
Jobe, Ron 160, 166
Johnson, Ingrid 80, 102, 104
Johnston, Rosemary Ross 72, 102
Jones, Esyllt W. 27, 69, 131
Jones, Gareth 148, 150, 152
Joosen, Vanessa 57, 63, 68
Jung, Carl Gustaw 113, 131

Kacer, Kathy 161, 225; *Louder Than Words* 21, 161, 169–170, 194, 195–200, 202–204, 212n28; *To Look a Nazi in the Eye: A Teen's Account of a War Criminal Trial* 209n14, 215
Kachak, Tetiana 76, 102
Kamboureli, Smaro 12
Kamińska-Maciąg, Sylwia 161, 166
Kaplita, Marek 7, 26
Katriuk, Vladimir 208–209n14
Kaye (Kysilewsky), Vladimir J. 34, 68
Keats, John 87

Keefer, Janice Kulyk 5, 13, 22n11, 23n16, 26, 223
Kerr, Phillip 170, 225
Kertzer, Adrianne 8, 26, 157, 166, 203, 215, 219, 222
KGB 168, 176, 208
Khanenko-Friesen, Natalie 65n16, 68
Kidd, Kenneth B. 8, 26, 76, 102
Kiefer, Barbara Z. 76, 102
Kil, Sang Hea 36, 68, 87, 102
Kim, Christine 18, 27–28, 69
King, Thomas 67, 130
Kiriak, Ilia 23n16
Kirk, Heather 148, 151
Kisluk, Serge 208
Klymasz, Robert B. 39–40, 68
kobzar 40–41
Kokkola, Lydia 8, 15, 21, 27, 117, 131–132, 150–151, 154, 157, 166, 183–184, 195, 197, 205–206, 213
Kononenko, Natalie 40–41, 64, 68
Konovalts, Yevhen 172
Korczak, Janusz 213n42
Kordan, Bohdan S. 27, 73, 102–103
Kornblatt, Judith D. 37, 68
Korteweg, Lisa 52, 68
Kosach-Kvitka, Larysa 64–65n15, 80; see also Ukrainka, Lesia (Lesya)
Kostash, Myrna 14, 34, 66, 68–69, 73, 101, 106, 125, 131
Kosyk, Volodymyr 173
Kozaczka, Grażyna J. 105–106, 119, 126n8, 131
Kozicka Simon, Anna 23
Krahn, Elizabeth 161, 166
Krawchenko, Bohdan 215
Krentsbach, Stella 208n10
Kruk, Laurie 5, 27, 61
kulak 142–148, 161–163; see also dekulakization
Kulish, Panteleimon 38
Kupchenko Frolick, Gloria 125, 129; 225; *Anna Veryha* 20, 23, 62–63, 105–106, 108, 110, 113, 115–120, 124–129, 131, 208, 223; *The Chicken Man* 125–126; *The Green Tomato Years* 125–126
Kurelek, William 11, 13, 20, 23, 25, 80, 113–114, 125, 127, 130–131, 134, 148
Kuryliw, Valentina 153, 161n20, 166

Lachmann, Renate 7, 27
Landsberg, Alison 2, 27; see also prosthetic memory

Langston, Laura 1, 18, 20, 27, 32–35, 43–46, 54–55, 60–61, 64, 69, 74, 80–82, 86, 88, 90, 102, 108–111, 143, 161, 223, 225
Lavrov, Sergey 207n1
Lawrence, Bonita 30, 47, 65n17, 69
Lazarenko, Joseph M. 10, 27
Lebensborn 11, 21, 175, 181, 207
Lebowitz, Jordana 209n14, 215; *see also* Kacer, Kathy
Leden, Laura 72, 103
Ledohowski, Lindy 11–12, 17–18, 23–24, 26–28, 31–32, 45–48, 50, 64, 69, 84, 103–104, 107–109, 125, 131
Ledwell, Jane 128, 131
Lenin, Vladimir 133, 139, 163
Lewis, David 99, 103
lieux de memoire 6; *see also* Nora, Pierre
Lilienfeld, Leibish 190
Litteken, Erin 164n33
Little, Jean 83, 99n9
London, Jack 59
Louie, Belinda 166
Lower, Wendy 171, 215
Luciuk, Kassandra 20, 82, 94, 99, 103, 223, 226
Luciuk, Lubomyr 12, 26, 73, 79, 103, 132
Luckhurst, Roger 178, 215
Lysenko, Adrian 159
Lysenko, Vera 18
Łebkowska, Anna 82, 102
Łuczak, Ewa 29

Maggi, Stefania 148, 158–159, 165
Mahovsky, Craig 73, 102
Makhno, Nestor 138–139, 141
Malko, Victoria A. 134–135, 155–156, 159–160, 163, 166
Mangan, Dan 219, 222
Mark, Inky 75; *see also* Act C-331 Internment of Persons of the Ukrainian Origin Recognition Act (Bill C-331)
Markowski, Michał Paweł 102
Marples, David R. 133, 137, 166, 171, 174, 215
Marsh, Katherine 159, 164n32
Marshall, Joan 23, 27
Marshman, Sophia 207, 215
Martchenko, Michael 19–20, 22n13, 63, 75–80, 99, 104, 149, 154, 167, 224, 226; *see also* Skrypuch, Marsha Forcuk
Martínez-Roldán, Carmen 76, 101
Martynowych, Orest T. 10, 27, 208, 215
Marunchak, Michael 92
Matusiak, Agnieszka 189, 194, 211, 216
Maydanyk, Jacob 107
McBride, Jared 208, 216
McCall, Sophie 18, 27, 32, 66, 69
McClintock, Anne 107, 131
McConnell, Taylor 14, 28
McCrina, Amanda 22n11, 207n2, 213n48, 225
McGonigal, James 76, 103
McKinney, Louise 126
Melnyk, Andrii 172
Melo, Vinicius 162n23, 166–167, 225
Mennonites 4, 17, 20, 138–142, 160
Messerchmidt, James W. 127n15, 130
Métis 19, 30–32, 40–42, 46–53, 57, 66, 122–124
Michułka, Dorota 202, 207, 212, 217
Mirchuk, Petro 173
Mitchell, Jean 128, 131
Mitchell, Shandi 63n8
Mochoruk, Jim 27, 68, 166, 215
Montgomery, L.M. (Lucy Maud) 1, 28, 30, 69, 97, 99, 103–104, 105–106, 108, 116, 131–132, 133, 166, 168, 216, 219, 222; *Anne of Green Gables* xi, 84, 106, 110, 116–117, 120, 128; *Rilla of Ingleside* 72–73, 77, 81, 83, 97, 102; *see also Anne of Green Gables*
Morton, Leah 27, 69, 131
Moss, Laura 12
Motyka, Grzegorz 173, 216
Motyl, Alexander J. 173, 207, 216, 220, 222
multiculturalism 9–16, 83–84; *see also* Canadian mosaic
multidirectional memory 6, 15, 137, 169–170, 176, 188, 197, 206, 219
Munsch, Robert 76
Mutala, Marion 13, 19–20, 46, 223–224, 226; *Baba's Babushka* 52, 66, 69, 105, 111–112; *Kokhum's Babushka: A Magical Meetis/Ukrainian Tale* 51–54, 66, 69, 131, 134; *My Dearest Dido: The Holodomor Story* 150, 151–153, 163, 166
Mycak, Sonia 16, 28

232 Index

Nasha Meri and *Katie* 20, 107–108, 115–124, 180; *see also* Swyripa, Frances
next-generation memory 1–7, 21, 31, 60, 74, 76, 82, 96–96, 106, 134, 138–140, 151, 153, 159, 168–169, 180, 206, 219, 222
Nielsen, Jennifer 20n27
Niewiadomska-Flis, Urszula 88, 103
Nikolajeva, Maria 35, 41, 69, 78, 99, 103
Nodelman, Perry 16, 28, 31, 33, 36, 42–44, 48, 50–51, 69, 78, 83, 99n8, 103
Nora, Pierre 6
Nuremberg trials 135
Nycz, Ryszard 102

O'Brien, Sharon 120, 131
Oberlander, Helmut 208–209n14
Odynsky, Wasyl 208–209n14
Oleskiw, Joseph (Oleskiv, Osyp) 34
Orange Revolution 173
Organization of Ukrainian Nationalists (OUN) 10–11, 14, 171–175, 179, 184, 186, 191, 216
Ostarbeiters 128, 175, 182, 207, 213
Ostashewski, Marcia 37–41, 69
Österlund, Mia 217
Oziewicz, Marek 161, 166

Palij, Ludia 125–126n1, 131
Palmer, Howard 70
Paluk, William 39, 61, 64, 70.
Paryż, Marek 29
patriarchy 107–115, 117, 126–127, 129; *see also* gender roles
Paul, Lissa 72, 102
Pauly, Matthew 163, 166
Pencie, Miranda de 128
Pernin, Muriel 161n17, 166, 212n35, 225
Perry, Adele 27, 69, 131
Pesonen, Jaana 150, 166
Petliura, Symon 139
Petryshyn, Jaroslav 34, 70, 82, 103, 136, 166
Pieracki, Bronisław 172
Plokhy, Serhii 9–10, 28, 37–40, 64, 70, 168, 171–173, 179, 207, 209, 216
pogroms 11, 137, 139, 160, 171, 173–176, 184, 189, 194–196, 212
Poniatowska, Patrycja 217
Poroshenko, Petro 174

picturebook 11, 22–23, 51–53, 75–78, 80, 99, 111, 149, 150, 162
Preis-Smith, Agata 29
prosthetic memory 2; *see also* Landsberg, Alison
Pukas, Ludviga (Nina) 194–195, 202, 215
Putin, Vladimir 168, 170, 174–175, 206–207, 216, 222
Pylypiw, Ivan 10
pysanka 13, 105, 107, 111–112, 124–125

Radzilowski, John 88, 103
Ravel, Edeet 207n2, 213n46, 216, 225–226
Razack, Sherene 45, 70
Red River Jig 53
Red Terror 134, 136, 138–142, 159
Reeder, Ellen D. 42, 70
Rees, Amber 66n22, 111, 131, 223, 226
Reimer, Mavis 16, 28, 33–34, 65, 67, 69–71, 72, 97, 103
Revolution of Dignity 162, 173
Richter, Miriam Verena 4–5, 7–9, 17–18, 28, 30, 47, 54, 61, 70, 116, 131, 151
Riel, Louis 46–47, 65
Righteous Among Nations 170, 188, 194, 202, 204
Robinson, Laura M. 116, 132
Rolle, Renate 42, 70
Rosenthal, Herman 64, 70
Rossoliński-Liebe, Grzegorz 171, 173, 176, 184, 191, 208–209, 216
Rothberg, Michael 4, 14–15, 28, 31, 46, 70, 73, 103, 136–137, 151–152, 166, 169–170, 174, 176, 179, 181, 184, 188, 197, 206, 216, 219, 220, 222
Rozumnyj, Jaroslav 68
Rud-Volga, Iryna 161
Rudling, Per Anders 11, 14, 24, 28, 152, 159, 162, 165, 173, 216

Saltman, Judith 13, 25, 76, 101
Samchuk, Ulas 159n2
Samosenko, Ivan 196
Satzewich, Vic 10–11, 28, 85, 103, 134, 136–137, 166, 175–176, 208, 216
Schmidt, Carola 66n24, 162n23, 166–167, 225
Schmuhl, Hans-Walter 15, 28

Schwebel, Sara L. 8, 28, 138, 183, 188, 216
Scott, Carole 78, 99, 103
Scythians 19, 31–33, 42, 46, 55–57
Seaton, Albert 37, 70
Second World War 168–214, 219–221
second-generation memory 2–3
Semchuk, Sandra 65, 70, 75, 82, 98n5, 103
Sheptyts'kyi, Andrei 212–213n41
Shevchenko (Ševčenko), Taras 38–41, 64–65, 71, 162–163
Shkandrij, Myroslav 133–136, 152, 167, 171–172, 175, 179, 184–185, 189, 194, 208, 211, 217
Siemens, Wendy 66, 69, 111, 131, 223, 226
Siemerling, Winfried 22, 28
Sifton, Clifford 10, 34
Sikora, Tomasz 28
Sikorska, Kateryna 190
simulacrum 31–32, 61, 62n4, 77, 143, 158; see also Baudrillard, Jean
Singh, Kanishka 220, 222
Skórka, Abraham 207
Skrypuch, Marsha Forchuk 8, 18–23, 28, 32, 46, 70, 74, 169–170, 217, 221, 224, 226; *Dance of the Banished* 65, 70, 75, 98–99, 101, 104; *Don't Tell the Enemy/Don't Tell the Nazi*s 185–186, 189–194, 196–197, 199, 200–202, 204–205, 209, 211, 213; *Enough* 20, 23, 149, 154, 167; *Hope's War* 21, 106, 149, 153, 176–182, 184, 188, 208–209, 211; *The Hunger* 100, 127–128; *Making Bombs for Hitler* 12, 197, 200, 203, 209, 211, 217; *Prisoners in the Promised Land: The Ukrainian Internment Diary of Anya Soloniuk* 19–20, 23, 31, 35–36, 50–54, 63, 65, 70, 75, 82–85, 87–88, 92–93, 96, 99, 100, 102, 104, 105, 108, 111–115, 132, 182, 186; "The Rings" 23, 149, 161–162; *Silver Threads* 63, 75–83; 99, 104; *Stolen Child* 100, 177, 181–182, 186, 203–205, 209, 217; *Traitors Among Us* 168, 177, 182–188, 200–202, 204–205, 209–211; *Trapped in Hitler's Web* 65, 128, 183, 185–186, 189–190, 197, 200–201, 204–205, 209–210, 214; *Underground Soldier/The War Below* 177, 18, 182, 184–188, 192–193, 197, 205, 209, 214, 217; "An Unexpected Visitor" 75, 95, 104; *Winterkill* 159
Smucker, Barbara 20, 99, 139–141, 147, 158, 160n7, 167, 225–226; see also Mennonites
Snyder, Timothy 15, 28, 168, 170, 171, 184–185, 192–194, 200, 202, 208, 213, 217, 220, 222
Sojka, Eugenia 21, 24, 28
Sontag, Susan 133, 156, 167
Spiegelman, Art 2, 219, 222
Spielberg, Steven 200
Spradlin, Michael P. 22, 225
Stalin, Joseph 10, 14, 40, 67, 133–136, 141–149, 151, 153–159, 161–166, 168, 171, 197, 205, 207, 210, 214
Stephens, John 4, 22, 29
Stets'ko, Iaroslav 191
Story, Norah 10, 29, 70, 98, 100, 104, 132
Styles, Morag 99, 101
Subtelny, Orest 175–176, 212, 217
Suchacka, Weronika 17, 23n16, 23n17, 29, 109, 132
Suffragettes 112, 126
Sugars, Cynthia 6, 12, 17, 26–27, 29, 69
Sullibanm, William M. 24
Sundmark, Björn 217
Swindler, Ann 24
Swyripa, Frances 10–13, 29, 34, 37–40, 54, 65, 68, 70, 73–75, 84, 87, 92, 96, 104, 107–110, 117, 119, 123, 126, 129, 132, 140, 142, 160, 167; see also *Nasha Meri* and *Katie*; *baba*
Šubrtová, Milena 164, 167, 188, 217

Tabarovsky, Izabella 220, 222
Tarnawsky, Yuri 64n14
Taylor, William Desmond 128
Tector, Amy 72, 104
Thompson, Angela 99n16, 104
Tipton, Steven M. 24
Titova, Lyudmila 212n35
Tottle, Douglas 136
transculturalism 8, 21; see also multiculturalism
travelling memory 4; see also Erll, Astrid
Trudeau, Pierre 12, 18, 22n9, 53
Trzeszczyńska, Patrycja 5, 11, 29
Ty, Eleanor 7, 17, 29, 167

Ukrainian Insurgent Army (UPA) 11, 14, 65, 170–179, 183–188, 190–191, 200–204, 206, 208–210, 213
Ukrainka, Lesia (Lesya) 64–65n15, 80; Kosach-Kvitka, Larysa
Ulanowicz, Anastasia 2–3, 18, 21, 29, 37, 63, 71, 100, 104, 106, 113, 127, 132, 135, 149, 153, 167, 180, 217; see also ghost images; second-generation memory
Umland, Andreas 174, 217

Vardanian, Maryna 29
Verbytsky, Mykhailo 210
Viatrovych, Volodymyr 173.
Vice, Sue 177, 217
Victoria, Queen 119
Vital, David 196, 217
Volhynia (1943) 209n17, 209n18
Vyshnevetsky, Dmytro (Bayda) 40–41; see also Cossack

Wakeham, Pauline 26, 27, 102–103
Walley-Beckett, Moira 128
War Measures Act 73–74, 98; see also internment of Ukrainians in Canada
War Times Election Act 73–74; see also internment of Ukrainians in Canada
Warner, Martina 145, 167
Warner, Natalie 162n22, 165, 223, 225
Warnqvist, Åsa 217
Warren, Patricia Nell 64n14
Warwaruk, Larry 18–20, 71, 85, 224, 226; *Andrei and the Snow Walker*
30–43, 45–51, 55–61, 66, 93, 108–109, 114, 122, 132, 140–143, 167; *Brovko's Amazing Journey* 20, 31–32, 42, 47, 50, 58–60, 65, 71, 93, 122–124, 129–130, 132
Weatherly, Frederic 86
Weaver, John 113
Webb, Peter 72–73, 104
Wesseling, Elizabeth 65, 71
Wesselius, Janet 116, 132
Wilson, Janet 23, 223
Wilson, Seymour V. 22n9, 29
Wiltse, Lynne 80, 104
Wójcik-Dudek, Małgorzata 207, 217
Wylęgała, Anna 170–174, 208, 217–218; see also entangled bystander

Yefimenko, Hennadiy 135, 137, 167
Yekelchyk, Serhy 9, 29, 66, 133, 136, 148, 167, 175, 218
Yesypenko, Dmytro 66
Yevtushenko, Yevgeny 212n35
Yokota, Junko 5, 29
Yom Kippur 190, 196
Yurchuk, Yuliya 173–174, 184–185, 211n29, 217–218
Yushchenko, Victor 173

Zabuzhko, Oksana 39–40, 65, 71
Zacharasiewicz, Waldemar 22, 29
Zacharias, Robert 139–140, 167
Zapata-Barrero, Ricard 21n2, 29
Zecker, Robert M. 36, 71
Zelenskyy, Volodymyr 168, 207, 215
Zhuk, Sergei I. 14–15, 29, 136, 167–168, 176, 208, 218
Żurek, Sławomir 213, 218